Photoshop
Elements 3

THE MISSING MANUAL

*The book that
should have been
in the box*

OTHER DIGITAL MEDIA RESOURCES FROM O'REILLY

Related titles

Adobe Encore DVD: In the Studio

Digital Photography Hacks

Digital Photography Pocket Guide

iPhoto 5: The Missing Manual

Adobe Photoshop CS One-on-One

Photoshop Elements 3 One-on-One

Adobe InDesign CS One-on-One

Digital Photography Pocket Guide

Digital Photography: Expert Techniques

DVD Studio Pro 3: In the Studio

oreilly.com

oreilly.com is more than a complete catalog of O'Reilly books. You'll also find links to news, events, articles, weblogs, sample chapters, and code examples.

oreillynet.com is the essential portal for developers interested in open and emerging technologies, including new platforms, programming languages, and operating systems.

Conferences

O'Reilly brings diverse innovators together to nurture the ideas that spark revolutionary industries. We specialize in documenting the latest tools and systems, translating the innovator's knowledge into useful skills for those in the trenches. Visit *conferences.oreilly.com* for our upcoming events.

Safari Bookshelf (*safari.oreilly.com*) is the premier online reference library for programmers and IT professionals. Conduct searches across more than 1,000 books. Subscribers can zero in on answers to time-critical questions in a matter of seconds. Read the books on your Bookshelf from cover to cover or simply flip to the page you need. Try it today with a free trial.

Photoshop Elements 3

THE MISSING MANUAL

Barbara Brundage

POGUE PRESS™
O'REILLY®

Beijing · Cambridge · Farnham · Köln · Paris · Sebastopol · Taipei · Tokyo

Photoshop Elements 3: The Missing Manual
by Barbara Brundage

Published by O'Reilly Media, Inc., 1005 Gravenstein Highway North, Sebastopol, CA 95472.

O'Reilly books may be purchased for educational, business, or sales promotional use. Online editions are also available for most titles (*safari.oreilly.com*). For more information, contact our corporate/institutional sales department: (800) 998-9938 or *corporate@oreilly.com*.

Editor:	Peter Meyers
Production Editor:	Philip Dangler
Cover Designer:	Ellie Volckhausen
Interior Designer:	Melanie Wang

Printing History:

March 2005:	First Edition.

 This book uses RepKover,™ a durable and flexible lay-flat binding.

ISBN: 0-596-00453-2
[C]

Table of Contents

Part Six: Additional Elements

Part Seven: Appendixes

The Missing Credits

About the Author

 **Barbara Brundage** has taught people how to use Photoshop Elements since it first came out in 2001. She's also a member of Adobe's Elements 3 pre-release group. Barbara first got interested in Elements for creating graphics for use in her day job as a harpist, music publisher, and arranger. Along the way she joined the large group of people who are finding a renewed interest in photography thanks to digital cameras. If she can learn to use Elements, you can, too!

About the Creative Team

Peter Meyers (editor) works as an editor at O'Reilly Media on the Missing Manual series. He lives with his wife and cat in New York City. Email: *peter. meyers@gmail.com*.

Linley Dolby (copy editor) spent several years in the production department at O'Reilly before moving to Martha's Vineyard to pursue a freelance career. She now helps whip technical books into shape for several companies, including O'Reilly and Pogue Press. Email: *linley@gremlinley.com*.

Grant Dixon (tech editor) is constantly amazed at how much creativity Elements can unleash once a little time is applied to learn the program. He is the creator of the Elements Challenge at *http://www.cavesofice.org/~grant/Challenge/*.

Galen Fott (tech editor) is a writer, animator, puppeteer, and the co-author (with Deke McClelland) of several books on Photoshop Elements. He also reviews software for *PC Magazine* and *Macworld*. Visit him at: *www.grundoon.com*.

Bryan O'Neil Hughes (tech editor) has been a Software Quality Engineer on Adobe's Photoshop Team since 1999. He has helped test and develop several releases of Photoshop and Photoshop Elements.

Rose Cassano (cover illustration) has worked as an independent designer and illustrator for twenty years. Assignments have ranged from the nonprofit sector to corporate clientele. She lives in beautiful Southern Oregon, grateful for the miracles of modern technology that make working there a reality. Email: *cassano@uci. net*. Web: *www.rosecassano.com*.

Philip Dangler (production editor) maintains a vintage Apple Macintosh museum in his office at O'Reilly. In his free time, he rolls his katamari around the world and goes snowboarding.

Acknowledgements

Many, many thanks to Galen Fott, Grant Dixon and Bryan Hughes for reading this book and giving me the benefit of their advice and corrections, and also to Rich Coencas for his help.

Special thanks also to graphic artist Jodi Frye (*www.frontiernet.net/~jlfrye/Jodi_ Frye*) for allowing me to reproduce one of her Elements drawings to show what can be done by those with more artistic ability than I have. Thanks also to Florida's botanical gardens, especially Mckee Botanical Garden (*www.mckeegarden. org*), Historic Bok Sanctuary (*www.boktower.org*), and Harry P. Leu Gardens (*www.leugardens.org*), for creating oases of peace and beauty in our hectic world. Finally, I'd like to thank everyone in the gang over at the Adobe Photoshop Elements support forum for letting me pester them with questions as I was writing.

The Missing Manual Series

Missing Manuals are witty, superbly written guides to computer products that don't come with printed manuals (which is just about all of them). Each book features a handcrafted index; cross-references to specific page numbers (not just "see Chapter 14"); and RepKover, a detached-spine binding that lets the book lie perfectly flat without the assistance of weights or cinder blocks.

Recent and upcoming titles include:

Mac OS X: The Missing Manual (Panther and Tiger editions) by David Pogue

Excel: The Missing Manual by Matthew MacDonald

FileMaker Pro 7: The Missing Manual by Geoff Coffey

iPhoto 5: The Missing Manual by David Pogue

GarageBand 2: The Missing Manual by David Pogue

iPod and iTunes: The Missing Manual by J.D. Biersdorfer

iMovie 4 HD and iDVD 5: The Missing Manual by David Pogue

Google: The Missing Manual by Sarah Milstein and Rael Dornfest

Switching to the Mac: The Missing Manual by David Pogue

Mac OS X Power Hound, Panther Edition by Rob Griffiths

Dreamweaver MX 2004: The Missing Manual by David Sawyer McFarland

Office 2004 for Macintosh: The Missing Manual by Mark H. Walker and Franklin Tessler

AppleWorks 6: The Missing Manual by Jim Elferdink and David Reynolds

Windows XP Home Edition: The Missing Manual by David Pogue

Windows XP Pro: The Missing Manual by David Pogue, Craig Zacker, and Linda Zacker

Applescript: The Missing Manual by Adam Goldstein

iLife '05: The Missing Manual by David Pogue

Home Networking: The Missing Manual by Scott Lowe

Introduction

All of a sudden, everyone in the world seems to be getting a digital camera. And no wonder. When you go digital, you get instant gratification—you can preview your photos as soon as you take them, and there's no more wondering how many duds you're going to get back from the photo store.

You save a bundle on printing, too, since you can pick and choose which photos to print. Or maybe you're thinking that printing's pretty 20th century. Maybe you want to post your photos on a Web site, email them to friends, or create a really cool slideshow with fancy transitions and music.

If the digital camera bug has bitten you, you're probably aware of something else: the image-editing and picture-organizing software that comes with most cameras can be pretty limited when it's time to spruce up your digital photos. Even if you're scanning in old prints and slides, you'll want a program that'll help you rejuvenate these gems and eliminate the wear and tear of all those years.

Enter Photoshop Elements 3: an all-in-one program that can help you improve your photos, keep them organized, and make top-notch prints and truly nifty creative projects.

Why Photoshop Elements?

Adobe's Photoshop is the granddaddy of all image-editing programs. It's the Big Cheese, the industry standard against which everything else is measured. Every photo you've seen in a book or magazine in the past 10 years or so has almost certainly passed through Photoshop on its way to being printed. You just can't buy anything that gives you more control over your pictures than Photoshop does.

But Photoshop has some big drawbacks—it's darned hard to learn well, it's horribly expensive, and many of the features in it are just plain overkill if you don't plan to work on pictures for a living.

For several years, Adobe tried to find a way to cram all of Photoshop's marvelous powers into a package that normal people could use. Finding the right formula was a slow process. First there was PhotoDeluxe, a program that was lots of fun but came up short when you wanted to fine-tune *how* the program worked. Then Adobe tried again with Photoshop LE, which many people felt just gave you all the difficulty of full Photoshop but still too little of what you needed to do top-notch work.

Finally—sort of like the "The Three Bears"—Adobe got it just right with Photoshop Elements, which took off like crazy, because it offers so much of the power of Photoshop in a program that almost anyone can learn to use. With Elements, you too can work with the same wonderful tools that the pros use.

With the first two versions of Elements, there was something of a learning curve. It was a super program but not one where you could just sit down and expect to get perfect results right off the bat.

In this new version, Photoshop Elements 3, Adobe has added lots of push-button–easy ways to correct and improve your photos without taking away any of the features in the earlier versions. If you've been scared of Elements because of what you've heard about how tricky it is, you can stop worrying and jump right in.

What You Can Do with Elements 3

Besides making Photoshop Elements 3 easier for beginners, Adobe has greatly expanded what the program can do. The Windows version of Elements 3 now includes all the organizing capabilities of *another* Adobe program called Photoshop Album (Adobe figured that anyone owning a Mac is probably using iPhoto to store their photos). Elements also comes with lots of new ways to share your photos. The list of what Elements can do is pretty impressive. You can:

- Enhance your photos by editing, cropping, and color correcting them, including fixing exposure and color problems

- Add all kinds of special effects to your photos, like turning a garden-variety photo into a drawing, a painting, or even a tile mosaic

- Combine photos into a panorama or a montage

- Move someone from one photo to another, and even remove people (your ex?) from last year's holiday photos

- Repair and restore old and damaged photos

- Organize your photos and assign keywords to them so you can search by subject or name

- Add type to your images and turn them into things like greeting cards and flyers

- Create slideshows to share with your friends, regardless of whether they use Windows, Mac, or even a Palm or Pocket PC device

- Automatically resize photos so that they're ready for email. If you're using Windows, Elements lets you send your photos inside specially designed emails

- Create digital artwork from scratch, even without a photo to work from

- Create and share professional-looking Web photo galleries and email-ready slideshows that will make your friends actually ask to see the pictures from your latest trip

- Create and edit graphics for Web sites, including making animated GIFs (pictures that move animation-style)

It's worth noting, though, that there are still a few things Elements *can't* do. While Elements 3 is much better at handling text than previous versions, it's still not really a substitute for PageMaker or any other desktop publishing program. And Elements can do an amazing job of fixing problems in your photos, but only if you give it something to work with. If your photo is totally overexposed, blurry, and the tops of everyone's heads are cut off, there may be a limit to what even Elements can do to help you out. (C'mon, be fair.) As a matter of fact, though, you're more likely to be surprised by how much Elements *can* fix than by what it can't.

What's New in Elements 3

This book is about Photoshop Elements 3. If you have an earlier version of Elements, you'll find a fair number of similarities. But the program's been given a pretty thorough overhaul, especially the *Quick Fix* feature, which gathers the basic editing tools into one window and lets you easily apply, well, quick fixes. Quick fix has several remarkable new tools—including the one-button Auto Smart Fix and the Shadows/Highlights tool for fixing areas of your photo that are too dark or too light—and finally a usably large preview window so you don't have to squint to see the potential results of your changes. Finally, the Windows version of Elements 3 is *very* different from previous versions. (See the next section, "The Big Difference.")

Some of the main changes in Elements 3 are:

- The dramatically redesigned Quick Fix window. Not only do you get more space to preview your changes, but the newly added tools really make what you're seeing worth looking at. In fact, you may find that the Quick Fix window becomes your main Elements workspace (Chapter 4).

- The Red-Eye tool has been redesigned. No more hours of trying to figure out why vampire-red eyes just turned werewolf gray. Now you can get great results with just one click (Chapter 4).

- You can scan as many photos as will fit onto your scanner, and Elements will automatically cut them apart, trim them, and straighten them up for you (Chapter 3).

- Help has been beefed up, too. There's help all over the place, even in the *tooltips* text, the little floating windows that pop up when your mouse hovers over an object on your screen.

- There are some useful *new* tools in Elements 3. The much sought-after Healing brush has been brought over from Photoshop, and it's even easier to use in Elements. Now you can just brush away blemishes (Chapter 9). The Shadow/Highlight tool, which helps correct exposure errors, also made it over from Photoshop (Chapter 4), as has the filter gallery (Chapter 11), which lets you change the order in which filters are applied. The new Color Replacement brush (Chapter 9) is also a great timesaver. And Elements has its own new Cookie Cutter tool, which makes it a snap to crop photos so they fit into shapes like stars or hearts (Chapter 11).

- Lots of high-end photographer's tools from Photoshop have made it into this version of Elements. Photographers who shoot in RAW format will be thrilled to have a version of the Photoshop plug-in for opening and correcting photos right in Elements without using another program. Noise Reduction helps combat the graininess that is the bane of the newer high-megapixel digital cameras, and photo filters, which work just like the filters you used to attach to your film camera for correcting light or for special effects, are now part of Elements (Chapter 8).

- The batch-processing feature has lots more options. Now you can process groups of photos not only when converting file types, but also to apply basic retouching, add captions, and insert copyright notices (Chapter 8).

- Text handling has been beefed up, too. For the first time, you can enter more than one line of text without spending hours getting the lines equally spaced (Chapter 12).

- For the technically inclined, Elements now lets you work in 16-bit color depth. You're still pretty limited in the kinds of edits you can make using this extra color information, but at least you can make your most important corrections and save your photos in 16-bit so that you'll have access to the extra detail in the future.

- Photoshop Elements 3 is based on Photoshop CS (the latest version of Photoshop), while Elements 2 is based on Photoshop 7 (Elements 1 is based on Photoshop 6). The tools in each version of Elements have the same general abilities and limitations as their big brother equivalents. This is important because it means you can use plug-ins and brushes designed to work with CS that haven't been compatible with earlier versions of Elements.

- No going back now—the Windows version requires at least Windows 2000 with Service Pack 4, or Windows XP with Service Pack 1. For those using Macs: Elements 3 only works with Mac OS X 10.2.8 or higher (Adobe actually recommends 10.3 for best performance). If you have older versions of either operating system, you'll have to stick with Elements 2 or go for a system upgrade.

A quick way to tell which version of Elements you've got is to look for the version number on the CD. If the program is already installed, see page 1 for help figuring out which version you have.

Incidentally, all three versions are totally separate programs, so you can run all of them on the same computer if you like, as long your operating system is compatible. So if you prefer the older version of a particular tool, or if you are a Mac veteran who has plug-ins that work only in Classic, you can still use them. If you've been using Elements 2 or Elements 1, you'll still feel right at home in Elements 3. You'll just have some terrific new toys to play with.

> **TIP** If you have a Mac, you can run multiple versions of Elements simultaneously if you want, but you'll probably find you need to start the older versions *before* you launch Elements 3.
>
> For Windows, running multiple versions of Elements works for some people but not for others, and Adobe doesn't recommend trying to run more than one version at the same time.

The Big Difference

There's one enormous difference between Elements 3 and earlier versions (and for that matter, between Elements and the vast majority of other Adobe products).

Adobe has abandoned its long-standing policy of making the Macintosh and Windows versions as much alike as possible. There are some big differences in what you get with Elements 3 depending on which platform you're on.

This book covers both the Windows and Mac versions. You'll see a lot of separate sections in the first three chapters and in Chapters 14 through 16, because getting photos into Elements and sending them out again, to share with other people, have some major platform differences. But the heart of the book—how to use Elements to fix, create, or improve your images—is still exactly the same regardless of whether you're on a Mac or a PC. Here's a quick look at the key differences.

Windows

Adobe has merged Photoshop Album, its photo-organizing software, into the Windows version of Elements and is now calling it the *Organizer*. You'll use the Organizer to store your photos, assign keywords (called *tags*) to search for them, and set up many different ways of viewing your files.

The best part of the Organizer is the *Create* feature, where you can quickly make slideshows, cards, album pages, VCDs (video CDs), and lots of other fun projects. You'll also use the Organizer to access an online ordering service (at *Ofoto.com*) for prints and books.

If you currently use Photoshop Album or you've wanted to try it, you'll be in heaven with Elements 3. On the other hand, if you're not an Album fan, or you're content with your own organizing system, you can ignore a fair amount of the Organizer's features. But whether you like it or not, you will get dumped back into the Organizer for certain tasks, like printing a contact sheet or creating a Web Gallery.

Macintosh

So, Mac folks, should you be snarling with disappointment and feeling defrauded that you don't get the Organizer? Yes, no, and maybe.

For starters, you have total freedom of choice about how organized you want to be. iPhoto integrates well with Elements, or you can use any other organizing program, or none at all if you prefer.

Also, the Mac version of Elements 3 is closer to Photoshop CS than its Windows counterpart. For instance, while you don't get Organizer, you do get all the functionality of the wonderful Photoshop File Browser, which lets you assign and manage keywords right in the File Browser itself without going to another window to do it. Windows folks don't get all the File Browser functions because they've got Organizer for things like assigning keywords.

Elements on the Mac also offers the Photoshop versions of the Web Gallery (for creating Web pages to display your photos) and the Picture Package (for printing multiple photos at once).

Really, about all you're missing is the handy Date view option in the Organizer, the built-in online print ordering, the easy CD backup feature, and the projects in Create. These are a loss. There are some very fun things you can do with Create, although many of them have some sort of iPhoto equivalent, so it's actually just the convenience of doing it all in one window that you lose.

Two other things lacking on the Mac side are the ability to burn a VCD within Elements, and some fonts that are included for the Create projects. You'll still need a program like Toast to burn a VCD, but really that's an iffish format on either platform, so it's not a great loss.

If you use a Mac, you'll also probably be a little annoyed by some features of the interface, which is decidedly Windows-y, even in the Mac version. For example, you'll have to get used to Windows "X" buttons to close some windows.

The Mac folks who'll be most unhappy are those who've been yearning for Photoshop Album for the Mac platform. If you're one of them, you might want to consider that File Browser keywords do pretty nearly everything Organizer does (although you still will need to jump through a few more hoops to back your photos up). If you need a really heavy-duty image organizing system, Organizer is probably not it anymore than iPhoto. On either platform, you may still prefer a third-party solution, like JAlbum or iView Media. It depends on how elaborate your requirements are.

For actual photo editing, there is still no real difference between the two platforms. The differences are at both ends of the process—how you get your photos into Elements and keep them organized, and how you send them out to share when you're done. The real work areas are still the same for both Mac and Windows, and equally competent for both.

Overall, the Mac version is still a pretty nice update from Elements 2, and it's cheaper than the Windows version, too. If you still aren't satisfied, of course, you can always let Adobe know how you feel.

Elements Versus Photoshop

It's very easy to get confused about the differences between Elements and the full version of Adobe Photoshop. Because Elements is so much less expensive, and because many of the program's more advanced controls are tucked away, a lot of Photoshop aficionados tend to view Elements as some kind of toy version of their program.

They could not be more wrong. Elements *is* Photoshop, but it's Photoshop adapted for use with your home computer printer and for the Web. The most important difference between Elements and Photoshop is that Elements does not let you work or save in CMYK mode, which is the format used for commercial color printing. (CMYK stands for Cyan, Magenta, Yellow, and blacK).

Elements also lacks several tools that are basic staples in any commercial art department, like Actions or scripting (to help automate repetitive tasks), the extra color control you can get from Curves, and the Pen tool's special talent for creating vector paths. (Chapter 17 will show you lots of ways to add some of these features to Elements). Also, for some special effects, like creating drop shadows or bevels, the tool you'd use—Layer Styles—doesn't have as many settings in Elements as it does in Photoshop. The same holds true for a handful of other Elements tools.

And although Elements is all most people will need to create graphics for the Web, it doesn't come with the ImageReady component of Photoshop, which lets you do things like automatically slice images for faster Web display. If you use Elements, you'll have to do those tasks manually or look for another program to help out.

The Key to Learning Elements

Elements may not be quite as powerful as Photoshop, but it's still a complex program, filled with more features than most people will ever end up using. The good news is that the Quick Fix window lets you get started right away, even if you don't understand every last option that Quick Fix presents you with.

As for the program's more complex features, the key to learning how to use Elements—or any other program, for that matter—is to focus only on what you need to know for the task you're currently trying to accomplish.

For example, if you're trying to use Quick Fix to adjust the color of your photo and crop it, don't worry that you don't get the concept of "layers" yet. You won't learn to do everything in Elements in a day or even a week. The rest will wait for you till you need it. So take your time, and don't worry about what's not important to you right now. You'll find it much easier to master Elements if you go slowly and concentrate on one thing at a time.

If you're totally new to the program, you'll find only three or four big concepts in this book that you really have to understand if you want to get the most out of Elements. It may take a little time for some concepts to sink in—resolution and layers, for instance, aren't the most intuitive concepts in the world—but once they click, they'll seem so obvious that you'll wonder why things seemed confusing at first. That's perfectly normal, so persevere. You *can* do this, and there's nothing in this book that you won't be able to understand with a little bit of careful reading.

The very best way to learn Elements is just to dive right in and play with it. Try all the different filters to see what they do. Add a filter on top of another filter. Click around on all the different tools and try them. You don't even need to have a photo to do this. See page 27 for how to make an image from scratch in Elements. Get crazy—you can stack up as many filters, effects, and layer styles as you want without crashing the program.

About This Book

Elements is such a cool program and so much fun to use, but figuring out how to make it do what you want is another matter. Amazingly, there's not even a complete manual included with Elements 3. All you get is the brief "Getting Started" guide. The Elements Help files are very good, but of course you need to know what you're looking for to use them to your best advantage.

You'll find a slew of Elements titles at your local bookstore, but most of them assume that you know quite a bit about the basics of photography and/or digital imaging. It's much easier to find good intermediate books about Elements than books designed to get you going with the program.

Which is where the Missing Manual comes in. This book is intended to make learning Elements easier by avoiding technical jargon as much as possible, and explaining *why* and *when* you'll want to use (or avoid) certain features in the program. That approach is as useful to people who are advanced photographers as it is to those who are just getting started with their first digital camera.

You'll also find tutorials throughout the book that refer to files you can download from the Missing Manual Web site (*www.missingmanuals.com*) so you can practice the techniques you're reading about. And throughout the book, you'll find several different kinds of sidebar articles. The ones labeled "Up to Speed" help newcomers to Elements do things or explain concepts that veterans are probably already familiar with. "Power Users' Clinics" cover more advanced topics that won't be of much interest to casual photographers.

About the Outline

This book is divided into six different sections, each of which focuses on a certain kind of task you might want to do in Elements.

Introduction to Elements

The first section of this book helps you get started with Elements. Chapter 1 shows you how to navigate Elements' slightly confusing layout and mishmash of programs within programs. You learn how to decide which window to start from, as well as how to set up Elements so it best suits your own personal working style. You'll also learn about some important basic keyboard shortcuts and where to look for help when you get stuck. Chapter 2 covers how to get photos into Elements, the basics of organizing them, and how to open files and create new images from scratch. Chapter 3 looks at how to save and back up your images, and explains the concept of resolution.

Elemental Elements

Chapter 4 tells you how to use the Quick Fix window to dramatically improve your photos. Chapters 5 and 6 cover two key concepts—making selections and layers—that you'll use throughout the book.

Retouching

Having Elements is like having a darkroom on your computer. In Chapter 7, you'll learn how to make basic corrections, such as exposure, color adjustments, sharpening, and removing dust and scratches. Then in Chapter 9 you'll move on to some more sophisticated fixes, like changing the light, using the clone stamp to make repairs, making your photos more lively with hue/saturation, and changing the colors in an image. Chapter 8 covers topics unique to digital camera users, like RAW conversion and batch processing your photos.

Artistic Elements

This section covers the fun stuff—painting on your photos and drawing shapes (Chapter 11), using filters and effects to create a more artistic look (Chapter 12), and adding type to your images (Chapter 13).

Sharing Your Images

Once you've created a great image in Elements, you'll want to share it, so this section is about how to get the most out of your printer (Chapter 14), how to create images for the Web and email (Chapter 15), how to make slideshows and Web Galleries with your photos (Chapter 16), and for Windows owners, all the fun projects in Create.

Additional Elements

There are literally hundreds of plug-ins and additional tools you can get to customize your copy of Elements and increase its abilities, and the Internet and your local bookstore are chock full of additional information. Chapter 17 offers a look at some of these, as well as information about using a graphics tablet in Elements and some resources for after you've finished this book.

The Very Basics

This book assumes that you know how to perform basic activities on your computer like clicking and double-clicking your mouse and dragging objects on-screen. Here's a quick refresher: to *click* means to move the point of your mouse or trackpad cursor over an object on your screen and press the mouse or trackpad button once. To *double-click* means to press the button twice, quickly, without moving the mouse between clicks. To *drag* means to click on an object and use the mouse to move it, while holding down the button so you don't let go of it. If you're comfortable with basic concepts like these, you're ready to get started with this book.

Windows and Mac Commands

Throughout this book, commands are given with their Windows version first, followed by the Mac equivalent. So if you see "Press Ctrl+S (⌘+S) to save your file," that means, if you're using Windows, press the Control key and the S key, while on a Mac you'd use the Command key and the S key. You'll read about the differences between the two operating systems wherever they're relevant.

Also, this book assumes you're using Windows XP or Mac OS X 10.3, and that's what you'll see in the screenshots in the illustrations. There are only a few differences if you're using an older version of either operating system, and you should be able to figure them out pretty easily.

About → These → Arrows

Throughout *Photoshop Elements 3: The Missing Manual* (and in any Missing Manual for that matter) you'll see arrows that look like this: "Go to Applications → Adobe Photoshop Elements → Plug-Ins → Import/Export."

This is a shorthand way of helping you find files, folders, and menu choices without having to read through excruciatingly long, bureaucratic-style instructions. So, for example, the sentence in the previous paragraph is a short way of saying: "Double-click your Applications folder to open it, then navigate to the folder labeled 'Adobe Photoshop Elements 3.' Open that folder and then look for another folder called 'Plug-Ins,' where you'll find the folder called 'Import/Export.'" The arrows work the same way for menus, too, as shown in Figure 0-1.

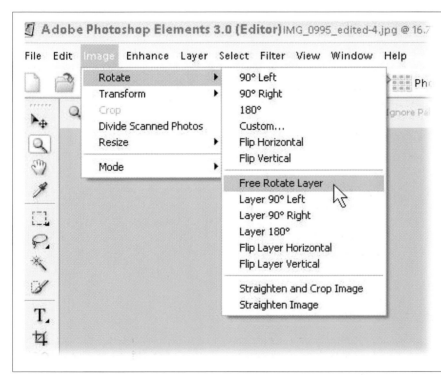

Figure 0-1:
In a Missing Manual, when you see "Select Image → Rotate → Free Rotate Layer," that's a quicker way of saying "Go to the menu bar and click Image, then slide down to Rotate, and choose Free Rotate Layer from the pop-out menu.

About MissingManuals.com

If you head on over to the Missing Manual Web site (*www.missingmanuals.com*) you can find links to downloadable images for the tutorials mentioned in this book, if you want to practice without using your own photos. (Or maybe you never take pictures that need correcting?)

A word about the image files for the tutorials: to make life easier for folks with dial-up Internet connections, the file sizes have been kept pretty small. This means you probably won't want to print the results of what you create (since you'll end up with a print about the size of a match book). But that doesn't really matter since the files are really meant for onscreen use.

At the Web site, you can also find articles, tips, and updates to the book. If you click the Errata link, you'll see any corrections to the book's content, too. If you find something, feel free to report it by using this link. Each time the book is printed, we'll update it with any confirmed corrections. If you want to be certain that your own copy is up to the minute, this is where to check for any changes. And thanks for reporting any errors or corrections.

Safari® Enabled

 When you see a Safari® Enabled icon on the cover of your favorite technology book, that means the book is available online through the O'Reilly Network Safari Bookshelf.

Safari offers a solution that's better than e-books. It's a virtual library that lets you easily search thousands of top tech books, cut and paste code samples, download chapters, and find quick answers when you need the most accurate, current information. Try it for free at *http://safari.oreilly.com*.

Part One:
Introductory Elements

1

Finding Your Way Around Elements

Photoshop Elements lets you do practically anything you want to your digital images. You can colorize black and white photos, remove demonic red-eye stares, or distort the facial features of people who've been mean to you. The downside is that finding your way around the program has gotten a lot more complicated than it used to be, especially if you're using the Windows version.

This chapter helps get you oriented in Elements. You'll learn about what to expect when you start up the program, and how to use Elements to fix your photos with just a couple of keystrokes—a great new feature in this version.

Along the way, you'll find out about some of Elements' basic controls and how to get hold of the program's Help files if you need them. Elements is absolutely crammed with help at every turn. Adobe did their best to make it as easy for you as possible.

UP TO SPEED

Which Version of Elements Do You Have?

This book covers Photoshop Elements 3. If you're not sure which version of Elements you have, the easiest way to find out is to look at the program's icon (the file you click on to launch Elements).

You can use this book if you have an earlier version of Elements, because a lot of the basic editing procedures are the same, but there are some pretty substantial differences between Elements 3 and the earlier versions, much more so than between Elements 1 and Elements 2.

The Welcome Screen

When you launch Elements for the first time, you get a veritable smorgasbord of options, all neatly laid out for you in the Welcome screen (the Windows version is shown in Figure 1-1 and the Mac version in Figure 1-2).

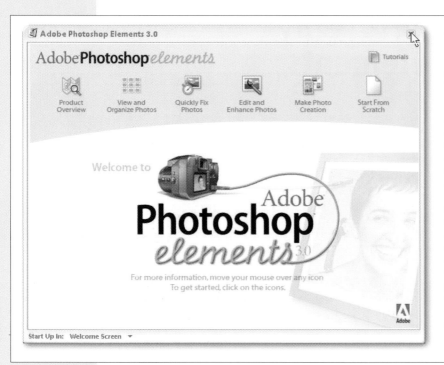

Figure 1-1:
The Windows Welcome screen gives you six main activities to choose from (there's also a Tutorials link in the upper-right corner). Hold your cursor over any of these options for more details about each choice. You can't bypass the Windows Welcome screen just by clicking the Close button. If you do, the screen goes away—but so does Elements. Fortunately, you've got options: the box on page 6 tells you how to permanently get rid of the Welcome screen.

Windows Version

Interestingly, the Windows Welcome screen is not actually Elements. It's a launching pad that, depending on the button you click, will start up one of two different programs:

- **Organizer,** which lets you store and organize your image files.

- **Editor,** which lets you edit your images.

It's quite easy to get back and forth between the Editor and the Organizer—which you might call the two different faces of Elements—and you probably won't do much in one without eventually needing to get into the other. But in some ways, they still function as two separate programs. In any case, the Welcome screen offers you no less than six choices for how to get into Elements:

- **Product Overview** offers a round-up of all the features inside Elements.

- **View and Organize Photos** takes you to the Organizer, where you can store and sort all your images.

- **Quickly Fix Photos** brings you to the wonderful new Quick Fix window (which is actually part of the Editor) where you can perform amazing color corrections with just a click.

- **Edit and Enhance Photos** takes you to the Editor, which is the digital darkroom/art studio where you can perform your most extensive edits.

- **Make Photo Creation** enables you to use your photos in a wide variety of projects like greeting cards and slideshows. You perform all these tasks in the Organizer.

- **Start From Scratch** provides you a new blank document in the Editor to noodle away on.

> **TIP**   The boxed version of Elements for Windows includes a half-hour video introduction to the program, led by Photoshop guru Deke McClelland. It's a good overview of some of the main features of Elements. To see it, fire up the Elements CD, click past the legal stuff, and click Product Overview. Windows Media Player launches, and Deke speaks.

If you start in the Organizer, once you've located a photo to edit, you have to wait while the Editor loads. And if you have both the Editor and the Organizer running, quitting the Editor doesn't close the Organizer. You have to close both programs independently.

UP TO SPEED

Where the Heck Did Elements Go?

If you know that you've installed Elements but you can't seem to figure out how to launch it, no problem.

In Windows: There should be a shortcut to Elements on your desktop once you've installed the program, or go to the Start menu and click the Adobe Photoshop Elements 3 icon. If you don't see Elements in the Start menu, click the arrow next to "All Programs," and you should find it in the pop-up menu.

On a Mac: Go to Applications → Adobe Photoshop Elements 3 and double-click the Photoshop Elements icon to launch the program. Elements usually creates its own Dock icon on its first launch. If you don't want this icon in your Dock, just drag it off and watch it vanish in a puff of smoke.

Mac Version

If you have a Mac, on the other hand, life is far less complex, since you only have one program to deal with: Elements. You'll either use Elements' File Browser or iPhoto to organize your photos. Adobe's made the reasonable guess that Mac fans will prefer to use iPhoto for many of the tasks Organizer handles for Windows folks, like online print and book ordering, or any other organizing program you might already be using.

Elements on the Mac opens right into the Standard Edit window and presents the Welcome screen, as shown in Figure 1-2, which lets you choose to connect to your camera or scanner, browse for files, start a new file, or open a recent one.

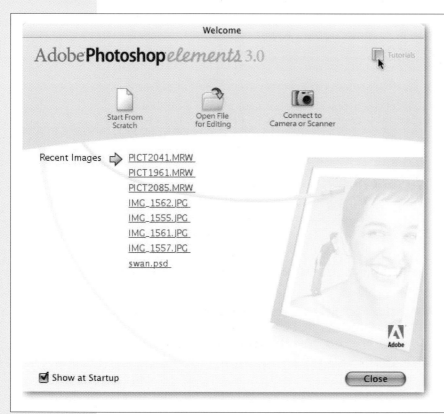

Figure 1-2:
If you're using a Mac, click the Tutorials button to go to Adobe's online tutorials for Elements. Also, after you've actually had some photos open in Elements, you'll see a list of recent items, like the ones shown here, on the Welcome screen. Just click any file to open it.

WHAT'S NEW

Getting Rid of the Welcome Screen

If you get to feeling like you've been welcomed enough, you can turn off the Welcome screen in Elements on either platform. Then you don't have to click through it every time you start the program.

Windows: In the Welcome screen's lower-left corner you can choose where you want Elements to start when you launch the program: Editor, Organizer, or Welcome screen. Pick the one you want, and from now on, that's what opens first in Elements.

To get the Welcome screen back, from either the Editor or the Organizer, choose Window → Welcome.

Mac: Turn off "Show at start-up" at the bottom of the Welcome Screen window. If later on you decide you want the Welcome screen back, go to Window → Welcome to turn it on again.

Organizing Your Photos

How you organize your photos depends a lot on whether you're using a Windows PC or a Mac. In Windows, you can import and organize your images directly within Elements' Organizer program, while most Mac people will probably use iPhoto if they want to keep their photos organized.

Windows Organizer

If you're using Windows, the Organizer is where your photos come into Elements and go out again. The Organizer stores and catalogs your photos, and you automatically come back to it for any activities that involve sharing your photos, like printing a photo package or making a slideshow. The Organizer has three main sections, as shown in Figure 1-3:

- **Photo Browser** lets you view your photos, sort them into collections, and assign keyword tags to them.

- **Date View** is a fun feature that lets you see your photo imports organized by the date you brought them into the Organizer. It's even laid out like a calendar.

- **Create** is where you come after you've finished editing your photos and are ready to use them in slideshows, album pages, greeting cards, and other projects.

The Organizer has lots of really cool features, and in the body of this book you'll meet them when they're relevant to the image-editing task at hand. The next chapter shows you how to use the Organizer to import and organize your photos, and Appendix A covers all the Organizer's different menu options.

Photo Downloader

Actually, the Windows version of Elements has one other component, which you might have seen already if you've plugged your camera into your computer since you installed Elements: the Photo Downloader (Figure 1-4).

This bumptious little program is meant to help you get your photos into the Organizer, and it's more zealous than a personal-injury lawyer on the scene of an accident. It sniffs out any device you attach to your computer that might possibly contain photos and races to the scene, elbowing the Explorer dialog box out of the way. Depending on the speed of your computer, it may show up before the Explorer dialog box or slightly after it. You have to dismiss the Downloader first if you want to use another program to import your photos.

You may love the Downloader or you may hate it. You can read more about it in the next chapter (page 22), including how to send it away for good if you want to. If you plan to use the Organizer to catalog your photos and assign keywords to them, reading the section on the Downloader in Chapter 2 can help you avoid some forehead-smacking moments.

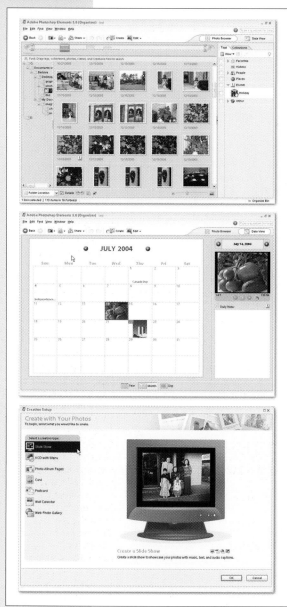

Figure 1-3:
*The Organizer gives you two main ways to look at your
images: Photo Browser (top) and the Date View (middle).
You can switch back and forth between them by clicking
their buttons in the upper-right corner of the Organizer
window.*

*The main Create window (bottom), which you get to by
clicking the Create button in the Shortcuts bar, gives you a
wide choice of projects that you can use to show off your
images. You can click Cancel to get back to the main
Organizer if you change your mind about starting a
project.*

Macintosh

Most people of the Mac persuasion who want to organize their photos will probably use iPhoto (See Figure 1-5 for how to make iPhoto use Elements as its image-
editing program). You can also assign keywords to photos using the Elements File
Browser (which is covered on page 39), or any other third-party organizing software you may have. But whichever method you choose, Elements does not automatically import your photos. You just open them in Elements when you're ready
to work on them or assign keywords.

Figure 1-4:
The Adobe Photo Downloader is yet another program that you get when you install the Windows version of Elements. Its role in life is to pull your photos from your camera (or other storage device) into the Organizer. The Downloader runs even if Elements isn't currently open (although, as you'll learn in Chapter 2, you can disable the Downloader if you don't like it). After the Downloader does its thing, you end up in the Organizer.

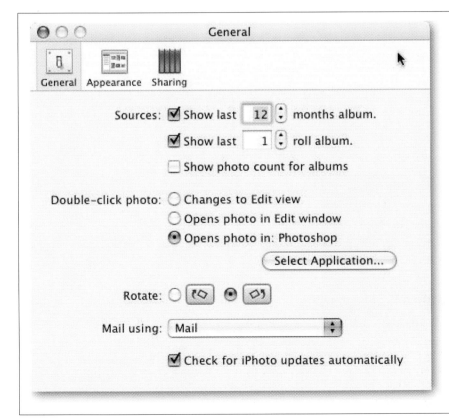

Figure 1-5:
You can set iPhoto so that double-clicking an image opens it in Elements, as shown here. Go to iPhoto → Preferences → General, choose "Double-click photo: opens photo in," click Select Application, and choose Photoshop Elements. Note that the dialog box only displays the first word "Photoshop." If you have both Photoshop and Elements on your Mac you'll either need to remember which program you chose, or just double-click a photo to find out.

Editing Your Photos

In addition to the Organizer, the other main section of Elements is what Adobe now calls the Editor. If you've used Elements in the past, this is the Elements you're used to, although it also has some added features in this version, most notably a hugely improved Quick Fix window.

Photo editing is exactly the same whether you're using Windows or Mac OS X. There are some differences in what you can do from the File Browser, which is where you can start projects like panoramas on a Mac, but otherwise there's not a jot of difference in how you edit a photo. You can see how much alike they are in Figure 1-6.

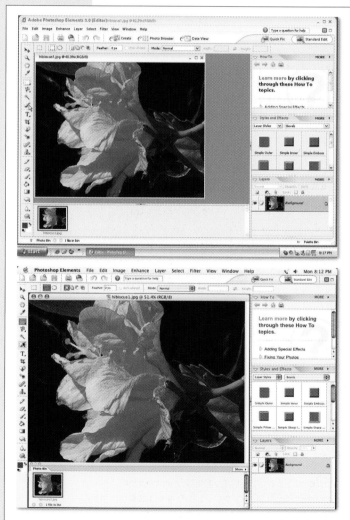

Figure 1-6:
As you can see, there's almost no difference between the Standard Edit window in Windows (top) and Mac OS X (bottom), except for the basic differences between the two operating system controls. Your tools are exactly the same and so are the techniques for using them. The long, skinny strip down the extreme left side of the screen is the Toolbox.

You can operate the Editor in either of two different modes:

- **Quick Fix.** For many beginners, this may end up as your main workspace. Adobe has gathered together the basic tools you need to improve most photos and it's the one place in Elements where you can have a before-and-after view while you work. Chapter 4 discusses using the Quick Fix in detail.

- **Standard Edit.** The Standard Edit window gives you access to Elements' most sophisticated tools. There are far more ways to work on your photo in Standard Edit than in the Quick Fix, and if you're fussy, it's where you'll do most of your retouching work. Most of the Quick Fix commands are also available via menus in the Standard Edit window.

The rest of this chapter covers some of the basic concepts and key tools you'll come across in the Editor.

Your Elements Tools

Elements gives you an amazing array of tools to use when working on your photo. You get almost two dozen primary tools to help you select, paint on, and otherwise manipulate your photos, and many of the tools have as many as four subtools hiding beneath them (see Figure 1-7). Bob Vila's workshop probably isn't any better stocked than the Elements' virtual toolbox.

> **TIP**   If you want to explore every cranny of Elements, you need to open a photo (in the Editor, choose File → Open). Lots of the menus are grayed out if there's no file opened.

The long, skinny strip on the left side of the Standard Edit window is the main Elements Toolbox, as you can see in Figure 1-6. It stays perfectly organized so that you can always find what you want without ever having to lift a finger to straighten it up. And what's more, if you should forget what a particular tool does, just hold your mouse over the tool's icon and a label appears. You activate a tool by clicking on it, as shown in Figure 1-7. And any tool that you select comes with its own collection of options, as shown in Figure 1-8.

Other windows in Elements, like the Quick Fix and the RAW converter (see Chapter 8) also have toolboxes, but none are as complete as the one in Standard Edit.

Don't worry about learning the names of every tool right now. It's easier to remember what a tool is once you've used it. And don't be concerned about how many tools there are. You probably have a bunch of allen wrenches in your garage toolbox that you don't use more than a couple of times a year, and you'll find that you tend to use certain Elements tools more than others.

> **TIP**   You can activate any tool with a keyboard shortcut, thereby saving a *ton* of time, since you don't have to interrupt what you're doing to trek over to the Toolbox. To see a tool's shortcut key, hover your mouse over the icon. It's the letter in parentheses in the tooltip's text that pops up.

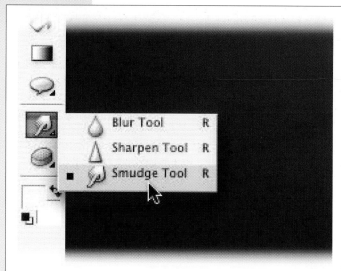

Figure 1-7:
Like any good toolbox, the Elements Toolbox has lots of hidden drawers tucked away in it. Many of the Elements tools are actually groups of tools, which are represented by tiny black triangles on the lower-right side of the tool icon. Clicking these triangles brings out the hidden subtools. The little black square next to the Smudge tool means it's the active tool right now.

POWER USERS' CLINIC

Doubling Up

Old Elements hands: If you prefer the double-columned Toolbox you're used to from previous versions, good news: tear the Toolbox loose from its moorings and collapse it into a double row by grabbing its top edge and pulling it off the Options bar. But keep in mind that a double-columned Toolbox is a bit of a quirky creature. If you put it too close to the left edge of the screen, it springs back to its original form.

In Windows, the Toolbox behavior also changes depending on whether you're in Maximize view.

Figure 1-8:
When a tool is active, the Options bar changes to show its available settings. Elements tools are highly customizable for the task at hand.

The Always-On Toolbox

Do I always have to have a tool selected?

Yes. When looking at the Toolbox you may notice that the Marquee tool icon (the little dotted rectangle) is highlighted, indicating that the tool is active. You can deactivate it by clicking a different tool. But what happens when you don't want any tool to be active? How do you fix things so that you don't have a tool selected?

You don't. In the Editor, one tool must always be selected, so you'll probably want to get in the habit of choosing a tool that won't do anything damaging to your image if you click it accidentally. For instance, the Pencil tool, which leaves a spot or line where you click, is probably not a good choice. The Marquee selection tool, the Zoom tool, and the Hand tool are the safest choices.

Bins and Palettes

In the Editor, the two big space-consuming objects hogging the bottom and right side of your screen are called *bins*. The Photo bin, as shown in Figure 1-9, helps you keep track of which images are currently open.

Figure 1-9:
The Photo bin runs across the bottom of your screen. It holds a thumbnail for every photo you have open. If you happen to have 73 photos open at once, you can scroll the bin to the left and to the right by clicking on either of the two triangle arrow buttons. To change which photo is active, just click the thumbnail of the one you want and it will open in the Editor.

The Photo bin is a useful feature, but unless you have a gigantic monitor, you might rather have the space for your editing work. To close the bin, click the Minimize button, just to the left of the phrase Photo Bin. (On the Mac: click the red button to close it, or click the green button to minimize it.) One very cool thing about the Windows Photo bin is that even when it's closed, you can use the left and right arrows (the ones to the right of the Minimize button) to rotate through the open photos until you find the one you want

The long wide strip down the right side of your screen is the Palette bin. Elements stores *palettes* in this bin to let you do things like keep track of what you've done to your photo (Undo History) and apply special effects to your images (Styles and Effects).

Taming the Palette bin

It's possible that you'll like the Palette bin, but many people don't. Most people find it wastes too much desktop acreage, and in Elements, you need all the working room you can get. Fortunately, you don't have to keep your Palettes in the bin; you can close the bin and just keep your Palettes floating around on your desktop or minimize them.

You open and close the bin by clicking the Palette Bin button at the bottom of your screen (in Windows) or you can click on the Palette Bin's left edge (anywhere along the thin vertical bar). You can also pull palettes out of the bin by dragging the tab of any palette. Figure 1-10 shows how to make your palettes even smaller once they're out of the bin. Freestanding palettes can also be combined with each other, as shown in Figure 1-11.

WHAT'S NEW

Tab No More

In earlier versions of Elements, you could use the Tab key to hide most everything in Elements except your image. Press Tab once, all you saw was your photo, sans distracting palettes and toolbars. Press Tab again and everything returned.

Windows veterans of Elements may be annoyed to learn that as of Elements 3, the Tab key only does this if you're on a Mac. In Windows, Tab hides any free-floating palettes that you've pulled out of the bin, but the anchored parts of the Elements program aren't going anywhere. You can help things a little by pulling the Toolbox loose, as described in the box on page 12. Alternatively, some people prefer to switch to the Organizer and press F11 for a full-screen view.

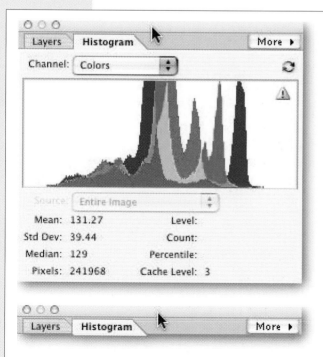

Figure 1-10:
You can free up even more space by collapsing your palettes, accordion-style, once they're out of the bin. To do so, double-click the palette's top bar (top). In Windows, you can also toggle back and forth between expanded and contracted views by clicking the palette's Minimize button. On a Mac, you can do the same thing by clicking the palette's green circle. The bottom figure shows a shrunken palette.

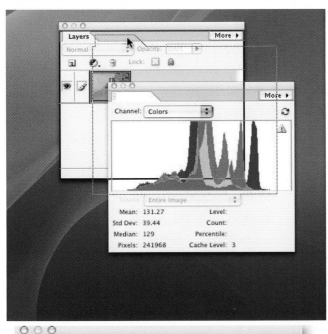

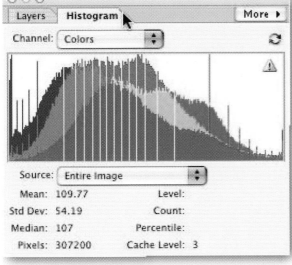

Figure 1-11:
You can combine two or more palettes together once you've dragged them out of the bin.

Top: The Histogram palette is being pulled into, and combined with, the Layers palette. (Note that as you drag a palette, its name temporarily disappears.) To combine palettes, drag one of them (by clicking on the palette's name tab) and drop it onto the other palette (notice the dark black border that appears on the Layers palette, signaling it's "ready" to accept the Histogram palette).

Bottom: To switch from one palette to another after they're grouped, just click the tab of the one you want to use. To remove a palette from a group, just drag it off the palette window. If you want to return everything to how it looked when you first launched Elements, go to Window → Reset Palette Locations.

Only three palettes are in the Palette bin to start with (How To, Layers, and Styles and Effects). To see how many more palettes you actually have, check out the Window menu. When you select a new palette, by choosing it in the Window menu, it may appear in the bin first. If you've hidden the bin, it jumps back out at you with the new palette on display, and you'll have to haul the palette out if you don't want to use the bin. Some palettes, like Undo History, show up already floating and you have to drag them into the bin if you want to corral them there.

NOTE If you've been going crazy because you're trying to get rid of one of the bin's original palettes, but every time you close it, it just hops back into the bin, click the More button in the upper-right corner of the palette, and turn off "Place in Palette bin." Next time you close the palette, it goes away and won't return till you choose it again from the Window menu.

Elements Shortcuts

One thing that makes Elements kind of bewildering is the number of ways there are to perform almost any action. You can navigate from menus, use the Shortcuts bar, or, as most people find easiest, use keyboard shortcuts. In this book, if there's a keystroke that you can use to do something, that's usually the method you'll see. But often there are other ways to do the same thing that are equally good. It's your choice.

For instance, on the top of your screen, just below the menu bar is the Shortcuts bar. If you're the kind of person who likes to click a button to make things happen, this is your part of Elements. If you pass your mouse over the Shortcut bar icons, you can see tooltips that tell you what each button does. Some people love the Shortcuts bar; some ignore it completely.

NOTE Elements 3 has one palette-related quirk. In the Window menu, visible palettes should have a check next to their names. But if you collapse a palette, even though the palette's name stays on your desktop, it is unchecked in the Window menu. If you lose a collapsed palette (they tend to get hidden behind the Options bar when you switch back and forth from Standard Edit to Quick Fix or the Organizer), just select the palette's name again in the list to bring the palette back to the front where you can reach it. If all else fails, choosing Reset Palette Locations in the Window menu puts everything back to its original position.

Getting Help and the How To Palette

Wherever Adobe found a stray corner in Elements, they stuck some help into it. You can't move anywhere in this program without being offered some kind of guidance. Here are some of the ways you can summon assistance if you need it:

- **Options bar.** Click the Question Mark button or enter a search term in the Help box, as shown in Figure 1-12.

- **Tooltips.** The text that pops up under your mouse as you move around Elements is linked to the appropriate section in Elements Help. Click a tooltip for more information about whatever your mouse is hovering over.

- **Dialog box links.** Most dialog boxes have links to Elements Help. If you get confused about what the settings for a filter do, for instance, just click the blue link text for a reminder.

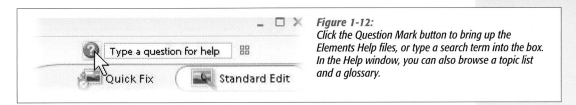

Figure 1-12:
Click the Question Mark button to bring up the Elements Help files, or type a search term into the box. In the Help window, you can also browse a topic list and a glossary.

The How To palette

If you need help figuring out where to begin a project, the Editor's How To palette gives instructions for lots of things you're likely to want to do in Elements (Figure 1-13). You can get directions for everything from making a photo look old-fashioned to creating fancy warped text effects.

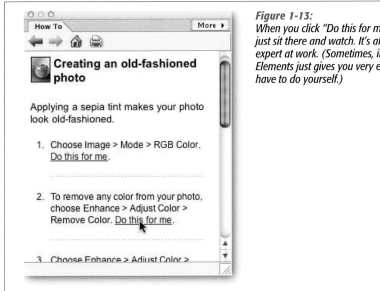

Figure 1-13:
When you click "Do this for me" Elements runs the show while you just sit there and watch. It's always helpful to be able to watch an expert at work. (Sometimes, instead of doing the work for you, Elements just gives you very explicit directions for something you have to do yourself.)

Escape Routes

Photoshop Elements has a couple of really wonderful features to help you keep from making irrevocable screw-ups: the Undo command and the Undo History palette. After you've gotten used to them, you'll probably wish it were possible to use these tools in all aspects of your life, not just Elements.

Undo

No matter where you are in Elements, you can almost always change your mind about what you just did. Just press Ctrl+Z (⌘-Z) and the last change you made goes away. This works even if you've just saved your photo but only while it's still open. (If you close your picture, your changes are permanent.) Keep pressing Ctrl+Z (⌘-Z) and you keep undoing your work, step by step.

If you want to redo what you just undid, just press Ctrl+Y (⌘-Y). These keystroke commands are great for toggling changes on and off while you decide whether you really want to keep them.

> **NOTE** You do have some control over the keys you use for Undo/Redo, if you go to Edit → Preferences → General (Photoshop Elements → Preferences → General). Elements gives you two other choices, both of which involve the Z key in combination with the Control, Alt, and Shift keys.

Undo History palette

In the Standard Edit window, you get even more control over the actions you can undo, thanks to the Undo History palette (Figure 1-14), which you open by choosing Window → Undo History.

Figure 1-14:
For a little time travel, just slide the pointer up and watch your changes disappear one by one. You can only go back sequentially. Here, for instance, you can't go back to Crop without first undoing the Paint Bucket and the Eraser. Slide the pointer forward to redo your work.

This palette holds a list of the changes you've made since the last time you saved your image. Just push the slider up and watch your changes disappear one by one as you go. Undo History even works if you've saved your file: as long as you haven't closed your file, the palette tracks every action you take.

Be careful, though. You can only back up as many steps as you've set Elements to remember. Elements lets you keep track of as many as 1,000 actions. You can regulate this number in Preferences, as explained in Figure 1-15.

The one rule of Elements

As you're probably beginning to see, Elements lets you work in lots of different ways. What's more, most people who use Elements will approach projects in different ways. What works for your neighbor with his pictures may be quite different from how you would choose to work on the very same shots.

However, there's one suggestion you'll hear from almost every Elements veteran, and it's an important one: **Never, ever work on your original. Always, always, always make a copy of your image and work on that.**

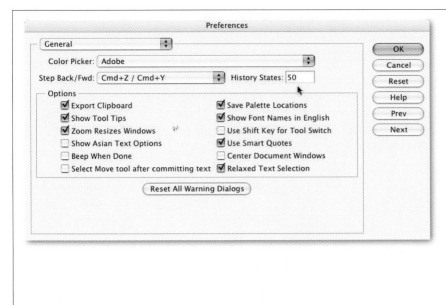

Figure 1-15:
You can set the number of steps the Undo History palette remembers in Edit → Preferences → General. Elements initially sets it to 50 by default, but it can be set as high as 1,000. Beware, though— remembering even 100 steps may slow your system to a crawl if you don't have a super-powered processor, plenty of memory, and loads of disk space. If Elements runs slowly on your machine, reducing the number of history states it remembers (try 20) may speed things up a bit.

If you have your original safely put away, you can go to town with your edits and know that you can always start over again if you want to.

Adobe recognizes the value of working from a copy. Elements does this automatically when you edit a photo that's cataloged in the Organizer, so that you can always revert to your original. iPhoto does something similar, but without the refinements of the Organizer's *versions,* which are explained in Figure 1-16.

If you store your photos in the Organizer, you don't need to worry about accidentally trashing your original. If you don't, or if you're using a Mac, the safest approach is to make a copy of your photo before you begin making any changes.

To make a copy of your image in Elements:

1. **Right-click the title bar of the Image window and choose Duplicate (Windows) or go to File → Duplicate (Windows or Mac).**

   The Image window is the small window within the Editor where your photo appears.

2. **Name the duplicate, and click the close button on the original.**

   Now the original's safely tucked out of harm's way.

3. **Save the duplicate, using Ctrl+S (⌘-S).**

   Choose Photoshop (.psd) as the file format when you save it. (You may want to choose another format after you've read Chapter 3 and understand more about your different format options.)

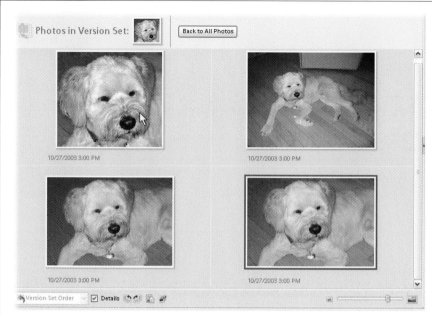

Figure 1-16:
In the Windows version of Elements, if you turn on the "Save in Version Set with Original" option, the Organizer will stack up as many copies of the different states of your photo as you want to save. You can choose to open any version at any time. See page 435 for more about Version sets.

Now you don't have to worry about making a mistake or changing your mind, because you can always start over if you want to.

Getting Started in a Hurry

If you're the impatient type and you're starting to squirm because you want to be up and doing something to your photos, here's the quickest way to get started in Elements. You can adjust the brightness and color balance all in one step.

1. **While you're in the Editor, open a photo.**

   Press Ctrl+O (⌘-O) and navigate to the image you want, then click Open.

2. **Press Alt+Ctrl+M (Option-⌘-M).**

   You've just applied Elements Auto Smart Fix tool.

Voila! You should see quite a difference in your photo, unless the exposure, lighting, and contrast were almost perfect before. The Auto Smart Fix tool is one of the many easy-to-use new features in Elements 3. (Of course, you may not like what just happened to your photo, but that's why you bought this book.)

If you're the really impatient type, you can jump right to Chapter 4 to learn about using the Quick Fix commands. But it's worth taking the time to read the next two chapters so you understand which file formats to choose and how to make some basic adjustments to your images, like rotating and cropping them.

Importing and Managing Your Photos

Now that you've had a look around Elements, it's time to start learning how to get photos *into* the program, and also how to keep track of where these photos are stored. As a digital photographer, you may no longer be facing shoeboxes stuffed with prints, but you've still got to face the menace of photos piling up on your hard drive. Fortunately, Elements gives you some great tools for organizing your collection and quickly finding individual pictures.

In this chapter, you'll learn how to import your photos from cameras, digital card readers, and scanners. You'll also find out how to import individual frames from videos, how to open files that are already on your computer, and how to create a new file from scratch. After that, you'll learn how to organize and find your pictures once they're in Elements, either by using the Organizer (Windows), or the Editor's File Browser (Mac and Windows).

Importing from Cameras

Elements gives you lots of different ways to get photos into your computer, but if you're using Windows, the simplest tool is the Adobe Photo Downloader. If you don't like the Downloader or if you're using a Mac, later in this section you'll learn about other ways to import your photos.

> **NOTE**   Regardless of your operating system, first carefully read the instructions from your camera manufacturer. These directions should always take precedence over anything you read here that might seem to suggest doing something differently.

The Photo Downloader (Windows Only)

If you're using Windows, you may have already made the acquaintance of the Photo Downloader, since it automatically appears whenever you connect a camera or card reader—even if Elements isn't running.

> **NOTE** If you're already in the Organizer, you'll see the "Get Photos" window instead. Its window is identical to that of the Downloader, except that you can't choose a different catalog if you have more than one (catalogs are covered on page 30).

The Downloader window is divided into two main parts (see Figure 2-1). On the left side are the thumbnails of your photos. The little checkmarks next to each image indicate which photos will be imported; just uncheck the ones you don't want to bring into the Organizer. If you've already imported some of the images, the Organizer tells you so and doesn't import them again.

The right side of the window is where you can adjust the settings for where your pictures are stored and how their folders are named.

Image size slider

Figure 2-1:
The Photo Downloader is the easiest way to get your photos into the Windows Organizer. If you want to control how many photos appear in the Downloader's main window, use the image size slider to adjust the size of the thumbnail photos. (You'll see a similar slider in all the main Organizer windows, too.)

Move the slider all the way to the left for the smallest possible thumbnails. As you move it to the right, the thumbnails get progressively larger so that you see fewer and fewer at once. You can also enlarge a thumbnail to maximum its size by double-clicking it.

> **NOTE** The Organizer only keeps a record of where your photos are; it doesn't actually make copies for its own use. So if you use a program like Windows Explorer to delete a photo from your hard drive, you'll have deleted it permanently.

The photos themselves are stored in a folder named after the date and time you imported them. (This folder is located inside the directory *C:\your user name\My Documents\My Pictures\Adobe\Digital Camera Photos*.) But you can also adjust where your files are saved and what they're named, by changing any of the settings in the Save Files section of the Photo Downloader window:

NOTE   Although this section usually talks about importing your pictures from a camera, most card readers work the same way. Use a card reader if you have one, since you'll spare your camera's batteries and you'll subject your camera to less wear and tear.

- **Location.** If you want to change where your photos are headed, click the Browse button and choose another location. You can permanently change the standard location by going to Organizer → Edit → Preferences → Camera or Card Reader. Set a new location, and from now on, the Downloader always puts your photos in the folder you chose.

- **Create Subfolder.** If you want to put your files into a subfolder with a name you pick, instead of a date-stamped one, this is where you do it.

TIP   If you give the folder a descriptive name, you can apply that name as a descriptive tag to all the photos in the folder with just one click (once you're in the Photo Browser window). There's much more on tags later in this chapter.

- **Rename Files to.** Turn this checkbox on to give all the photos the same name, plus a three-digit number. So if you type *obedience_school_graduation,* you get photos named *obedience_school_graduation001,* *obedience_school_graduation002,* and so on.

- **Advanced Options.** Click this if you have multiple catalogs and you want to specify which one gets the photos (catalogs are covered on page 30).

Once you're done adjusting these settings, click Get Photos, and the Downloader gets your photos and launches the Organizer so you can review your pictures. Elements also asks whether you want to keep or delete the photos on the device you're importing from (see Figure 2-2).

Figure 2-2:
The Downloader offers to delete the files from your card or other device once they've been imported. This seems like a handy feature, but prudent people might want to think twice about whether to actually delete the files. Very rarely, the Downloader is a little wonky in its importing, and it's not a bad idea to wait until you've been through all your photos before deleting the originals.

Disabling the Photo Downloader

If you use Windows and you don't want to use the Photo Downloader, you can kill the Downloader by going to Organizer → Edit → Preferences → Camera or Card Reader and turning it off. You can still use the Get Photos command when you're in the Organizer, even if you turn off the Downloader.

The Downloader runs as a *service,* a behind-the-scenes program that Windows always keeps running. If you're not going to use the Downloader, you might as well turn it off completely and maybe give your system a little boost by reclaiming the resources it uses.

To do that, go to *Control Panel\Administrative Tools\Services\Photoshop Elements Device Connect*. Highlight the Downloader in the list and go to Action → Properties and set the Startup to Manual.

If you disable the Downloader, you can still use any of the standard Windows photo-opening options, like Windows Imaging Assistant, or just copy the files to a folder via the system dialog box that pops up when Windows detects your camera or card reader.

NOTE You can tell the Organizer to "watch" folders that you often bring graphics (or even sound files or video) into. When you set a watched folder, Elements keeps an eye on it and lets you know when there are new photos there. Elements either imports the new files or tells you they're waiting for you, depending on which option you choose. See page 431 for more about watched folders.

Photo Importing Options for the Mac

If you're a Mac owner, you probably want to use iPhoto to import your photos—but that's not your only choice. You can also use Image Capture or just drag the photos from your camera or card to the desktop without using any program at all.

iPhoto and Elements

The first time you connect a camera or card reader to your Mac, iPhoto opens and offers to download your photos. This is the easiest method to choose if you plan to use iPhoto to catalog your images. Just let it take over.

Sometimes people get confused about using Elements and iPhoto together. The thing to remember is that if your photos are already in iPhoto, you don't need to import them into Elements or export them from iPhoto to work on them.

You can set up iPhoto so that double-clicking your photos opens them in Elements for editing. This also makes it a lot easier for iPhoto to keep track of what you're doing (and lets you preserve iPhoto's ability to let you revert to your original image at any point). Just go to iPhoto → Preferences → General. In the "Double-click photo" section choose the third option ("Opens photo in:") and then use the Select Application button to navigate to Applications → Adobe Photoshop Elements 3 folder → Adobe Photoshop Elements 3.

Image Capture

Image Capture is a built-in program that comes with your Mac and lets you determine which program, if any, imports your photos. To use it, launch Image Capture when you don't have a camera or card reader connected to your computer, and go to the Preferences menu. (Don't close the No Image Capture Device Connected window first or you'll quit the program.) If you want to select a program that isn't one of the standard choices, select "Other" and navigate to the program you want to use, then quit Image Capture. From now on, that's the program that will open when you hook up your camera.

Photoshop Elements

You can also pull photos directly into Elements from a camera. Just click "Connect to Camera or Scanner" in the Welcome Screen or go to File → Import while your camera's attached. Choose your camera from the list of options and then select the photo you want to import. (You'll learn about scanning images into Elements later.)

Opening Stored Images

If you've got photos already stored on your computer, you have several options for opening them with Elements. If the file format is set to open in Elements, just double-click the file's icon to launch Elements and open the image. (If you want to change which files automatically open in Elements, see the box on page 26. You've also got a few ways to open files from within Elements:

- **From the Organizer (Windows only).** Go to File → Get Photos → From Files and Folders, or press Ctrl+Shift+G, then select your file. The other options in the Get Photos menu (like opening files stored on a mobile phone) are covered in Appendix A.

- **From the Editor (Mac and Windows).** Go to File → Open or press Ctrl+O (⌘-O) and select your file. To bring up the Editor's File Browser so you can choose from a thumbnail view of your photos, press Ctrl+Shift+O (Shift-⌘-O) and navigate to the photo you want. There's more about the File Browser later in this chapter.

- **From the Welcome window (Mac only).** The Mac Welcome screen includes a list of recently opened photos, or you can click the Open File for Editing button to bring up the File Browser window.

TIP   Elements can open PDF files (choose File → Open), but if they're longer than one page, Elements lets you open only one page at a time. If you need to extract a particular graphic from a PDF file, or all the graphics from a multi-page PDF file, go to File → Import → PDF Image, and Elements extracts all the graphics from the file for you.

FREQUENTLY ASKED QUESTION

Picking the File Types Elements Opens

How do I stop Elements from opening all my files?

Many people are dismayed to discover that once they install Elements, it opens every time they double-click any kind of graphics file—whether they want the file to open in Elements or not.

If you're using the Windows version of Elements, you can control the file types associated with Elements by going to Edit → File Association in the Editor. Alternatively, both the Windows and Mac operating systems also let you adjust which program opens when you double-click a file. On either platform, first find a file of the type you want to change and:

In Windows:

1. Right-click the icon of the closed file.

2. From the pop-up menu, choose Properties.

3. Click the Change button next to the application and select the application you want to open the file. Turn on "Always use this application" to change the program for all files of this type.

On the Mac:

1. Click the icon of the closed file.

2. Press ⌘-I for the Get Info window.

3. Go to "Open with:" and choose the application you want. To change the setting for all files of that type, click "Change All."

Scanning Photos

Elements comes bundled with many scanners, because it's the perfect software for making your scans look their best. There are two main ways of getting scans into Elements. Some scanners come with a *driver plug-in,* a small utility program that lets you scan directly into Elements. Look on your scanner's installation software for information about Elements compatibility or check the manufacturer's Web site for a Photoshop plug-in to download. (If you can scan into Photoshop, you should be able to scan into Elements.) You may also be able to scan into Elements if your scanner uses the *TWAIN interface,* which is an industry standard used by many scanner manufacturers.

If you don't have any of these, you'll need to use the scanning program that came with your scanner. Then, once you've saved your scanned image in a format that Elements understands, like TIFF (.tiff, .tif) or Photoshop (.psd), open the file in Elements like any other photo.

To control your scanner from within Elements, in the Editor, go to File → Import and you'll find your scanner's name on the list that appears. In Windows, you can also scan from the Organizer by choosing File → Get Photos → From Scanner, or by pressing Ctrl+U.

TIP   If you do a lot of scanning, check out the "Divide Scanned Photos" command (page 47) for helpful tips on how to quickly scan in lots of photos at the same time.

Also, you can save yourself a lot of drudgery in Elements if you make sure your scanner glass and the prints you're scanning are both as dust-free as possible before you start.

Capturing Video Frames

Elements lets you capture a single frame from a video and use it the way you would any still photo. This feature works best if you choose a movie that's already on your computer.

Elements can read many popular video file formats, including .avi, .wmv, and .mpeg. You do need to have a program on your computer (besides Elements) that's capable of viewing the video file. For example, to view a QuickTime movie, you need to have QuickTime installed on your PC.

TIP   The video capture tool in Elements isn't really designed for use with long movies. You'll get the best results with clips that aren't more than a minute or two long, at most.

To import a video frame go to File → Import → Frame From Video, and then in the Video import dialog box:

1. **Find the video that contains the frame you want to copy.**

   Click the Browse button and navigate to the movie you want. After you choose the movie, the first frame should appear in the window in the Frame From Video dialog box.

2. **Navigate to the frame you want.**

   Either click the Play button or use the slider below the window to move through the movie until you see what you want.

3. **Copy the frame you want by clicking "Grab Frame."**

   You can grab as many frames as you want. Each frame shows up in the Elements Editor as a separate file.

4. **When you have everything you need, click Done.**

While this is a very fun thing to be able to do, it does have certain limitations. Most important, your video is going to be at a fairly low resolution, so you're not going to get a great print from a video frame.

Creating a New File

You can also create a new blank Elements document. You'd want to do this when you're using Elements as a drawing program or when you're combining parts of other images together, for example.

To create a new file, go to the Editor, and choose File → New → Blank File (or press Ctrl+N [⌘-N]) to bring up the New File dialog box. You have lots of choices to make each time you start a new file; they're all covered in the following sections.

Picking a Document Size

The first thing you need to decide, logically enough, is how big you want your document to be. You can choose inches, pixels, centimeters, millimeters, points, picas, or columns as your unit of measurement. Just pick the one you want in the Width and Height pull-down menus and then enter a number. Or you can choose one of the many preset sizes shown in Figure 2-3.

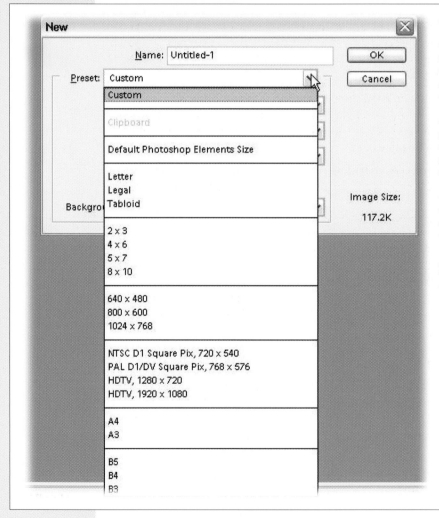

Figure 2-3:
The list of preset document sizes is divided into groups, each of which features popular file sizes and resolution settings for a variety of common uses. For example, the fourth group from the top includes traditional photo print sizes, and the group after that lists widely used choices for onscreen graphics. The default Photoshop Elements size is 5" x 7" at 72 pixels per inch, which works well if you're just playing around and trying things out.

Choosing Resolution

If you decide not to use one of the presets, you need to choose a resolution for your file. There's a lot more about resolution in the next chapter, but a good rough guide is to choose 72 pixels per inch (ppi) for files that you'll look at only on a monitor and 300 ppi for files you plan to print.

Choosing Color Mode

Elements gives you lots of color choices throughout the program, but this is probably your most important one because it determines which tools and filters you can use in your document. The three choices available in the Color Mode menu are:

• **RGB Mode.** Choosing RGB (which stands for red, blue, and green) means that you're creating a color document, as opposed to a black and white one. You'll probably choose this most of the time, even if you don't plan on having color in your image, because RGB gives you access to all of Elements' tools. Chapter 7 has lots more about picking colors.

• **Grayscale Mode.** Black and white photos are called *grayscale*, because they're really made up of many shades of gray. In Elements, you can't do as much editing on a grayscale photo as you can in RGB (for example, you can't use most of the filters on a grayscale photo).

• **Bitmap Mode.** Every pixel in a bitmap mode image is either black or white. Use this mode for true black and white images—shades of gray need not apply here.

> **NOTE**   Sometimes you may need to change the color mode of an existing file to use all of Elements tools and filters. For example, there are quite a few things you can do only if your file is in the RGB color mode. So if you need to use a filter on a black and white photo and your choice is grayed out, go to Image → Mode and select RGB Color. This won't suddenly colorize your photo. It just changes the way Elements handles the file. You can always change back to the original color mode when you're done. If you have a 16-bit file (see page 199), you need to convert it to 8-bit color, or you won't have access to many of the commands and filters in Elements. Make the change by choosing Image → Mode → Convert to 8 Bits/Channel.

Choosing Your File's Contents

The last choice you have to make when you start a new file is the *contents* of the file. This is where you tell Elements the color to use for the empty areas of the file, like the background. You can be a traditionalist and choose white (almost always a good choice), or else choose a particular color or transparency. More about transparency in a minute.

If you want to choose a color other than white, use the Foreground/Background color squares to do it, as shown in Figure 2-4.

The third option is the most interesting: transparent. To understand transparency and why it's such a wonderful invention, you need to know that every digital

Figure 2-4:
To choose a new Background color, just click the Background color square (the green one shown here) to bring up the Color Picker. Then choose the color you want. Your new color appears in the square, and the next time you do something that involves using a Background color, that's the shade you get. The whole process of picking colors is explained in much more detail in Chapter 7.

image, every single one, is either rectangular or square. A digital image *can't* be any other shape.

But digital images can *appear* to be a different shape—sunflowers, sailboats, or German Shepherds, for example. How? By placing your object on a transparent background so that your object looks like it was cut out, so that only its shape appears, as shown in Figure 2-5. The actual photo is still a rectangle, but if you placed it into another image, you'd see only the shell and not the surrounding area, because the rest of the photo is transparent.

To keep the clear areas transparent when you move your image, you need to save the image in a file format that allows transparency. JPEGs, for instance, automatically fill transparent areas with solid white, so they're not a good choice. TIFFs, on the other hand, let the transparent areas stay clear. You can find out about which formats allow transparency on page 76.

The Organizer

If you use Windows, the Organizer is where you keep track of your photos and start most of your projects for sharing your photos. You can see all your photos in the Organizer, assign keywords (called *tags*) to make it easier to find the pictures you want, and search for your photos in many different ways.

There are three main windows in the Organizer. Create is where you make calendars, greeting cards, album pages, and other fun stuff. Date View is an alternate way to look at and search for your photos, as explained in Figure 2-6. The Photo Browser is the most versatile of the three and your main Organizer workspace—that's what the rest of this section is about.

The Organizer stores the information about your photos in a special database called a *catalog*. You don't have to do anything special to get started—Elements

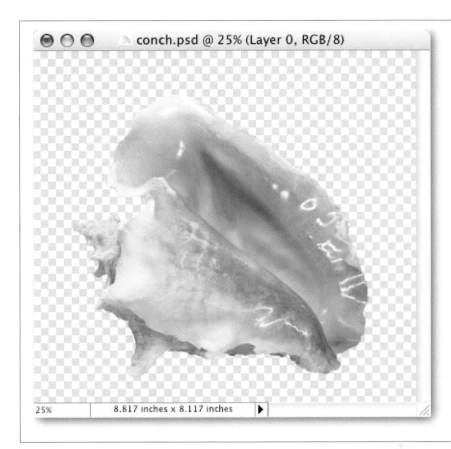

Figure 2-5:
The checkered background is Adobe's way of indicating that an area is transparent. (It doesn't mean you've somehow selected a patterned background.) If you place this photo into another image, all you'll see is the shell itself, not the checkerboard or the rectangular outline of the photo.

If you don't like the size and color of the grid, you can adjust them in Edit → Preferences → Transparency (Photoshop Elements → Preferences → Transparency).

creates your catalog (named *My Catalog*) automatically the first time you import photos. It's possible to have more than one catalog, but most people don't, since you can't search more than one catalog at a time.

Your catalog can include photos stored anywhere on your computer, and even photos that you've moved to remote disks and CDs. There aren't any limits on where your originals can be located, but once your photos appear in the Organizer, it's better to move them from within the Organizer as opposed to using another method (like Windows Explorer).

> **TIP** The Organizer lets you choose to edit in programs other than Elements by going to Organizer → File Preferences → Editing → Use a Supplementary Editing Application. So if you want to supplement Elements with a program like Paint Shop Pro, or even Photoshop, it's easy to do.

The Photo Browser

The Photo Browser may look a little intimidating the first time you see it, but it's really very logical. Figure 2-7 shows the Photo Browser's main components.

Figure 2-6:
Date View offers you the same menu options as the main Photo Browser window, but instead of a contact sheet–like view of your photos, you see them laid out on a calendar. Click a date, and in the upper-right corner of the screen, you can step through a slideshow view of that day's pictures. Date View is fun, and sometimes handy for searching, but it doesn't offer many useful functions that aren't also in the Photo Browser.

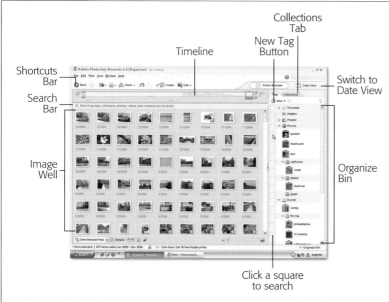

Figure 2-7:
The Photo Browser is your main Organizer workspace. You can customize it by dragging the dividers to make any area larger or smaller. If you go to View → Arrange, you can change the way your photos are sorted in the Photo Browser.

At the top of your screen, just below the Menus, is the Shortcuts bar, your main navigational tool in the Organizer. By clicking the relevant icons, you can choose to import photos, print them, share them, create projects, edit your photos, or switch over to Date View.

The Timeline is just below the Shortcuts. Each little bump on the Timeline represents a group of photos (based on the sorting method you chose in View → Arrangement). The higher a bar is, the more photos in that batch. Click a bar to see thumbnails of all the photos from that date in the main window, which Adobe calls the *Image Well.* Directly below the Timeline is the Search Bar, one of many ways to look for your photos.

On the right side of the Photo Browser is the *Organize bin.* That's where you *tag,* or label, your photos with keywords for easy searching. (Tagging is probably the first thing you'll want to do to your photos in the Organizer; you'll find directions on how to tag later.)

If you'd like to get a simultaneous look at the folders on your PC, go to View → Arrangement → Folder Location. A new pane on the left side of the Photo Brower's window appears, showing the folder structure, including the exact location of the current batch of photos. Click a folder's icon to see the photos it contains displayed in the Image Well.

You can also move your photos and folders in this pane by dragging them, if you want the Organizer to keep track of where they are (Figure 2-8).

> **TIP** Once you get your photos into the Organizer, you can use Review Photos and Compare Photos to see a larger view of your photos and choose the ones you want to print or edit. See Appendix A.

Creating Categories and Tags

The Organizer's got a great system for quickly finding photos, but it works only if you use special keywords, called *tags,* which the Organizer uses to track down your pictures.

A tag can be a word, a date, or even a rating (as explained in the box on page 34). When you import photos to the Organizer, the photos are automatically tagged with the date of import, but you may want to add more tags to make it easier to search for the subject of the photo later on. You can give a photo as many tags as you like.

Tags are grouped into *categories.* You get a certain number of preset categories, like People, Places, and Events, but you can create your own categories, too. You can also create as many subcategories within categories as you like. You might have a category of "Vacations," with "China trip" and "Cozumel" as subcategories, for instance. Your photos in those categories might have the tags "Jim and Helen," "silk factory," or "snorkeling."

Working with tags and categories

Elements gives you a few generic tags to help you get started, but you'll want to learn how to create your own tags, too. After all, by the time you've got 5,000 or so photos in the Organizer, searching for "Family" probably isn't going to help narrow things down.

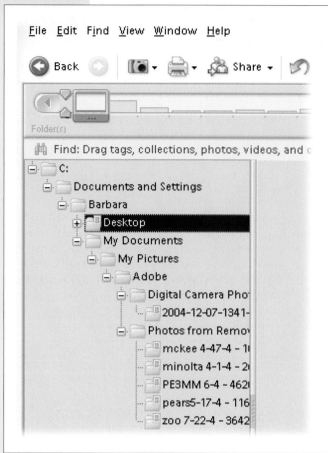

Figure 2-8:
If you want to move photos and folders after you've brought them into the Organizer, either go to File → Move or drag them in this pane of the Photo Browser. If you move photos around when you're not in the Organizer, Elements can't easily find them again. If Elements loses track of a photo, you can use the Reconnect command (File → Reconnect) to help Elements find it again.

ORGANIZATION STATION

Special Tags

Elements starts you off with two special kinds of tags:

- **Favorites.** Favorites let you assign a one- to five-star rating to your photos. It's a good way to mark the ones you want to print or edit. Ratings are a great searching tool.

- **Hidden.** If you apply the Hidden tag to a photo, the photo isn't displayed in the Photo Browser until you click the search square next to the Hidden tag icon. The Hidden tag is useful for archiving those photos that didn't come out quite right but that you're not ready to trash. You can save these pictures (just in case) without having them cluttering up your screen while you're working with your good photos.

To Kill the Organizer

Nobody is neutral about Adobe's decision to include the Organizer with Elements 3. People either love the Organizer or they absolutely hate it. If you're in the latter group you might try to see if you can come to terms with the Organizer, because it does have some very useful features.

But if you just can't learn to love the Organizer and you're willing to lose all the Organizer-specific features, like contact sheets and Web Galleries, here's what you need to do to disable it:

1. Quit Elements if it's running and then follow the steps for disabling the Photo Downloader as a service, listed earlier in the chapter. While you're in Services, do the same thing for "Adobe Active File Monitor" (this is what runs the watched folders part of the Organizer).

2. Go to My Documents and delete the Adobe folder directory after first confirming that there's nothing in there that you want to keep.

3. Go to the Program files for Elements and rename the .exe file for the Organizer so that Elements can't find it.

4. Make a direct shortcut to the Editor .exe file and use that to launch Elements in the future.

Several people have reported that this successfully hides the Organizer from the Editor and eliminates the checkboxes for version sets. Your mileage may vary, of course, and you may need to reinstall Elements to get it working again, but if you're an Organizer loather, it's worth a try.

When you're ready to create a new tag:

1. **Call up the Create Tag dialog box.**

   Press Ctrl+N, or from the Tags pane in the Organizer bin, click the New drop-down menu and choose New Tag. The Create Tag dialog box appears. (You also create new categories and subcategories from this dialog box.)

2. **Name the new tag and assign it to a category.**

   Enter the name you want to use in the text box where it says Name. Then, assign the tag to a category by picking from the Category pull-down menu. (You can change the category later if you want.) You can also edit the icon for your tag, as explained in Figure 2-9. Many people like to edit the icons Elements uses to represent different tags; this can make it easy to search for a tag visually as well as by its name.

To assign the tag to a photo, just drag the tag's icon from the Organize bin onto the photo's thumbnail. It's as easy as that.

You can also delete tags, rearrange their order by dragging them, and even change the size of your tag icons by right-clicking a tag and choosing what you want to do

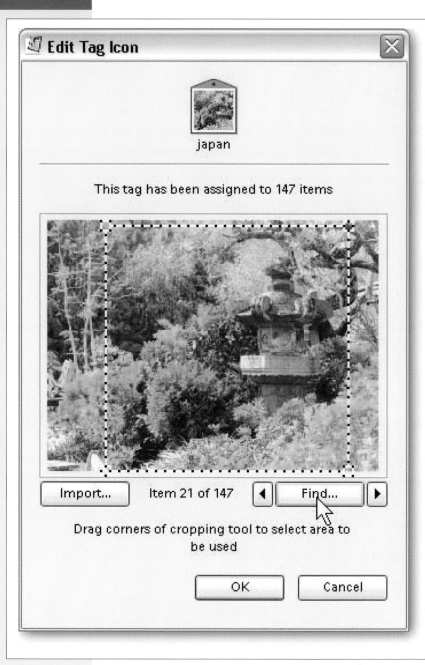

Edit Tag Icon

japan

This tag has been assigned to 147 items

Import...   Item 21 of 147   ◄   Find...   ►

Drag corners of cropping tool to select area to be used

OK   Cancel

Figure 2-9:
Many people like to edit the icons Elements uses to represent different tags; this can make it easy to search for a tag visually as well as by its name. To change the picture associated with a tag, right-click the tag in the Organize bin. Then from the pop-up menu, choose "Edit [Tag Name] tag..." and click the Edit Icon button.

In the Edit Tag Icon dialog box, the arrows on either side of the Find button let you step through all the photos that use that tag (the Find button shows you those photos all at once). Or you can click the Import button to use a different image stored on your computer. Once you've chosen the picture you want, drag the dotted square to use only a certain part of your photo.

from the pop-up menu. You can also drag tags from one category to another in the Organize bin.

If you decide you want to remove a tag from a photo after you've assigned it:

- **From a single photo.** Right-click the photo's thumbnail, select Remove Tag, and then choose the tag you want to get rid of.

- **From a group of photos.** Select the photos, right-click one of them, select Remove Tag from Selected Items, and then choose the tag you want to remove.

> **TIP** When an image first gets imported into the Organizer, you'll see an icon in the upper-right corner of the Image Well called "Instant Tag." Clicking it assigns the photo's folder name as a tag.

Creating Collections

You can also group your photos into *collections*, which are handy containers for storing multiple pictures. Collections are great for gathering together pictures taken at a particular event. They can also be used to prepare groups of photos that you plan on using in one of the Create projects, like slideshows or Web Galleries (covered in Chapter 16).

Collections can hold as many pictures as you want to put in them; and individual pictures can be included in multiple collections. Photos inside a collection can appear in any order you choose, which is important, for instance, if you want to control the order of photos in a slideshow.

> **TIP** Collections are also good for gathering together groups of photos you want to export for use with another program.

You work with collections very much the way you do with tags, but you start by clicking the Collections tab in the Organize bin. From there, the procedure works pretty much the same way as creating or editing a tag or a category.

Searching for Photos

Anyone who's been diligent enough to assign tags to all (or most) of their photos will be pleased to learn how easy Elements makes finding tagged photos. And as for the untagged masses? The good news is that Elements still gives you a few helpful ways to find your pictures. The next few sections take you through all your options.

Browsing through photos

When you don't know exactly which photo you're looking for, Elements gives you a few ways to search through groups of pictures. These methods are also great if you're just looking to browse but don't want to look through your entire collection.

- **Folders.** You can navigate through the folders stored on your computer, just as you would when using a program like Windows Explorer. First, turn on Folder view if you haven't done so earlier (View → Arrangement → Folder Location). Navigate by expanding the folders you want and working your way down to the ones that contain the photos you want. When you reach a folder that contains photos, the photos appear in the Image Well.

- **Timeline.** Each bar in the Timeline represents a group of photos. Click a bar, and you see the photos that were in that batch. The way the photos are grouped changes to match what you've chosen in View → Arrangement.

- **Date View.** You see your photos, listed by date, on a calendar page. Just click the date of the group you want to see.

> **TIP** The Find menu, which is covered in Appendix A, also lets you search for photos with similar colors. Choose Find → By Color Similarity with Selected Photo(s). This option is great when you're looking for similarly toned graphics to use in a project

Using tags and categories to find photos

Of course, when you're looking for a particular picture, you can use all the previously listed ways to find photos and just keep clicking through groups of photos until you find the one you want. But searching by tags and categories is the easiest way to find a particular photo.

- **Organize bin.** Click the empty square next to a tag or category, and Elements finds all the photos associated with those tags and categories. (A pair of binoculars appears inside the square to indicate it's being used to search for photos.) Click as many tags and categories as you want, and Elements searches for them all.

  You can exclude a tag from a search by right-clicking the tag's name and, in the menu, choosing to exclude it. So you could search for photos with the tags "sports" and "rock-climbing," but not "broken leg," for instance.

- **Search bar.** The Organizer's Search bar is another way to perform a tag search. Figure 2-10 shows how to use it.

- **Editor File Browser.** You don't have to be in the Organizer to find photos. The Editor has a browser of its own, the File Browser, where you can also search. The next section explains how to use it.

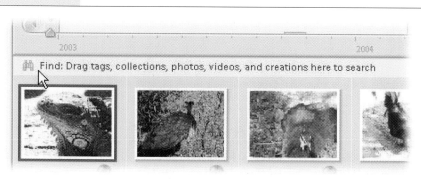

Figure 2-10:
To use the Search bar to find individual pictures, just drag any tag (or category) onto the bar with the binoculars. Your tag can hit the bar anywhere, not just on the binoculars icon itself.

Viewing Data About Your Images

The Organizer is just packed with information about your images. From captions you've written to statistics captured by your camera, the Properties window is chock full of interesting tidbits. To launch it, select any photo in the Organizer and press Alt+Enter, or right-click any photo and choose Properties from the pop-up menu. You get four different kinds of information to choose from, each of which you get to by clicking the icon on the top of the Properties window:

- **General.** This is information that includes the file's name, location (on your PC), size, date you took the picture, caption (just put your cursor in the box and start typing to add one), and a link to any audio files associated with it (page 413). You can also change the photo's file name here by highlighting the name and typing in a new one.

- **Tags.** If you've assigned any tags to your photo, they're listed here.

- **History.** History tells you when the file was created, imported, and edited, and also where you imported it from (your hard drive, for instance).

- **Metadata.** *Metadata* is information about the photo that's stored in the photo file itself. Most notably, this is where you view your *EXIF* data. EXIF data is information that your camera stores about your photos, including the camera you used, when you took the picture, the exposure, the file size, the ISO speed, aperture setting, and much more.

By paying attention to your EXIF data you can learn lots about what works for making good shots...and what doesn't.

The Metadata screen includes many other kinds of information besides the EXIF data. Click the Complete button at the bottom of the window to see the full listing (clicking the Brief button shows you highlights only). You can search your metadata very thoroughly from the Editor's File Browser, as explained in the next section.

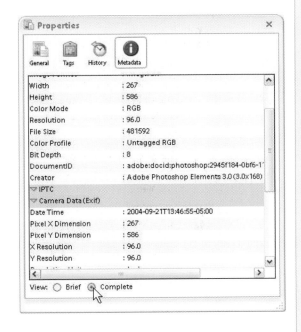

The File Browser (Mac and Windows)

The Organizer isn't the only place to rummage through your photos. The Editor also includes a File Browser that lets you look through thumbnail images of all your photos as well as search for particular images. Being able to search while working in the Editor is a great timesaver, since it can save you from having to switch back to the Organizer.

NOTE   If you have a Mac, the File Browser is where you assign keywords to your photos. The Mac File Browser is very similar to the one that comes with Photoshop CS, while the Windows version doesn't contain quite as many capabilities. The Mac-specific information comes later in this section. For now, everything applies to both platforms.

The File Browser is organized a little like the Organizer's Folder view. Starting at the top of the File Browser, down the left side of the window you see the folder hierarchy of your hard drive (the Folders palette), a Preview palette, and at the bottom, a palette for your metadata (page 39) (and keywords, covered later, if you're on a Mac). Your thumbnails appear in the main window on the right.

You can choose how much space to give to each palette as explained in Figure 2-11.

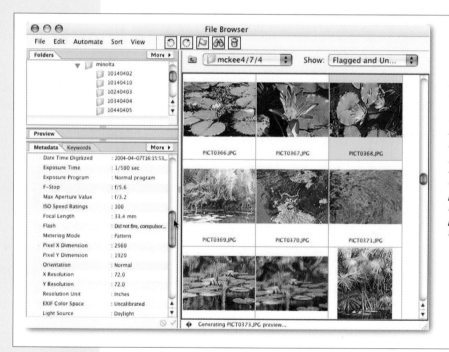

Figure 2-11:
You can customize the view in the File Browser the same way you can in the Photo Browser: by dragging the dividers to make an area bigger or smaller. If you want more space to see your EXIF info (page 39), drag the top bar of the Metadata palette upward. Double-clicking a palette's title collapses the palette.

NOTE   Although Elements calls them "palettes," you can't move them around like regular palettes—they stay tethered to the File Browser.

Opening and Modifying Files

To call up the File Browser, just press Ctrl+Shift+O (⌘-Shift-O) while you're in either Quick Fix or Standard Edit mode. If you have a Mac, you can also launch the File Browser by clicking "Open file for editing" in the Welcome screen.

It's very easy to use the File Browser. Navigate through the Folders palette the way you would go through a folder view anywhere else on your computer. Click a folder, and the main File Browser window displays thumbnails of any photos in the folder (you'll also see any subfolders that contain graphics files). You can open any of the folders that show up in the main window by double-clicking them.

Select files in the File Browser the way you would anywhere else—click a file, Shift-click or Ctrl+click (⌘-click) to select multiple files. To open a photo for editing, double-click its thumbnail or press Enter (Return) if you've already selected the thumbnail.

Above the File Browser's thumbnails window, you see the name of the current folder and to its left, an icon that looks like a folder with a bent arrow on it. Click the icon to go back up one level from the folder you're currently in. If you click the folder name, you'll get a pop-up menu showing the folders you've recently explored.

> **TIP** The pop-up menu also offers you a list of favorite folders. Creating a favorite folder is very handy if you're doing a lot of work in one folder and want to be able to come back to that folder quickly. Just press the Up One Level icon, so that you can see the folder itself in the window (rather than the files it contains). Highlight the folder and select "Add Folder to Favorites" from the File Browser's Edit menu. The Folder you chose now appears in the list of folder names just above the recent folders. To get rid of a Favorite folder, just choose "Remove Folder from Favorites."

The File Browser also gives you a very complete view of your file's metadata, as shown in Figure 2-12.

> **TIP** If you regularly want to add similar file information to lots of different photos—copyright info and your name, for instance—you can create a *Metadata template,* which lets you quickly assign one file's metadata to additional photos. Start by entering the metadata for one file (in the File Browser, go to File → File Info). Then click the arrow at the upper-right corner of the window and choose "Save Metadata template." The next time you open File → File Info for a new photo, choose "Show templates," and select the one you want. You can then make any changes to the data when it pops into the new window.

Despite its relatively simple look, the File Browser lets you modify and manage your files in many ways. You can:

- **Rotate photos.** Select the photo(s) you want to rotate by clicking one of the Rotation buttons in the File Browser's menu bar. When you click either of these buttons, Elements rotates the thumbnail view, but doesn't rotate the actual photo until you open and save the image. The thumbnail shows a curved arrow as a reminder that you rotated the file.

- **Delete photos.** Select the photo(s) you don't want, then click the Trash icon at the top of the window or drag the files directly onto the Trash icon. Elements sends them to your computer's regular Recycle Bin (Trash), so you're really throwing them away for good. You can retrieve them from the Recycle Bin as long as you don't empty it first. Once you empty the Recycle Bin (Trash), the photos are gone.

Figure 2-12:
The File Browser displays an amazing amount of information about your photos. If it's a bit overwhelming, you can manage it by clicking the More button on the Metadata palette and choosing "Metadata Display Options." That brings up this window where you can turn on or off items you want to show or hide. You can also increase the font size in the More menu if the fine print bothers you.

- **Rename files and folders.** You can change the name of a file or folder by high-lighting it and typing the replacement name, just as you would elsewhere on your computer.

- **Move files and folders.** You can rearrange your photos right in the File Browser by dragging them in the Folder view. You can also haul photos right into and out of the File Browser. If you drag from the File Browser to your desktop, you copy the file to the desktop.

- **Create new folders.** If you want to add a new folder, just go to File Browser → File → New Folder or right-click (Control-click) anywhere in the File Browser's main window and choose New Folder from the pop-up menu.

- **Batch rename and convert the format of files.** Elements lets you modify groups of photos simultaneously, doing things like renaming, making file format changes, and performing basic color correction (see page 203 for more details on batch processing).

TIP   The File Browser can slow down over time (and slow Elements down, too), as its collection of thumbnail images grows. Once in a while, it's a good idea go to File → Purge Cache to dump the old thumbnails, which will speed things back up again.

Searching with the File Browser

The File Browser offers some powerful searching tools, including the ability to sort your photos according to everything from resolution to photo height. To do so, start by going to the Sort menu where you'll see the different ways you can choose to rank your photos. Turn Ascending on or off to see them in the order you prefer: ascending or descending. In addition to sorting your photos, the File Browser makes it easy to search for individual photos or groups of pictures.

You can choose to search by using lots of different combinations of information, ranging from the date a file was last modified to files whose "name starts with" a given word, number, or letter, for example, that you provide—a great help when you can't quite remember the exact file name.

To search from the File Browser:

1. **Start searching by clicking the binoculars at the top of the File Browser window.**

    The Search window shown in Figure 2-13 appears.

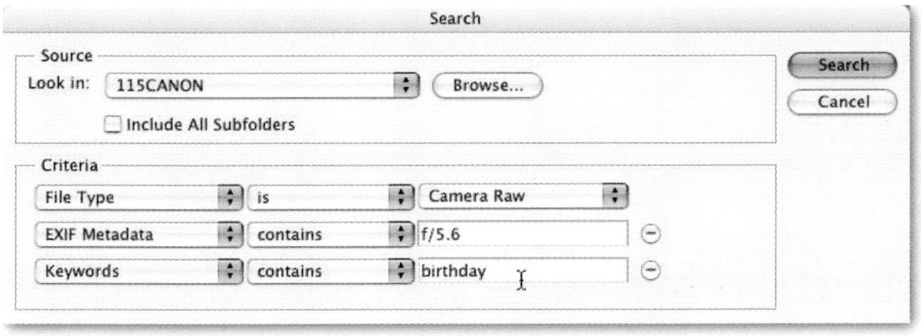

Figure 2-13:
The File Browser search window lets you search by up to three different criteria at once. To add to your search, just click the plus button to add other criteria. Be sure to turn on the "Include All Subfolders" checkbox or Elements searches only at the current folder level. You can search any folder on your computer, not just the ones that are currently open in Elements.

2. **Choose a folder to search within.**

    Click the Browse button and, in the window that pops up, navigate to the folder you want to search through. Select it and click Choose.

3. **Choose your search criteria.**

    Select a category from the pop-up menu, type in your search term, and click Search.

TIP   If you choose "EXIF Metadata" as your criteria and then enter a particular number as your search value, you can find all the photos you took at a certain ISO, or all the photos you took at f/5.6, and so on. This method is great for making comparisons, like which shutter speeds work best under certain conditions, for example.

Assigning Keywords (Mac Only)

If you have a Mac, it's very easy to assign keywords to your photos in the File Browser. You can do most of the things that your Windows counterparts get to do with tags, and you get to do the tagging right in the Editor.

NOTE   The keywords you assign in iPhoto are not the same as Elements keywords. The two programs don't read each other's keywords, unfortunately, so you can't assign a keyword in iPhoto and expect to search for it in Elements, or vice versa.

Start from the Keywords tab on the Metadata palette (see Figure 2-14). The Keywords tab can be dragged into one of the other File Browser palettes, if you prefer. So if you want to be able to see metadata and keywords at the same time, for instance, you can park your Keywords in the Preview palette instead.

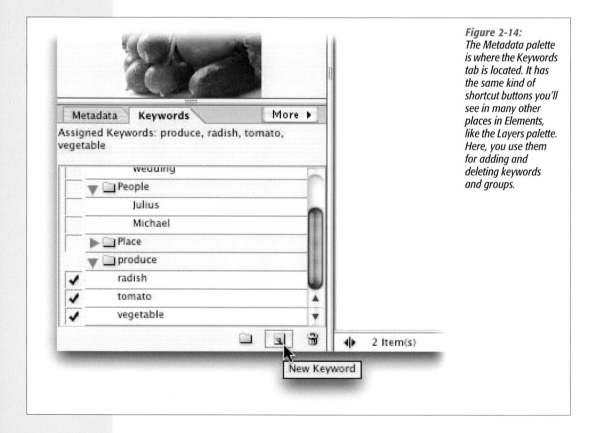

Figure 2-14:
The Metadata palette is where the Keywords tab is located. It has the same kind of shortcut buttons you'll see in many other places in Elements, like the Layers palette. Here, you use them for adding and deleting keywords and groups.

Here's some basic information about how to get started with keywords:

- **Create a keyword.** To set up a keyword so that you can assign it to a photo, start by clicking the New Keyword button on the Metadata/Keywords palette, or go to the Keyword palette, click More, and choose New Keyword. In either case, a new line appears in the palette with the cursor blinking, all ready for you to type in the new keyword. Press Return to create the keyword.

- **Assign a keyword.** To attach a keyword to a photo, first select the photo. Then in the Metadata/Keywords palette, click the box next to the keyword you want, or double-click the keyword itself. A checkmark appears next to the keywords assigned to the photo.

- **Remove a keyword.** If you want to remove a keyword from a particular image, first select the photo in the File Browser. Click the box again, or double-click the keyword again. The check goes away. This removes the keyword from that particular photo only.

- **Delete a keyword.** If you want to completely get rid of all instances of a keyword, click the keyword in the palette to select it, then click the Delete Keyword icon (the little trash can.) This deletes the keyword throughout Elements, not just from the current photo.

- **Rename a keyword.** Did you assign the keyword "dummies" to photos of your boss and now he wants a copy of one? Click the keyword in the palette to select it, then click the More button and choose "Rename." (This doesn't change the way the keyword displays on photos it's already been assigned to, though. In the boss scenario, you're probably safer deleting the old keyword altogether and assigning a new one.)

You can also create keyword sets, which are groups of keywords, more or less equivalent to the Organizer's categories. By applying a set to a photo, you add all the keywords in that set at once.

- **Create a keyword set.** To start a new keyword set, click the New Keyword Set button (the folder) at the bottom of the Metadata palette. Then enter the name for the set and press Return.

- **Create a new keyword in a set.** If you want to create a brand new keyword and include it as part of an existing set, click the name of the set, then click the New Keyword button. Your new keyword appears as soon as you name it and press Return.

- **Move a keyword.** To move a keyword into or out of a set, just drag it up or down to wherever you want to relocate it.

Once you create a keyword set, you can apply all the keywords in it to a photo by highlighting the photo and clicking the box next to the keyword set's name. Removing and renaming sets uses the same steps you'd use for single keywords.

NOTE If you get photos from someone else who uses Elements, the keyword sets show up as regular keywords. You'll need to recategorize things if you want to keep the same hierarchy.

Flagging files

Another useful feature that's unique to the Mac is the ability to flag your files, which places a little flag right below the file's thumbnail image. You might want to flag files that are good enough to print or maybe the files that you think are stinkers but don't want to trash just yet.

You can choose to view only flagged or unflagged files in the File Browser, too. This lets you focus your attention on flagged files without having to root through the rest of your collection. To do so, go to the View menu to make your choice:

- **Flag a file.** If you want to flag a photo or a group of photos, select the file or files you want to flag and click the Flag icon in the File Browser's menu bar.

- **Remove a flag.** If you want to remove a flag, select the photo or photos, and then click the Flag icon again. The flag disappears from the photo.

Rotating, Resizing, and Saving

Last chapter, you learned how to get your photos into Elements. Now it's time to look at how to trim off unwanted areas, straighten out crooked photos, and save your files. You'll also learn how to change the overall size of your images and how to zoom in and out, to get a better look at things while you're editing.

> **NOTE** Windows folks: from here until Chapter 14, you need to be in the Elements Editor. If you're still in the Organizer, press Ctrl+I to go to the Standard Edit window.

Straightening Scanned Photos

Almost everyone knows the frustration of carefully placing a photo on a scanner, only to find that your scan has come out crooked. Elements includes a wonderful command—Divide Scanned Photos—that solves this problem. Not only that, but you can scan several photos at once, and Elements straightens them out and chops them apart for you. Anyone who's slogged their way through digitizing generations of ancient snapshots will testify that this a very big deal indeed, almost worth the whole price of Elements.

Figure 3-1 shows how you can use Elements to help save time. Put as many photos on the scanner bed as you can fit, and once you've gotten your scan into Elements, you can use Divide Scanned Photos to separate and straighten the individual images.

Start by scanning in a group of photos. The only limit on the number of photos is how many you can fit on your scanner. It doesn't matter whether you scan directly into Elements or use your scanner's own software. (See Chapter 2 for more about scanning images into Elements.)

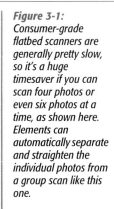

Figure 3-1:
*Consumer-grade
flatbed scanners are
generally pretty slow,
so it's a huge
timesaver if you can
scan four photos or
even six photos at a
time, as shown here.
Elements can
automatically separate
and straighten the
individual photos from
a group scan like this
one.*

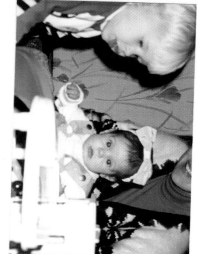

NOTE   Sometimes it pays to be crooked. Divide Scanned Photos does its best work if your photos are really crooked, so don't waste time trying to be precise when placing your pictures on the scanner.

Divide Scanned Photos works the same way whether you've got a Windows computer or a Mac.

1. **Open your scanned image file in the Editor.**

   It doesn't matter what file format you used to scan in your group of photos.

2. **Divide, straighten, and crop the individual photos.**

Go to Image → Divide Scanned Photos. Sit back and enjoy the view as Elements carefully calculates, splits, straightens out, and trims each image. You'll see the individual photos appear and disappear as Elements works through the group.

3. **Name and save each separated image.**

When Elements is done, you'll have the original group scan as one image and a separate image file for each photo Elements has carved out. If you're using Windows, you can import the cut-apart photos into the Organizer (page 30). Just make sure that "Add to Organizer" is turned on in the Save As dialog box.

Elements usually does a crackerjack job of splitting up your photos, but once in a while, it chokes, leaving you with an image file that contains more than one photo. Figure 3-2 shows you how to deal with images that Elements didn't succeed in splitting up.

Figure 3-2:
Sometimes Elements just can't figure out how to split up your photos, and you wind up with something like these two not-quite-split-apart images. Rescan the photos that confused Elements, only this time, make sure they're more crooked on the scanner and leave more space between them. Elements should then be able to split them correctly.

Elements can also straighten out and crop (trim) a single scanned image. After you've scanned in your photo, go to Image → Rotate → Straighten and Crop Image, and Elements tidies things up for you. You can also choose just Straighten if you'd rather crop the edges yourself. (Cropping is explained later in this chapter.)

Rotating Your Images

Owners of print photographs aren't the only ones who sometimes need a little help straightening out their pictures. Digital photos sometimes need to be rotated. For example, not all cameras output photos so that Elements (or any other image-editing program, for that matter) knows the correct orientation for your picture. Some cameras send portrait-orientated photos out on their side, and it's up to you to straighten things out.

Fortunately, Elements has rotation commands just about everywhere you go in the program. If all you need to do is get Dad off his back and stand him upright again, here's a list of where you can perform a quick 90-degree rotation on any open photo:

- **Quick Fix (page 83).** Click either of the Rotation buttons at the top of the Control Panel.

- **Standard Edit (page 11).** Select Image → Rotate → Rotate 90° Left (or Right).

- **File Browser (page 39).** Click the left or right arrow at the top of the File Browser window.

    > **NOTE**   Remember that in the File Browser, you're actually rotating a thumbnail replica of your image; the actual image won't be rotated until you open the image file.

- **RAW Converter (page 189).** Click the left or right arrow at the bottom of the Preview window.

- **Organizer (Windows only; page 30).** You can rotate a photo almost any time in the Organizer by pressing Ctrl+the left or right arrow key. Another way to rotate is to go to Edit → Rotate 90° Left (or Right). Finally, there's a pair of Rotate buttons to click at the bottom of the Photo Browser window.

Those commands all get you one-click, 90-degree changes. But Elements has all sorts of other rotational tricks up its sleeve, as explained in the next section.

Rotating and Flipping Options

Elements gives you several ways to change the orientation of your photo. To see what's available, in the Editor, go to Image → Rotate. You'll notice two groups of Rotate commands in this menu. For now, it's the top group you want to focus on. (The second group does the same things, only those commands work on layers, which are explained in Chapter 6.)

In the first group of commands, you'll see:

- **Rotate 90° Left or Right.** This gets you the same rotation as the rotate buttons explained earlier. Use these commands for digital photos that come in on their sides. (Remember you can also apply these commands in the File Browser [page 39] before you open your photo in Elements.)

- **Rotate 180°** turns your photo upside down and backward.

- **Flip Horizontal.** Flipping a photo horizontally means that if your subject was gazing soulfully off to the left, now she's gazing soulfully off to the right.

- **Flip Vertical.** This turns your photo upside down without changing the left/right orientation (which is what "Rotate 180°" does).

NOTE When you're flipping photos around, remember you're making a mirror image of everything in the photo. So someone's who's writing right-handed becomes a lefty, any text you can see in the photo is backward, and so on.

- **Custom Rotate.** Selecting this one brings up a dialog box where if you're mathematically inclined, you can type in the precise number of degrees to rotate your photo.

Figure 3-3 shows these commands in action.

Figure 3-3:
Even the most uncooperative cat will turn somersaults for you if you use the rotate commands. Here, in the top row, from left to right, you see the original, the photo rotated 90 degrees to the right, and the photo rotated 180 degrees. The bottom row shows the photo flipped horizontally (left), and flipped vertically (right).

Free Rotate

What about all those photos you've taken where the content isn't straight? You can flip those pictures around forever, but if your camera was off-kilter when you snapped the shot, your subjects are going to lean like a certain tower in Pisa.

Elements has planned for this, too. The rotate command that's best for this is Free Rotate Layer, which lets you grab your photo and turn it until the content is where you want it. If you aren't sure where straight is, Elements gives you some help figuring it out, as shown in Figure 3-4.

All the rotate commands are also available for use on individual layers, incidentally. (Chapter 6 tells you all about layers, but you don't have to understand layers to use the Free Rotate Layer command.)

To use Free Rotate Layer:

1. **Go to Image → Rotate → Free Rotate Layer.**

   Elements asks you if it should "make this background a layer." Say yes. (Again, Chapter 6 tells you everything you need to know about layers.)

Figure 3-4:
If you need some help figuring out where straight is, go to View → Grid to toggle these handy guidelines on and off. You can adjust the grid spacing in Edit → Preferences → Grid (Photoshop Elements → Preferences → Grid).

2. **Name the layer if you want to.**

   A dialog box appears, giving you a chance to name the layer if you want. Then click Okay.

3. **Use the curved arrows to adjust your photo (Figure 3-5).**

   Your picture may look kind of jagged while you're rotating. Don't worry about that—Elements smooths things out once you're done.

Figure 3-5:
To straighten the contents of your photo, or even to spin it around in a circle, grab these little arrows and start turning. Just grab the corner and adjust your photo the way you'd straighten a crooked picture on your wall. The arrows appear when you move your mouse near a corner of the photo.

4. **When you've got your image positioned where you want it, press Enter (Return).**

Now you've got a nice straight picture, but the edges are probably pretty ragged because of the slanting present in the original, unrotated sides. You can take care of that by cropping your photo, which is covered in the next section.

Cropping Pictures

Whether or not you straightened your digital photo, sooner or later you'll probably need to *crop* it—trim it to a certain size. There are two main reasons for cropping your photos. If you want to print on standard sizes of photo paper, you usually need to trim off part of your image so it fits onto the paper. The other important reason for cropping your photo is to enhance it. You can crop away distracting objects in the background or other people you don't want in the picture, for instance.

A few cameras produce photos that are proportioned exactly right for printing to a standard size like 4"×6". But most cameras give you photos that aren't the same proportions as any of the standard paper sizes like 4"×6" or 8"×10". (The width-to-height ratio is also known as the *aspect ratio*.)

The extra area most cameras provide gives you room to crop wherever you like. You can also crop out different areas for different size prints (assuming you save your original photo). Figure 3-6 shows an example of a photo that had to be cropped to fit on a 4"×6" piece of paper.

Figure 3-6:
When you print onto standard sized paper, you may have to choose the part of your digital photo you want to keep. This photo came from the camera as you see it in the left figure; it had to be cropped down to make it the right shape for a 4" x 6" print.

If your photo isn't in the Organizer, it's best to perform your crops on a copy, since trimming is going to throw away the pixels outside the area you choose to keep. And you never know—you may want those pixels back someday.

Using the Crop Tool

You can use the Crop tool in either the Standard Edit or Quick Fix window. The Crop tool includes a helpful list of preset sizes to make cropping easier. If you don't need to crop to an exact size, here's how to perform basic freehand cropping:

1. **Activate the Crop tool.**

   Click the Crop icon in the Toolbox or press C.

2. **Drag anywhere in your image to select the area you want to keep.**

   The area outside the boundaries of your selection is covered with a dark shield. The dark area is what you're discarding. To move the area you've chosen, just drag the selected area to wherever you want it.

NOTE   You may find the Crop tool a little crotchety sometimes. See the box on page 56 for help in making it behave.

3. **To resize your selection, drag one of the little handles on the sides and corners.**

   They look like little squares, as shown in Figure 3-7.

PICT0875.MRW @ 25%(Background, RGB/8)

Figure 3-7:
If you want to change your selection from horizontal to vertical, or vice versa, just move your cursor outside the cropped area and you'll see the rotation arrows. Grab and rotate them, the same way you would an entire photo. Doing this doesn't rotate your photo–just the boundaries of the crop.

4. **If you make a mistake in dragging, press Cancel (the No symbol) in the Options bar.**

   That undoes the selection so you can start over.

5. **When you're sure you've got the crop you want, press Okay (the Checkmark) in the Options bar or double-click inside the cropping mask, and you're done.**

Cropping Your Image to an Exact Size

You don't have to eyeball things when cropping a photo. You can enter any dimensions you want in the width and height boxes in the Options bar, or you can choose one of the Presets, which automatically enters the relevant numbers for you. Figure 3-8 shows you a timesaver: how to quickly switch the width and height numbers.

When you crop using this method, the crop mask is constrained to the size you entered.

Crop Tool Idiosyncrasies

The Crop tool can be a little crotchety sometimes. People have called it "bossy," and that's a good word for it. Here are some settings that may help you control it better.

- **Snap to Grid.** You may find that you just cannot get the crop exactly where you want it. Does the edge keep jumping slightly away from where you put it? Like most graphics programs, Elements uses a grid of invisible lines—called the *autogrid*—to help position things exactly. Sometimes a grid can be a big help, but in situations like this, it can be a nuisance.

  If you hold down Ctrl (⌘), you can temporarily disable the autogrid. To get rid of it permanently, or to adjust the spacing on it, go to the View menu and turn off Snap to Grid. You can adjust the grid settings in Preferences → Grid

- **Front Image.** If you look in the Options bar when the Crop tool is active, you'll see two buttons in the middle of the bar: Front Image and Clear.

  Front Image is a great help when you're cropping multiple photos to the same size and resolution. If you have a picture that's already the size and resolution you want, make it the active image and click Front Image. The Crop tool automatically uses the information from this photo as the guide for subsequent crops.

- **Clear.** This one, logically enough, clears any information entered in the boxes in the Options bar. Remember that fact, because just erasing any numbers you've entered in the dimension boxes doesn't always make Elements let go of that information.

If the Crop tool won't let you drag where you want and keeps insisting on creating a particular sized crop, press the Clear button again. If that doesn't work, in the Options bar, choose "Reset tool" as shown in the illustration. This clears the Crop tool settings more completely than the Clear button does.

There's also a bug in the Elements 3 Crop tool that makes it run away from you whenever you get too near the edge of your photo. Fortunately, this happens only in Maximize view, so if you switch to one of the other views (Window → View), you can make it stop scrolling.

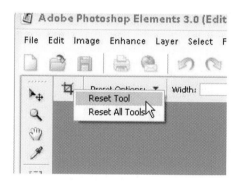

WARNING   If you put a number in the Resolution box, the Crop tool resamples your image to match that resolution, if it's not the same as the existing resolution of your photo. See the section on Resampling (page 71), which explains why that's not always a good thing.

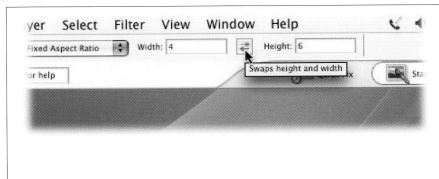

Figure 3-8:
If you want to change which number is the width setting and which is the height, just click these little arrows to swap them. So if you chose 8" x 10" from the presets but you want a landscape orientation, click the arrows to get 10" x 8" instead.

Cropping with the Marquee Tool

The Crop tool is very handy, but it wants to make the decisions for you about several things you may want to control yourself. For instance, the Crop tool may decide to resample the image (see page 71) whether you want it to or not—even if you don't enter a resolution in the Options bar. The Crop tool gives you no warning about this: it just resamples.

For better control, and also for making elliptical crops (great for oval vignettes), you might prefer to crop by using the Marquee tool. It's no harder than using the Crop tool, but you get to make all the choices yourself this way.

There's one other big difference between using the Marquee tool and the Crop tool: with the Crop tool, all you can do with the area you selected is crop it. The Marquee tool, in contrast, lets you do anything else you want to your selected area, like adjust the color, which you may want to do before you crop.

To make a basic crop with the Marquee tool:

1. **Activate the Marquee tool.**

   Click it in the Toolbox (the little dotted square) or press M. Figure 3-9 shows you the shape choices you get within the Marquee tool.

2. **Drag the selection marquee across the part of your photo you want to keep.**

   When you let go, your selected area is surrounded by the dotted lines shown in Figure 3-10. These are sometimes called "marching ants." The area inside the marching ants is the part of your photo you're keeping. (There's a lot more about making selections in Chapter 5.) If you make a mistake, press Ctrl+D (⌘-D) to get rid of the selection and start over.

3. **Crop your photo.**

   Go to Image → Crop. The area outside your selection disappears, and your photo is cropped to the area you selected in step 2.

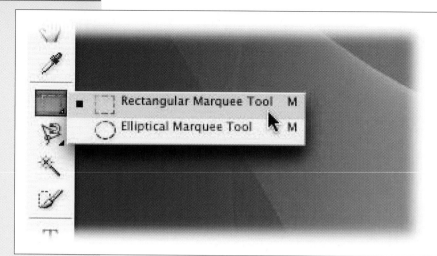

Figure 3-9:
Click the Marquee tool, and you can choose the shape from this menu, or by clicking your choice in the Options bar when the tool is active. They both do the same thing.

If you want to crop your photo to a particular aspect ratio, you can do that easily. Once the Marquee tool is active, but before you drag, go to the Options bar. In the Mode menu, choose Fixed Aspect Ratio. Then enter the proportions you want in the Width and Height boxes. Drag and crop as described earlier. Your photo will be in exactly the proportions you entered in the Options bar.

You can also crop to an exact size with the Marquee tool:

1. **Check the resolution of your photo.**

   Go to Image → Resize → Image Size and check to see that the number in the Resolution box is somewhere between 180 and 300 pixels per inch (ppi). 300 is best, for reasons explained later in the section about resizing your photos. Make sure that the box that says "Resample Image" is turned off.

2. **Activate the Marquee tool.**

   Click the Marquee tool in the Toolbox (the little dotted square) or press M. Choose the Rectangular Marquee tool.

3. **Enter your settings in the Options bar.**

   First go to the Mode menu and choose Fixed Size. Next, enter the dimensions you want in the Width and Height boxes.

4. **Drag in your image.**

   You get a selection the exact size you chose in the Options bar.

5. **Crop your Image.**

   Go to Image → Crop.

The Cookie Cutter tool also gives you a way to create really interesting crops, as shown in Figure 3-11.

PICT1103.MRW @ 16.7%(Background, RGB/8)

Figure 3-10:
When you let go after
making your Marquee
selection, you see the
"marching ants"
around the edge of
your selection.

TIP   If you're doing your own printing, there's really no reason to tie yourself down to standard photo sizes like 4" x 6"—unless of course you need the image to fit in a frame or album that only accommodates that size. But most of the time, your images could just as well be square, or long and skinny, or whatever proportions make the most effective photo. This is doubly true for images for the Web. So don't feel that every photo you take has to be straitjacketed into a standard size.

Figure 3-11:
*With the Elements
Cookie Cutter tool, you
don't have to be
square anymore. The
Cookie Cutter tool lets
you crop your images
to a variety of different
shapes, from the kind
of abstract border you
see here, to heart- or
star-shaped outlines.
You can read more
about how to use the
Cookie Cutter tool on
page 301.*

Changing Your View of Your Image

Sometimes, rather than changing the size of your photo, all you want to do is change its appearance in Elements so you can get a better look at it. For example, you might want to zoom in on a particular area, or zoom out, so you can see how edits you've made have affected your photo's overall composition.

This section is about how to adjust the view of your image inside Elements. Nothing you do with the tools and commands in this section changes anything about your actual photo. You're just changing the way you see it. Elements gives you lots of tools and keystroke combinations to help with these new views; soon you'll probably find yourself making these changes without even thinking about them.

Image Views

Before you start resizing your view of your photos, Elements gives you several different ways to position your image windows. When you first use Elements, if you have more than one photo open at a time, your photos tile themselves so that you can see them all simultaneously. If you have two photos open, for instance, each photo window spreads itself out to take half the available space on your desktop. You're not stuck with this layout, though.

When you go to Window → Images, you get several choices for how your image windows should display:

- **Maximize.** Each photo window takes up the entire Elements desktop. You can also click the large square at the right of the Editor shortcuts bar to switch to this view.

- **Cascade.** Your image windows appear in overlapping stacks. Most people find this the most practical view when you want to compare or work with two images.

- **Tile.** Your image windows appear edge to edge so that they fill the available desktop space. With two photos open, each gets half the window, with four photos each gets one quarter of it, and so on. If you click the four squares in the Shortcuts bar you get this view.

- **Match Zoom.** All your windows get the same magnification level as the active image window.

- **Match Location.** You see the same part of each image window, like the upper-right corner or the bottom left. Elements matches the other windows to the active window.

If you've got the Mac version of Elements, you also get the option to minimize windows to the dock. You can also use the regular ⌘-M keystroke to minimize. Everyone, on Mac and Windows, also gets four handy commands for adjusting the view of your active image window. Go to the View menu, and you see:

- **New Window for…** Choose this and you get a separate, duplicate window for your image. This is a terrific help when you're working on very fine detail. You can zoom way in on one view while keeping the other window in a regular view.

- **Fit on Screen.** This makes your photo as large as it can be while still keeping the entire photo visible. You can also press Ctrl+0 (⌘-0) for this view.

- **Actual Pixels.** This is the most accurate look at the onscreen size of your photo. If you're creating graphics for the Web, this is the size your image will be in your Web browser.

- **Print Size.** This view is really just a guess by Elements, because Elements doesn't know exactly how big a pixel is on your monitor.. But it's a rough approximation of the size your image would be if you printed it at the current resolution. (Resolution is explained in the section on resizing your actual photo.)

To adjust the view of a particular image, Elements gives you three useful tools: the Zoom tool, the Hand tool, and the Navigator palette. These are explained in the following sections.

The Zoom Tool

Some of the Elements' tools require you to get a very close look at your image to see what's going on. Sometimes you may need to see the actual pixels as you work, as shown in Figure 3-12. The Zoom tool makes it easy to zoom your view in and out.

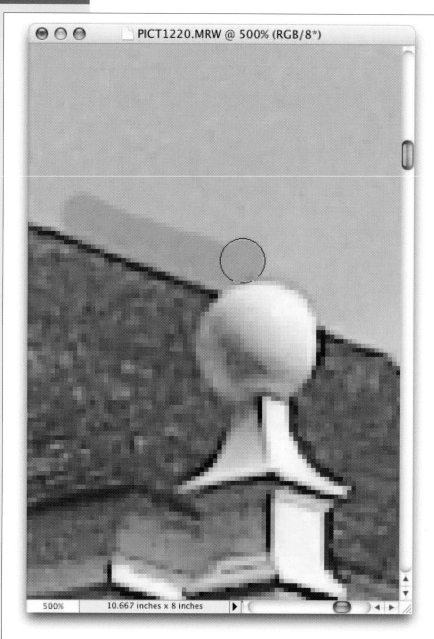

PICT1220.MRW @ 500% (RGB/8*)

500%   10.667 inches x 8 inches

Figure 3-12:
There are times when you want to zoom way, way in when working in Elements. You may even need to go pixel by pixel in tricky spots, as shown here.

The Zoom tool's Toolbox icon is the little magnifying glass with a plus sign on it. Click it or press Z to activate the tool. To use the Zoom tool, you just click the place in your photo where you want the zoom to focus. The point where you clicked becomes the focus, and the view increases by 10 percent each time you click.

You can also select the Zoom Out tool in the Options bar, by clicking the magnifying glass with the minus sign on it.

> **TIP**   If you hold Alt (Option) as you click, either Zoom tool zooms in the opposite direction—out rather than in, for instance, with the regular Zoom tool.

The Zoom tool has several Options bar settings you can use as well:

- **Zoom percent.** Enter a number here and the view immediately jumps to that percentage. 1600 percent is the maximum.

- **Resize Windows to fit.** Turn this on, and your image windows get larger and smaller along with the image size as you zoom. The image always fills the entire window with no gray space around it.

- **Ignore Palettes.** This setting lets windows resize so that they don't stop getting larger when they reach the edge of a palette. Instead, they continue resizing underneath the palette. This choice is not available until you turn on "Resize Windows to fit."

- **Zoom all windows.** If you have more than one image window, turn this on and the view changes in all the windows in synch when you zoom one window.

> **TIP**   You can hold down the Shift key while you zoom, and all your windows zoom together. You don't need to go to the Options bar to activate this feature.

The buttons for Fit on Screen, Actual Pixels, and Print Size are the same as the menu commands described in the preceding section.

> **NOTE**   You don't need to bother with the actual Zoom tool at all. You can zoom without letting go of the keyboard by pressing Ctrl+= (⌘-=) to zoom in and Ctrl+– (⌘--) to zoom out. Just hold down Ctrl (⌘) and keep tapping the equal or minus sign until the view is what you want.
>
> It doesn't matter which tool you're using at the time—you can always zoom in or out this way. Since you'll do a lot of zooming in Elements, this keyboard shortcut is one to remember.

The Hand Tool

With all that zooming, sometimes you're not going to be able to see your entire image at once. Elements includes the Hand tool to help you adjust which part of your image you can see. It's very easy to use. Just click the little hand in the Toolbox or press H to activate the Hand tool.

When the Hand tool is active, your cursor turns to the little hand as shown in Figure 3-13. Drag with the hand to move your photo around in the window. This can be very helpful when you're zoomed in or working on a large image.

The Hand tool gives you the same Scroll All Windows option you have for the Zoom tool, but you don't have to use the Options bar to activate it. Just hold down Shift while using the Hand tool, and all your windows scroll in synch. The Hand

IMG_0688.JPG @ 25% (RGB/8*)

25%   12.622 inches x 9.467 inches

Figure 3-13:
The easiest way to activate the Hand tool is to press the Space bar on your keyboard. No matter what you're doing in Elements, that calls up the Hand tool until you release the Space bar. Then the tool you were previously using returns.

tool also gives you the same three buttons (Fit on Screen, Actual Pixels, and Print Size) that the Zoom tool does. Once again, they're the same as the menu commands described at the beginning of this section.

Figure 3-14 shows the Hand tool's somewhat more sophisticated assistant, the Navigator palette, which is very useful for working in really big photos or when you want to have a slider handy for micro-managing the zoom level. Go to Window → Navigator to call it up.

Changing the Size of Your Image

The previous section was about how to resize the view of your image as it appeared on your monitor. Sometimes you need to change the size of your actual image, and that's what this section is about.

Resizing your photo brings you up against a pretty tough concept in digital imaging: *resolution*. Resolution is the term for the amount of detail your image can show, and it's dependent on the number of pixels in your photo. Where it gets confusing is that resolution for printing and for onscreen use (like email and the Web) are quite different.

Figure 3-14:
*Meet the Navigator.
You can travel around
your image by
dragging the little red
rectangle—it marks the
area of your photo
that you can see
onscreen. You can also
enter a percent
number for the size
you want your photo
to display at, or move
the slider or click the
zoom in/out
magnifying glasses on
either side of it to
change the view. The
Navigator's just great
for keeping track of
where you are in a
large image.*

Print resolution and onscreen resolution are measured in different terms. The
number of pixels you need for best results is quite different depending on what
you want to do with your photo. For example, you need many more pixels to create a good-looking print than you do for a photo that's going to be viewed only
onscreen. A photo that's going to print well almost always has too many pixels in it
for onscreen display, and its file size is usually pretty hefty for emailing. So you
often need two different copies of your photo for the two different uses. If you
want to know more about resolution, a good place to start is *www.scantips.com*.

This section gives you a brief introduction to both screen and print resolution as
they pertain to using the Resize Image dialog box correctly. You'll also learn how
to add more canvas (more blank space) around your photos. You'd add canvas to
make room for captions below your image, for instance.

To get started, open a photo you want to resize and go to Image → Resize → Image
Size. This brings up the Image Size dialog box, shown in Figure 3-15.

Resizing Images for Email and the Web

It's important to learn how to size your photos so that they show up clear and easy
to view onscreen. Have you ever gotten an emailed photo that was so huge you
could see only a tiny bit of it on your monitor at once? That happens when someone sends an image that isn't optimized to be viewed on a monitor. It's very easy to
avoid that problem—once you know how to correctly size your photos for
onscreen viewing.

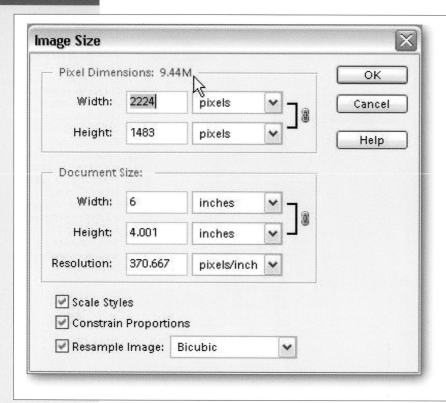

Figure 3-15:
The Pixel Dimensions section of the Image Size dialog box contains the settings you'll need when preparing a photo for onscreen viewing. The number immediately to the right of Pixel Dimensions (9.44 M) indicates the current size of your file in megabytes. The Document Size section has the settings you'll use when you want to prepare photos for printing.

If you look at the Image Size dialog box, you'll see that there are two main sections. The top one says Pixel Dimensions, and below that is Document Size. You'll use the Pixel Dimensions settings when you know your image is only going to be viewed onscreen. (Document Size is for printing.)

A monitor is concerned only with the size of a photo as measured in pixels, known as the *pixel dimensions*. On a monitor, a pixel is always the same size. (This is unlike a printer, which can change the size of the pixels it prints out.) Your monitor doesn't know anything about pixels per inch (ppi), and it can't change the way it displays a photo even if you change the photo's ppi settings, as shown in Figure 3-16. (It's true that graphics programs like Elements can change the size of your onscreen view, but most programs, like your Web browser, can't.)

All you have to decide is how many pixels long and how many pixels wide you want your photo to be. You control those measurements in the Pixel Dimensions section of the Image Size dialog box.

What dimensions should you use? That depends a little on who's going to be seeing your photos, but as a general rule, small monitors today are usually 1024×768 pixels. Some monitors, like the largest Dell and Apple models, have many more pixels than that, of course. Still, if you want to be sure that everyone who sees your photo won't have to scroll, a good rule of thumb is choose no more than 650 pix-

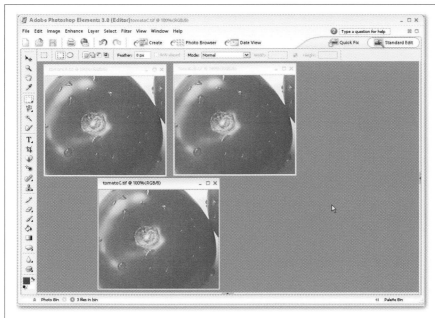

Figure 3-16:
This screenshot demonstrates how your monitor doesn't care about the ppi settings you enter. One of these photos was saved at 100 ppi, the second at 300 ppi, and the last at 1000 ppi. Can you tell which? No. They all display at exactly the same size on your monitor, because they all have exactly the same pixel dimensions, which is the only resolution setting your monitor understands.

els for the longer side of your photo, whether that's the width or the height. If you want people to be able to see more than one image at a time, you might want to make your photos even smaller. Also, some people set their monitors to display only 600×800 pixels, so you might want to make even smaller images to send to them.

> **TIP**   To get the most accurate look at how large your photo truly displays on a monitor, go to View → Actual Pixels.

Also, although a photo is always the same pixel dimensions, you really can't control the exact inch dimensions at which those pixels display on other people's monitors. A pixel is always the same size on any given monitor, but different monitors have different sized pixels these days. Figure 3-17 may help you grasp this concept.

> **NOTE**   In the following sections, you'll be learning what to do when you want to *reduce* the size of an image. It's much easier to get good results making a photo smaller than larger. Elements does let you *increase* the size of your image, using a technique called upsampling (explained later), but you may get mediocre results. The section on resampling explains why.

To resize your photos, start by making very sure you're not resizing your original. You're going to be shedding pixels that you can't get back again, so do this on a copy (File → Duplicate).

Figure 3-17:
Both these computers have a screen resolution of 1024 x 768 pixels, and the photo they're displaying takes up exactly the same percentage of each screen. But the picture is larger on the left, because the monitor is physically larger—in other words, the pixels are bigger.

1. **Call up the Image Size dialog box.**

   Go to Image → Resize → Image Size.

2. **In the Pixel Dimensions area, enter the dimension you want for the longer side of your photo.**

   Usually you'd want 650 pixels or less. Be sure that pixels show as the unit of measurement. You just need to enter the number for one side. Elements figures it out for the other side as long as "Constrain Proportions" is turned on down near the bottom of the dialog box.

3. **Check the settings at the bottom of the dialog box.**

   Constrain Proportions should be turned on. (Scale Styles doesn't matter. Leave it on.) Resample Image should be turned on. (*Resampling* means changing the number of pixels in your image.) Choose Bicubic Sharper from the pull-down menu. Adobe recommends Bicubic Sharper when you're making an image smaller, but you may want to experiment with the other menu options if you don't like the results with Bicubic Sharper.

4. **Click Okay.**

   Your photo is resized, although you may not immediately see a difference onscreen. Go to View → Actual Pixels, before and after you resize, and you can see the difference. Save your resized photo to make your size change permanent.

Sometimes Elements resizes for you—for example when you use Attach to E-mail (see Chapter 15). But the method described here gives you more control over your results than letting Elements make your decisions for you.

> **NOTE** If file size is a concern, use Save for Web (described on page 386), which helps you create smaller files.

Resizing for Printing

If you want great prints, you need to think about your photo's resolution quite differently than you do for images that you're emailing. For printing, as a general rule, the more pixels your photo has, the better. That's the reason camera manufacturers keep packing more megapixels into their new models—the more pixels you have, the larger you can print your photo and still have it look terrific.

> **NOTE** Even before you take your photos, you can do a lot toward making them print well if you always choose the largest size and the highest quality setting (typically Extra Fine, Superfine, or Fine) on your camera.

When you print your photo, you need to think about two things: the size of your photo in inches (or whatever your preferred unit of measurement is) and the resolution in pixels per inch (ppi). Those settings work together to control the quality of your print.

Your printer is a virtuoso that plays your pixels like an accordion. Your printer can squeeze the pixels together and make them smaller, or spread the pixels out and make them larger. Generally speaking, the denser your pixels, the higher your ppi. The higher the resolution of your photo is, the better it looks.

If you don't have enough pixels in your photo, the print will appear pixelated—very jaggy and blurry looking. The idea is to have enough pixels in your photo so that they'll be packed fairly densely—ideally at about 300 ppi.

The ppi setting is critical for getting a good print. If you try to print a photo at 72 ppi it usually looks terrible, because the pixels just aren't dense enough. 300 ppi is considered optimum. You usually don't get a visibly better result if you go over 300 ppi, just a larger file size. Depending on your tastes, you may be content with your results at a lower ppi. For instance, some Canon camera photos come into Elements at 180 ppi, and you may be happy with how they print. But 200 ppi is usually considered about the lowest density for an acceptable print. Figure 3-18 demonstrates why it's so important to have a high ppi setting.

> **NOTE** Your printer has its own resolution settings, which are measured in dots per inch (dpi). This isn't the same as your image resolution. Your 300 ppi photo will usually look much better at a very high dpi, but dots don't directly equate to pixels in your image. If your printer prints at 2400 dpi, you still only need a 300 ppi image to start with.

To set the size of an image for printing:

1. **Call up the Image Size dialog box.**

   Go to Image → Resize → Image Size.

2. **Check the resolution of your image.**

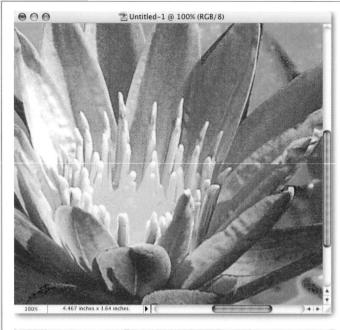

Figure 3-18:
Different resolution settings can dramatically alter the quality of a printout.

Top: A photo with a resolution of 300 ppi.

Bottom: The same photo, with resolution set to 72 ppi. Too few pixels stretched too far causes this kind of blocky, blurry printing. When you can see the individual pixels, a photo is said to be pixelated.

You want to look at the Document Size section of the dialog box. Start by checking the ppi setting. If it's too low, like 72 ppi, go to the bottom of the dialog box and turn off Resample Image. Then enter the ppi you want in the Document Size area. The dimensions should become smaller to reflect the greater density of the pixels. If they don't, click Okay and then open the dialog box again.

3. **Check the physical size of your photo.**

Look at the numbers in the Document Size area. Are they what you want? If so, you're all done. Click Okay.

4. **If your size numbers aren't right, resize your photo.**

If the proportions of your image aren't what you want, crop the photo using one of the methods described earlier, then come back to the Image Size dialog. Don't try to reshape an image using the Image Size dialog box.

Once you've returned to the Image Size dialog box, go to the bottom of the window and turn on Resample Image. Choose Bicubic Smoother in the menu. (This is Adobe's recommendation, but you may find that you prefer one of the other resampling choices.)

Now enter the size you want for the width or height. Make sure that Constrain Proportions is turned on. If it is, Elements will calculate the other dimension for you. (Scale Styles doesn't matter. Leave it on.)

5. **Click Okay.**

Your photo is resized and ready for printing.

Resampling

Resampling means changing the number of pixels in an image. When you resample, your results are permanent, so you want to avoid resampling an original photo if you can help it. As a rule, it's easier to get good results when you *downsample,* i.e., make your photo smaller, than when you *upsample,* i.e., make your photo larger.

This is because when you upsample, you're adding pixels to your image. Elements has to get them from somewhere and so it makes them up. Elements is pretty good at this, but these pixels are never as good as the pixels that were in your photo to begin with, as you can see from Figure 3-19.

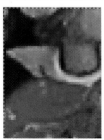  

Figure 3-19:
Here's a close-up look at what you're doing to your photo when you resample it. You can do this as an experiment with one of your own photos, too. (Just be sure it's not your original, if you don't use the Organizer.)

The photo as it came from the camera

Downsampled to 72 ppi

Unsampled back to the original resolution. See how soft the pixels look compared to the original?

When you enlarge an image to more than 100 percent of its original size, you'll definitely lose some of the original quality. So, for example, if you try to stretch a photo that's 3" wide at 180 ppi to an 8" × 10" print, don't be surprised if you don't like the results.

Elements 3 includes some new resampling methods, and they're very good compared to what was previously available. You select them in the Resample Image menu in the Image Size dialog box. Adobe recommends choosing Bicubic Smoother when you're upsampling (enlarging) your images and Bicubic Sharper when you're downsampling (reducing) your photos, but you may prefer one of the others. It's worth experimenting with them all to see which you prefer.

Adding Canvas

Just like the works of Monet and Matisse, your photos appear in Elements on a digital "canvas." Sometimes you may want to add more canvas to make room for text or if you're combining photos into a collage.

To make your canvas larger, go to Image → Resize → Canvas Size. You can change the size of your canvas using a variety of measurements, If you don't know exactly how much more canvas you want, choose Percent. Then you can guesstimate that you want, say, 2 percent more canvas or 5 percent more. Figure 3-20 shows how to get your photo into the right place on the new canvas.

> **NOTE** Changing the size of your canvas doesn't change the size of your picture any more than pasting a postcard onto a full-sized sheet of paper changes the size of the postcard. In both cases, all you get is more empty space around your picture.

Saving Your Work

After all your editing and resizing effort, you want to be sure that you don't lose any of those files you struggled so hard to create. Saving your work is easy in Elements. When you're ready to save your file, press Ctrl+Shift+S (⌘-Shift-S) to bring up the Save As dialog box. The Windows version is shown in Figure 3-21.

The top part of the Save As window is pretty much the same as it is for any program—you choose where you want to save your file, what you want to name it, and the file format you want. (There's more about file formats later.) You also get some important choices that are unique to Elements:

- **As a Copy.** When you save an image as a copy, Elements makes the copy, names it "[OriginalFileName] copy," and puts the copy away. You still have the original on your desktop. If you want to work on the copy, you must open it. Sometimes Elements forces you to save as a copy: for instance, if you want to save a layered image and you turn off the layers option. (See Chapter 6 for more about layers.)

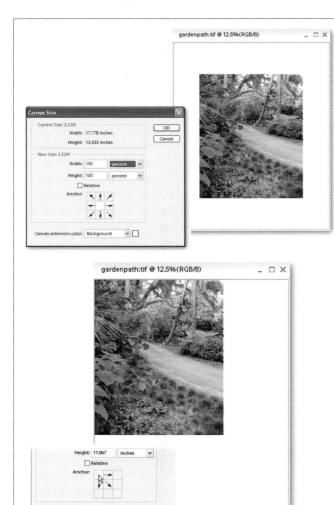

Figure 3-20:
The Add Canvas dialog box isn't as complicated as it looks. The strange little Anchor grid with arrows pointing everywhere lets you decide exactly where to add new canvas to your image. The white box represents your photo's current position. By clicking in any of the surrounding boxes, you tell Elements where to position your photo on the newly sized canvas. In the top pair of images, the new canvas has been added equally around all sides of the existing image. In the bottom pair, the new canvas has been added below and to the right of the existing image.

- **Layers.** If your image has layers, turn on this checkbox to keep them. If you turn off this setting, Elements usually forces you to save as a copy. To avoid having to save as a copy, flatten your image (page 145) before saving it.

- **Color profile (Mac)/ICC Profile (Windows).** You can choose to embed a color profile in your image. Chapter 7 explains color profiles.

If you have the Windows version of Elements, you've also got a few other choices:

- **Include in Organizer.** This checkbox always appears turned on. Leave it on and your photo gets saved in the Organizer. Turn it off if you don't want the new file to go to the Organizer.

Finding a Size that Fits

Here's a brief list of resolutions you might use for different projects. Of course, you're not bound to them, but a good guiding principle to keep in mind is that you can always dump extra pixels if you decide you don't need them, but once you've cut pixels, they're gone forever.

- **Scans that will only be viewed onscreen (and not printed).** 72 ppi is generally considered enough for onscreen viewing. Just remember that if you scan at this low resolution, you won't get a good print at a decent size if you change your mind later on. If there's any chance you'll want to print your image, you're better off scanning at a print resolution (see the next bullet list item) and then creating a separate, downsized copy for onscreen viewing. Better yet, just look at the pixel dimensions of your scan.

- **Scans for printing.** 300 ppi is pretty standard, unless you're going to enlarge the image or you need to do a lot of really close editing work on it.

- **Scans to make very large prints.** Try 600 ppi for these.

- **Scans for detailed close-up retouching.** 600 ppi, then downsample to 300 ppi before you make your final print. The extra pixels give you a more detailed view when zooming way in, but add little or nothing to the print quality.

- **Digital photos to email.** You can get away with the lowest image quality settings on your camera for these, but you risk kicking yourself later if you happen to get a shot that you want to print.

- **Digital photos for printing.** Use the Fine or Superfine settings on your camera and the largest photo size available. You can always size them down later if you don't need all those pixels.

- **Save in Version Set with Original.** This option tells the Organizer to save your image (including any edits you've made) as a new version, separate from your original. Your photo gets the name of the original plus an ending to indicate it's an edited version.

  You can create as many versions as you want. Then you can go directly to any state that you've saved your image in. It's a very handy feature. When you choose to start a version set, from now on, you'll get the Save As dialog box every time you save (instead of being able to just save your changes). Elements does that to give you the chance of creating a new version each time.

- **Use Lower Case Extension.** This just causes Elements to save your file as yourfile.jpg rather than yourfile.JPG, for example. Leave this setting on unless you have a reason to turn it off.

When you save a file with layers (see Chapter 6), you may see the warning shown in Figure 3-22. If you choose to turn on the "Maximize compatibility" checkbox, a flattened composite image gets added to your file for the benefit of programs that may not understand Elements Layers. Doing so makes for a substantially larger file, so it's up to you how much you care about being able to open your image at some future date without a version of Elements handy.

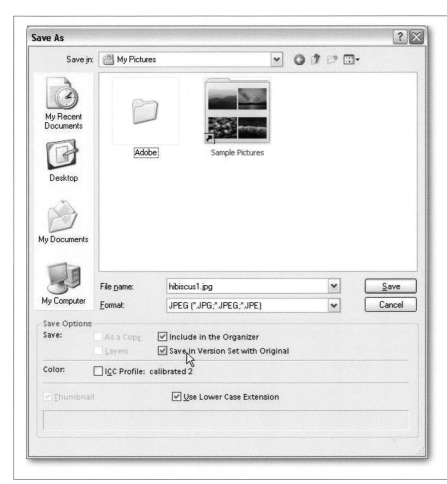

Figure 3-21:
The Elements Save As dialog box actually varies a little depending on just what you're saving, but this example is pretty typical. If you click the Format pull-down menu, you'll see a long list of file formats. (Macs have the same menu, too.)

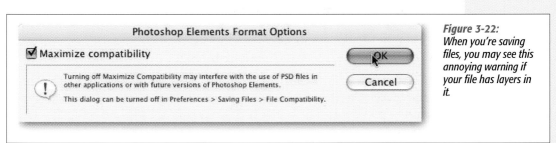

Figure 3-22:
When you're saving files, you may see this annoying warning if your file has layers in it.

The File Formats Elements Understands

Elements lets you save your file in a great many formats. Your best choice depends on how you plan to use your image. These are your choices when working in Elements:

Opening Obscure File Formats

Once in a great while, you may run into a file that was created in a format that Elements doesn't understand. Sometimes you can fake Elements out and con it into opening the document by changing the file extension to a more common one.

For the few file formats that make Elements throw up its hands in despair, try the free software programs Irfanview for Windows (*www.irfanview.com*) or Graphic Converter (*www.lemkesoft.com*) for Macs. Graphic Converter is shareware, but it comes bundled with many Macs, so you may already have it. Check your Applications folder.

Very rarely, you'll run across a file that makes even Irfanview or Graphic Converter give up. If that happens, try a Google search (use the file's three or four letter extension as your search term). It's unlikely to help you open it, but if you can figure out what it is, you can probably figure out where it came from and ask whoever sent it to you to try again with a more standard format.

- **Photoshop (.psd, .pdd).** The native file format for Elements or Photoshop. It's a good idea to save your files as .psd files before you work on them. A .psd file can hold lots of information, and you don't lose any data by saving in this format. Also, it allows you to keep layers, which is very important, even if you haven't used them for much yet.

- **TIFF (.tif, .tiff).** Another format that doesn't cause loss of information and allows you to save layers. TIFF files are used extensively in print production, and some cameras allow you to choose TIFF as a shooting option. Like Photoshop files, TIFFs can be very large.

- **JPEG (.jpg, jpeg, .jpe).** Almost everyone who uses a computer has run into JPEGs at one time or another. Most digital cameras offer the JPEG format as an option. Generally, when you bring a JPEG into Elements, you want to to use another format when you save it, to avoid data loss. Keep reading for more about why.

- **JPEG 2000 (.jpf, .jpx, .jp2).** This is a newer variation of the JPEG format that makes small files without losing any data and also supports transparency. There aren't many Web browsers that can display these files, though, so it's not a good choice for the Web.

- **PDF (.pdf, .pdp).** Adobe invented PDF, or Portable Document Format, which lets you send files to people with Adobe Reader (formerly, Acrobat Reader) so they can easily open and view the files. Elements uses PDF files to create presentations like slideshows.

- **Compuserve GIF (.gif).** These are used primarily for Web graphics and work well mainly for files without a lot of subtle shadings of color. See page 386 for more on when to choose GIFs. They're also used for Web animations, called animated GIFs, which Elements can help you create (see page 392).

- **PICT (.pct).** PICT is an older Mac format that is still used by some applications. AppleWorks, for example, handles PICTs better than any other graphics format. Also, sometimes larger file formats like TIFFs generate their thumbnail previews as PICT resource files.

- **BMP (.bmp).** An old Windows standby. The small size of .bmp files makes them fast to display, so they are used for many graphics tasks by the Windows operating system.

- **PNG.** Another Web graphic format. See page 386 for more information about these files.

- **EPS (.eps).** Encapsulated Post Script format. Used to share documents among different programs, but generally you get best results with these if they're going to a Post Script Printer.

The not-so-common file formats

Besides the garden-variety formats in the previous list, Elements lets you save in some formats you may never have heard of. Here's a list, and then you can forget all about them, probably.

- **Filmstrip.** This format's for use with Premiere, Adobe's video-editing program. You won't even see this option if Premiere isn't installed on your computer.

- **PIXAR.** Yup, *that* Pixar. This is the special format for the movie studio's high-end workstations, although if you're working on one of those, it's extremely unlikely that you're reading this page.

- **Scitex CS.** A format used for prepress work in the printing industry.

- **Raw.** This isn't the same as your camera RAW file, but rather an older Photoshop format that consists of uncompressed data.

- **Targa TGA,** or Targa, is a format developed for systems using the Truevision video board, but it has become a popular graphics format, particularly for Windows.

- **PCX.** A bitmap format used on different platforms.

About JPEGs

You remember what you read earlier in this chapter about how throwing away pixels can lead to shoddy looking pictures? Well, certain file formats were designed to make your file size as small as possible. They do this by throwing out information by the bucketful. These formats are known as *lossy,* since they throw out, or lose, some of the file's data every time you save it, to make the file as small as possible.

Sometimes you want that to happen, like when you want a small-sized picture for a Web site. So many of the file formats that were developed for the Web, most notably JPEG, are designed to favor smallness over any other quality. They compress the file sizes by allowing some data to escape.

NOTE Formats that preserve all your data intact are called *non-lossy* formats, regrettably enough. (You'd think they could have found a better name than that.) Photoshop and TIFF are your usual choices for non-lossy saves.

If you save a file using the JPEG format, every time you hit the Save button, your computer is squishing pixels out of the image. You don't want to keep saving as a JPEG over and over again. Every time you do, you lose a little more potential detail from your image. You can usually get away with saving as a JPEG once or twice, but if you keep it up, sooner or later you start to wonder what happened to your picture.

It's okay that your camera takes JPEGs. Those are pretty enormous JPEGs, usually. Just importing a JPEG won't hurt your picture. But once you get your files into Elements, save your pictures as Photoshop or TIFF files while you work on them. If you want another JPEG as the final result, change the format back to JPEG *after* you're done editing it.

TIP Your camera may give you several different JPEG compression options to help you fit more pictures on your memory card. Always choose the least compression possible. Your photos will be slightly larger, but the quality is much, much better. It's worth sacrificing the space.

UP TO SPEED

File Formats

After you've spent hours creating a perfect image, you want other people to be able to see your picture, too. If everyone who wanted to view your images needed a copy of Elements, you probably wouldn't have a very large audience for your creations. So Elements lets you save in lots of different *file formats.*

What does that mean? It's pretty simple, really. A file format is a way in which your computer saves information so that a program or another computer can read and use the file.

Because there are many different kinds of programs, and several different computing platforms, the kind of file that's best for one use may be a really poor choice for doing something else. That's why many programs, like Elements, can save your work in a variety of different formats, depending on what you want to do with your image. There are many formats, like TIFF and JPEG, that many different programs can read. Then there are other formats, like the .pub files that Microsoft Publisher creates, that can be easily read only by the program that created the file.

Changing the File Format

It's very easy to change the format of a file in Elements. Just go to Save → Save As and, from the Format pull-down menu, select the format you want. Elements makes a copy of your file in the new format and asks you to name it.

Backing Up Your Files

With computers, you just never know what's going to happen, so "Be prepared" is a good motto. If your computer crashes, it won't be nearly so painful if all your photos are safely backed up someplace else.

Saving to CDs and DVDs

Elements makes it very easy to save your files to any add-on storage device like a Zip drive or an external hard-drive. Of course, you can just do a Save As and choose your storage device as the destination, but it's also easy to back up to CDs (and DVDs, if you have a DVD burner).

Both Windows XP and Mac OS X also have CD-burning utilities built right into the system. The box on page 81 explains how to use them. But if you have a Windows computer, you're in for a treat with the Elements Organizer. It lets you burn CDs or DVDs right from the Organizer and gives you many different options for backing up your photos and catalogs (page 30). All those options are covered in the next section.

You can also burn directly from iPhoto if you prefer, but the discs you burn in iPhoto can't be read by Windows computers or most commercial photo processors.

Organizer Backups

If you're using Windows, the Organizer offers you a simply swell way to back up your photos. It's one of the best parts of the Organizer, and it's certainly very thorough, even going so far as to label the CD you create (Figure 3-23).

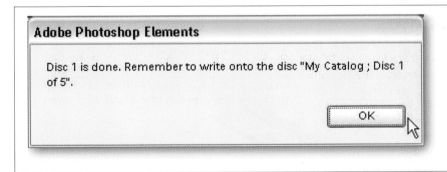

Figure 3-23:
The Organizer walks you through every step of backing up your photos. It doesn't forget a thing, even reminding you to write the disc's name on it when you're done. Okay, Mom.

NOTE If you have a Mac, iPhoto also has its own backup utility, if you use that program.

1. **In the Organizer, select the files you want to back up.**

   If your images are scattered throughout your catalog, (page 30), you might want to gather them together into one collection for simplicity's sake.

You don't have to back up every photo in the group. Control-click to select only the ones you want. You can also press Ctrl+A to select all your photos and then Shift+click to deselect the ones you don't want.

2. **Choose to burn or back up your files.**

Go to File → Backup or File → Burn. Both commands take you to the same window. The only difference is which radio button is preselected when you get there. You can perform this step from either the Photo Browser or Date View, but you can't pick and choose the photos in Date View. So switch over to the Photo Browser if you don't want all the photos from a particular date.

3. **Tell Elements whether to move your files or just back them up.**

Choose Copy/Move or Backup Catalog and click Next. Copy/Move is for backing up just your photos (or videos) themselves. Backup Catalog backs up everything—all your cataloging info, any Create projects you might have made in that catalog, any audio files, and so on.

4. **If you chose Copy/Move, decide whether you want Elements to leave your files where they are.**

Copy just makes a backup copy of your files. Your originals are still right where they were on your hard drive. If you want to copy them, leave the Move checkbox turned off.

Move means what it says. Elements puts the files on the disc and your originals are gone from the hard drive, leaving only thumbnails. This is a great feature if you're a prolific photographer. The cataloging info stays, and Elements remembers the name of the disc the originals are on. If you want one of those photos, you find the thumbnail and Elements tells you which CD to put in the drive. (Keep this in mind when you set up your cataloging system.)

There are also checkboxes for moving all the files in a stack or version set (page 435). They'll be grayed out unless the files you select include a stack or photo with versions.

If you chose to back up your catalog, Elements offers to check for any missing files and reconnect them (page 34). Take Elements up on this offer. Click Reconnect and go get a cup of coffee while Elements searches for all the files you've moved. If Elements can't find the files, it offers you a chance to try to find the missing files yourself. You can also let the backup continue without the missing files.

5. **If you chose Backup, tell Elements what kind of backup to make.**

Choose Full Backup or Incremental Backup. This option is really cool. Full Backup backs up *everything* in your catalog. Pick that one the first time you make a backup, or if you're backing up everything to move to a new computer. Incremental backup finds only the stuff that's new since the last time you made a backup, and that's all it copies—a major time and space saver.

Other Ways to Back Up

Windows XP: You can easily burn your files to a CD in Windows XP if you don't want to use the Organizer's backup feature. You might want to do so after downloading images from your camera, if you don't use the Adobe Downloader.

To back up to a CD, first be sure that burning is enabled for your CD burner. Go to *My Computer\E Drive\Properties* and turn on "Enable CD burning for this device." Oh, and no, you can't burn a CD without a CD burner. You'd be surprised how many people get confused by that. Then:

1. Put a blank CD in your CD tray.

2. Attach your camera or memory card reader.

3. Choose either to create a folder (if you are going to back up all your photos) or Shift+click the photos you want and then click "Burn these files to a CD" in the preview window.

4. After your files have been copied, click the pop-up window in the System Tray to see them and select the Burn option.

Mac OS X: Burning a CD in OS X is also very simple. Once your camera's plugged in, or your card's attached to the computer:

1. Put a blank CD in the drive. When the window opens and asks what to do, choose "Finder" and give the CD a name.

2. Drag your files to the CD's icon when it appears on the desktop.

3. Go to File → Burn Disc. Make sure the CD icon is highlighted first or the Burn option is grayed out.

You can also burn directly from iPhoto if you prefer, but the discs you burn in iPhoto can't be read by Windows computers or most commercial photo processors.

---

6. **Whether you're Copy/Moving or backing up, put a blank CD or DVD in the drive when Elements asks you to.**

Elements needs to know what kind of discs you're using for backup so it can calculate how many discs you need and how long it will take. (Yes, Elements even tells you how many CDs or DVDs you need.)

7. **Enter a name for the CD/DVD.**

If you don't enter a name, the disc gets named after the current Elements catalog (page 30), even if you're copying only one photo. As Elements burns each disc it asks if you want Elements to verify the disc to be sure it's okay. You do. Elements prompts you to feed it more discs if your backup doesn't all fit on one disc.

NOTE If you're backing up to a DVD, pay very close attention to what Backup is doing. There's a bug in which you might end up with an empty DVD, even when Elements claims to have burned and verified the DVD. If your DVD is ready in a few seconds, you know something is wrong.

The Quick Fix

One of the most significant improvements in Elements 3 is the way you can dramatically improve the appearance of a photo with just a click or two—even if you have no idea of what you're doing. The Quick Fix window gathers together easy-to-use tools that can help you adjust the brightness and color of your photos and make them look sharper. You don't need to understand much about what you're doing, either. You just need to know how to click a button or slide a pointer with your mouse, and then decide whether you like the look of what you just did.

If, on the other hand, you *do* know what you're doing, you may still find yourself adjusting things like shadows and highlights in the Quick Fix window because it's the only place in Elements that gives you a before-and-after view as you work.

In this chapter, you'll learn how to use all the tools available to you in the Quick Fix window. You'll also learn about what order to apply the fixes so you get the most out of all the tools.

> **TIP**   If an entire chapter on Quick Fix is unsatisfyingly slow, you may want to start off by trying out the ultra-fast Auto Smart Fix: a quick-fix tool for the truly impatient. Page 20 tells you everything you need to know.

The Quick Fix Window

Getting to the Quick Fix window is easy. If you're in the Editor, go to the Shortcuts bar and click the Quick Fix button. If you're in the Organizer, on the Shortcuts bar, click the Edit button's drop-down triangle, and choose "Go to Quick Fix." The Quick Fix window looks like a stripped-down version of the Standard Editor (see Figure 4-1).

Figure 4-1:
The Quick Fix window. If you have several photos open when you come into the Quick Fix window, you can use the Photo bin to choose the one you want to edit. You can also call up the Editor's File Browser (page 39) by pressing Ctrl+Shift+O (⌘-Shift-O) to search for new photos without leaving the Quick Fix window.

Your tools are neatly arranged on both sides of your image: on the left side, there's a four-item Toolbox, and on the right side, there's a collection of quick-edit palettes stored inside the Control Panel. First, you'll take a quick look at what tools Quick Fix provides you with. Then, later in the chapter, you'll learn how to actually use them.

The Quick Fix Toolbox

The Toolbox holds an easy-to-navigate subset of the larger tool collection you'll find in the Standard Edit window. All the tools work the same way in both modes, and you can also use the same keystrokes to switch tools here, too. From top to bottom, the Quick Fix Toolbox holds:

- **The Zoom tool** lets you telescope in and out on your image so that you can get a good close look at details or pull back to see the whole photo. (See page 61 for more on how the Zoom tool works.)

- **The Hand tool** helps move your photo around in the image window—just like grabbing it and moving it with your own hand (page 63).

- **The Crop tool** lets you change the size and shape of your photo. You crop off the areas you don't want (page 54).

- **The Red Eye tool** makes it a snap to fix those horrible red eyes you see in flash photos (page 87).

The Quick Fix Control Panel

The Control Panel, on the right side of the Quick Fix window, is where you'll make most of your adjustments. Elements helpfully arranges everything into four palettes—General Fixes, Lighting, Color, and Sharpen—listed in the order you'll typically use them. In most cases, it makes sense to start at the top and work your way down until you get the results you want. (See page 97 for more suggestions on what order to work in.)

The Control Panel always fills the right side of the Quick Fix screen. There's no way to hide it, and you can't drag the palettes out of the Control Panel as you can in Standard Edit mode. But you can expand and collapse them, as explained in Figure 4-2.

> **NOTE** If you go into Quick Fix mode before you open a photo, you won't see the pointers in the sliders, just empty tracks. Don't worry–they'll automatically appear as soon as you open a photo and give them something to work on.

Figure 4-2:
Clicking any of these triangles collapses or expands that section of the Control Panel. If you have a small monitor and you're bothered by the way the Sharpen slider scrapes the bottom of the window, close one of the upper sections to bring it up onto your screen when you need to reach it.

Different Views: After vs. Before and After

When you open an image in Quick Fix your picture first appears by itself in the main window with the word *After* above it. Elements keeps the Before version— your original photo—tucked away, out of sight. But you can pick from three other different layouts, which you can choose at any time: Before Only, Before and After (Portrait), and Before and After (Landscape). The Before and After views are especially helpful when you're trying to figure out if you're improving your picture— or not, as shown in Figure 4-3. Switch between views by picking from the pop-up menu just below your image.

Figure 4-3:
The Before and After view in the Quick Fix window makes it easy to keep an eye on just how you're changing your photo. You can use the Zoom tool to change the size of your photos, but the windows themselves are a little buggy—sometimes they resize along with the view percentage and sometimes they don't. If your window gets stuck, try switching to the After view and then back to the Before and After view.

MACS ONLY

Quick Fix Navigation

Windows veterans will probably find the Quick Fix window pretty normal since it takes over your whole screen. But if you're on a Mac, the first thing you may notice in Quick Fix is that you can't see your desktop anymore. This is just the way Adobe designed Elements.

Mac owners may feel trapped here since you can't easily click on the desktop and get back to the rest of your computing life. And tabbing doesn't hide the Control Panel the way it hides the Palette bin in Standard Edit.

To escape from Quick Fix and get back to where you can see your desktop, click the Standard Edit button in the Options bar to return to a more Mac-like view. Or, if you want to hide Elements completely, press ⌘-Ctrl-H. To bring the program back onscreen again, click its icon in the dock. Also, clicking the X in the upper-right corner of the Quick Fix screen closes your photo but not Elements.

NOTE Quick Fix limits the amount of screen space available for your image. If you want a larger view while you work, you need to click over to Standard Edit.

Editing Your Photos

The tools in the Quick Fix window are pretty simple to use. You can try one or all of them—it's up to you. And whenever you're happy with how your photo looks, you can leave Quick Fix and go back to the Standard Editor.

If you want to rotate your photo, you can do it here by clicking the appropriate Rotate button at the top of the Control Panel. (See page 49 for more about rotating photos.)

> **NOTE** If you click the Quick Fix Reset button, just above your image, you'll return your photo to the way it looked *before* you started working in Quick Fix. This button undoes *all* Quick Fix edits, so don't use it if you only want to undo a single action. For that, just use the regular undo command: Edit → Undo or Ctrl+Z (⌘-Z).

Fixing Red Eye

Everyone who's ever taken a flash photo has run into the dreaded problem of *red eye*—those glowing, demonic pupils that make your little cherub look like something out of an Anne Rice novel. Red eye is even more of a problem with digital cameras than with film, but luckily, Elements has a simple and terrific Red Eye tool for fixing it. All you need to do is click the red spots with the Red Eye tool, and your problems are solved.

To use the Red Eye tool (Figure 4-4):

1. **Open a photo.**

   The Red Eye tool works the same whether you get to it from the Quick Fix Toolbox or the main Toolbox in Edit mode.

2. **Zoom in so you can see where you're clicking.**

   Use the Zoom tool to magnify the eyes. You can also switch to the Hand tool if you need to drag the photo so that the eyes are front and center.

3. **Activate the Red Eye tool.**

   Click the Red Eye icon in the Toolbox or press Y.

4. **Click in the red part of the pupil with the Red Eye tool (see Figure 4-4).**

   That's it. Just one click should fix it. If a single click doesn't fix the problem, you can also try dragging over the pupil with the Red Eye tool. Sometimes one method works better than the other. You can also adjust two settings on the Red Eye tool: Darken Amount and Pupil Size, as explained later.

5. **Click in the other eye.**

   Repeat the process on the other eye, and then you're done.

If you need to adjust how the Red Eye tool works, the Options bar gives you two controls, although 99% of the time you can ignore them:

- **Darken Amount.** If the result is too light, increase the percentage in this box.

- **Pupil Size.** Increase or decrease the number here to tell Elements how much area to consider part of a pupil.

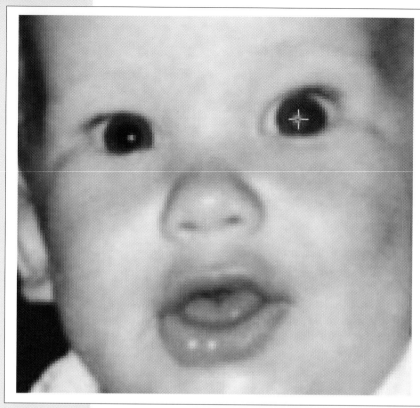

Figure 4-4:
Zoom in when using the Red Eye tool so you get a good look at the pupils. The eye on the left side of the picture has already been fixed. Don't worry if your photo looks so magnified that it loses definition—just make the red area large enough for a bulls-eye (so to speak). Notice what a good job the Red Eye tool does of keeping the highlights (called catchlights) in the eye that's been treated.

POWER USERS' CLINIC

Other Red Eye Fixes

The Red Eye tool does a great job most of the time but it doesn't always work and it doesn't work on animals' eyes. There are a couple of other ways you can fix red eye that work in almost any situation. Here's one:

1. Zoom way, way in on the eye. You want to be able to see the individual pixels.

2. Use the Eyedropper tool (page 177) to sample the color from a good area of the eye, or from another photo. Confirm that you've got the color you want by checking the Foreground color picker.

3. Get out the Pencil tool (page 280) and set its size to 1 pixel.

4. Now click in the bad or empty pixels of the eye to replace the color with the correct shade. Remember to leave a couple of white pixels for a catchlight.

This solution works even if the eye is blown out (i.e., all white with no color information left.)

If you understand layers, you can also fix Red Eye by selecting the bad area, creating a Hue/Saturation adjustment layer and desaturating the red area, but this method doesn't work so well if the eye is blown out.

Smart Fix

The secret weapon in the Quick Fix window is the Smart Fix command, which automatically adjusts a picture's lighting, color, and contrast, all with one click. You don't have to figure anything out. Elements does it all for you.

You'll find the Smart Fix in the General Fixes palette, and it's about as easy to use as hitting the speed dial button on your phone: click the Auto Smart Fix button, and if the stars are aligned, your picture will immediately look better. (Figure 4-5 gives you a glimpse of its capabilities.)

> **TIP** You'll find Auto buttons scattered throughout Elements. Elements uses them to make a best-guess attempt to implement whatever change the Auto button is next to (Smart Fix, Levels, Contrast, etc.). It never hurts to at least try clicking these Auto buttons since if you don't like what you see, you can always perform the magical undo: Edit → Undo, or Ctrl+Z (⌘-Z).

If you're happy with the Auto Smart Fix button's changes, you can move onto a new photo, or try sharpening your photo a little (see page 96) if the focus appears a little fuzzy. You don't need to do anything to accept the Smart Fix changes.

But if you're not ecstatic with your results, take a good look at your photo. If you like what Auto Smart Fix has done, but the effect is too strong or too weak, press Ctrl+Z (⌘-Z) to undo it, and try the Smart Fix Amount slider instead. The Amount slider does the same thing the Auto Smart Fix does, only you control the degree of change.

Watch the image as you move the slider to the right. If your computer is slow, there's a certain amount of lag time, so go slowly to give it a chance to catch up. If you happen to overdo it, sometimes it's easier to press the Reset button above your image and start again. Figure 4-6 explains how to use the checkmark and the cancel button (which appear next to the General Fixes label) to accept or reject your changes.

> **TIP** Usually you get better results with a lot of little nudges to the Smart Fix slider than by moving it way over to the right and back again.

Incidentally, these are the same Smart Fix commands you see in two places in the Editor's Enhance Menu: Enhance → Auto Smart Fix (Ctrl+M, or ⌘-Option-M) and Enhance → Adjust Smart Fix (Ctrl+Shift+M, or ⌘-Shift-M).

Sometimes Smart Fix just isn't smart enough to do everything you want it to do, and sometimes it does things you don't want it to do to your photos. The Smart Fix is better with photos that are underexposed than photos that are overexposed, for one thing. Fortunately, you still have several other editing choices to try, and they're covered in the following sections. If you don't like what Smart Fix has done to your photo, undo it before going on to make other changes.

Figure 4-5:
The Auto Smart Fix button produced the bottom photo with just one click. (A click of the Auto Sharpening button, explained later on page 96, was added to really make it look spiffy.)

NOTE   You can also get to the Smart Fix command from within the Organizer; the box on page 98 shows you how.

Adjusting Lighting and Contrast

The Lighting palette lets you make very sophisticated adjustments to the brightness and contrast of your photo. Sometimes problems that you thought stemmed from exposure or even focus may right themselves with these commands.

Figure 4-6:
When you move a slider in any of the Quick Fix palettes, the cancel and checkmark buttons appear in the palette you're using. Clicking the cancel symbol undoes the last change you made, while clicking the checkmark applies the change to your image.

If you make multiple slider adjustments, the cancel symbol undoes everything you've done since you clicked the checkmark. So, for example, if you lightened shadows and adjusted the midtone contrast, clicking cancel removes both changes. But if you adjusted the shadows, then clicked the checkmark, and then made the contrast adjustment, canceling the contrast adjustment would cancel just that without affecting the shadows' change.

Levels

If you want to understand how Levels really works, you're in for a long technical ride. On the other hand, if you just want to know what it can do for your photos, the short answer is that it adjusts the brightness of your photo by redistributing the color information; Levels changes (hopefully fixes!) both brightness and color at the same time.

If you've never used any photo-editing software before, this may sound rather mysterious, but photo-editing pros can tell you that Levels is one of the most powerful commands for fixing and polishing up your pictures. To find out if its magic works for you, click the Auto Levels button. Figure 4-7 shows what a big difference it can make to your photo.

What Levels does is very complex. Chapter 7 contains loads more details about what's going on behind the scenes and how you can apply this command much more precisely.

Contrast

The main alternative to Auto Levels in Quick Fix is Auto Contrast. Most people find that their images tend to benefit from one or the other of these. Contrast adjusts the relative darkness and lightness of your image without changing the color, so if Levels made your colors go all goofy, try adjusting the contrast instead.

Figure 4-7:
A quick click of the Auto Levels button can make a very dramatic difference in how vivid your photo is. The original photo of the squirrel (left) isn't bad, and you might not realize how much better the colors could be. But the photo on the right shows how much more effective your photo can be once Auto Levels has balanced the colors.

You activate Contrast just as you do the Levels tool: just click the Auto button next to its name.

Shadows and Highlights

The Shadows and Highlight tools do an amazing job of bringing out the details that are lost in the shadows or bright areas of your photo. Figure 4-9 shows what a difference these tools can make.

The Shadow and Highlight tools are a collection of three sliders, each of which controls a different aspect of your image:

- **Lighten Shadows.** Nudge the slider to the right and you'll see details emerge from murky black shadows.

- **Darken Highlights.** Use this slider to dim the brightness of overexposed areas.

- **Midtone Contrast.** After you've adjusted your photo's shadows and highlights, your photo may be very flat looking with not enough contrast between the dark and light areas. This slider helps you bring a more realistic look back to your photo.

   TIP   You may think you only need to *lighten* shadows in a photo, but sometimes just a smidgen of Darken Highlights may help, too. Don't be afraid to experiment by using this slider even if you've got a relatively dark photo.

Be discreet. Getting overenthusiastic with these sliders can give your photos a very washed out, flat look.

Figure 4-8:
The top photo shows a classic vacation picture problem: the day is bright, the scenery's beautiful, but everyone's faces are hidden in the dark shadows cast by their hats.

In the bottom photo, the Shadow and Highlight tools brought back everyone's faces, but now they look a bit jaundiced. Use the color sliders to make them look healthy again.

FREQUENTLY ASKED QUESTION

Calibrating Your Monitor

Why do my photos look awful when I open them in Elements?

Do you find that when you open your photos in Elements they look really terrible, even though they look decent in other programs? Maybe your photos are all washed out looking, or reddish or greenish, or even black and white?

If that's the case, you need to calibrate your monitor, as explained on page 160. It's easy to do and it makes a big difference.

Elements is what is known as a *color-managed* application. You can read all about color management in Chapter 7.

For now, you just need to understand that color-managed programs pay much more attention to the settings for your monitor than regular programs like word processors.

It makes programs like Elements a little more trouble to set up initially, but it also means that you can get truly wonderful results if you invest a little time and effort when you are getting started. Also, if you don't calibrate your monitor, Elements can show its displeasure in odd ways that don't seem to have anything to do directly with color.

Color

The Color palette lets you—surprise, surprise—play around with the colors in your image. In many cases, if you've been successful with Auto Levels or Auto Contrast you won't need to do anything here.

Auto Color

Once again, there's another one-click fix available—Auto Color. Actually, in some ways this one should be up in the Lighting section. Like Levels, it simultaneously adjusts color and brightness, but it looks at different information in your photos to decide what to do with them.

When you're first learning to use Quick Fix, you might want to try all three—Levels, Contrast, and Auto Color to see which generally works best for your photos. Undo between each change and compare your results. Most people find that they like one of the three most of the time, but you usually don't need to apply all three to the same photo.

Auto Color may be just the ticket for your photos, but you may also find that it shifts your colors in strange ways. Give it a click and see what you think. Does your photo look better or worse? If it's worse, just click Reset or Ctrl+Z (⌘-Z) to undo it, and go back to Auto Levels or Auto Contrast. If they all make your colors look a little wrong, or if you want to tweak the colors in your photo, move on to the Color sliders, which are explained in the next section.

Using the Color sliders

If you want to adjust just the colors in your photo without changing the brightness, then you want to check out the Color sliders. For example, your digital camera may produce colors that don't quite match what you saw when you took the picture, you might have scanned an old print that's faded or discolored, or you might just want to change the colors in a photo for the heck of it. If so, the sliders below the Auto Color button are for you.

There are four ways to adjust your colors here:

- **Saturation** controls the intensity of the color in your photo. For example, you can turn a color photo to black and white by moving the slider all the way to the left. Move it too far to the right and everything glows with so much color that it looks radioactive.

- **Hue** changes the color from, say, red to blue or green. If you aren't looking for realism, you can have some fun with your photos by really pushing this slider, as you saw back in Figure 4-3.

- **Temperature** lets you adjust color from cool (bluish) on the left to warm (orange-ish) on the right. You'd use this for things like toning down the warm glow you see in photos taken in tungsten lighting, or just for fine-tuning your color balance.

• **Tint** adjusts the green/magenta balance of your photo, as shown in Figure 4-9.

Figure 4-9:
The greenish tint in the top photo is a drastic example of a very common problem caused by many digital cameras. A little adjustment of the Tint slider clears it up in a jiffy (bottom). It's not always as obvious as it is here that you need a tint adjustment. If you aren't sure, the sky is often a dead giveaway. Is it robin's egg blue? If the photo's sky is that color and the real sky was just plain blue, tint is what you need.

You probably won't use all these sliders on a single photo, but you can use as many of them as you like. Remember to click the checkmark that appears in the Color palette if you want to accept your changes. Chapter 7 has much more information about how to use the full-blown Editor to really fine-tune your image's color.

TIP If you look at the color of the slider's track, it shows you what happens if you move in that direction. So there's less and less color as you go left in the Saturation track, and more and more to the right. Looking at the tracks can help you know where you want to move the slider.

Sharpening

Now that you've finished your other corrections, it's time to *sharpen,* or improve the focus, of your photo. Most digital camera photos need some sharpening, since the sharpening your camera applies is usually deliberately conservative. Once again, a Quick Fix Auto button is at your service. Give the Auto Sharpen button a try to get things started (Figure 4-10).

You should understand, though, that the sad truth is that there really isn't any way to actually improve the focus of a photo once it's taken. Software sharpening just increases the contrast where the program perceives edges, so using it first can have strange effects on other editing tools and their ability to understand your photo.

If you don't like what Auto Sharpening does (you very well may not), you can undo it (click the Cancel button on the Sharpen palette) and try the slider. If you thought the Auto button overdid things, go very gently with the slider and stop and look at where the Auto button moved the slider to. Changes vary from photo to photo, but usually Auto's results fall at around the 40 to 50 percent mark on the slider.

NOTE If you see funny halos around the outlines of objects in your photos, or strange flaky spots (making your photo look like it has eczema), those are artifacts from too much sharpening.

Figure 4-10:
On the left, you can see the original image, then what Auto Sharpen did (middle), and finally, the results of using the Sharpen slider (right) to achieve stronger sharpening than Auto was willing to perform.

Always try to view Actual Pixels (View → Actual Pixels) when sharpening, because that gives you the clearest idea of what you're actually doing to your picture. If you don't like what the button does, undo it and try the slider. Zero sharpening is all the way to the left. Moving to the right increases the amount of sharpening applied to your photo.

As a general rule, you want to sharpen more for photos you plan to print than for images for Web use. You can read lots more about sharpening on page 182.

> **TIP** If you've used photo-editing programs before, you might be interested to know that the Auto Sharpen button applies the Unsharp Mask filter to your photo. The difference is, you don't have any control over the settings, as you would if you applied the mask from the Filters menu. But the good news is that if you want it, you can get this control—even from within Quick Fix. Just go to the Filters menu and choose Sharpen → Unsharp Mask.

At this point, all that's left is cropping your photo, if you'd like to reduce its size. Page 53 tells you everything you need to know about cropping.

Quick Fix Suggested Workflow

There're no hard and fast rules for what order you need to work in when using the Quick Fix tools. As mentioned earlier, Elements lays out the tools in the Control Panel, from top to bottom, in the order that usually makes sense. But you can pick and choose which tools you want, depending on what you think your photo needs. But if you're the type of person who likes a set plan for fixing photos, here's one order in which to apply the commands the Quick Fix has to offer:

1. **Rotate your photo (if needed).**

   Use the buttons at the top of the Control Panel.

2. **Fix red eye (if needed).**

3. **Try Auto Smart Fix and/or the Smart Fix slider. Undo if necessary.**

   Pretty soon you'll get a good idea of how likely it is that this fix will do a good job on your photos. Some people love it; some people think it makes their pictures too grainy looking.

4. **If Smart Fix wasn't smart enough, work your way down through the other Lighting and Color commands until you like the way your photo looks.**

   Read the sections earlier in this chapter to understand what each command does to your photo.

5. **Sharpen.**

   Try to perform sharpening as your last adjustment, because other commands can give you funky results on photos that have already been sharpened.

6. **Crop.**

   You might also want to crop as a first step sometimes, depending on the photo. If you've got a lot of overexposed sky that you plan to cut out anyway, you may get better results from the Lighting and Color tools if it's gone already.

NOTE When you're in Quick Fix mode, you can always switch back to the Standard Editor at any point if you want tools or filters not available in Quick Fix.

GEM IN THE ROUGH

Performing Quick Fixes from the Organizer

If you're using Windows, you don't even need to be in the Quick Fix window to perform one-button fixes. In the Organizer, on the Shortcuts bar, if you choose Edit → Auto Fix Window, you'll see the dialog box shown here. All the commands are identical to their equivalents in the Quick Fix window. Clicking "More Editing…" will take you to the Standard Edit window.

Incidentally, if you take a look at the illustration, you can see a dire-looking warning right above the image. It tells you that the photo contains data for Print Image Matching that you may lose if you edit your photo. Print Image Matching, or P.I.M., is a special technology that supposedly can give you better prints when you print your photo without editing it.

You need to have a P.I.M. enabled camera and an Epson Printer to use Print Image Matching. If you want to try P.I.M. printing from Elements, you need to go to the Goodies folder on the install disc, find and install the plug-in, and read the PDF, which gives detailed instructions for how to do this kind of printing. The plug-in doesn't install automatically when you install Elements.

The bottom line is that Elements is warning you that if you edit your photo, you won't have an unedited file anymore to use for P.I.M. Fortunately, the Organizer's Auto Fix window is the only place in Elements where you're likely to run into the warning.

Part Two:
Elemental Elements

2

Making Selections

One of Elements' most impressive talents is its ability to let you *select* part of your image and make changes only to that area. Selecting something tells Elements, "Hey, *this* is what I want to work on. Just let me work on this part of my picture and don't touch the rest of it." You can select your entire image or any part of it.

By using selections, you can fine-tune your images in very sophisticated ways. You could change the color of just one rose in a whole bouquet, for instance, or change your nephew's festive purple hair color back to something his grandparents would appreciate. Graphics pros will tell you that good selections make the difference between shoddy amateurish work and a slick professional job.

> **TIP** The big secret to selecting is to take the time to be accurate. It's tempting to make your selections too quickly when you're first trying your hand at this, but you'll get better results if you don't rush.

Elements offers you a whole bunch of different selection tools to work with. You can draw a rectangular or a circular selection with the Marquee tools, for instance, or paint a selection on your photo with the Selection brush. For most jobs there's no right or wrong tool; with experience you may find you tend to prefer working with certain tools more than others. Often you'll use more than one tool to create a perfect selection. Once you've read this chapter you'll understand all the different selection tools and how to use each one.

> **TIP** It's much easier to select an object that's been photographed against a plain background. So, if you know you're going to want to select a bicycle, for example, shoot it in front of a blank wall rather than a hedge.

Making Quick Selections

Sometimes the only thing you want to do is select your entire photo. For instance, if you want to copy and paste your whole photo you need to select all of it. Elements gives you some useful commands to help you make basic selections in a snap:

- **Select All** (**Select → All or Ctrl+A [⌘-A]**) tells Elements to select your entire image. You'll see the "marching ants" around the outer edge of your entire picture, as shown in Figure 5-1.

  If you want to copy your image into another program, this is the fastest way to select the entire image. If your photo contains layers, which you'll learn about in Chapter 6, you might not be able to get everything you want with the Select All shortcut. In that case, page 142 (merging layers) explains what to do.

  TIP   If you're planning on copying an image to another program, like Microsoft Word or PowerPoint, make sure you've got "Export Clipboard" turned on in Preferences → General.

- **Unselect Everything** (**Select → Deselect or Ctrl+D [⌘-D]**) removes any current selection. Remember the keystroke combination, because it's one you'll probably use over and over again in Elements.

- **Reselect** (**Select → Reselect or Shift+Ctrl+D [Shift-⌘-D]**) tells Elements to reactivate the selection you just canceled. Use this if you realize you still need a selection you just got rid of. Or you can just press Ctrl+Z (⌘-Z) to back up a step.

- **Hide a Selection** (**Ctrl+H [⌘-H]**) keeps your selection active while hiding its outline. Sometimes the marching ants around a selection make it hard to see what you're doing, or they can be distracting. To see the ants again, press Ctrl+H (⌘-H) again.

  TIP   It's easy to forget you have a selection sometimes. When a tool acts goofy or won't do anything, start your troubleshooting by pressing Ctrl+H (⌘-H) to be sure you don't have a hidden selection you forgot about.

Selecting Rectangular and Elliptical Areas

Selecting your whole picture is all very well and good, but many times your reason for making a selection is precisely because you *don't* want the whole image involved in what you plan to do. How do you select just part of the picture?

Well, the easiest way is to use the Marquee tools. You already made the acquaintance of the Rectangular Marquee tool back in Chapter 3, in the section on cropping. If you want to select a block of your image or a circle or an oval from it, the Marquee tools are the way to go. As the winners of "Most frequently used Selection tools," they get top spot in the Selection area of the Editor's Toolbox. You can

bell.tif @ 25% (RGB/8)

25%

Figure 5-1:
The popular name for these dotted lines is "marching ants" because of the way they march around your selections to show you where the edges lie. When you see the ants, your selection is active, meaning what you do next happens only to the selected area.

modify how they work, like telling them to create a square instead of a rectangle, as explained in Figure 5-2.

To use the Marquee tools to make a selection:

1. **Press M or click the Marquee tool's icon in the Toolbox to activate it.**

   The Marquee tool is the little dotted square right below the Eyedropper icon.

gardenarchway.psd @ 25%(RGB/8)

Figure 5-2:
The Marquee tools usually make oval or rectangular selections. To make a perfectly circular or square selection, hold down the Shift key while you drag. To draw your selection from the center, hold down Alt (Option). It's easier to do it that way when you know the central point you want to include but aren't sure how much of the surrounding area you want.

UP TO SPEED

Paste vs. Paste Into

Newcomers to Elements are often confused by the fact that there are two Paste commands in Elements: Paste and Paste Into Selection. Knowing what each one does will help you avoid problems.

- **Paste.** 99 percent of the time, Paste is the one you want. This command simply places your copied object wherever you paste it. Once you've pasted your object, you can move whatever you've pasted by moving the selected area.

- **Paste Into Selection.** This is a special command for pasting a selection into *another* selection. Your pasted object only appears *within* the bounds of the selection you're pasting into.

When you use Paste Into Selection, what you paste can still be moved around, but it won't be visible anywhere outside the edges of the selection you're pasting into. This is very handy if you want to do something like putting a beautiful mountain view outside your window. You can maneuver the mountain photo around till it's properly centered. And if you move it outside the boundary of your window selection, it just disappears.

2. **Choose the Shape you want to draw: rectangle or ellipse.**

   In the Options bar or in the Toolbox pop-out menu for the Marquee tools, choose the rectangle or the ellipse to set the shape.

3. **Choose a feather value if you want one.**

   Feathering makes the edges of your selection softer or fuzzier. See the box on page 106 for a look at how feathering (and anti-aliasing) work.

4. **Drag in your image to make your selection.**

   Wherever you initially place your mouse becomes one of the corners of your rectangular selection or a point on the outer edge of your ellipse (unless you're using the "draw from center" option explained in Figure 5-2). The selection outline expands as you drag your mouse.

   If you make a mistake, just press the Escape key. You can also press either Ctrl+D (⌘-D) to get rid of all current selections, or Ctrl+Z (⌘-Z) to remove the most recent selection.

The mode choices in the Options bar give you three ways to control the size of your selection: Normal lets you manually control the size of your selection; Fixed Aspect Ratio lets you enter proportions in the Width and Height boxes; and Fixed Size lets you enter specific dimensions in these boxes.

Once you've made your selection, you can move the selected area around in the photo by dragging it (see page 117), or you can use the arrow keys to nudge your selection in the direction you want to move it. Changing the size of a Marquee selection once you've made it is pretty tricky and it's far easier to just start over again, but you can add to or subtract from any selection you make in Elements. The section "Controlling the Selection Tools" tells you how.

Selecting Irregularly Sized Areas

It would be nice if you could always get away with making simple rectangular or elliptical selections, but is life really ever that neat? You aren't always going to want to select a block-shaped chunk of your image. If you want to change the color of one fish in your aquarium picture, selecting a rectangle or square isn't going to help you any more than selecting the entire photo.

Thankfully, Elements gives you other tools that make it easy for you to make very precise selections—no matter their size or shape. In this section, you'll learn how to use the rest of the Selection tools. But first you need to understand the basic controls that they (almost) all share.

Controlling the Selection Tools

If you're the kind of person who never makes a mistake and you also never change your mind, you can skip this section. If, on the other hand, you're human, you need to know about the mysterious little squares you see in the Options bar when the Selection tools are active (see Figure 5-3).

These selection squares don't look like much, but they tell the Selection tools how to do their job: whether to start a new selection with each click, to add to what

Feathering and Anti-Aliasing

If you're old enough to remember what supermarket tabloid covers looked like before there was Photoshop, you probably had many a laugh at the obviously faked photos. Anyone could see where the art department had physically glued a piece cut from one photo onto another picture.

Nowadays, of course, the pictures of Elvis's and Cher's vampire baby from Mars are *much* more believable looking. That's because with Photoshop (and Elements) you can add *anti-aliasing* and *feathering* whenever you're making selections.

Anti-aliasing is a way of smoothing the edges of a digital image so that it's not jagged looking. When you make selections, the Lasso tools and the Magic Wand let you decide whether to use anti-aliasing. It's best to leave anti-aliasing on unless you have a reason to want a really hard-looking edge on your selection.

Feathering blurs the edges of a selection. When you make a selection that you plan to move to a different photo, a tiny feather can do a lot to make it look like it's always been part of the new photo. The selection tools let you set a feather value before you use them, except for the Selection brush. Generally a 1- or 2-pixel feather gives your selection a more natural-looking edge without visible blurring.

If you apply a feather value that is too high for the size of your selection, you see a warning that says "No pixels are more than 50% selected." Reduce the feather number to placate it.

A larger feather gives a soft edge to your photos. Old-fashioned vignettes like the one above are a classic example of where you'd want a fairly large feather. In this figure, the feather is 15 pixels wide.

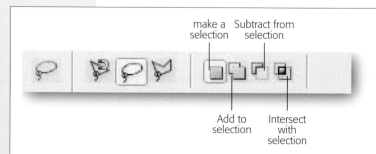

make a selection   Subtract from selection

Add to selection   Intersect with selection

Figure 5-3:
These cryptic squares can save you hours of time once you understand how to use them to tell the Selection tools how to behave.

you've already got, or to remove things from your selection. They're available for all the Selection tools except the Selection brush, which has its own set of options. From left to right, here's what they do:

- **Select** is the standard selection mode that you'll probably use most of the time. If you click this button, every time you start a new selection your previous selection disappears.

- **Add to Selection** tells Elements to add what you select next to what you've already selected. Holding down the Shift key while you use a Selection tool does the same thing. Most people need this one a lot, because it's not always easy to get a perfect selection on the first try.

- **Subtract from Selection** removes what you select next from any existing selection. By holding down Alt (Option) while selecting the area you want to remove, you can accomplish the same thing directly from the keyboard.

- **Intersect with Selection** is confusing. It lets you take a selected area, make a new selection, and wind up with only the areas where both overlap as your final selection. See Figure 5-4. The keyboard equivalent is Alt+Shift (Option-Shift).

Figure 5-4:
Intersect with Selection lets you take two separate selections and select only the area where they intersect. If you have an existing selection and you choose this mode, when you select again you wind up with a selection that includes only the overlapping area.

Here, the top blueish-purple rectangle is the first selection, and the bottom purple square represents the second selection. The light area shows what's left selected after you let go of the mouse button.

The Magic Wand

The Magic Wand is a slightly temperamental—and occasionally highly effective—tool for selecting an irregularly shaped, but similarly colored, area of an image. If you have a big area of a particular color, the Magic Wand can find its edges in one click. It's not actually all that magical: all it does is search for pixels with similar color values. But if it works for you, you may decide it should keep the "magic" in its name because it's a great timesaver when it cooperates, as Figure 5-5 shows.

macaw.psd @ 33.3%(RGB/8)

Figure 5-5:
Just one click with the Magic Wand created this selection. If there isn't a big difference between the color of the area you want to select and the colors of neighboring areas, the Wand isn't as effective as it is here.

Using the Magic Wand is pretty straightforward. You just click anywhere in the area you want to select. Depending on your *tolerance* setting (explained in the following bullet list), you may nail the selection at once or it may take several clicks to get everything. If you need to click more than once, remember to hold down Shift so that each click adds to your selection.

The Magic Wand does its best job when you offer it a good solid block of color that is clearly defined and doesn't have a lot of different shades in it. But it can be frustrating trying to select colors that have any shading or tonal gradations. You have to click and click and click. There are two Options bar settings that you can adjust to help the Wand do a better job:

- **Tolerance** adjusts the number of different shades that the tool selects at once. A higher tolerance includes more shades (resulting in a larger selection area), while a lower tolerance gets you fewer shades (and a more precise selection area). If you set the tolerance too high, you'll probably select a lot more of your picture than you want.

- **Contiguous** makes the Magic Wand select only color areas that actually touch each other (see Figure 5-6). It's on by default, but sometimes you can save a lot of time by turning it off.

Figure 5-6:
In the left photo, Contiguous is checked. By turning it off, as in the photo at right, you can select all the orange hats with just one click. If you want all the orange hats, it's easier to leave Contiguous turned off and then quickly clean up the selection afterwards with the Selection brush (which is covered on page 113).

The Lasso Tool

The Magic Wand is great, but it only works well when your image has clearly defined areas of color. A lot of the time, you'll want to select something from a cluttered background that the Magic Wand just can't cope with. Sometimes you might think the easiest way would be if you could just draw around the object you want to select.

Enter the Lasso tool. The Lasso is actually three tools: the Lasso tool, the Polygonal Lasso tool, and the Magnetic Lasso tool. Each tool lets you select an object by tracing around it.

You activate the Lasso tools by clicking their icon in the Toolbox (it's just below the Marquee tool) or by pressing L, and then selecting the particular variation you want in the Options bar or the Toolbox pop-out menu. You then drag around the outline of your object to make your selection. The following sections cover each Lasso tool.

The basic Lasso tool

The theory behind the basic Lasso tool is very simple. You click in your photo and your cursor changes to the lasso shape shown in Figure 5-7. Just drag around the outline of what you want to select. When the end of your selection gets back around to join up with the beginning, you've got a selection.

dresser.psd @ 143%(RGB/8)

Figure 5-7:
The end of the rope, and not the lasso loop, is the working part of the basic Lasso tool. If the cursor's shape bothers you, you can change it to crosshairs by pressing the Caps Lock key. You need to press Caps Lock when the Lasso tool is active, but before you have actually begun your selection.

In practice, it's not always so easy to make an accurate selection with the Lasso, especially if you're using a mouse. A graphics tablet is a big advantage when using this tool, since tablets let you draw with a pen-shaped pointer. (There's more about graphics tablets in Chapter 17.) But even if you don't happen to have a graphics tablet lying around, you can make all the tools work just fine with your mouse once you get used to their quirks.

It helps to zoom the view way in and to go very slowly when using the Lasso. (See page 60 for more information on changing your view.) Many people use the regular Lasso tool to quickly select an area that roughly surrounds their object and then go back with the other selection tools, like the Selection brush or the Magnetic Lasso, to clean things up.

If you want to draw a straight line for part of your border, hold down Alt (Option) as you drag. If you want to get out of the Lasso tool before finishing your selection, press Escape. Once you have a selection, press Ctrl+D (⌘-D) to get rid of it.

The Magnetic Lasso

The Magnetic Lasso is a very handy tool, especially if you were the kind of kid who never could color inside the lines or cut paper chains out neatly. The Magnetic Lasso snaps to the outline of any clearly defined object you're trying to select, so you don't have to follow the edge exactly.

The Magnetic Lasso does its best work on objects with clearly defined edges. You won't get much out of it if your subject is a furry animal, for instance. The Magnetic Lasso also likes a good strong contrast between the object and the background. (You can change the cursor shape with the Caps Lock key, just as with the regular Lasso.)

Click to start a selection. Then move your cursor around the perimeter of what you want to select; click again back where you began to finish your selection. You can also Ctrl+click (⌘-click) at any point, and the Magnetic Lasso will immediately close up whatever area you've surrounded. You can also adjust how many points the Magnetic Lasso puts down and how sensitive it is to the edge you are tracing as shown in Figure 5-8.

The Magnetic Lasso comes with four additional settings in the Options bar:

- **Width** tells the Magnetic Lasso how far away to look when it's trying to find the edge. The value is always in pixels, and you can set it as high as 40.

- **Edge Contrast** controls how sharp a difference the Magnetic Lasso should look for between the outline and the background. A higher number looks for sharper contrasts, a lower number for softer ones.

- **Frequency** controls how fast Elements puts down the fastener points you see in Figure 5-8.

- **Pen Pressure** doesn't do anything unless you have a graphics tablet. If you do and you turn this on, how hard you press controls how Elements searches for the edge of objects you're trying to select. When you bear down harder, it's more precise. When you press more lightly you can be a bit sloppier and Elements will still find the edge.

Many people live full and satisfying lives paying no attention whatsoever to these settings, so don't feel like you need to be fussing with them all the time. You can usually ignore them unless the Magnetic Lasso misbehaves.

trafficbarricade.tif @ 100%(RGB/8)

Figure 5-8:
One nice thing about the Magnetic Lasso is that it's easy to back up as you're creating your selection. As you go, it lays down the little boxes shown in this figure, which are called anchor or fastening points. If you make a mistake with the Magnetic Lasso, pressing Backspace/Delete takes you back one point each time you press the key.

If the Magnetic Lasso skips a spot or won't grab on to a spot where you want it to, you can force it to put down an anchor point by clicking once where you want the anchor to appear.

TIP You get better results with the Magnetic Lasso if you go more slowly than if you speed around the object. Like most people, the Magnetic Lasso does better work if you give it time to be sure of where it's going.

The Polygonal Lasso

At first, this may seem like a totally stupid tool. It works like the Magnetic Lasso, but it only creates perfectly straight segments. So you may think, "Well that's great if I want to select a Stop sign, but otherwise, what's the point?"

Actually, if you're one of those people who just plain *can't* draw and you even have a hard time following the edge of an object that's already on the screen, this is the tool for you. The trick is to use very short distances between clicks. Figure 5-9 shows the Polygonal Lasso in action.

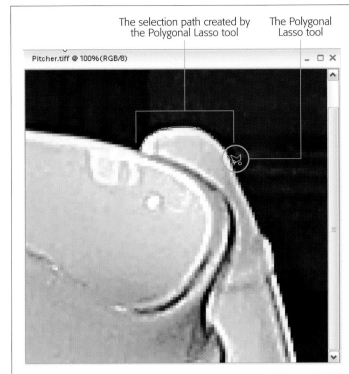

The selection path created by
the Polygonal Lasso tool

The Polygonal
Lasso tool

Pitcher.tiff @ 100% (RGB/8)

Figure 5-9:
*If you have limited dexterity, the Polygonal
Lasso tool and a lot of clicks eventually get
you a nice accurate selection. You need to
zoom way, way in to use this tool to select an
object that doesn't have totally straight sides.
Here, the Polygonal Lasso easily made it
around the curve of the handle by clicking to
make extremely short segments.*

The big advantage of using the Polygonal Lasso over the Magnetic Lasso is that it's much easier to keep it from getting into a snarl.

The Selection Brush

The Selection brush is one of the greatest tools in Elements. It makes it much, much easier to make complex selections and to clean up the selections you've got.

With the Selection brush, you just paint over what you want to select. To do that, you drag over the area you want. You can let go, and each time you drag again, you automatically add to your selection. There's no need to change modes in the Options bar or hold down the Shift key the way you do with the other Selection tools.

Not only that, but the Selection brush also has a Mask mode, in which you see what *isn't* part of your selection. This is great for finding tiny spots you might have missed and for checking the accuracy of your selection outline. In Mask mode, anything you paint over gets *masked* out. In other words, it's protected from being selected.

Masking can be a little confusing at first, but you'll soon see what a useful tool masking is. Figure 5-10 shows the same selection made with and without Mask mode.

Figure 5-10:
The same selection with the brush in Selection mode (left), and in Mask mode (right). The red covers everything that is not part of your selection. In the top figure, you see a standard selection marquee just as you'd get using any of the other selection tools.

The Selection brush is pretty simple to use:

1. **Click the Selection brush in the Toolbox, or press A.**

   The Selection brush is located in the Toolbox just below the Magic Wand. Choose either Selection mode or Mask mode and the brush size you want.

2. **Drag over the area you want.**

   If you are in Selection mode, the area you drag over becomes part of your selection. If you are in Mask mode, the area you drag over is kept from becoming part of your selection.

The Selection brush gives you several choices in the Options bar:

- **Brush.** You can use many different brushes depending on whether you want a hard- or soft-edged selection. If you want a different brush, just choose it from the menu here. (For more about brushes, see Chapter 8.)

- **Size.** To change the brush size, type a size in the box, click the arrow, and use the slider. Or just press the close bracket key (]) to increase the size (keep tapping it until you get the size you want). The open bracket key ([) decreases the size of your brush.

   TIP The bracket key shortcut works with any brush, not just the Selection brush.

- **Mode.** This is where you tell Elements whether you are creating a selection (Selection) or preventing an area from being part of a selection (Mask).

- **Hardness.** This controls two things: the sharpness of the edge of your selection and its opacity. See Figure 5-11.

Switching between Selection and Mask mode is a good way to see how well you've done when you finish making your selection. In Mask mode, the parts of your

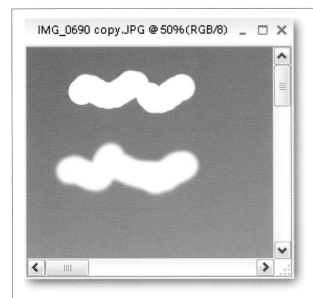

IMG_0690 copy.JPG @ 50%(RGB/8)

Figure 5-11:
The top selection was made at 100 percent hardness, the bottom one at 50 percent. (The selected area was then deleted to show you the outline more clearly.)

image that are *not* part of your selection have a red film over them, so that you can clearly see the selected area only.

> **TIP**   You don't have to live with the red mask color if you don't want to. To change the color of the mask: click the Overlay Color box in the Options bar while the Selection brush is active. Use the Color Picker (see page 175) to choose the color you prefer.

You can temporarily make the Selection brush do the opposite of what it has been doing by holding down Alt (Option) while you drag. For example, if you're in Selection mode and you've selected too large an area, Alt+drag (Option-drag) over the excess to remove it. If you're masking out an area, Alt+drag (Option-drag) to add an area to the selection. This may sound confusing, but some things are easier to learn by doing.

> **TIP**   The Selection brush is great for fine-tuning selections made with the other selection tools. Quickly switching to the Selection brush in Mask mode is a great way to check for spots you might have missed—the red makes it really easy to see them.

Changing and Moving Selections

Now that you know all about how to make selections, it's time to learn about some of the finer points of using and manipulating them. Elements gives you several handy options for changing the areas you've selected and for actually moving images around once they're selected. You can even save a tough selection so you don't have to do *that* again.

Inverting a Selection

One thing you often want to do with a selection is *invert* it. That means telling Elements, "Hey, you know the area I've selected? Well, I want you to select everything *except* that area."

Why would you want to do that? Well, sometimes it's easier to select what you *don't* want. For example if you have an object with a complicated outline, like the group of buildings shown in Figure 5-12. Say you want to put this building on your letterhead, it might be difficult to select. But the sky is just one big block of color. It's a lot easier to select the sky with the Magic Wand than to try to get an accurate selection of the building itself.

Figure 5-12:
Say you want to put this building on your letterhead. You could spend half an hour meticulously selecting it, or instead just select the sky with a click of the Magic Wand and invert your selection to get the silos.

In the left figure, the sky has the marching ants around it to show that it's the active selection-but that's not what you want. Inverting the selection gives you the ants around the buildings without the trouble of tracing out all the ladders and pipes on the silos.

To invert a selection:

1. **Make a selection.**

   Usually, you first select what you *don't* want if you're planning to invert your selection. You can select with any tool that suits your fancy.

2. **Go to Selection → Inverse.**

   Now the part of your image that you *didn't* select is selected.

Making a Selection Larger or Smaller

What if you want to tweak the size of your selection? Sometimes you may want to move the outline of a selection outward a few pixels to expand it. Figuring out how to do so confuses people because Elements offers two similar-sounding ways to do it: Grow and Expand. They sound like they should do the same thing, but there's a slight but important difference between them.

Smoothing and Bordering

Elements includes a couple of specialist commands for tweaking the edges of your selections.

- **Smoothing** (Selection → Smooth) is a sometimes-dependable way to clean up ragged edges on a selection. You enter a pixel value, and Elements evens out the edges of your selection based on the number you entered, by searching for similarly colored pixels.

  If you enter 5 pixels, Elements looks at a 5-pixel radius from the edge of your selection. In areas where most of the pixels are already selected, it adds in the others. Where most pixels aren't selected, it deselects the ones that are selected to get rid of the jagged edges.

This can be handy, but smoothing is sometimes hard to control. Usually it's easier to clean up your selection by hand with the Selection brush than to use Smoothing.

- **Bordering** (Select → Modify → Border) adds an antialiased, invisible border to your image. You might say it selects the selection's outline. You would use it when your selection's edges are too hard and you want to soften them. Choose a border size, and click Okay. Only the border is selected so you can also apply a slight Gaussian blur (see page 318) to soften it more if you like.

- **Grow** (Select → Grow) moves your selection outward to include more similar contiguous colors, no matter what shape your original selection was. Grow doesn't care about shape; it just finds more matching contiguous pixels.

- **Expand** (Select → Modify → Expand) preserves the shape of your selection and just increases the size of it by the number of pixels you specify.

- **Similar** (Select → Similar) does the same thing as Grow but looks at all pixels, not just the adjacent ones.

- **Contract** (Select → Modify → Contract) shrinks the size of a selection.

So what's the big difference between Expand and Grow? Look at Figure 5-13 to see how differently they behave.

Moving Selections

Often you make selections because you want to move objects around—like putting that dreamboat who wouldn't give you the time of day next to you in your senior year class photo. You can move a selection in several ways.

Here's the simplest, tool-free way to move something from one image to another:

1. **Select it.**

   Make sure you've selected everything you want. It's really annoying when you paste a selection from one image to another and find you missed a spot.

2. **Press Ctrl+C (⌘-C) to copy it.**

   Or you could use Ctrl+X (⌘-X) if you want to cut it out of your original. Just remember that Elements leaves a hole if you do it that way.

Stopsign.tif @ 100%(RGB/8)

Figure 5-13:
Top: In the original selection, everything in the Stop sign has been selected except the small white border on the outside of the sign.

Bottom Left: If you use Grow to enlarge the selection, you also get parts of the building that are similar in tone. Your selection isn't shaped like a Stop sign anymore.

Bottom Right: But if you use Expand instead, the selection still has the exact shape of the sign, only now the edges of the selection move outward to include the white border area of the sign.

TIP If you copy and paste a selection and you see it's got partially transparent areas in it, back up and go over your selection again with the Selection brush using a hard brush, then copy and paste again.

3. **Go to File → New from Clipboard.**

This creates a new document with just your selection in it. Or you can use Ctrl+V (⌘-V) to paste it into another image or a document in another program. (Be sure you've turned on Export Clipboard in Preferences → General.)

The Move tool

You can also move things around *within* your photo by using the Move tool, which lets you cut or copy selected areas. Figure 5-14 shows how to use the Move tool to conceal distracting details in photos.

The Move tool lives at the very top of the Standard Edit Toolbox. To use it:

1. **Make a selection.**

   Make sure your selection doesn't have anything in it that you don't want to copy.

2. **Switch to the Move tool.**

   Click the Move tool or press V. Your selection stays active but is now surrounded by a rectangle with box-shaped handles on the corners.

3. **Move the selection and press Enter/Return when you're satisfied with its position.**

   As long as your selection is active, you can work on your photo in other ways and then come back and reactivate the Move tool. If you're worried about losing a complex selection, save it as described in the next section. If you're not happy with what you've done, just press Ctrl+D (⌘-D) to deselect everything, and you can start over again.

You can move a selection in several different ways:

- **Move it.** If you just move a selection by dragging it, you leave a hole in the background where the selection was. The Move tool *truly* moves your selection. So unless you have something under it that you want to show through, that's probably not what you want to do.

- **Copy it and move the copy.** If you press the Alt (Option) key as you're moving, you'll copy your selection, so your original remains where it was. But now you'll have a duplicate to move around and play with.

- **Resize it.** You can drag the Move tool's handles to resize or distort your copy, which is great when you need to change the size of your selection. The Move tool lets you do the same things you can do with Free Transform (see page 263).

- **Rotate it.** The Move tool lets you rotate your selection the same way you can rotate a picture using Free Rotate (see page 51). Just grab a corner and turn it.

> **TIP**   You can save a trip to the Toolbox and move selections without activating the Move tool. To move a selection without copying it, just place your cursor in the selection, hold down Ctrl (⌘), and move the selection.
>
> To move a copy of a selection, follow the same procedure but hold down the Alt (Option) key as well. You can drag the copy without damaging the original. To move multiple copies, just let go, then press Ctrl+Alt (⌘-Option) again and drag once more.

yellowsweater.psd @ 26.6%(RGB/8)

yellowsweater.psd @ 26.6%(RGB/8)

Figure 5-14:
Let's say you wanted to get rid of the window in the upper-right corner of the top photo. By copying and moving pieces of the wall (bottom), you can cover up the window and create a simpler background to put the focus on the woman rather than the building.

Holding down the Alt (Option) key while using the Move tool copies a selected area. If you use the Move tool without this keystroke modifier, Elements cuts away the selection, leaving a hole in your photo.

Saving Selections

You can tell Elements to remember the outline of your selection so that you can reuse it again later on. This is a wonderful timesaver and it's easy to do, too.

> **TIP** Elements' saved selections are the equivalent of Photoshop's *alpha channels*. Keep that in mind if you decide to try tutorials written for Photoshop. Incidentally, alpha channels saved in files in Photoshop show up in Elements as saved selections.

To save a selection:

1. **Make your selection.**

2. **Choose Select → Save Selection, give your selection a name, and save it.**

   When you want to use the selection again, go to Select → Load Selection and there it is, waiting for you.

Making changes to a saved selection

It's probably just as easy to start your selection over if you need to tweak a saved selection, but it is possible to make changes if you want. This can save you some time if your original selection was really tricky to create.

Say you've got a full-length photo of somebody and you've created and saved a selection of the person's face (called, naturally enough, "Face"). Now, imagine that after applying a filter to the selection, you decide it would look silly to change only the face and not the person's hands, too.

So you want to add the hands to your saved selection. There are a couple of ways to do this.

The simplest is just to load up "Face," activate your selection tool of choice, put the tool in Add to Selection mode (page 107), and then save the selection again with the same name.

But how about if you've already selected the hands and you want to add *that* new selected area to the existing facial selection? Here's what you'd do:

1. **Go to Select → Save Selection.**

   Choose your saved "Face" selection. All the radio buttons in the dialog box become active.

2. **Choose "Add to Selection."**

   What you just selected is added to the original selection and saved, so now your "Face" selection also includes the hands.

Layers: The Heart of Elements

If you've been working mostly in the Quick Fix window so far, you've probably noticed that once you close your file, the changes you've made are permanent. You can undo actions while the file's still open, but once you close it, you're stuck with what you've done.

Well, in Elements, you can keep your changes and still revert to the original image if you use *layers*, a nifty system of transparent sheets that keep each element of your image on a separately editable sliver. Layers are one of the greatest image-editing inventions ever. By putting each change you make on its own layer, you can constantly rearrange the composition of your image, or add and subtract changes whenever you want.

If you use layers, you can save your file and quit Elements and come back days or weeks later and still undo what you did or change things around some more. There's no statute of limitations for the changes you make when using layers.

Some people resist learning about layers because they fear they're too complicated. But they're actually very easy to use once you understand how they work. And once you get started with layers, you'll realize that using Elements without them is like driving a Ferrari in first gear. This chapter gives you the information you need to get comfortable working with layers.

Understanding Layers

Layers aren't that complicated, but it may help to first think about an example from the real world to understand how they work. Imagine you've got a drawing of a room you're thinking about redecorating. Say the drawing features a few of the objects that you know will be in the room, like the walls, the windows, and a piece of furniture or two. To get an idea of your different decorating possibilities, imagine that you've also got a bunch of clear plastic sheets, each of which has some image on it that changes the room's look: a couch, a few different colors for the carpet, a standing lamp, and so on. Your decorating work is now pretty easy, since you can add and remove, and mix and match, the plastic sheets with ease.

Layers in Elements work pretty much the same way. With layers, you can add and remove objects and also make changes to the way your image looks. And with any of these changes, you can modify or discard them later on.

If you look at Figure 6-1, you can see an Elements file that includes layers. Each object in that flyer is on a different layer, so you can easily remove anything any time you want, or change the appearance or rearrange the location of any object in the image.

Figure 6-1:
Every object on this flyer—the background, the scarecrow, the pumpkins, each block of text—is on its own layer, which makes changing things a snap. Want to change the background, get rid of the pumpkins, or change the phone number? With layers, it's easy to do any of these things.

Harvest Fest

❀ Rides
❀ Livestock Show
❀ Square Dancing
❀ Crafts Fair

It's that time of year again! Everybody's favorite weekend for appple bobbing, corn husking, pumpkin pie eating, and general merriment is almost here. Get your crops in and come join us the last weekend in October for our annual town festival and fair. The fun starts at 8 am Saturday.

For more information and livestock show entry forms, please call 555-9876.

Saturday, October 30
County Fairgrounds
8 am till Midnight

You can also use layers for many adjustments to your photos, giving yourself the chance to tweak or eliminate those adjustments later. For instance, say you used the Quick Fix's Hue slider but then decided the next day you didn't like what you did: you're stuck (unless you can dig out a copy of your original). But if you'd used a Hue/Saturation adjustment *layer* to make the change, you could just throw out that layer and keep all your other changes intact (you'll learn about adjustment layers later in this chapter). You can also use layers to combine parts of different photos together, as shown in Figure 6-2.

Figure 6-2:
Layers make it easy to combine elements from different photos. You may not be able to afford to send your grandparents on a real trip to Europe, but once you understand layers, you can give them a virtual vacation.

Once you understand how to use layers, you'll feel much more comfortable making radical changes to an image, because mistakes are much easier to fix. Not only that, but by using layers you can easily make lots of very sophisticated changes that are otherwise very difficult and time-consuming.

> **TIP**   Once you've been through this chapter, if you'd like a little more experience working with layers, Elements gives you an excellent tutorial. Launch Help and go to Contents → Tutorials → Harness the Power of Layers.

The Layers Palette

The Layers palette is your control center for any kind of layer-related action you want to perform, like adding, deleting, or duplicating layers. Figure 6-3 shows you the Layers palette for an image that already has lots of layers.

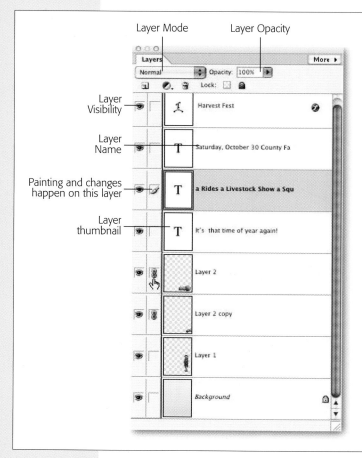

Figure 6-3:
Here's the Layers palette for the illustration in Figure 6-1. Each row lists a separate layer in the image. The presence of the tiny paintbrush icon indicates that any painting or changes you make will happen on this layer.

It's important to have access to the Layers palette whenever you work with layers, not only for the information it gives you, but because most layer manipulating can be done more easily from the palette than working directly in your image.

Managing the Layers Palette

The Layers palette lives in a fairly inconvenient location at the very bottom of the Palette bin. The flippy triangle to the left of its name lets you open (or close) the palette; sometimes on small monitors the palette contents are hidden below the bottom edge of the bin.

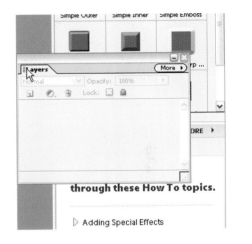

The Layers palette is important, so you probably want to get it out where you can see it all the time, at least while you're working with layered files. To do so, just grab the top bar of the palette near the name and pull it out of the bin onto your desktop, as shown in the illustration. (For keeping track of the Layers palette once it's out of the bin, take a look at page 13.)

You can collapse the Layers palette once it's on the desktop, but Elements gurus usually like to keep it easily accessible.

If you have a big monitor and you can see all the contents and have room to keep the Palette bin open while you work, it's fine to leave the Layers palette in the bin if you prefer. The idea is to get that palette where you can see it all the time and easily get to it with your mouse.

Each layer displays its name and a little thumbnail icon in the palette showing the layer's contents. You can adjust the size of the icon or turn it off altogether if you prefer, as shown in Figure 6-4.

The Layers palette always contains one layer that's active, meaning that any action you take, like painting, is going to happen on that layer (and that layer only). In Windows, the active layer is dark gray, while on the Mac, it's blue. The little paintbrush in the Layers palette in the square to the right of the eye icon also indicates which layer is currently active.

When you look at an image that contains layers, you're looking down on the stack of layers from the top, just the way you would with the overlays on the drawing. The layers appear in the same order in the Layers palette—the top layer of your image is the top layer in the stack in the Layers palette. (Layer order is important, because whatever is on top can obscure what's beneath it.)

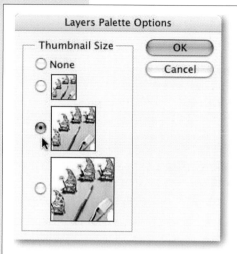

Figure 6-4:
If you want to change the size of the thumbnail icons in the layers palette, call up the Layers Palette Options dialog box by clicking the More button at the upper-right corner of the Layers palette. Then select "Palette Options" from the bottom of the menu.

There are many things you can do in the Layers palette. You can turn the visibility of layers off and on, change the order in which layers are stacked, link layers together, change the opacity of layers, add and delete layers—the list goes on and on. The rest of this chapter covers all these options, and more.

The Background

The bottom layer of any image is a special kind of layer called the background. If you bring any image or photo into Elements, the first time you open it, you'll see its one existing layer is called "Background." (That's assuming that nobody else has already edited the file in Elements and changed things.)

> **NOTE** There are two exceptions to the first-layer-is-always-the-background rule. First, if you create a new image by copying something from another picture, you'll just have a layer called "Layer 0." And background layers can't be transparent, so if you choose the Transparency option when creating a file from scratch, you'll have a Layer 0 instead of a background layer then, too.

That's logical enough, if you think about it for a minute. Whatever else you do is going to come in on top of this layer, so it's reasonable to call it the background. Content-wise the background can be totally plain or busy, busy, busy. A background layer doesn't mean that it literally contains the background of your photograph—your entire photo can be a background layer. It's entirely up to you what's on your background layer and what you place on other, newly added layers. A common strategy for photographs is to keep your photo's image on the background layer, and then perform adjustments and other embellishments (like adding type) on other layers.

Whatever you choose, there are a few things you can't do to backgrounds: if you want to change its blending mode (page 137), opacity (page 135), or position in the layer stack, you need to convert the background into a regular layer.

> **TIP** The Background and Magic Erasers automatically turn a background layer into a regular layer when you click a background with them. If you have a single object on a solid background and you want transparency around the object, one click with the Magic Eraser turns your background into a layer, eliminates a solid-colored background, and replaces it with transparency. (There's more on the Eraser tools in Chapter 11.)

You can change a background to a regular layer by double-clicking the background in the Layers palette. Or, if you attempt to make certain kinds of changes to the background (like moving its position), Elements will prompt you to change the background to a regular layer.

You can also transform a regular layer into a background layer if you want. The main reason to do this would be to send a layer zipping down to the bottom of the stack in a many-layered file. To do so:

1. **Click in the Layers palette on the layer you want to convert to a background.**

2. **Select Layer → New → Background from Layer.**

   It may take a few seconds for the program to finish calculating and respond after you tell it what to do. The layer you've changed moves down to the bottom of the layer stack in the Layers palette, and automatically gets renamed "Background."

> **NOTE** You can't have more than one background layer in an image. So what do you do if you want to change a regular layer to a background layer, and you've already got a background layer? Well, you need to change the existing background into a regular layer first. Otherwise, the command is unavailable.

Creating Layers

Your image doesn't automatically have multiple layers. Lots of newcomers to Elements expect the program to be smart enough to put each object in a photo onto its own layer. It's a lovely dream, but even Elements isn't that brainy. To experience the joy of layers, you first need to add at least one layer to your image, which is what you'll learn how to do in the next few sections.

> **TIP** It might help you to follow along through the next few sections if you get out a photo of your own or create a new file to use for practice. (See page 27 for details on how to create a new file.) If you create a new file, choose a white background.

Which File Types Can Use Layers?

You can add layers to any file you can open in Elements, but not every file format lets you save those layers for future use.

For instance, if your camera shoots JPEGs, you can open the JPEG in Elements and create lots of layers, but when you try to save the file, you'll see a warning reminding you that you can't have layers in a JPEG.

Usually you'll want to choose either Photoshop (.psd) or TIFF as your format when saving an image with layers, because they both let you keep your layers for future use. PDF files can also have layers.

If someone using Photoshop sends you an image that has layers, you'll see them in the Layers palette when you open the file in Elements. Likewise, Photoshop can see layers you create in Elements.

If someone sends you a Photoshop file with *layer sets* (a way to group layers into what are essentially folders in the layers palette), Elements doesn't understand those, so ask the sender to expand the layer sets or convert the set to regular layers before sending you the file.

Adding a Layer

Elements gives you several different ways to add new layers. You can use any of the following methods:

- Select Layer → New → Layer.

- Press Ctrl+Shift+N (⌘-Shift-N).

- In the Layers palette, click the New Layer icon (the little square shown in Figure 6-5).

When you create a new layer using any of these commands, the layer starts out empty. You won't see a change in your image until you use the layer for something (pasting something into the empty layer or painting on it, for example). If you look at the Layers palette, you'll see that any new layer you add appears just above the layer that was active when you created the new layer.

> **NOTE**   The only limit to the number of layers your image can have is your computer's processing power. But if you find yourself regularly creating projects with upwards of 100 layers, you might want to upgrade to Photoshop CS, which has tools that make it easier to manage large numbers of layers.

Some actions create new layers automatically. For instance, if you drag an object in from another photo (see page 149 for an explanation of how to do this), the object automatically comes in on its own layer. And that's very handy for arranging the new item just where you want it, without disturbing the rest of your composition.

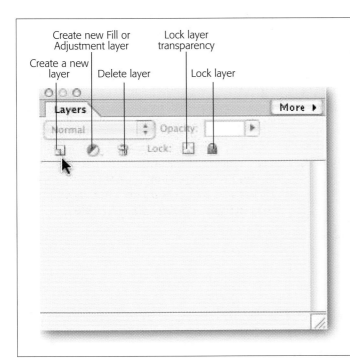

Create a new Fill or
Adjustment layer

Create a new
layer

Delete layer

Lock layer
transparency

Lock layer

Figure 6-5:
More controls on the Layers palette. Click the little New Layer icon on the left side of the Layers palette when you want to quickly add a new layer.

Deleting Layers

It's very easy to delete layers. Figure 6-6 shows the simplest way.

There are a few other ways to delete a layer. You can also:

• Select Layer → Delete Layer.

• Right-click (Control-click) the layer in the Layers palette and choose "Delete Layer" from the pop-up menu.

• Click the More button on the Layers palette and choose "Delete Layer" from the pop-up menu.

Duplicating a Layer

Duplicating a layer can be very useful. Many Elements commands, like filters or color modification tools, won't work on a brand new *empty* layer. This poses a dilemma, because if you apply those changes to the layer containing your main image, you'll alter it in ways you can't undo later. The workaround is to create a duplicate layer and make your changes on that new layer. Then you can ditch the duplicate later if you change your mind, and your original layer is safely tucked away unchanged.

If all this seems annoyingly theoretical, try going to Enhance → Adjust Color → Adjust Hue/Saturation, for example, when you're working on a new blank layer, and see what happens. You'll see the dialog box shown in Figure 6-7 if you try to work on a blank layer.

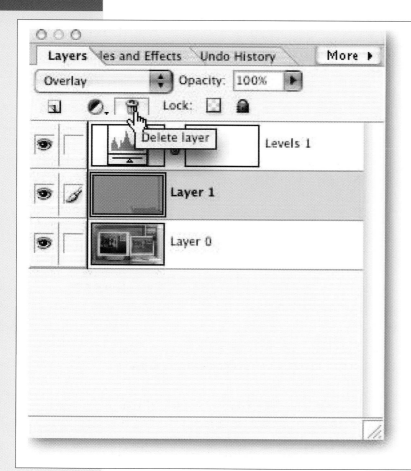

Figure 6-6:
To make a layer go away, you can either drag the layer to the Trash can icon on the Layers palette or, after selecting the layer, just click the icon itself. Elements asks if you want to delete the active layer. Say yes, and it's history. Once you delete a layer, it's gone forever.

There are a few of ways to duplicate an existing layer and its content. Select the layer you want to duplicate to make it the active layer, and then do one of the following:

- Choose Layer → Duplicate Layer.

- Right-click (Control-click) the Layer in the Layers palette and choose "Duplicate Layer" from the pop-up menu.

- Click the More button on the Layers palette and choose "Duplicate Layer."

Creating a new layer by any of these methods copies the entire contents of the active layer into the new layer. You can mess with the duplicate as much as you want without damaging the original layer.

Copying and Cutting from Layers

You can also make a new layer that consists only of a *piece* of an existing layer. But first you need to decide whether you want to *copy* your selection or *cut it out* and place it on the new layer.

What's the difference? It's pretty much the same as copying vs. cutting in your word processing program. When you make a New Layer via Copy, the area you select appears in the new layer while remaining in place in the old layer, too. On the other hand, New Layer via Cut removes the selection from the old layer and places it on a new layer, leaving a corresponding hole in the old layer. Figure 6-8 shows the difference.

Once you've selected what you want to move or copy, your new layer is only a couple of keystrokes away.

- **New Layer via Copy.** The easiest way to copy your selection to a new layer is to press Ctrl+J (⌘-J). You can also go to Layer → New → Layer via Copy. Whichever you use, if you didn't select anything before you use these keystrokes, your whole layer gets copied, so it's also a good shortcut for making a duplicate layer.

- **New Layer via Cut.** To cut your selection out of your old layer and put it on a layer by itself, press Ctrl+Shift+J (⌘-Shift-J), or go to Layer → New → Layer via Cut. Just remember that you'll leave a hole in your original layer when you do this.

If for some reason you want to cut and move the entire contents of a layer, you can press Ctrl+A (⌘-A) first, although usually it's easier just to move your layer instead.

car.tif @ 66.7%(Layer 1, RGB/8)

Figure 6-8:
The difference between New Layer via Copy and New Layer via Cut becomes obvious when you move the new layer so you can see what's beneath it.

Top: The original light is still in place in the underlying layer.

Bottom: When New Layer via Cut is used, the light leaves a hole behind.

car.tif @ 66.7%(Layer 1, RGB/8)

Managing Layers

The Layers palette lets you manipulate your layers in all kinds of ways, but first you need to understand a few more of the palette's cryptic little icons. Some of the things you can do with layers may seem tiresomely obscure when you first read about them, but once you're actually using layers, you'll quickly see why many of these options exist. The next few sections explain how to manipulate your layers in several different ways: how to hide them, how to group them together, how to change the way you see them, and how to combine layers together.

Making Layers Invisible

You can turn the visibility of layers off and on at will. This is a tremendously useful feature, if you think about it. If the image you're working on has a busy background, for example, it's often hard to see what you're doing when you're working on a particular layer. Making the background invisible can really help you focus on the layer you're interested in. To turn off visibility, first select the layer you want to hide and then click the eye icon in the Layers palette.

> **TIP** If you have a bunch of hidden layers and you decide you don't want them anymore, go to Layers Palette → More → Delete Hidden Layers to get rid of them all at once.

GEM IN THE ROUGH

Naming Layers

You might have noticed that Elements isn't terribly creative when it comes to naming your layers. You get "Layer 1," "Layer 2," and so on. Fortunately, you don't have to live with those. It's quite easy to rename your layers in Elements.

Maybe renaming layers sounds like a job for people with too much time on their hands, but if you get started on a project that winds up with many layers, you may find that you can pick out the layers you want more quickly if you give them descriptive names.

Incidentally, you can't rename a background layer. You have to change it to a regular layer first. Also, Elements

helps you out with Text layers (see Chapter 13) by naming them using the first few words of the text they contain. To rename a layer:

1. **Double-click its name in the Layers palette.** The name turns to an active text box.

2. **Type in the new name.** You don't even need to highlight the text–Elements does that for you automatically.

As with any other change, you have to save your image afterward if you want to keep the name.

Adjusting Transparency

Your choices for layer visibility aren't limited to on and off. You can create immensely cool effects in Elements by adjusting the *opacity* of layers. In other words, you can make a layer partially transparent so that what's underneath shows through it.

To adjust the opacity of a layer, just click the layer in the Layers palette and then either:

• Click in the Opacity box and type in the percentage of opacity you want.

• If you'd rather make the adjustment visually (as opposed to entering numbers), click the triangle to the right of the Opacity percentage and adjust the pop-out slider, as shown in Figure 6-9.

Figure 6-9:
You can watch the opacity of your layer change as you move the slider back and forth. Different blend modes (see the section, "Blend Mode") often give the best effect if you adjust the opacity of their layers.

Fading in Elements

One great thing in Photoshop that Elements lacks is the ability to *fade* special effects and filters. This gives you great control over how much these tools change an image. (Often, filters generate harsh-looking results, and Photoshop's fade tool helps adjust a filter's effect until it's what you intended.)

In Elements, you can approximate the fade tool by applying filters, effects, or layer styles to a duplicate layer. Then, reduce the layer's opacity till it blends in with what's below (and change the blend mode if necessary) to give you exactly the result you're looking for.

When you create a new layer using either the keyboard shortcut (Ctrl+Shift+N (Control-Shift-N)) or the menu (Layer → New → Layer), you can set the opacity right away in the New Layer dialog box. If you create a new layer by clicking the New Layer icon in the Layers palette, you won't see the dialog box. To change opacity when using that method, Alt+click (Option-click) the New Layer icon, and the New Layer dialog box appears.

You can't change the opacity of a background layer. You have to convert it first to a regular layer (see page 129).

Locking Layers

You can protect your image from yourself by *locking* any of the layers. Locking keeps you from changing a layer's contents. You can also lock just the transparent parts of a layer if you want. When you do that, the transparent parts of your layer stay transparent no matter what you do to the rest of it (see Figure 6-10).

To lock the transparent parts of a layer, select the layer and then click the little checkerboard in the Layers palette. It works like a button—when it's active it looks pushed-in and is slightly darker than it is when it's off. To unlock, just click the checkerboard again.

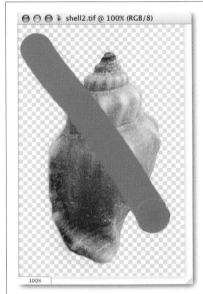 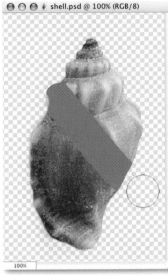

Figure 6-10:
After you've isolated an object on its own layer, sometimes you want to paint only on the object—and not on the transparent portion of the layer. Elements lets you lock the transparent part of a layer, making it easy to paint only the object itself.

Left: On a regular layer, paint goes wherever the brush does.

Right: With the layer's transparency locked, the stroke stops at the edge of the shell, even though the brush is now on the transparent portion of the layer.

To lock the contents of a whole layer so that no changes can be made to it, click the little Lock icon in the Layers palette next to the checkerboard. Now if you try to paint on that layer or use any other tools, your cursor turns into the shape of the universal "no" symbol as a reminder that you can't edit that layer. You'll also see a Lock icon next to the layer name in the Layers palette. To unlock the layer, just click the Lock icon once more.

> **NOTE** Locking only preserves the layer from edits. It doesn't keep the layer from being merged into another layer or flattened, and it won't keep your image from being cropped.

Blend Mode

You also see another little menu in the Layers palette that says "Normal" or, in the New Layer dialog box, "Mode: Normal." This is the setting for your *blend mode*. Blend modes are a way of controlling how an image is affected by the use of different tools. When used with layers, blend modes control how the objects in a layer blend with the objects in the layer beneath it. By using different blend modes, you can make your image lighter, darker, or even make it look like a poster, with just a few bold colors in it.

Blend modes are an awful lot of fun once you understand how to use them. You can use them to fix under- or overexposed photos, or to create all kinds of special visual effects. You can also use some of the tools, like the Brush tool, in different blend modes to achieve different effects. The most common blend mode is Normal, in which everything you do behaves just the way you would expect: an object shows its regular colors, paint acts just like, well, paint.

Chapter 11 has lots more about how to use blend modes. For now, take a look at Figure 6-11, which shows how you can totally change the way a layer looks just by changing the layer's blend mode.

The blend modes are grouped together in the menu in categories according to the way they affect your image, but not every mode makes a visible change in every circumstance. Some of them may seem to do nothing—that's normal. It just means that you don't have a condition in your current image that's responding to that particular mode change. See the "The Sharpen Filters" section on page 182 in the next chapter for one example of a situation where a mode change makes an enormous difference.

Rearranging Layers

One of the truly amazing things you can do with Elements is move your layers around. You can change the order in which layers are stacked so that different objects appear in front of or behind each other. For example, you can position one object behind another if they're both on their own layers. Just grab the layer in the Layers palette and drag it to where you want it to be.

> **NOTE** Remember, you're always looking down onto the layer stack when you look at your image, so moving something up in the list moves it toward the front of the picture.

Figure 6-12 shows the early stages of the flyer for a Fall Harvest Festival (originally shown in Figure 6-1). The pumpkins are already in place, and the scarecrow was dragged in from another image. The scarecrow comes in at the top of the stack, in front of the pumpkins. You can put the scarecrow behind the pumpkins by simply dragging the scarecrow layer beneath the pumpkin layer in the Layers palette.

> **NOTE** The only kind of layer you can't move is a background layer. If you want to bring a background layer to another spot in the layer stack, first convert the background layer to a regular layer (page 129), and then you can move it.

You can also move layers by going to Layer → Arrange and choosing the command of your choice:

- **Bring to Front** sends the selected layer to the top of the stack so the layer's contents appear in the foreground of your image.

- **Bring Forward** moves the layer up one level in the Layers palette, so it appears one step closer to the front of your image.

Figure 6-11:
Here you see the leaves photo from Figure 6-9 with a Pattern fill layer over them. In normal mode, the pattern would completely hide the leaves, but by changing the blend mode of the pattern layer you can create very different looks. (There's more about Pattern layers in the section, "Fill and Adjustment Layers") From top to bottom, the different modes are: normal, dissolve, and hard mix. Notice how dissolve gives a grainy effect and hard mix a vivid, posterized look.

- **Send Backward** moves the layer down one level so it's sent back one step in the image.

- **Send to Back** puts the layer directly above the background layer so it appears as far back as you can move anything.

Figure 6-12:
Notice how the scarecrow moves from in front of the pumpkins (left) to behind them (right). That's thanks to the magic of changing the order of the layers.

Grouping and Linking Layers

What if you want to move several layers at once? For instance, in the Harvest Festival image there are two layers with pumpkins on them. It's kind of a pain to drag each one individually if you need to move them in front of the scarecrow, for instance. Fortunately, you don't have to.

Linking layers

You can link layers together, and then they'll travel as a group, as shown in Figure 6-13.

If you want to remove a link between layers, just click the chain icon to turn it off again. You can always merge the layers (covered in the next section) into one layer if you want. Sometimes, though, you'll want to keep layers separate, while still being able to move the layers as a group. Linking is the way to do that.

Grouping layers

An even more powerful way to combine separate layers is to *group* them. Grouping enables you to let one layer influence the other layers it's grouped with. Grouping layers isn't at all the same as linking them. It's probably easiest to understand grouping by looking at the example shown in Figure 6-14, which shows how you can crop an image on one layer using the shape of an object on another layer.

> **TIP**   If you group two layers together, the bottom layer determines the opacity of both layers.

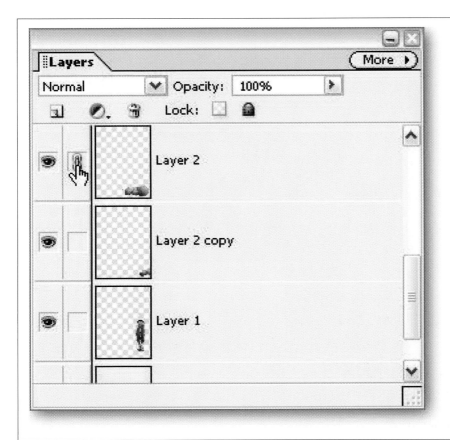

Figure 6-13:
Click the little square
where the cursor
appears in the figure
to link two layers
together (you're
linking the layer to
whatever layer is
currently active). The
chain icon appears to
indicate they'll move
as a group.

Once the layers are grouped, you can still slide the top layer around with the Move tool to reposition it so that you see exactly the part of it that you want. So in Figure 6-14, the beach layer was maneuvered around till the sandpipers showed in the bottom of the shell shape.

To group two layers together, make the top layer (of the two you want to group) the active layer. Then choose Layer → Group with Previous. You can also group layers using the keyboard. First, make sure the top layer is the active layer, then press Ctrl+G (⌘-G). Another way to group is to do it right in the Layers palette. Hold Alt (Option) and in the Layers palette, move your cursor over the dividing line between the layers. Click when you see two linked circles appear by your cursor. Now your layers are grouped.

You can also use grouping for very sophisticated photo corrections, like grouping a Levels Adjustment layer and a Gradient Fill layer, so that your Levels adjustment fades out to one side, for instance.

If you get tired of the layer grouping or you want to delete or change one of the layers, you can select Layer → Ungroup or press Ctrl+Shift+G (⌘-Shift-G) to remove the grouping.

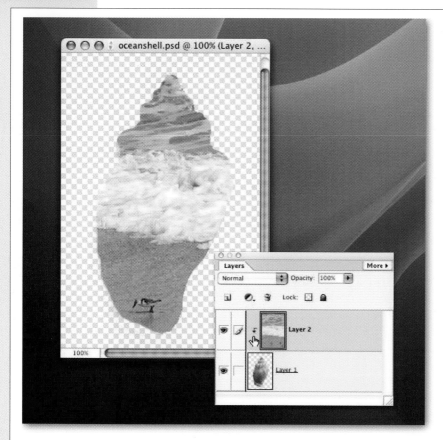

Figure 6-14:
This image began with a picture of a shell on one layer and a beach scene on the layer above it. At first, the beach image totally hid the shell, but interesting things happen when you group the layers. The beach layer gets cropped to the shape of the bottom layer, the shell. The little downward-bent arrow in the Layers palette indicates the beach layer is grouped with the shell layer, below it.

Merging and Flattening Layers

By now, you've probably got at least an inkling of how useful layers are. But there is a downside to having layers in your image: they take up a lot of storage space, especially if you have lots of duplicate layers. Layers make files bigger. Fortunately, you aren't committed forever to keeping layers in your file. You can reduce your file size quite a bit—and sometimes also make things easier to manage—by merging layers or flattening your image.

Merging layers

Sometimes you may have two or more separate layers that really could be treated as one layer, like the pumpkins shown in Figure 6-15. You aren't limited to linking those layers together—once you've got everything arranged to your satisfaction, you can merge them together into one layer. Also, if you want to copy and paste your image, many times the standard copy and paste commands (explained in Chapter 5) will copy only the top layer. So it helps to get everything into one layer, at least temporarily.

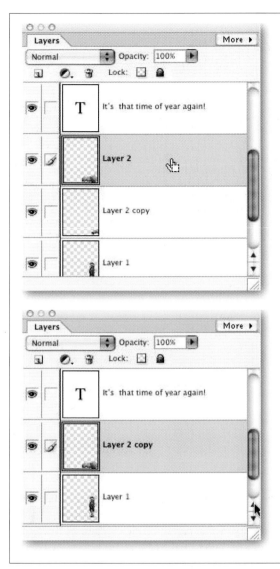

Figure 6-15:
Those pumpkins again. If you no longer need two separate pumpkin layers, you can merge the layers together.

Top: The Layers palette with the two separate pumpkin layers.

Bottom: The pumpkin layers merged into one layer.

You'll probably merge layers quite often when you're working with multi-layered files (for example, when you're working with multiple objects that you want to edit simultaneously).

To merge layers, you have a few different options, depending on what is active in your image at the time. You can get to any of the following commands from the Layers menu, or from the More button on the Layers palette.

- **Merge Down** combines the active layer and the layer immediately beneath it. If the layer just below the active layer is hidden, you won't see this option in the list of choices.

- **Merge Visible** combines all the visible layers into one layer. If you want to combine layers that are far apart, just temporarily turn off visibility (by clicking the Eye icon) for the ones in between and for any other layers that you don't want to merge.

- **Merge Linked.** Click any of your linked layers and you see this command, which joins the linked layers into one layer.

- **Merge Clipping Mask.** You need to select the bottom layer of a group to see this command. Choose it, and the grouped layers join into one layer.

It's important to understand that once you merge layers and save and close your file, you can't just un-merge them again. You can of course use any of the undo commands (page 17), but once you've gotten past your undo limit, you're stuck with your merged layers.

> **TIP**   The box "Stamp Visible" shows you another way to combine all your layers, while still keeping a separate copy of the individual layers.

Sometimes if your layer contains type or shapes drawn with the Shape tool, you won't be able to merge the layer right away. Elements asks you to *simplify* the layer first. Simplifying a layer means that you have converted its contents to a raster object. In other words, now it's just a bunch of pixels, subject to the same resizing limitations as any photo would be. So for example, if you have a type layer, you can still apply filters to the type or paint on it, but you can no longer edit the words. (See Chapter 11 for more about simplifying and working with shapes, and see Chapter 13 for working with type.)

POWER USERS' CLINIC

Stamp Visible

There are times when you want to perform an action on all the visible layers of your image without permanently merging them together. You can easily do this—and do it quickly, too, even if you have dozens of layers in your file—by using what Adobe calls the "Stamp Visible" command. This combines the contents of all your layers into a new layer at the top of the stack.

Stamp Visible lets you work away on the new combined layer while still preserving your existing layers untouched, in case you want them back later on. To use Stamp Visible, first create a new blank layer and make it the top layer of your image.

Next, either press Control+Shift+Alt+E (⌘-Shift-Option-E) or hold down Alt (Option) while selecting the "Merge Visible" command from the Layers menu (or from the More menu in the Layers palette). You'll see the top layer fill itself with the combined contents of all your other layers.

If you want to keep a layer or two from being included in this new layer, just turn off the visibility of those you don't wish to include before using the Stamp Visible command.

Flattening an image

While layers are simply swell when you're working on an image, they can be a headache when you want to share your image, especially if you're sending it to a photo-printing service (their machines usually don't understand layered files). And even if you're printing at home, the large size of a layered file can make it take forever to print. Also, if you plan to use your image in other programs, very few non-Adobe programs are totally comfortable with layered files, so you may get some odd results if you feed them a layered file.

In these cases, you may want to squash everything in your picture into a single layer. It's very easy to do this in Elements. You simply flatten your image. Do so by going to Layer → Flatten Image, or on the Layers palette, choose More → Flatten Image.

> **NOTE** Saving your image as a JPEG file automatically gets rid of layers, too.

There's no keystroke shortcut for flattening, because it's something you don't want to do by accident. Like merging, flattening is a permanent change. Many cautious Element veterans always do a "Save As," instead of a plain Save, before flattening. That way you have a flattened copy and still have your working copy with the layers intact, just in case. Organizer version sets (page 435) can help you here, too, since they allow you to save different states of your image. So you could have a version with layers and a flattened version, too.

Fill and Adjustment Layers

Fill layers and *Adjustment layers* are special types of layers. Adjustment layers let you manipulate a layer's lighting, color, or exposure. If you're mainly interested in Elements to spruce up your photos, you'll probably use Adjustment layers more than any other kind. Adjustment layers are great, because they give you the ability to undo or change your edits later on if you want to.

You can also use Adjustment layers to take the changes you've made on one photo and reapply those changes to another photo (see the box on page 146). And after you've created an Adjustment layer, you can limit future edits so they affect only the area of your photo covered by the Adjustment layer.

You'll find out much more about all the things you can do with Adjustment layers in the next few chapters of this book. For now, you just need to learn how to create and manipulate them.

Fill layers are just what they sounds like: layers filled with a color, a pattern, or a gradient (a rainbow-like range of colors). There's more about gradients in Chapter 12 (page 325).

NOTE   Photo filter Adjustment layers are a useful new feature in Elements 3. They let you digitally make the sort of adjustments that you used to do by attaching a colored piece of glass to the front of your camera's lens. You can read more about what you can do with photo filters in Chapter 8.

GEM IN THE ROUGH

Adjustment Layers for Batch Processing

Chapter 8 shows you how to perform *batch* commands: simultaneously applying adjustments to groups of photos. The drawback with Elements' batch tool is that you have access only to some of the auto commands there. So what do you do if you're a fussy photographer who's got 17 shots that are all pretty much the same and you'd like to apply the same fixes to all of them? Do you have to edit each one from scratch?

Not in Elements. You can open the photos you want to fix and then drag an Adjustment layer from the first photo onto each of the other photos (page 149 shows you how to drag layers between images). The new photo gets the same adjustments at the same settings. It's not as fast as true batch processing, but it saves a lot of time over editing each photo from scratch.

Adding Fill and Adjustment Layers

Creating an Adjustment or Fill layer is easy. In the Layers palette, just click on the black and white circle, as shown in Figure 6-16. The button displays a menu of all the Adjustment and Fill layer choices one list (the first three choices are Fill layers; the rest are Adjustment layers).

Whichever type of layer you choose, you get a dialog box that lets you tweak the layer's settings (the exception is Invert layers, which doesn't give you any choices). After you make your choices, click Okay, and the new layer appears.

You get only three Fill layer choices: Solid color, Gradient (a rainbow-like range of colors), and Pattern. There's more about patterns in Chapter 9 and about gradients in Chapter 12.

The kinds of Adjustment layers you can select from are:

- **Levels.** This is a much more sophisticated way to apply Levels than using the Auto Levels button in the Quick Fix or the Auto Level command from the Enhance menu. Page 163 has more information about using Levels. For most people, Levels is the most important Adjustment layer.

- **Brightness/Contrast.** This does pretty much the same things as the Quick Fix adjustment (covered on page 83).

- **Hue/Saturation.** Again, it's very much like the Quick Fix command (page 83), only with slightly different controls.

- **Gradient Map.** This is very tricky to understand and is explained in detail on page 335. It applies a gradient based on a map of the luminosity values in your image. That means you can apply a gradient so that the colors aren't just distributed in a straight line across your image.

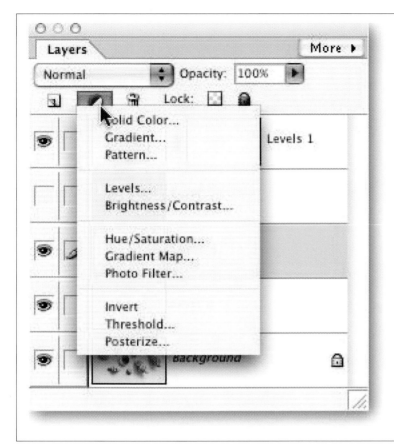

Figure 6-16:
To create a new Adjustment or Fill layer, click the black and white circle for a pop-up menu. Use the menu to choose the type of Adjustment or Fill layer you want. If you'd rather work from the menu bar, go to Layer → New Adjustment Layer (or Layer → New Fill Layer) and choose the layer type you want.

- **Photo Filter.** Use this to adjust the color balance of your photos by adding warming, cooling, or special effects filters, just like you might attach to the lens of a film camera. See page 201.

- **Invert.** This reverses the colors of your image to their opposite values, for an effect similar to a film negative. See page 246.

- **Threshold.** Use this to make everything in your photo pure black or pure white. See page 248.

- **Posterize.** Reduces the numbers of colors in your image to give a poster-like effect. See page 248.

You can change the settings for a Fill or Adjustment layer by highlighting it in the Layers palette, and then going to Layer → Content Options. The layer's dialog box reappears, and you can adjust its settings. Deleting Fill and Adjustment layers is a tad different from deleting a regular layer, as explained in Figure 6-17.

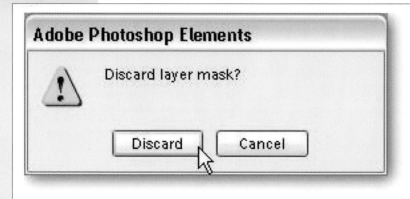

Figure 6-17:
When you click the Layers palette Delete icon, Elements asks you if you want to "Discard layer mask?" Click Discard. Then you have to click the Trash icon again to fully delete the layer. If you want to get rid of the layer in one go, you've got a few choices: use the Layer menu (Delete Layer), right-click (Control-click) the layer in the Layers palette, or use the More button to delete it. There's more about layer masks in the next section.

Layer Masks

Adjustment and Fill layers use something called a *layer mask*, which dictates which parts of the layer are affected (see Figure 6-18). By changing the area covered by the layer mask you can control which part of your image the layer adjustments affect.

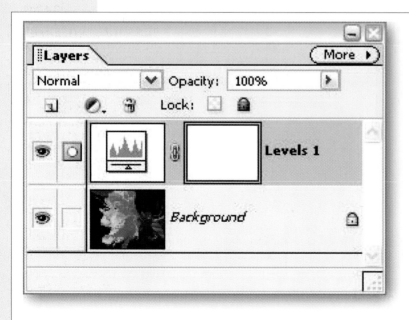

Figure 6-18:
Adjustment and Fill layers, like the Levels 1 layer shown here, always have two icons in the Layers palette: the left side shows what kind of adjustment the layer is making (Levels, in this case). You can double-click that icon to bring up the dialog box to make changes to your settings after the layer is in place. The right icon is for the Layer Mask, and you can use it to control the area that is covered by the adjustment.

Full Photoshop uses layer masks for many other purposes, but in Elements without any of the add-ons (See Chapter 17), these layers are the only place you encounter a layer mask. The great thing about layer masks is that you can edit them by painting on them, as explained on page 239. In other words, you can go back later and change the part of your image that the Adjustment layer affects.

Incidentally, the term layer *mask* may be a bit confusing if you're thinking about masking with the Selection brush. With the Selection brush, masking prevents something from being changed. A layer mask really works the same way, but by definition, it starts out empty; in other words, the mask can be used to prevent your adjustment from affecting parts of the layer, but not until you mask out parts of your image by painting on the layer mask. So to begin with, your entire layer is affected by your change.

Moving Layers Between Images

If you use layers, it's extremely easy to combine parts of different photos together. Just put what you want from photo A into its own layer and then drag it onto photo B. The trick is that you have to drag the layer *from the Layers palette*. If you try to drop one photo directly onto another photo's window, you'll just wind up with a lot of windows stacked up on top of each other. Figure 6-19 shows you the correct way to move a layer between photos.

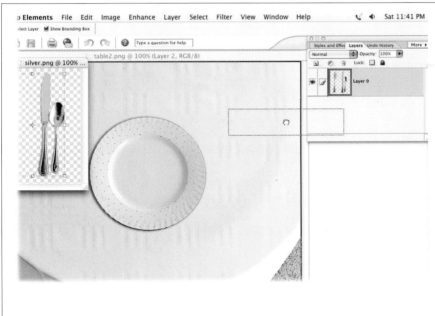

Figure 6-19:
This figure shows how to move objects from one photo to another. Here, the goal is to get the silverware from photo A (whose Layers palette is visible) onto the tablecloth in photo B (whose image is visible). You always drag from the Layers palette onto a photo window when you combine parts of different images into a composite. (If you try to drag from a photo to a photo, it won't work.) You can use the Move tool to adjust your object's placement once you've dropped it into the image.

Here are a few points to keep in mind when you're copying a layer from one image to another:

- Watch out for conflicting resolution settings (page 64). The bottom image (i.e., the one receiving the moved layer) controls the resolution. So if you bring in a layer that's set to 300 pixels per inch (ppi), and place it on an image that's set to 72 ppi, the object you're moving will now be set to 72 ppi.

- Lighting matters. Objects that are lit differently will stand out if you try to combine them. If possible, plan ahead and choose similar lighting for photos you're thinking about combining.

- Feather with care. A little feathering (page 106) goes a long way towards creating a realistic result.

NOTE If you'd like more practice using layers, visit the "Missing CD" page at *www.missingmanuals.com* and download the Table Tutorial. It walks you through most of the basic layer functions.

3

Part Three: Retouching

Basic Image Retouching

You may be perfectly happy for a very long time using Elements only in Quick Fix mode. And that's fine, as long as you understand that you've hardly scratched the surface of what Elements can do for you. Sooner or later, though, you're probably going to run across a photo where your best Quick Fix efforts just aren't good enough. Or you may just be curious to see what else Elements has under its hood. That's when you finally get to put all your image-selecting and layering skills to good use.

Elements gives you a heap of ways to fix your photos beyond the limited options in Quick Fix. This chapter guides you through how to fix basic exposure problems, shows you new ways of sharpening your photos, and most important, helps you understand how Elements can improve the colors in your photos.

If you want to get the best possible results from Elements, you need to understand a little about how your camera, computer, and printer think about color. Next to resolution, color is the most important concept in Elements. After all, almost all the adjustments Elements makes actually consist of changing the color of pixels. So quite a bit of this chapter is about understanding how Elements—and by extension, you—can manipulate your image's color.

> **NOTE** Most of Elements' advanced-fixes dialog boxes have a "preview" checkbox, which lets you watch what's happening to your image as your adjust the settings. It's a good idea to keep these checkboxes turned on so you can make sure you like the changes you're making.

Fixing Exposure Problems

Incorrectly exposed photos are *the* number one problem all photographers face. No matter how carefully you set up your shot and how many different settings you try on your camera, it always seems like the picture you really, really want to keep is the one that is over- or underexposed.

UP TO SPEED

Understanding Exposure

What exactly *is* exposure, anyway? You almost certainly know a poorly exposed photo when you see it: either it's too light or it's too dark. But what exactly has gone wrong?

Exposure refers to the amount of light your film (or the sensor in your digital camera) received when you released the shutter.

A well-exposed photo shows the largest amount of detail in *all* parts of your image—light and dark. In a properly exposed photo, shadows aren't just pits of blackness, and bright areas show more than washed out splotches of white.

The Quick Fix commands (Chapter 4) can really help your photo, but if you've tried to bring back a picture that is badly over- or underexposed, you've probably run into the limitations of what Quick Fix can do. Similarly, the Shadows/Highlights command can do a lot, but it's not intended to fix a photo with totally whacky exposure—just ones where the contrast between light and dark areas needs a bit of help. And if you push Smart Fix to its limits, your results may be a little strange. In those situations, you need to move on to some of Elements' more powerful tools to help you get your exposure straightened out.

Deciding Which Exposure Fix to Use

When you open a poorly exposed photo in Elements, the first thing you need to do is figure out what's wrong with it, just like a doctor diagnosing a patient. If the exposure's not perfect, what exactly is wrong? Here's a list of common symptoms to help you figure out where to go next:

- **Everything is too dark.** If your photo is really dark, try adding a Screen layer, as explained later. If it's just a bit too dark, try using Levels (see page 163).

- **Everything is too light.** If the whole photo looks washed out, try adding a Multiply layer (explained below.) If it's just a bit too light, try Levels (page 163).

- **The photo is mostly okay, but your subject is too dark or the light parts of the photo are too light.** Try the Shadows/Highlights adjustment (page 156).

Of course, if you're lucky (or a skilled photographer), you may not see any of these problems, in which case, you can skip to "Using Levels" (page 163), if you want to do something to make your colors pop.

NOTE You might've noticed that you didn't see Brightness/Contrast mentioned anywhere in the previous list. A lot of people tend to jump for the Brightness/Contrast controls when facing a poorly exposed photo. That's logical—after all, these dials usually help improve the picture on your TV. But in Elements, about 99 percent of the time, you've got a whole slew of powerful tools—like Levels and the Shadows/Highlights command—that can do much more than Brightness/Contrast can.

Fixing Major Exposure Problems

If your photo is completely over- or underexposed, you need to add special layers to correct the problems. You follow the same steps to fix either problem. The only difference is the layer blend mode (page 137) you choose: Multiply layers darken your image's exposure while Screen layers lighten it. Figure 7-1 shows Multiply layers in action (and also gives you an idea of the limitations of this technique if your exposure is really far gone).

Be careful, though. If your entire photo isn't out of whack, using Multiply or Screen layers can ruin the exposure of the parts that were okay to start with. You lose definition in those areas if you add too many layers. So if your exposure problem is spotty (rather than image-wide), try Shadows/Highlights first. If your whole photo needs an exposure correction, here's how to use layers to fix it:

1. **Create a duplicate layer.**

   Open your photo and press Ctrl+J (⌘-J) or go to Layer → Duplicate Layer. Check to be sure the duplicate layer is the active layer.

2. **In the Layers palette, change the Mode for the new layer in the pop-up menu.**

   Choose Multiply, if your photo is overexposed, or Screen, if it's underexposed. Make sure you change the mode of the duplicate layer, not the original layer.

3. **Adjust the opacity of the layer if needed.**

   If the effect of the new layer is too strong, in the Layers palette, move the Opacity slider to the left to reduce the new layer's opacity.

4. **Repeat as necessary.**

   You may need to use as many as five or six layers if your photo is in really bad shape. If you need extra layers, you'll probably want them at 100 percent opacity, so you can just keep pressing Ctrl+J (⌘-J), which will duplicate the current top layer.

You're more likely to need several layers to fix overexposure than you are for underexposure. And, of course, there are limits to what even Elements can do for a blindingly overexposed image. Overexposure is usually a tougher fix than underexposure, especially if the area is blown out, as explained in the box on page 157.

Figure 7-1:
For those who think photographically, each Multiply layer you add is the equivalent to stopping your camera down one f-stop.

Top: This photo is totally overexposed, and it looks like there's no detail there at all. Multiply layers darken things down enough to bring back a lot of the washed out areas. This technique can bring up the detail quite a bit.

Bottom: As you can see in the corrected photo, even Elements can't do much in areas where there's no detail at all.

The Shadows/Highlights Command

The new Shadows/Highlights command is one of the biggest stars in Elements 3. With it, you can zip through corrections that would have been darned near impossible in previous versions of Elements. It's an incredibly powerful tool for adjusting only the dark or light areas of your photo without messing up the rest of it. Figure 7-2 shows what a great help it can be.

Avoiding Blowouts

An area of a photo is *blown out* when it's so overexposed that it appears as just plain white—in other words, your camera didn't record any data at all for that area. (Elements isn't all that great with total black, either, but that doesn't happen quite so often. Most underexposed photos have some tonal gradations in them, even if you can't see them very well.)

A blowout is as disastrous in photography as it is when you're driving. Even Elements can't fix blowouts, because there's no data for it to work from. So you're stuck with the fixes discussed in this chapter, which are never as good as a good original.

So when you're taking pictures, remember that it's generally easier to correct underexposure than overexposure. Keep that in mind when choosing your camera settings. If you live where there is extremely bright sunlight most of the time, you might want to make a habit of backing your exposure compensation down a hair. Depending on your camera, your subject, and the average ambient glare, you might try starting at –.3 and adjusting from there.

You can also try *bracketing* your shots—taking multiple shots of exactly the same subject with different exposure settings. Then you can combine the two exposures for maximum effect (the box on page 200 explains how to combine images).

The Shadows/Highlights command in the Standard Editor works pretty much the same way it does in Quick Fix (page 92). The single flaw in this great tool is that you can't apply it as an Adjustment layer (page 145). Because of that you might want to apply Shadows/Highlights to a duplicate layer. Then, later on, you can discard the changes if you want to take another whack at adjusting the photo. In any case, it's not difficult at all to make amazing changes to your photos with Shadows/Highlights. Here's how:

1. **Open your photo and duplicate the layer (Ctrl+J [⌘-J]) if you want to.**

   Duplicating your layer makes it easier to undo Shadows/Highlights later on if you change your mind.

2. **Go to Enhance → Adjust Lighting → Shadows/Highlights.**

   Your photo immediately becomes about 30 shades lighter. Don't panic. As soon as you select the command, the Lighten Shadows setting automatically jumps to 50 percent, which is way too much for about 80 percent of your photos, probably. Just shove the slider back to 0 to undo this change before you start making your corrections.

3. **Move the sliders around until you like what you see.**

   The sliders do exactly what they say: Lighten Shadows makes the dark areas of your photo lighter, and Darken Highlights makes the light areas darker. Pushing the slider to the right increases the effect for either one.

Figure 7-2:
Shadows/Highlights can bring back details from photos where you were sure there was no information at all.

Top: The original photo is extremely backlit.

Bottom: Shadows/Highlights brings out the hidden detail and reduced the background glare. If you look closely at the mouths of the bells and the wooden supports just below them, you can see the kind of noise that often lurks in underexposed areas. Those problems mean you still may need to tweak the saturation (page 225) once you're done using Shadows/ Highlights or use some noise reduction on the formerly shadowed areas (page 313).

4. **Click Okay when you're happy.**

The Shadows/Highlights tool is very easy to use, because you just go by what you're seeing. Here are a couple of tips to help you get more out of Shadows/Highlights:

- You may to want to add a smidgen of the opposite tool to balance things out a little. In other words, if you are lightening shadows, you may get better results by giving the Darken Highlights slider a teeny nudge, too.

- Midtone Contrast is there because your photo may look kind of flat after you're done with Shadows/Highlights, especially if you've made big adjustments. Move the Midtone Contrast slider to the right to increase the contrast in your photo. It usually adds a bit of a darkening effect, so you may need to go back to one of the other sliders to tweak your photo after you use it.

> **TIP** If the Shadow/Highlights tool looks like it washed out your photo's colors—making everyone look like they've been through the laundry too many times—you might adjust the color intensity with one of the Saturation commands, either in Quick Fix or in the Standard Editor (as described on page 225). Watch people's skin tones when increasing the saturation—if the subjects in your photo start looking like sunless-tanning lotion disaster victims, you've gone too far.

Controlling the Colors You See

You want your photos to look as good as possible and to have beautiful, breathtaking color, right? That's probably the reason you bought Elements. But now that you've got the program, you may be having a little trouble getting things to look the way you want. Do either of these situations sound familiar?

- Your photos look great onscreen but your prints are washed out, too dark, or the colors are all a little wrong.

- Your photos look just fine in other programs like Word or Windows Explorer, but they look just awful in Elements.

What's going on? The answer has to do with the fact that Elements is a *color-managed* application. That means that Elements uses your monitor for guidance when deciding how to display images. Color management is the science of making sure that the color in your images is always exactly the same, no matter who opens your file or what kind of hardware they're viewing it on or printing it from. If you think of all the different monitor and printer models out there, you get an idea of what a big job this is.

Graphics pros spend their whole lives grappling with color management, and you can find plenty of books about the finer points of color management. On the most sophisticated level, color management is complicated enough to make you curl up, whimpering, into the fetal position and swear never to create another picture.

Luckily for you, Elements makes color management a whole lot easier. Most of the time, you have only two things to deal with: your monitor calibration and your color space. This chapter covers both.

> **NOTE** There are a couple of other color-related settings for printing, too, but you can deal with those when you get ready to print. Chapter 14 explains them.

Calibrating Your Monitor

Most of your applications pay no attention to what your monitor thinks, but a color-managed application like Elements relies on the *profile*—the information your computer stores about the settings of your monitor—when it decides how to print or display a photo onscreen. If that profile isn't accurate, neither is the color in Elements.

So you may need to *calibrate* your monitor, which is a way of adjusting its settings. A properly calibrated monitor makes all the difference in the world for getting great-looking results. If your photos look bad only in Elements or if your pictures in print don't look anything like they look onscreen, the place to start is by calibrating your monitor.

Getting started with calibrating

Calibrating a monitor sounds horribly complicated, but it's actually not that difficult to do and it's even kind of fun. You get an extra added benefit in that your monitor may look about a thousand times better than you thought it could. Calibrating might even make it easier to read text in Word, for instance, because the contrast will be better.

The monitor-calibrating approach you take depends on the kind of computer you're using:

- **In Windows:** Adobe gives you the Adobe Gamma Utility. It installs right along with Elements. To get to it, go to Start → Control Panel → Appearance and Themes → Adobe Gamma. Click the utility and follow the onscreen directions. Figure 7-3 shows you the Adobe Gamma window.

- **On the Mac:** In System Preferences, you'll find the calibrator, which you should use rather than the Adobe Gamma. Go to System Preferences → Displays → Color → Calibrate. Turning on the "Expert Mode" box gives you many more options, and Panther has a much more detailed calibrator than Jaguar.

If you have an LCD (flat panel) monitor, the bad news is that Adobe Gamma isn't really designed to work with LCDs. The good news is that sometimes it does help (despite Adobe's claims that it won't work LCDs). It's certainly worth a try, and the odds are that you can improve your view at least a little, even if you can't make it perfect. If that doesn't help, you might want to try a third-party monitor-calibrating solution. Most of the good ones for LCDs use special hardware, so expect to spend some money if you need to go that route. Luckily, prices for calibration systems have dropped dramatically in the past year or two.

If your photos still look a little odd even after you've calibrated your monitor, you may need to turn on the "Ignore EXIF" setting in the Editor's preferences. See Figure 7-4.

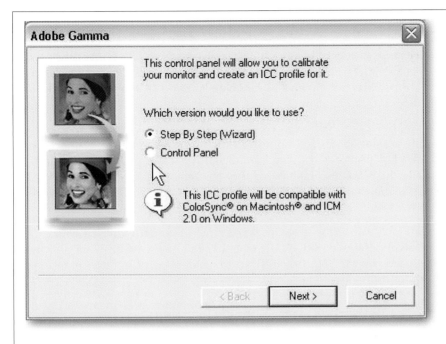

Figure 7-3:
Despite its name, the Adobe Gamma Utility is actually fairly easy to use, as you can see from this straight-forward first screen. Choose the wizard, if you've never calibrated your monitor before.

If you want a step-by-step guide to using the Adobe Gamma Utility, Photoshop guru Ian Lyons has an excellent tutorial on his Web site at www.computer-darkroom.com/ps8-colour/ps8_2.htm. (It was written for Photoshop, but Adobe Gamma works the same no matter which program you use.)

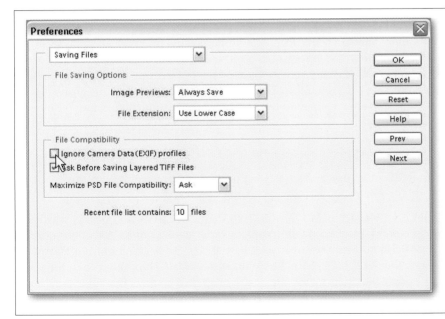

Figure 7-4:
If you still see a funny color cast (usually red or yellow) on all your digital camera photos, go to Edit → Preferences → Saving Files (Elements → Preferences → Saving Files) and turn on "Ignore Camera Data (EXIF) profiles." Some cameras embed nonstandard color information in their files, and the Elements Ignore EXIF utility just tells Elements to pay no attention to it, allowing your photos to be properly displayed and printed.

Choosing a Color Space

The other thing you may need to do to get good color from Elements is to check the *color space* Elements is using. Color space refers to which standard (out of several possibilities) Elements is using to define your colors. Color space can seem pretty abstruse the first time you hear about it, but it's simply a way of defining what colors mean. For example, when someone says "green," what do you envision: a lush emerald color, a deep forest green, a bright lime?

Choosing a color space is a way to make sure that everything—Elements, your monitor, your printer—that handles a digital file sees the same colors the same way. Over the years, the graphics industry has agreed on standards so that everyone has the same understanding of what you mean when you say red or green—as long as you specify which set of standards you're using.

There are only two color spaces that you need to concern yourself with in Elements: sRGB (also called sRGB IEC61966-2.1) and Adobe RGB. When you choose a color space, you tell Elements which set of standards you want it to apply to your photos.

If you're happy with the color you see on your monitor in Elements and you like the prints you're getting, you don't need to make any changes. If, on the other hand, you aren't perfectly satisfied with what Elements is giving you, you'll probably want to modify your color space, which you can do in the Color Settings dialog box. Go to Edit → Color Settings (Photoshop Elements → Color Settings) or press Ctrl+Shift+K (⌘-Shift-K). Here are your choices:

- **No Color Management.** Elements respects any information that your file already contains, like color space information from your camera, and doesn't attempt to add any color info to the file data. (When you do a Save As, there's a checkbox that offers you the option of embedding your monitor profile. Don't turn this on, since your monitor profile is best left for the monitor's own use, and putting the profile into your file can make trouble if you ever send the file someplace else for printing.)

- **Limited Color Management.** Choose this and you're looking at your photo in the sRGB color space, which is what most Web browsers use, so this is a good choice for when you're preparing graphics for the Web.

- **Full Color Management.** This one uses the Adobe RGB color space, which is a wider color space than sRGB. In other words, it allows more gradations of color than sRGB. Sometimes this is your best choice for printing but not always. So despite the note you'll see in the Color Settings dialog box about "best for printing," don't be afraid to try one of the other two settings instead. Many home inkjet printers actually cope better with sRGB or no color management than with Adobe RGB.

So what's your best option? Once again, if everything's looking good, leave it alone. Otherwise for general use, you're probably best by starting with No Color Management. Then try the other two if that didn't work well for you.

If you choose one of the other two options, when you save your file, Elements attempts to embed a *tag*, or information about the color space, into your file for the space you're in—either Adobe RGB or sRGB. (Incidentally, this tag is not related to the Organizer tags that you read about in Chapter 2.) It's up to you whether you let Elements do that. If you don't want a color tag in your file, just turn off the checkbox before you save your file. Figure 7-5 shows what you may see when you open a file that doesn't have a color tag or one that's tagged with a different color space than the one you're currently using.

Figure 7-5:
When you open an untagged file (one that isn't assigned to a particular color space), Elements asks if you want to convert it to the current color space. You can safely leave the file untagged if you prefer not to assign a profile to it, and in many cases, this is your best bet for maximum flexibility. (Assigning a profile is sometimes helpful, because then any program that sees your file knows what color standards you were working with. But if you're new to Elements, you'll usually have an easier time if you don't start embedding profiles in files without a good reason.)

NOTE If you're comfortable with the whole concept of assigning color tags to your image, you can use the Missing Profile dialog box to assign a different color profile to a file. If your photo already has a color space, save it as an untagged file (turn off the color profile checkbox before saving). Now reopen the photo (in the color space you want instead), and perform Save As again. Make sure that the "assign profile" box *is* turned on in the Save As dialog box this time.

Using Levels

People who've used Elements for awhile will tell you that the Levels command goes right at the top of any list of the program's most essential tools. You can fix an amazing array of problems simply by adjusting the level of each color channel. (On your monitor, each color you see is composed of red, green, and blue. In Elements, you can make very precise adjustments to your images by adjusting these *color channels* separately.)

Just as its name suggests, Levels adjusts the level of each color within your image. There are several different adjustments you can make using Levels, from general brightening of your colors to fixing a color cast (there's much more about color casts later). Most digital photo enthusiasts treat every picture they take to a dose of Levels, because there's no better way to polish up the color in your photo.

The way Levels works is fairly complex. A short explanation would be to start by thinking of the possible range of brightness in any photo on a scale from 0 (black) to 255 (white). Some photos may have pixels in them that fall at both those extremes, but most photos don't. And even the ones that do may not have the full range of brightness in each individual color channel. Most of the time, there's going to be some empty space at one or both ends of the scale.

When you use Levels, you tell Elements to consider the range of colors available in *your* photo as the *total* tonal range it has to work with. Elements redistributes your colors accordingly. Basically, you just get rid of the empty space at the ends of the scale of possibilities. This can dramatically readjust the color distribution in your photo, as you can see in Figure 7-6.

It's much, much easier to use Levels than to understand it, as you know if you've already tried Auto Levels in the Quick Fix (page 91). That command is great for, well, quick fixes. But if you really need to massage your image, Levels has a lot more under the hood than you can see there. The next section shows you how to get at these settings.

Understanding the Histogram

Before you can get started adjusting Levels, you first need to understand the heart, soul, and brain of the Levels dialog box: the Histogram, as shown in Figure 7-7.

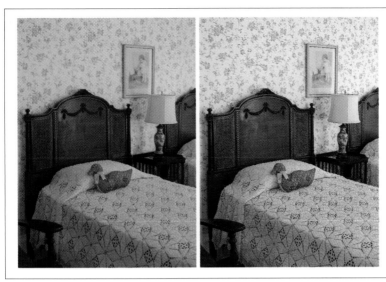

Figure 7-6:
A simple Levels adjustment can make a huge difference in the way your photo looks. Here, Levels not only got rid of the yellow cast in the left photo, but the right photo also gives the impression of having better contrast and sharpness, too.

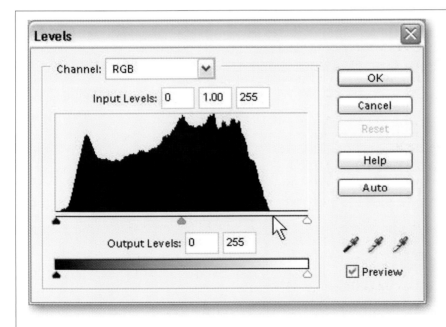

Figure 7-7:
One of the scariest sights in Elements, the Levels dialog box is actually your very good friend. If it frightens you, take comfort in knowing that you've always got the Auto button here, which is the same Auto Levels command as in the Quick Fix. But it's worth persevering: the other options here give you much better control of the end results.

The Histogram is the black bumpy mound in the window. It's really nothing more than a bar graph indicating the distribution of the colors in your photo. (It's a bar graph, but there's no space between the bars, which is what causes the mountainous look.)

From left to right, the Histogram shows the brightness range from dark to light (the 0 to 255 mentioned earlier this section). The height of the "mountain" at any given point shows how many pixels in your photo are that particular brightness. You can tell a lot about your photo by where the mound of color is before you adjust it, as demonstrated in Figure 7-8.

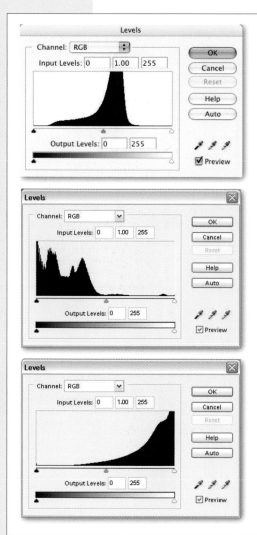

Figure 7-8:
Top: If the bars in your Histogram are all smushed together, your photo doesn't have a lot of tonal range. As long as you like how the photo looks, that's not important. But if you're unhappy with the color in the photo, it's usually going to be harder to get it exactly right than a photo that has a wider tonal distribution.

Middle: If all your colors are bunched up on the left side, your photo is underexposed.

Bottom: If you just have a big lump that's all on the right side, your photo is overexposed.

If you look above the Histogram, you can see that there is a little menu that says RGB. If you pull that down, you can also see a separate histogram for each individual color. You can adjust all three channels at once in the RGB setting (which those in the know call the *luminosity*), or change each channel separately.

The Histogram contains so much information about your photo that Adobe also makes it available in the Editor in its own palette so that you can always see it and use it to monitor how you're changing the colors in your image. The Histogram palette is shown in Figure 7-9. Once you get fluent in reading histogram-ese you'll probably want to keep this palette around.

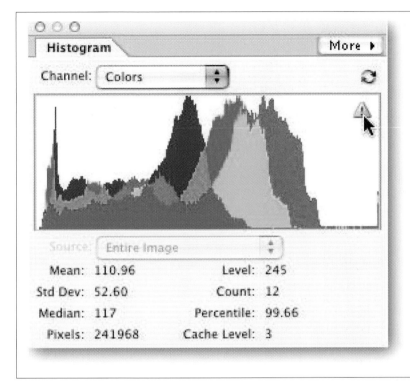

Figure 7-9:
If you keep the Histogram on your desktop, you can always see what effect your changes are having on the color distribution in your photo. To get this nifty Technicolor view, go to Window → Histogram and then choose Colors from the pull-down menu on the palette. To update a Histogram, click the triangle as shown.

If you're really into statistical information about your photo, there's a bunch of it available from this palette, but if you're not a pro, you can usually safely ignore these numbers.

The Histogram is just a graph, and you don't do anything to it directly. What you do when you use Levels is to use the Histogram as a guide so that you can tell Elements what to consider as the white and black points, i.e., the darkest and lightest points, in your photo. (Remember, you're thinking in terms of brightness values, not shades of color, for these settings.)

Once you've set the end points, you can adjust the *gamma*—the tones in between that would be gray in a black and white photo. If that sounds complicated, it's not—not when you're actually doing it. Once you've made a Levels adjustment, the next time you open the Levels dialog box, you'll see that your Histogram now runs the entire length of the scale, because you've told Elements to redistribute your colors so that they cover the full dark-to-light range.

The next two sections show you—finally!—how to actually adjust your image's Levels.

TIP   If you learn how to interpret the Histograms in Elements, you'll also be able to use the histogram in your camera, which is very helpful, since it's really hard to judge how well your picture turned out when all you have to go by is that tiny LCD screen in your camera. By looking at your camera's histogram you can tell how well exposed your shot was.

Adjusting Levels: The Eyedropper Method

One way to adjust Levels is to set the black, white, and/or gray points by using the eyedroppers on the right side of the Levels dialog box. It's quite simple—just follow these steps:

1. **Bring up the Levels dialog box. (Select Layer → New Fill or Adjustment Layer → Levels).**

   If for some reason you don't want a separate layer for your Levels adjustment, go to Enhance → Adjust Lighting → Levels or press Ctrl+L (⌘-L) instead. But making the Levels changes on an Adjustment layer gives you more flexibility for making changes in the future.

2. **Move the Levels dialog box out of the way so that you get a good view of your photo.**

   The dialog box loves to plunk itself down smack in the middle of the most important part of your image. Just grab it by the top bar and drag it to where it's not covering up a crucial part of your photo.

3. **In the Levels dialog box, click the black eyedropper.**

   From left to right, the eyedroppers are black, gray, and white. You can kind of see the colors if you look closely.

4. **Move your cursor back over your photo and click an area of your photo that should be black.**

   Should be, not is. That's a mistake lots of people make the first time they use this tool. They get the gray eyedropper, say, and click a spot that appears gray rather than one that *ought to be* gray.

5. **Repeat with the other eyedroppers for their respective colors.**

   In other words, now find a white point and a gray point. That's the way it's supposed to work, but it's not always possible to use all of them in any one photo. Experiment to see what gives you the best-looking results.

6. **When you're happy with what you see, click Okay.**

See, it's not so hard. If you mess up, just click the Reset button, and you can start over again.

Adjusting Levels: The Slider Controls

The eyedropper method works fine if your photo has spots that should be black, white, or gray, but a lot of the time, your picture may not have any of these colors.

Fortunately, the Levels sliders give you yet another way to apply Levels, and it's by far the most popular method. Using the sliders gives you maximum control over your colors, and it works great even for photos that don't have a white, black, or gray point to click.

If you look directly under the Histogram, you'll see three little triangles, called the Input sliders. The left triangle is the slider for setting the black point in your photo, the right slider sets the white point, and the middle slider adjusts your gamma (gray). You just drag them to make changes to the color levels in your photo, as shown in Figure 7-10.

When you move the left Input slider, you tell Levels, "Take all the pixels from this point down and consider them black." With the right slider, you're saying, "Make this pixel and all higher values white." The middle slider, the gamma slider, adjusts the brightness value that's considered medium gray. All three adjustments improve the contrast of your image.

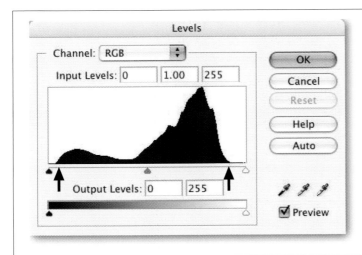

Figure 7-10:
Here's how to use the Levels sliders. You want to move the sliders from the ends of the track until they're under the outer edges of the color data in the graph. If there's empty space on the end, just move the slider until it's under the first mound of data. The large arrows in this figure show where you'd position the sliders for this photo.

NOTE If there are small amounts of data, like a flat line at the ends or if all your data is bunched in the middle of the graph, watch the preview in your photo to decide how far toward the mountain you should bring the sliders. Moving it all the way in may be too drastic. Your own taste should always be the deciding factor when you're adjusting a photo.

The easiest way to use the Levels sliders is to:

1. **Bring up the Levels dialog box.**

   Use one of the methods described in step 1 of the Eyedropper method (page 168).

---

2. **Move the Levels dialog box so you've got a clear view of your photo and then grab the black Input slider.**

   That's the one on the left side of the Histogram box.

3. **Slide it to the right, if necessary.**

   Move it over until it's under the left-most part of the Histogram that has a "mound" of color in it. If you glance back at Figure 7-10, you'd move the left slider to where the left large arrow is. (Incidentally, although you're adjusting the colors in your image, the Levels Histogram stays black and white no matter what you do—you don't get any color in the dialog box itself.)

   You may not need to move the slider at all if there's already a good bit of data at the end of the Histogram. It's not mandatory to adjust everything every time.

4. **Grab the white slider (the one on the right side) and move it left.**

   Bring it under the farthest right area of the Histogram that has a mound of data in it.

5. **Now adjust the gray slider.**

   This is called the *gamma* slider and it adjusts the midtones of your photo. Move it back and forth while watching your photo until you like what you see. Gamma makes the most impact on the overall result, so take some time to play with this slider.

6. **Click Okay.**

You can adjust your entire image or adjust each color channel individually. The most accurate way is to first choose each color channel separately from the Channel drop-down menu in the Histogram dialog box. Adjust the end points for each channel by itself, and then go back to RGB and tweak just the gamma slider.

> **TIP**   If you know the numerical value of the pixels you want to designate for any of these settings, you can type that information into the boxes. You can set the gamma value from .10 to 9.99. It is set at 1.00 automatically.

The last control you might want to use in the Levels dialog box is the Output Levels slider. Output Levels work roughly the same way as your brightness and contrast controls on your TV. Moving these sliders makes the darkest pixels darker and the lightest pixels lighter. Among pros, this is known as adjusting the tonal range of a photo.

Adjusting Levels will improve almost every photo you take, but if your photo has a bad *color cast*—if it's too orange or too blue—you may need something else. The next section shows you how to get rid of unwanted color.

Removing Unwanted Color

It's not uncommon for an otherwise good photo to have a *color cast*—that is, to have all the tonal values shifted so that the photo is too blue, like Figure 7-11, or too orange.

Figure 7-11:
Left: You may wind up with a photo like this every once in a while if you forget to change the white balance, your camera's special setting for the type of lighting conditions you're shooting in (common settings are daylight, fluorescent, and so on). This is an outdoor photo taken with the camera set for tungsten indoor lighting.

Bottom: Elements fixes that wicked color cast in a jiffy. The photo still needs other adjustments, but the color is back in the ballpark.

Elements gives you several ways to correct color cast problems:

• **Auto Color Correction** doesn't give you any control over how Elements works, but it often does a good job. To use it go to Enhance → Auto Color Correction, or press Ctrl+Shift+B (⌘-Shift-B).

• **Levels** gives you the finest control of the methods in this list. You can often eliminate a color cast by adjusting the individual color channels till the extra color is gone (as explained in the previous section). The downside is that Levels can be very fiddly for this sort of work, and one of the other ways may be much faster at getting you the results you want.

• **Remove Color Cast** is the special command for correcting a color cast with one-click ease. The next section explains how to use this tool.

• **The Color Variations** dialog box is helpful in figuring out which colors you need more or less of, but it has some limitations. It's covered later, on page 172.

• **The Photo Filter command** is new to Elements 3; it gives you much more control than the Color Cast tool, and you can apply Photo Filters as Adjustment layers, too. Photo Filters are covered in Chapter 8.

All these tools can be useful for fixing a color cast, depending on exactly what your problem is. Usually you'd start with Levels and then move on to the Color Cast tool or the Photo Filter.

Using the Color Cast tool

The Color Cast tool is another eyedropper sampling tool that adjusts the colors in your photo based on the pixels you click. In this case, you show Elements where a neutral color should be. As you saw with the heron in Figure 7-11, the Color Cast command can make a big difference with just one click. To use it:

1. **Go to Enhance → Adjust Color → Remove Color Cast.**

   Your cursor should change to an eyedropper when you move it over your photo. If it doesn't change, go to the dialog box and click the Eyedropper icon.

2. **Click an area that should be gray, white, or black.**

   You only have to click once in your photo for this tool to work. As with the Levels eyedropper tool, click an area that *should be* gray, white, or black (as opposed to looking for an area that's currently one of these colors). If several of these colors appear, you can try different spots in your photo, clicking Reset in between each sample, until you find the spot that gives you the most natural-looking color.

3. **Click Okay.**

The Color Cast tool works pretty well if your image has areas that should be black, white, or gray, even if they are very tiny. The tricky thing is when you have an image that doesn't have a good area to sample—when there isn't any black, white, or gray anywhere in the picture. If that's the case, consider using the Photo Filter, which is described on page 201.

> **TIP** After using the Color Cast tool, try using the Auto Color Correction command from the Enhance menu. Often this helps put the final touch on color cast removals. If you don't like what it does, just press Ctrl+Z (⌘-Z) to undo it.

Using Color Variations

The Color Variations window (Figure 7-12) is very appealing to many Elements beginners, because it gives you a visual clue about what to do to fix the color in your photo. You just click the little preview thumbnail that shows the color balance you like best, and Elements applies the necessary change to make your photo look like the thumbnail.

However, Color Variations has some pretty severe limitations, most notably, the microscopic size of the thumbnails. It's very hard to see accurately what you're doing, and with Elements 3, even newcomers can usually get better results in Quick Fix.

Still, Color Variations is useful for those times when you know something's not quite right in your color but you can't figure out exactly what to do about it. And since it's adjustable, Color Variations is good for when you do know what you want but you want to make only the tiniest sliver of a difference to the color of your photo.

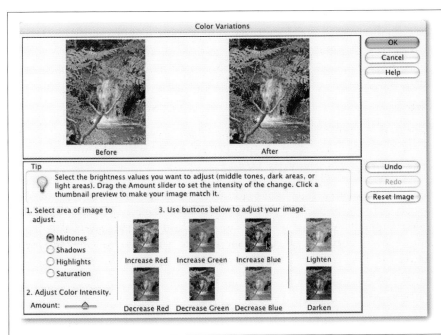

To use the Color Variations tool:

1. **Open your photo.**

   You may want to make a duplicate layer (page 131) for the adjustments, so that you'll have the option to discard your changes if you're not happy with them. If you don't work on a duplicate, keep in mind that the changes you make here aren't undoable after you've closed the photo.

2. **Go to Enhance → Adjust Color → Color Variations.**

   You see the dialog box pictured in Figure 7-12.

3. **On the lower-left corner of the dialog box ("Select area of image to adjust."), click a radio button to choose whether you want to adjust highlights, shadows, midtones, or saturation.**

   Color Variations begins by selecting midtones, which is usually what you want. But experiment with the other settings to see what they do. The Saturation button works just like Saturation in Quick Fix (page 94).

4. **Use the slider at the bottom of the dialog box to control how drastic the adjustment should be.**

   The farther you push the slider to the right, the more dramatic the change. Usually, just a smidgen is enough to make a noticeable change.

5. Just below where it says "Use buttons below to adjust your image," click one of the color buttons to make your photo look more like one of the thumbnail photos.

   You can always Undo or Redo using the buttons on the right side of the window, or use Reset Image to put your photo back to where it was when you started.

6. When you're happy with the result, click Okay.

Choosing the Color You Want

So far, the color corrections you've been reading about in this chapter have all done most of the color assigning for you. But a lot of the time you want to be able to *tell* Elements what colors you want to work with—like when you're selecting the color for a background or Fill layer (page 145), or when you want to paint on an image.

Although you can use any of the millions of colors your screen can display, Elements loads only two colors of your choosing at a time. You access these colors from the squares at the bottom of the Toolbox (see Figure 7-13). Adobe refers to the colors as your Foreground and Background colors.

Foreground and Background mean just what they sound like—use the Background color to fill in backgrounds, and use the Foreground color with the Elements tools, like the Brush or the Paint Bucket. You can use as many colors as you want, of course. You just have to change your settings in Foreground/Background to access these other colors.

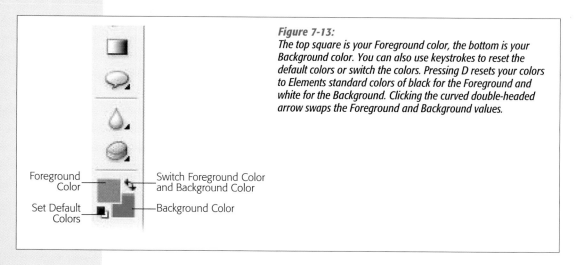

Figure 7-13:
The top square is your Foreground color, the bottom is your Background color. You can also use keystrokes to reset the default colors or switch the colors. Pressing D resets your colors to Elements standard colors of black for the Foreground and white for the Background. Clicking the curved double-headed arrow swaps the Foreground and Background values.

Foreground Color

Set Default Colors

Switch Foreground Color and Background Color

Background Color

The color-picking tools at the bottom of the Toolbox let you control the color you're using in a number of different ways:

- **Reset default colors.** Click the tiny black and white squares to return to the standard settings of black for the Foreground color and white for the Background color.

- **Switch Foreground and Background colors.** Click the little curved arrows above and to the right of the squares, and your Background color becomes the Foreground color, and vice versa. This is very helpful when you have inadvertently made your color selection in the wrong box. (For example, if you've set the Foreground color to yellow, but you actually meant to make the Background color yellow: just click these arrows, and you're all set).

- **Change either the Foreground or Background color to whatever color you want.** You can choose any color you like for either color square. Click either square to call up the Color Picker (explained later) to make your new choice. There's no limit on the colors you can select to use in Elements. Well, technically there is, but it's in the millions, so there are bound to be enough choices for anything you want to do.

You have a few different ways to tell Elements what colors you want to use as Foreground and Background colors. The next few sections show you how to use the Color Picker, the Eyedropper tool (to pick a color from an existing image), or the Color Swatches palette.

When you're working with some of the Elements tools, like the Type tool, you can choose a color in the tool's Options bar settings. Adobe knows that, given a choice, most people tend to prefer working with either the Color Swatches or the Color Picker, so they've come up with a clever way to accommodate both camps, as shown in Figure 7-14.

The Color Picker

Figure 7-15 shows you the Color Picker. It has an intimidating number of options, but most of the time, you don't need all of them. Picking a color is as easy as clicking when you see the color you want.

The Color Picker is actually pretty simple to use:

1. **Click the Foreground or Background color square in the Toolbox.**

   The Color Picker launches. Some other tools—like the Paint Bucket (page 281) and the mask color option for the Selection brush (page 113)—also use the Color Picker. It works the same way no matter how you get to it.

2. **Choose the color range you want to select from.**

   You do this with the vertical Color Slider in the middle of the Color Picker. Slide through the spectrum until you see the color you want in the Color Field.

Click here for
the Color Picker

Click here for
the Color Swatches

Figure 7-14:
*Whether you prefer using Color Swatches or the Color
Picker, Elements gives you your choice (for most tools) in
the Options bar. Click the color sample in the box to bring
up the Color Picker, or if you're a Swatcher, click the
arrow to the right of the box to pop out the Color
Swatches palette.*

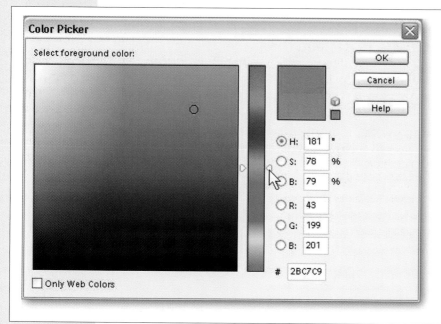

Figure 7-15:
*For most beginners,
the most important
parts of the Elements
Color Picker are the
slider in the middle
(called, oddly enough,
the Color Slider), and
the square window,
which Adobe calls the
Color Field. Use the
Slider to get the
general color you
want, then click in the
Field on the exact
shade.*

3. **Click the exact spot in the Color Field where you see the particular shade you want.**

   You can keep clicking around to watch the color in the top box in the window change to reflect the color you have chosen. The bottom box continues to show your original color for comparison.

4. **Click Okay.**

The color you selected is now your option in the Foreground or Background square in the Toolbox.

That's the basic way to use the Color Picker. See the box "Paint by Number" for ways to enter a numeric value for your color if you know it, or to change the shades the Color Picker is offering you.

TIP   You're not limited to Elements' color picker. Both Windows and Mac have their own, built-in color pickers. See the box on page 178 for how to use these.

POWER USERS' CLINIC

Paint by Number

The Elements Color Picker also includes some very sophisticated controls that you can probably ignore for a long time before you have to understand them. For the curious or more advanced, here's what the rest of the Color Picker does.

- **HSB buttons.** These numbers control the hue, saturation, and brightness of your color. The settings control pretty much the same values as the Hue/Saturation adjustment. (See page 223 for more about hue and saturation.)

- **RGB buttons.** The RGB buttons let you specify the amount of red, green, and blue you want in the color you're picking. Each button can have a numerical value anywhere from 0 to 256. A lower number means less of the color, a higher number means more. For example, 128, 128, 128 is neutral gray. By changing the numbers, you can change the blend of the color.

- **Hex number.** Below the radio buttons is a box that lets you enter a special six-character hexidecimal code that you use when you're creating Web graphics. These codes tell Web browsers which colors to display. You can also click a color in the window to see the hex number for that shade.

- **Only Web Colors checkbox.** Turning this button on insures that the colors you see in the main color box are drawn only from the 216 colors that antique Web browsers can display. For example, if you're creating a Web site and you're really worried about color compatibility with Netscape 4.0, this box is for you. If you see a tiny cube just to the left of the Help button, then the color you're using isn't deemed Web safe.

The Eyedropper Tool

If you've ever repainted your house you've probably had the frustrating experience of spotting the *exact* color you want—if only there were a way to capture that color. That's one problem you'll never run into in Elements, thanks to the handy Eyedropper tool that lets you sample any color you see on your monitor and then automatically make it the Foreground color in Elements. If you can get a color into your computer, Elements can grab it.

Sampling a color (i.e., snagging it for your own use) couldn't be simpler than it is with the Eyedropper. You just move your cursor over the color you want and click.

OUTSIDE ELEMENTS

A New Box of Crayons

Both operating systems include their own color pickers that you can use instead of the Adobe Color Picker. They're easy to select. Go to Edit → Preferences → General (Photoshop Elements → Preferences → General).

- **Windows:** The Windows color picker opens up looking pretty feeble—just a few colored squares and some plain white ones, but if you click "define custom colors," it expands, giving you access to most of the features in the Adobe picker. (The plain white squares are like little pigeonholes where your color choices are saved.)

- **Mac:** Apple includes a very deluxe color picker as part of its operating system. It includes the option to pick from a wheel rather than by using sliders as Adobe's does, and some people find that easier to do. The OS X color picker also includes a silly, fun way to pick your colors—from a box of crayons. (See the illustration.) You just click a crayon to choose a color like Asparagus or Maraschino to paint your magnum opus with.

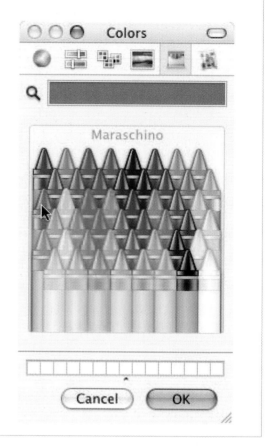

It even works on colors that aren't already in Elements, as explained in Figure 7-16.

By now, you may be thinking that Elements has more eyedroppers than your medicine cabinet. But this time, the Eyedropper in question is the Official Elements Eyedropper tool that has its own place in the Toolbox. It's one of the easiest tools to use:

1. **Click the Eyedropper in the Toolbox or just press I.**

   Your cursor changes into a tiny eyedropper.

2. **Move the Eyedropper over the color you want to sample.**

   You can watch the color change in the Foreground color box as you move the Eyedropper around.

Figure 7-16:
The secret to using the Eyedropper tool to sample colors outside of Elements: Start by clicking in your Elements file. Then, while still holding your mouse button down, move your cursor over to the non-Elements object, until the eyedropper is over the area you want to sample. Then you can let go, and you'll see the new color in the Elements color squares.

If you let go before you get to the non-Elements object, it won't work. Here, the Eyedropper has picked up the yellow of the Disk icon, but it could as easily have been a color from a Web page or a word processing document.

3. **Click when you see the color you want.**

Your color choice is loaded up, ready to use, as your Foreground color in the Color Squares. To make it a Background color instead, Alt+click (Option-click) the color in your source.

If you want to keep your color sample around so that you can use it another time without having to get the Eyedropper out again, you can save your color samples in the Swatches palette. Then you can quickly choose those exact colors again any time you want. See the next section for directions on how to do this.

NOTE Since there may be some slight pixel-to-pixel variation in a color, the Eyedropper actually samples a little block of pixels and averages them. In the Eyedropper Options bar settings, you can choose between a 3-pixel square average or a 5-pixel one. Oddly enough, this Eyedropper setting also applies to the Magic Wand. Change it here and you change it for the Wand, too.

The Color Swatches Palette

The Color Swatches palette holds several little preloaded libraries of sample colors for you to use in picking a color. Go to Window → Color Swatches to call up the Color Swatches palette. You can park the Color Swatches palette in the Palette bin just like any other palette, if you like, or leave it floating on your desktop. When you're ready to choose a color, just click the swatch you want and it appears in the Foreground color square or the color box of the tool you're using.

The Color Swatches palette is very handy when you want to keep certain color choices at your fingertips. For instance, you might put your logo colors into it, and then you always have those colors available for any graphics or ads you create in Elements.

There are several different libraries of Color Swatches available to you. Click the More button on the Swatches palette to see them all. A swatch you create appears at the bottom of the current library, and you can save it there, or you can create your own swatch libraries if you'd rather do that.

Using the Color Swatches to select your Foreground or Background color is as easy as using the Eyedropper tool was. Figure 7-17 shows you how.

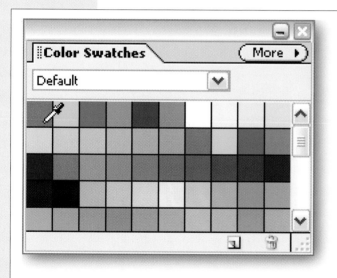

Figure 7-17:
When you move your cursor over the Color Swatches palette, it changes to an eyedropper. Click to select a color. The preloaded palettes include tooltips text with the color names, to help you be sure which shade is which. If you use the swatches a lot, you can choose "Place in palette bin" from the More menu so the Swatches palette is always there.

To use the Color Swatches palette:

- **To pick a foreground color:** Click the color you want. It appears as the Foreground color choice.

- **To pick a background color:** Ctrl+click (⌘-click) a color, and Elements makes it the Background color.

You can also change the way the Color Swatches palette displays swatch information, as shown in Figure 7-18.

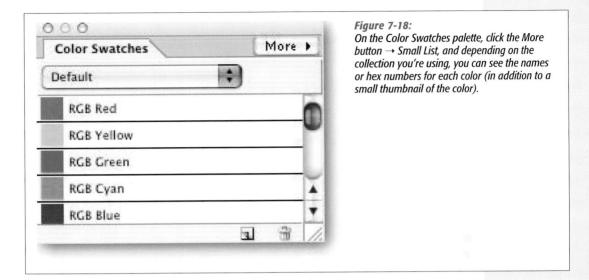

Figure 7-18:
On the Color Swatches palette, click the More button → Small List, and depending on the collection you're using, you can see the names or hex numbers for each color (in addition to a small thumbnail of the color).

Saving colors in the Swatches palette

Any colors you've picked using the Color Picker or Eyedropper tool, you can save as swatches. If you don't save them, you lose them as soon as you select a different library or close the palette.

To add a swatch, you can do one of two things:

- **Click the New Swatch icon at the bottom of the Color Swatch palette.** It's the same square that stands for "new" in the Layers palette.

- **Click the More button on the palette, and choose "New Color Swatch."**

In either case, you get a chance to name and save the new swatch. The name shows up as tooltips text when you hover your mouse over the swatch in the palette. (Don't change the save location if you want Elements to continue to recognize it as a swatch.) Your swatch gets saved at the bottom of the current swatch library. To delete a swatch that you've saved, drag it to the Trash icon in the Color Swatches palette.

You can also create your own libraries, if you want to keep your own swatches separate from the ones Elements gives you. Go to the More button on the palette and pick Save Color Swatches. Then give your new library a name and save it.

> **NOTE**   If you save a new swatch library, it doesn't show up in the list of libraries until the next time you start Elements.

Sharpening Your Images

Digital cameras are wonderful, but often it's hard to tell how well you've focused until you download the photos to your computer. Also, because of the way digital sensors process information, most digital image data usually needs to be sharpened. Sharpening gives the impression of improved focus. Even film shots may look just fine in a 4 × 6-inch print, only to be revealed as not so crisp once you scan them and zoom in.

Fortunately, Elements includes some almost miraculous tools for sharpening your images. (It's pretty darned good at blurring them, too, if you want—see page 306.)

Elements does include a Sharpen tool, but it turns out it's not the most useful solution available. That honor goes to the Unsharp Mask. Honorable mention goes to the High-Pass filter. All three are covered in the following sections.

The Sharpen Filters

Most of the time, the best way to sharpen an image is by using the sharpening filters. If you go to Filter → Sharpen, your choices are Sharpen, Sharpen Edges, Sharpen More, and something called Unsharp Mask. Although it sounds like the very last thing you'd want, the Unsharp Mask is actually by far the most capable and versatile of the sharpening tools, as well as having the most counter-intuitive name in all of Elements.

To be fair, it's not Adobe's fault. *Unsharp Mask* is an old darkroom term, and it actually does make sense if you know how they used to do it with film. Film developers would immediately know what to do with the Unsharp Mask, even if it confuses the heck out of everyone else. To see why Unsharp Mask trumps the other sharpening filters, take a look at Figure 7-19.

Figure 7-19:
Left: The photo was sharpened with the Sharpen filter. It's not bad, but it's not much different from the way the photo came from the camera, either.

Right: The photo was treated with a dose of Unsharp Mask. Notice how much clearer the individual hairs in the dog's coat are and how much better defined its eyes and mouth are.

The other sharpen filters are not complete slouches—they're just not as good as the mighty Unsharp Mask. Here's what they do:

- **Sharpen,** just as the name says, sharpens your image, but you have no control over anything. It's a take-it-or-leave-it command with no adjustments. You can apply it repeatedly to build up the effect.

- **Sharpen Edges** finds areas where significant color changes occur and sharpens the adjacent pixels. This filter tries to work only on edges (i.e., where two contrasting colors meet), without affecting the overall smoothness of the photo. Once again, there are no controls to let you tweak its effects.

- **Sharpen More** applies a more intense filter than the Sharpen filter. It's basically pretty similar to the Sharpen filter with the settings raised a bit. Depending on your photo, it may not make much difference, or it may sharpen it to the point where you start to see *artifacts* (explained in Figure 7-20).

The Unsharp Mask

While there's nothing wrong with the other sharpening tools, the Unsharp Mask is so much more powerful; it makes you wonder why Adobe bothered with the rest of them when Unsharp Mask is all you really need. It ranks right up there with Levels as a contender for most useful tool in Elements. The Unsharp Mask is the only sharpening tool that gives you any control over how much it sharpens, and that's crucial.

To use the Unsharp Mask, you want to first finish all your other corrections and changes. The Unsharp Mask (or any sharpening tool) can cause unpredictable results with other adjustments you make after you apply it, so always sharpen as the very last step. A good rule to remember is "last and once." Applying sharpening repeatedly degrades your image's quality.

If you're sharpening an image with layers, be sure the active layer has something in it. Applying sharpening to a Levels Adjustment layer, for example, won't do anything. Also, perform any format conversions (page 208) before applying sharpening. Finally, you might want a duplicate layer for the sharpening if you want the ability to undo your changes later on. Press Ctrl+J (⌘-J) to create the duplicate layer.

> **NOTE**   It's helpful to understand just exactly what Elements does when it "sharpens" your photo. It does not magically correct the focus. As a matter of fact, it doesn't really sharpen anything.
>
> What it does is deepen the contrast where colors meet, giving the impression of a crisper focus. So while Elements can dramatically improve a shot that's just faintly out of focus or a little soft, even Elements can't fix that old double exposure or a shot where the subject is just a blur of motion.

When you're ready to apply the Unsharp Mask:

1. **Go to Filter → Sharpen → Unsharp Mask.**

2. **Move the sliders until you like what you see.**

   In the Preview window, you can zoom in and out and grab the photo to adjust which part you see.

3. **When you're satisfied, click OK.**

The sliders for the Unsharp Mask work very much like the sliders in several of the other tools:

- **Amount.** This tells Elements how much to sharpen, in percent terms. A higher number means more sharpening.

- **Radius.** This tells Elements how far from an edge Elements should look when increasing the contrast.

- **Threshold.** This is how different a pixel needs to be from the surrounding pixels before Elements should consider it an edge and sharpen it. If the threshold is left at zero, the standard setting, Elements sharpens all the pixels in an image.

There are many, many different schools of thought about which values to plug into each box. Whatever works for you is fine. The one thing you want to watch out for is oversharpening. Figure 7-20 tells you how to know if you've gone too far.

Figure 7-20:
The perils of oversharpening. This lizard may have a suspicious attitude, but he didn't have a skin condition. The flaky look comes from over-applying sharpening, and the white flecks are called artifacts.

You'll probably need to do a bit of experimenting to find out which settings work best for you. Photos you want to print often need to be sharpened to an extent that makes them look over-sharpened when viewed on your monitor. Therefore, you may want to create separate versions of your photo (one for onscreen viewing and one for printing). Stacks in the Organizer are great for keeping track of multiple copies like this. (See page 435.)

> **TIP** If you are working on a group of images and want to apply a filter like the Unsharp Mask to all of them (using the same settings each time), look at the top of the Filter menu. You'll see the last filter you used listed first. If you choose a filter from there, Elements automatically applies the filter with the setting you used last time. You can also just press Ctrl+F (⌘-F) to automatically reapply the last filter and its settings.
>
> If you want to change the filter's settings, select the filter from its place in the list of filters instead.

The High-Pass Filter

Unsharp Mask is definitely the traditional favorite, but there's an alternative method that many people prefer because you do it on a dedicated layer and can back the effect off later by adjusting the layer's opacity if you like. It's called *High-Pass* sharpening. Both methods have their virtues, and you may find that you choose your method according to the content of your photo.

1. **Open your photo and make sure the layer you want to sharpen is the active layer.**

2. **Duplicate your layer by pressing Ctrl+J (⌘-J).**

   If you have a multilayered image and you want to sharpen all the layers, first flatten your image or use the Stamp Visible command (page 144), so it's all in one layer.

3. **Go to Filter → Other → High-Pass.**

   Your photo now looks like the victim of a mudslide, buried in featureless gray. That's what you want for right now.

4. **Move the slider until you can barely see the outlines of your subject.**

   Usually that means picking a setting somewhere roughly between 1.5 and 3.5. If you can see colors, your setting is too high. If you can't quite eliminate every trace of color without totally losing the outline, a tiny bit of color is okay.

5. **Click Okay.**

6. **In the Layers palette, set the blend mode for the new layer to Overlay.**

   Ta-da! Your subject is back again in glowing, sharper color, as shown in Figure 7-21.

Figure 7-21:
Top: The original photo.

Bottom: High-Pass sharpening using Vivid Light makes the colors more vivid, but the ripples are much harder-edged than they were in the original.

For high-pass sharpening, you can use any of the blend modes in the group with Overlay, except Hard Mix and Pin Light. Vivid Light can make your colors pop, but watch out for sharpening artifacts, since they'll be more vivid, too. Overlay gives a softer effect.

The Sharpen Tool

Elements also gives you a dedicated Sharpen tool (Figure 7-22). It's a special brush that sharpens instead of adding color to the areas you drag it over. To get to it, go to the Blur tool and choose the Sharpen tool from the fly-out menu.

The Sharpen tool has a couple of settings in the Options bar, in addition to the brush choices, which work the way they do for the regular Brush tool (see Chapter 11). The Strength setting adjusts how much the brush sharpens what it passes over. A higher number means more sharpening.

The Mode setting lets you increase the visibility of an object's edge by choosing Darken or Lighten, but usually Normal gives the most predictable results.

Figure 7-22:
The Sharpen tool is not meant to sharpen an entire photo, but it's great for detail sharpening. Here, it's being used to bring out the detail in the front strand of beads.

Approach this tool with caution; it's very easy to overdo things with it. One pass too many or a too-high setting, and you start seeing artifacts right away.

Elements for Digital Photographers

If you're a fairly serious digital photographer, you'll be delighted to know that in this version of Elements, Adobe hasn't just included new features to make the program easier for beginners. Your needs are provided for, too, thanks to some new advanced tools pulled straight from Photoshop CS.

Number one on the list is the famous *Adobe Camera RAW Converter,* which takes RAW files—a format some cameras use to give you maximum editing control—and lets you convert and edit them in Elements. In this chapter, you'll learn lots more about what RAW is, and why you might or might not want to use it in your own photography.

You'll also get to know the Photo Filter command, which helps adjust image colors by replicating the old-school effect of placing filters over a camera's lens. And last but not least, Elements now includes some truly useful batch processing tools, including features to help rename files, perform format conversions, and even apply basic retouching to multiple photos. Read on for more about the Elements tools and tricks that are most important for sophisticated digital photographers.

The RAW Converter

Probably the most popular thing Adobe has done for photography buffs in this version is including the celebrated Adobe Camera RAW Converter. For many people, this feature alone is well worth the price of the program, since you just can't beat the convenience of being able to perform conversions in the same program you use for editing.

If you don't know what RAW is, it's just a file format. But a very special one. Your digital camera actually contains a little computer that does a certain amount of processing to your photos right inside the camera itself. If you shoot in JPEG format, for instance, your camera has already made some decisions about things like sharpness, color saturation, and contrast before it saves the JPEG files to your memory card.

If your camera lets you shoot RAW files on the other hand, you get the mostly unprocessed data straight from the camera. Shooting in RAW lets you make your own decisions about how your photo should look, to a much greater degree than you can with any other format. It's something like getting a negative from your digital camera—what you do to it in your digital darkroom is up to you.

That's the big advantage of RAW—total control. The downside is that every camera manufacturer has its own proprietary RAW format, and the format may even vary between models from the same manufacturer. No regular graphics program can edit these files, and very few programs can even view them. Instead, you need special software to convert your RAW files to a format that you can work with. In the past, that usually meant you needed to use software from the manufacturer before you could move your photo into an editing program like Elements.

Enter Adobe Camera RAW, which now lets you convert your files right in Elements. Not only that, but the Adobe Camera RAW plug-in that comes with Elements lets you make very sophisticated corrections to your photos—before you even open them. Many times, you can do everything you need right in the converter, so that you're done as soon as you open your converted file. (You can, of course, still use any of Elements regular tools once you've opened a RAW file.) Using Adobe Camera RAW saves you a ton of time, and it's compatible with most cameras' RAW files.

> **NOTE** Adobe has updated the RAW plug-in since Elements 3 was released. You can download the latest version by going to *www.adobe.com/support/downloads* and scrolling down to the section for Photoshop CS. (Elements and Photoshop use the same plug-in, but you don't see all the features in Elements). Aside from support for newer cameras, the new plug-in also gives you the ability to use Adobe's new Digital Negative (.dng) format, an attempt to create a single, universal long-term storage format for all kinds of RAW files. Adobe regularly updates the RAW converter to include new cameras, so if your camera's RAW files don't open, check for a newer version of the plug-in.

Using the RAW Converter

For all the options it gives you, the RAW Converter is very easy to use. Adobe has designed it so that it *automatically* calculates and applies what it thinks are the correct settings for exposure, shadows, brightness, and contrast. You can accept the Converter's decisions or override them and do everything yourself—it's your call.

To get started, you must first open your images. You can keep track of RAW files in the Organizer (page 30), but the Organizer doesn't open them. You have to be

To Shoot in the RAW or Not

Should I shoot my pictures in the RAW format?

It depends. There are pros and cons to using the RAW format. It might surprise you to learn that some professional photographers choose *not* to use RAW. For example, not many journalists use RAW, and it's not common with sports photographers, either. Here's a quick look at the advantages and disadvantages to help you decide if you want to get involved with RAW.

On the plus side, you get:

- **More control.** With RAW you have a lot of extra chances to tweak your photos, and you get to call the shots, instead of your camera.

- **More fixes.** If you're not a perfect photographer, RAW is more forgiving—you can fix a lot of mistakes in RAW, although even RAW won't make a bad photo into a great photo.

- **No need to fuss with your white balance all the time while shooting.** Although you'll still get better input if your camera's white balance settings are correct.

But RAW also has some significant drawbacks. For one thing, you can't just open up a file and start using the photo the way you do with a JPEG file. You've always got to convert it first, whether you use the Elements Converter or one supplied by the manufacturer. Other disadvantages include:

- **Larger file size.** RAW files are smaller than TIFFs, but they're usually much bigger than the highest-quality JPEGs. Consequently, you'll need more memory cards if you regularly shoot RAW.

- **Speed.** It generally takes your camera longer to save RAW files than JPEGs—a significant consideration for action shots. Newer cameras have a buffer that holds a few shots and lets you keep shooting while the camera is working, but you'll hit the wall pretty quickly if you're using burst (rapid-advance) mode. Then you just have to wait.

- **Worse in-camera preview.** For many cameras, you have some pretty significant limitations for digitally zooming the view in the viewfinder when using RAW.

You might want to try a few shots of the same subject in both RAW and JPEG to see whether you notice a difference in your final results. Generally speaking, RAW offers the most leeway if you want to make significant edits, but you need to understand what you're doing. JPEG is easier if you're a beginner.

It's really your call. There are excellent photographers who wouldn't think of shooting in anything but RAW, and excellent photographers who think it's too time-consuming.

---

in the Editor to actually convert the files. Both the Organizer and the Editor's File Browser can display thumbnails of your RAW files before you open them so that you can choose the photo you want.

You can start converting your file in two places:

- **In the Organizer,** highlight the file and click Edit → Standard Editor (or press Ctrl+I).

- **In the Editor,** use the File Browser to locate the file you want and double-click the thumbnail of the photo you want. That brings up the Converter.

TIP You may not be able to open your RAW files by double-clicking them outside of Elements (from the Windows desktop or the Mac Finder). You'll probably get a message to the effect that your computer has no idea what program to use to open that file. You can make sure that Elements is the program that's always used to open your RAW files by following the steps described on page 26.

One important point about RAW files: Elements never overwrites your original files. As a matter of fact, Elements *can't* in any way modify the original RAW file. This means that your original is always there for you if you want to try converting your photo again later on using different settings. It's something like having a negative that you can always get more prints from.

NOTE The Organizer can store your RAW files with no problems, but the Photo Downloader tends to be very slow about importing them and has been known to choke when working with RAW files. You may well find you prefer to get your RAW photos into your computer using one of the other methods discussed in Chapter 2.

Adjusting the view

When the RAW Converter opens, you should see something like Figure 8-1. Before you decide whether to accept the auto settings that Elements offers or to perform further tweaking, you need to get a good close look at your image. The Converter makes it easy to do this by giving you a large preview of your image and a handful of tools to help adjust what you're looking at.

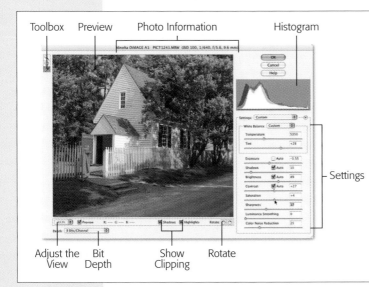

Toolbox   Preview   Photo Information   Histogram

Adjust the View   Bit Depth   Show Clipping   Rotate

Settings

Figure 8-1:
The Elements RAW Converter packs a number of powerful tools into one window. Besides the large preview window, you have a small Toolbox containing some old friends and a specialized tool for adjusting your white balance (explained later), as well as the panel on the right where you tweak your settings. There are more ways to adjust the view, including arrows for rotating your photo, below the preview area.

- **Hand and Zoom tools.** These are in the Toolbox at the upper-left corner of the Converter window. You use them here exactly the same way you would anywhere else in Elements. The keyboard shortcuts for adjusting the view (page 63) also work in the RAW Converter.

- **Rotation arrows.** If you need to rotate your photo, click one of the arrows below the lower-right corner of the preview window.

- **View percentage.** You get a pop-up menu with preset sizes below the lower-left corner of the preview window. Just choose the size you want.

Once you've gotten a good close look at your photo, you need to decide: did Elements do a good enough job of choosing the settings for you? If so, you're done, unless you want to sharpen your photo here (explained later). If you prefer to make adjustments to your photo in the Converter, read on.

The RAW Converter's Settings menu

The long strip down the right side of the RAW Converter gives you many ways to tweak and correct the color, exposure, sharpness, brightness, and noise level of your photo. When you first open a file in the Converter, Elements makes its best guess for the settings it thinks your photo needs.

That's a feature you'll either love or hate. The good news is that you don't have to live with the decisions Elements makes for you. If all this auto stuff drives you crazy, you can turn it off completely. You'll learn how in a minute.

If you look at the upper-right corner of the Converter, you see a Histogram at the top of the window. This helps you keep track of how your changes are affecting the colors in your photo. (Chapter 7 contains more information about reading Histograms on page 165.)

Just below the Histogram is a pull-down menu that says "Camera Default." It also offers you a couple of other options. Whatever is chosen in this menu determines how Elements converts your photo. Here's a look at what the choices mean:

- **Camera Default.** Elements contains a profile of normal RAW settings for your camera model that it uses as its baseline for the adjustments it makes. That's your Camera Default.

- **Selected Image.** Choose this after you've made changes in the Converter to revert to the settings you had when you first opened this photo.

- **Previous Conversion.** If you've already processed a photo and want to apply the same settings to this one, choosing this setting applies the settings from the last RAW image you opened (but only if it's from the same camera).

- **Custom.** Once you start changing settings, you see this instead of one of the other choices.

Since individual cameras of the same model may vary, the default settings may not be the best ones for *your* camera. You can override the default settings and create a new set of default settings for any camera. You also use pretty the much same procedure if you just want to get Elements out of Auto mode. In either case, you need to create your own default settings. This is very easy to do, using the pop-out menu shown in Figure 8-2.

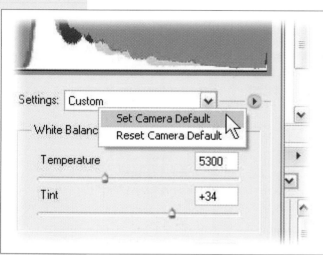

Figure 8-2:
If you don't like the way Elements converts your photos, you can turn off the Auto buttons or make any other changes to your settings. Then click the arrow inside the blue circle and select "Set Camera Default." From now on when you open a photo, you'll see the settings you've chosen.

- **To turn off the Auto settings:** If you just want to put Elements in manual mode, turn off all four checkboxes, then click the arrow and choose "Set Camera Default." You're still using the same basic settings, but Elements won't do the Auto thing anymore.

- **To change your camera's settings:** If you know that you always want a different setting for one of the sliders—like maybe your Shadows setting at 13 instead of the factory setting of 9—move all the sliders (not just the ones with Auto boxes) to where you want them and choose "Set Camera Default." From now on, Elements opens your photos with these settings as your starting point.

- **To revert to the original Elements settings for your camera:** If you want to go back to the way things were originally, click the arrow and choose "Reset Camera Default." This also turns the Auto settings back on.

If you have a lot of RAW files to process, Elements also gives you a few ways to speed up applying your settings.

- In the RAW Converter, Alt+click (Option-click) the Okay button to apply the current settings without actually opening the file.

- In the Editor's File Browser, if you double-click a RAW photo's thumbnail, you'll get the Converter. But if you highlight the thumbnail and press Enter (Return), the photo opens with its current RAW settings applied to it, skipping the Converter window.

- In the File Browser, highlight the files you want to change. Go to File → Apply Camera RAW Settings (Automate → Apply Camera RAW Settings). You get a dialog box where you can choose Selected Image, Camera Default, or Previous Conversion, all of which were described earlier.

White Balance

If you decide to adjust your photos yourself, the first control you'll see listed is for white balance. Adjusting white balance is often the most important change when it comes to making your photos look their best.

The White Balance control adjusts all the colors in your photo by creating a neutral white tone. If that sounds a little strange, stop and think about it for a minute. The color you think of as *white* actually changes depending on the current lighting conditions. In the late afternoon, white is much warmer because of the sun's low rays, while at noon, there's no warmth (no orange/yellow color) to the light at all. In the same way, tungsten lighting is much warmer than fluorescent lighting, which makes whites rather bluish.

Most digital cameras have a white balance setting on them, although you may have to take your camera out of Auto or Program mode to see it. Your camera white balance choices are usually something like Auto, Daylight, Cloudy, Tungsten, Fluorescent, and Custom. When you shoot JPEGs, getting the correct setting here really matters, because it's tough to readjust white balance, even in a program like Elements. With RAW, you can afford to be a little sloppier about setting your white balance, because you can easily tweak it in the RAW Converter.

Getting the white balance right can make a very big difference in how your photo looks, as you can see in Figure 8-3.

Elements gives you several ways to adjust the white balance in your image:

- **Pull-down menu.** The menu just below the Histogram starts out by displaying "As Shot," which means Elements is showing you your camera's settings. You can use the menu to change it, choosing from Auto, Daylight, Cloudy, and other options. From Daylight down through the other choices on the list, each setting is slightly warmer than the one above it. It's worth giving Auto a try, since it gets it right a surprising percent of the time for many cameras.

- **Temperature.** You can use this slider to make your photo warmer (more orange) or cooler (more blue). Moving the slider to the left cools your photo, while moving it to the right warms it. You can also type a temperature in the box in degrees Kelvin (the official measurement for color temperature) if you're experienced in doing this by the numbers. You'd use the Temperature slider and the Tint slider in conjunction for a perfect white balance.

- **Tint.** This adjusts the green/magenta balance of your photo, pretty much the way it does in the Quick Fix. Move it to the left to increase the green in your photo and to the right for more magenta.

Figure 8-3:
Top: The blue-green color seen in this photo is typical of photos with poor white balance.

Bottom: By using the tools Elements gives you, you can easily correct the white balance, which also makes your photo appear more vivid and improves the contrast.

- **Eyedropper tool.** The RAW window has its own special Eyedropper tool. You click a white or light gray spot in your photo with it, and Elements calculates the white balance based on those pixels. This is the most accurate method, but it may be hard to find white pixels to use it on.

If you're a good photographer, much of the time a good white balance and a little sharpening may be all your photo needs before it's ready to go out into the world.

Adjusting Exposure, Shadows, Brightness, and Contrast

The next group of settings includes the adjustments that Elements makes to your photo automatically: Exposure, Shadows, Brightness, and Contrast. If you like the Auto results, that's great, and Elements is fairly talented at making these adjustments. But you may find that for some photos, the Auto settings just don't work, as in Figure 8-4, or you may just prefer to tweak things yourself.

Figure 8-4:
Top: The RAW Converter's suggested settings for this moon shot. (If you've been wondering what noise is, this is an outstanding example of that annoying problem.)

Bottom: With a little bit of manual adjustment, this moon shot was salvaged.

Here's what each of the four settings does for your photo:

- **Exposure.** A properly exposed photo shows the largest possible range of detail. Shadows aren't so dark that you can't see detail in them, and highlights aren't so bright that all you're seeing is white. Move the slider to the left to decrease exposure and to the right to increase it. (The values on the scale are equivalent to f-stops.) Too high a choice here will *clip* some of your highlights. (They'll be so bright there's no detail in them.) See Figure 8-5.

Figure 8-5:
To help you get the Exposure and Shadows settings right, Elements includes checkboxes below the preview window where you can turn on special masks that show you where your highlights (in red) or your shadows (in blue) lose detail at your current settings. In this photo, Elements is warning that the areas where you see red will get clipped when you open the photo unless you change the settings.

- **Shadows.** This slider increases the shadow values and determines which pixels become black in your photo. Increasing the Shadows value may give an effect of increased contrast in your photo. Move the slider to the right to increase shadows or to the left to decrease them. A very little change here goes a long way. Move too far to the right and you'll clip your shadows. (In other words, they'll become plain black.)

- **Brightness.** This is somewhat similar to exposure in that moving the slider to the right lightens your image and moving it to the left darkens it. But the Brightness slider won't clip your photo the way the other two may. Use this slider to set the overall brightness of your image after you've used the Exposure and Shadows sliders to set the outer range of your photo.

- **Contrast.** This adjusts the midtones in your image. Move this slider to the right for greater contrast in those tones and to the left for less. It's usually the last of the four sliders to use.

Most of the time, you'll want to adjust all four of these sliders to get a perfectly exposed photo.

Adjusting Saturation, Sharpness, and Noise

Once you've got your exposure and white balance right, you may be almost done with your photo. But in most cases, you'll still want to make a stop in the bottom section of the RAW Converter for sharpening.

There are two other important adjustments available here as well: saturation and noise reduction. None of the adjustments in this section have Auto settings, although you can change the standard settings by moving their sliders where you want them and then creating a new camera default, as described earlier.

- **Saturation.** This controls how vivid your colors are. Most RAW files have lower saturation to start with than you'd see in the same photo shot as a JPEG, so it's common to want to boost their saturation a bit. Move the slider to the right for more intense color, to the left for more muted color.

- **Sharpening.** Use this slider to increase the edge contrast in your photo, which makes it appear sharper. If you're going to be done with your photo when you leave the RAW Converter, you can sharpen it here by dragging the slider to the right to increase sharpness.

   If you plan to go on to do more editing, drag the slider all the way down to the left to zero before leaving the Converter, or you may get strange results from some of your changes in the Editor. (It's fine to sharpen temporarily while you're working on your photo in the Converter. Just move the slider back to zero as a last step if you're going on to the Editor.)

   Sharpening should usually be the last step when editing your photo. If you do sharpen here, set the view to 100 percent so that you can get an accurate look at how you're changing your photo as you sharpen.

The next two settings work together to reduce the *noise* (or graininess) of your photo. Noise is a big problem in digital photos, especially with 5+ megapixel cameras that don't have the large sensors found in true SLR cameras. Elements gives you two adjustments here that may help.

- **Luminance Smoothing.** This setting reduces grayscale noise, which causes an overall grainy appearance to your photo—something like what you'd see in old newspaper photos. The slider is always at zero to start with, because you don't want to use it more than you can help. That's because moving to the right reduces noise, but it also softens the detail in your photo.

- **Color Noise Reduction.** If you look at what should be evenly colored areas of your photo, and you see obvious groups of differently colored pixels, this setting can help smooth things out. Drag the slider to the right to reduce the amount of color noise.

In most cases, it may take a fair amount of fiddling with these sliders to come up with the best compromise between sharpness and smoothness. It helps if you zoom the view up to 100 percent or more when using them.

Digital Blending

With most digital cameras, you're likely to hit the clipping point (page 197) in an image much sooner than you want to. If you up the exposure so that the shadows are nice and detailed, about half the time you've blown the highlights. On the other hand if you adjust your exposure settings down to favor the highlights, your shadows are murkier than an Enron annual report.

Photographers try to get around these limitations with a technique called *digital blending,* in which you *bracket* your shots, i.e., take two identical shots of your subject at different settings—one exposed for shadows and one for highlights—and then combine them, choosing the best bits of each one.

That technique is great for landscapes. But if you're shooting hummingbirds, roller-skating chimps, or toddlers, you know it's just about impossible to get two identical shots of a moving subject. And if you're like many amateur photographers, you may not realize you didn't capture what you wanted until you're home and see the shot on your computer.

If you shoot in RAW mode, you can use the Converter to help you fake digital blending, sort of. It's not as good as planning ahead, but you can often salvage another stop or two of detail. Just follow these steps:

1. Run your photo through the Converter twice, one time exposing for the highlights and once for the shadows.

2. Drag one image onto the other—the way you would if you were creating a new layer (page 129). Put the image with the largest area that you want to use on top, so you'll have less to change.

3. Use the Eraser tool (page 289) to rub out the bad spots on the top photo, revealing those areas in the bottom layer. The illustration shows this process in action: the blown-out sky in the top image is being erased to reveal the blue sky in the bottom layer. This is very similar to the procedure for creating spot color on page 236.

When you're done, you can merge the layers if you want.

If you'd like to try your hand at the real thing, you'll find an excellent tutorial at The Luminous Landscape at *http://luminous-landscape.com/tutorials/digital-blending.shtml.* Every digital photographer should bookmark this site. You're sure to find a ton of valuable information on this site, including lots of fine tutorials.

Choosing bit depth: 8 or 16 bits?

Once you've got your photo looking good, you have one more important choice to make: do you want to open it as an 8-bit or a 16-bit file? *Bit depth* refers to the number of pieces of color data, or *bits,* that each pixel in your image can hold. A single pixel of an 8-bit image can have 24 bits of information in it, 8 for each of the three color channels. A 16-bit image holds far more color information than an 8-bit photo. How much more? An 8-bit image can hold up to 16 million colors, while a 16-bit image can hold up to 281 *trillion* colors.

Most digital cameras produce RAW files with 10 or 12 bits per channel, although a few can shoot 16-bit files. You'd think it makes perfect sense to save your digital files at the largest possible bit depth, but the fact is you'll find quite a few restrictions for how much you can do to a 16-bit file in Elements. You can open it, make corrections, and save it, but that's about all. You can't work with layers or apply the more artistic filters, or use most of the Auto commands on a 16-bit file.

> **NOTE**   Your scanner may say it handles 24-bit color, but this is actually the same as what Elements calls 8-bit. Elements goes by the number of bits per color channel, whereas some scanner manufacturers try to impress you by giving you the total for all three channels (8 x 3 = 24). When you see very high bit numbers—assuming you aren't a commercial printer—you can usually get the Elements equivalent number by dividing by three.

Once you've decided between 8- and 16-bit color, just make your selection in the Depth drop-down menu (in the lower-left corner of the RAW Converter window). The RAW bit-depth setting is sticky, so if you change it, all your images open in that color depth until you change it again. If you ever forget what bit depth you've chosen, your image's title bar will tell you, as shown in Figure 8-6.

Figure 8-6:
You can always tell an image's bit depth by looking in the title bar of any image window. This image is 16-bit.

> **NOTE**   If you do decide to create a 16-bit image and you become frustrated by your lack of editing choices, you can convert your image to 8-bit by choosing Image → Mode → Convert to 8 bits. You can't convert an 8-bit image to 16-bit.

If you want to take advantage of any 16-bit files you may have, you might want to use either Save As or the Organizer's version set option (see page 20) for the copy you plan to convert to 8 bit. That way you'll still have the 16-bit file for future reference. Incidentally, your Save options are different for the two bit depths. JPEG, for instance, is available only for 8-bit files. If you wonder why you only have choices like JPEG 2000 when you save a file, then you've got yourself a 16-bit file.

Photo Filter

The Photo Filter command gives you a host of nifty new photo filters that are the digital equivalent of the many-colored lens-mounted filters used in traditional film photography. You can use them to correct problems with your image's white balance, as well as for a bunch of other fixes, from the seriously photographical to the downright silly. For example, you can correct a bad skin tone or dig out an old photo of your fifth-grade nemesis and make him green, literally. Figure 8-7 shows one Photo Filter in action.

Elements comes with about a dozen Photo Filters, but for most people, the important ones are the top four: two warming filters and two cooling filters. You use these to get rid of the color casts that come from a poor white balance (page 195).

Figure 8-7:
You can use the Photo Filter to correct the color casts you get from artificial lighting.

Left: This photo had a strong bluish tinge from nearby fluorescent lighting.

Right: The Warming Filter (85) took care of it. Use Cooling Filter (80) or Cooling Filter (82) to counteract the orange cast from tungsten lighting.

The filters are an improvement over the Color Cast eyedropper, because you can control the strength with which you apply them (using the Density slider, explained later). And you can also apply them as Adjustment layers (page 145), so you can tweak them later on. To apply a Photo Filter:

1. **Open the Photo Filter dialog box.**

   Go to Layer → New Adjustment Layer → Photo Filter, or to Filter → Adjustments → Photo Filter. The Photo Filter dialog box appears.

2. **Choose a filter from the pull-down list or click the Color radio button.**

   You get two choices. The pull-down list gives you a choice of filters in preset colors. If you want to choose your own custom color, click the Color button instead.

3. **If you chose the Color button, click the color square in the dialog box to bring up the Color Picker and choose the shade you want.**

You can also sample a color from your image. The cursor turns to an eyedropper when you move it from the dialog box into your photo. Just click the color you want for your filter, and that color appears in the color square in the dialog box.

4. **Move the Density slider to adjust the color.**

Moving the Density slider to the right increases the filter's effect; moving it to the left decreases it. If you leave Preserve Luminosity turned on, the filter won't darken your image. Turn Preserve Luminosity off and your photo gets darker when you apply the filter.

5. **Click OK.**

Processing Multiple Files

The formerly humble Batch Processor has gotten a makeover in Elements 3 with several additions to make it more useful for prolific photographers. It's also got a new name: Process Multiple Files. You can do a lot of very useful things with the new version, too, like adding copyright information or captions to multiple files or even using some of the Quick Fix auto commands, as well as renaming files and changing their formats.

To call up the batch processing window, go to File → Process Multiple Files in the Editor (Mac or Windows) or the Windows File Browser. In the Mac File Browser, go to Automate → Process Multiple Files. You see yet another of the headache-inducing giant Elements dialog boxes, but this one is actually pretty easy to understand. If you look closely, you see that the dialog box is divided into sections, each with a different specialty (see Figure 8-8).

> **TIP**   "Process *Multiple* Files" is the name of the command, but you can run it on just one photo
> if you want. Just open your photo, go to File → Process Multiple Files, and choose "Opened Files"
> as your source. You can even opt to save the new version to the desktop without overwriting your
> original.

The following sections cover each main section of the Process Multiple Files dialog box. You have to use the first section (which tells Elements which files you want to process), but you'll probably only want to make use of one or two of the other sections at any one time. (Of course, you can use them all, as shown in Figure 8-8.)

Choose Your Files

In the first section of the dialog box, in the upper-left corner, you identify the files you want to convert and then tell Elements where to put them once it's processed them. You have several options here: you can choose your currently open files, the

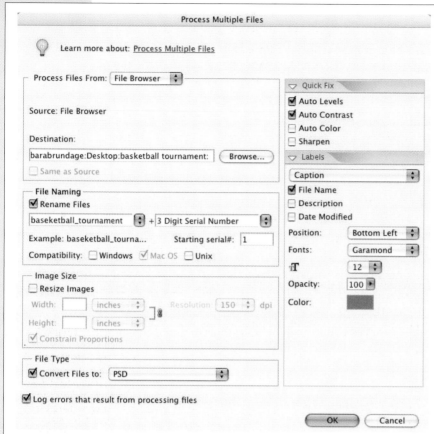

Figure 8-8:
Process Multiple Files could also be called "Run Multiple Processes" in Elements 3 because you can make so many changes at once. This dialog box is set up to apply the following changes: rename every file (from PICT8983 to basketball_ tournament001, for instance), change them to the .psd format, apply Auto Levels and Auto Contrast, and add the file name as a caption. All that happens by clicking the OK button.

contents of a folder, or the files at the current level of the File Browser (not the Photo Browser). You can also choose "Import," which brings up the same options you see when you go to File → Import, like your camera or scanner. Using this option, you can choose to convert your files as you bring them into Elements.

If you want to include files scattered around at different locations on your hard drive, you can speed things up by opening the files or gathering them into one folder. If you have a couple of folders' worth of photos to convert, you can save time by putting them all into one folder and using the "include all subfolders" option explained later. Then all the files get converted at once.

To get started, you first need to choose your files and tell Elements where to put the converted files. Here's how:

1. **Choose the files you want to convert.**

   Use the "Process Files From" pull-down menu to tell Elements which kind of files you want: open files, folder, files imports from your camera or scanner, or the files currently chosen in the File Browser.

2. **If you chose "Folder," tell Elements which folder you want.**

Click the Browse button and, in the dialog box that appears, choose the folder you want. Files for processing must be in a folder if they aren't already open, unless you chose the Browser option (page 39). In the Browser, Elements processes any files you've selected, or all the files at the current folder level, if you haven't made a selection.

If you have folders within a folder and you want to change the files in them all, turn on the "Include All Subfolders" checkbox. Otherwise, Elements changes only the files at the top level of the folder.

3. **Pick a destination.**

This is where the files will end up once they've been processed. Most of the time, you'll want a new folder for this, so click Browse, and then click New Folder in the window that opens. You can also choose an existing folder in the Browse window if you prefer. You need to be careful about choosing "Same as Source," as Figure 8-9 explains.

Figure 8-9:
If you turn on the "Same as Source" checkbox, Elements warns that it's going to replace your originals with the new versions. That's a timesaver, but it's dangerous, too. If something goes wrong, your originals might be messed up, so don't choose this unless you have a back-up copy someplace else.

File Renaming

Being able to rename a group of files all in one fell swoop is a very cool feature, but it does have a few limitations. Yes, you can rename your files here, but if you think that means you can give each photo a name like "Keisha and Gram at the Park," followed by "Fred's New Newt" for the next photo, you're going to be disappointed. (Unless of course your files already have those names and you just want to change the capitalization.)

To rename your files, turn on the Rename Files option in the dialog box. You then see two active text boxes with pull-down menus next to them. You can enter any text you like, and it will appear on every photo in the group, or you can choose any of the many options in the menus. (Both menus are the same.)

The menus offer you a choice of the document name (in three different capitalization formats), serial numbers, serial letters, dates, extensions, or nothing at all. Figure 8-10 shows the many choices you get.

> **NOTE** If you choose to add serial numbers, there's a box where you can designate the starting number. This defaults to 1. That's actually going to show up as 001, because the leading zeros are needed for your computer to recognize the file order. Ten would be 010, one hundred would be 100, and so on.

So if you type "tongue_piercing_day" in the text box and choose the 3-digit serial number, your photos will be named *tongue_piercing_day001.jpg, tongue_piercing_day002.jpg*, and so on.

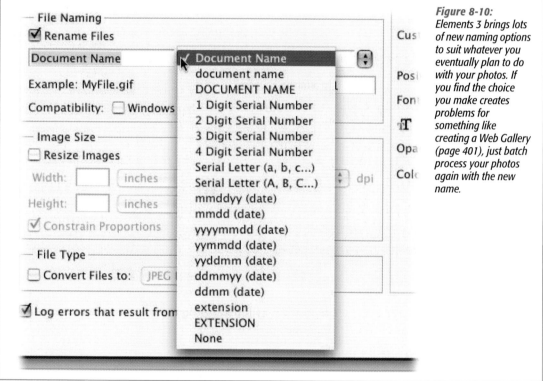

Figure 8-10:
Elements 3 brings lots of new naming options to suit whatever you eventually plan to do with your photos. If you find the choice you make creates problems for something like creating a Web Gallery (page 401), just batch process your photos again with the new name.

You also get to designate which operating systems' naming conventions Elements should respect when assigning the new names, as shown in Figure 8-11. If you send files to people or servers using other operating systems, you know how important this can be.

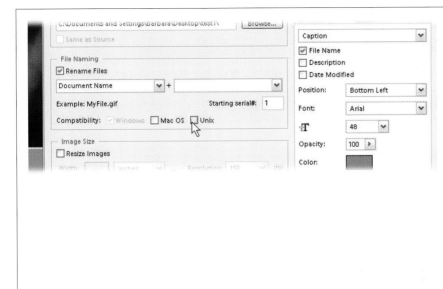

Figure 8-11:
The Compatibility checkboxes tell Elements to watch out for any characters that would violate the naming conventions of the operating systems you check. This is very handy if, say, your Web site is hosted on a Unix server and you want to be sure your file names won't create a problem for it. You can choose to be compatible with either or neither of the other operating systems, but your own operating system is always checked.

TIP   If all you want to do to your files is rename them, you don't have to deal with the entire Process Multiple Files window. The File Browser also offers an option to Rename Multiple Files. It's in the File menu in Windows or the Automate menu for Macs. The window is a stripped-down version of Process Multiple Files. Everything works the same way it does in the larger dialog box, so your naming options are exactly the same in both places.

Changing Image Size and File Type

The Image Size and File Type sections let you resize your photos and change your images' file formats. The Image Size settings work best when you're trying to reduce file sizes (for example, with a folder of images that you've converted for Web use but found are still too big).

NOTE   Before you make any big changes to a group of files, it's important that you understand the concept of how changes in an image's resolution and file size affect its appearance. See page 64 for a refresher.

To apply image size changes, turn on the Resize Images checkbox and then adjust the Width, Height, and Resolution settings, all of which work the same way as those described on page 64.

In the File Type section, you can convert files from one format to another. This is probably the most popular batching activity. If your camera creates JPEGs and you want TIFFs for editing work, you can change an entire folder at once. From the pull-down menu, just select the file type you want to create.

The final setting in the left half of the window is the checkbox for logging errors in processing your files. It's a good idea to turn this checkbox on, as explained in Figure 8-12.

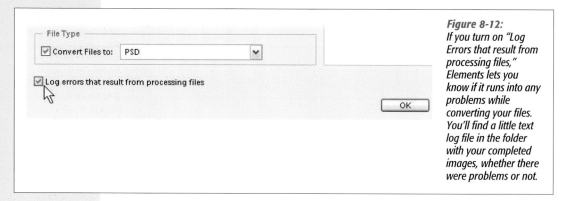

Figure 8-12:
If you turn on "Log Errors that result from processing files," Elements lets you know if it runs into any problems while converting your files. You'll find a little text log file in the folder with your completed images, whether there were problems or not.

Applying Quick Fix Commands

In the upper-right corner of Process Multiple Files, you'll find some of the same Quick Fix commands you have in the regular Quick Fix window. If you consistently get good results with the Auto commands there, you can run them on a whole folder at once here.

You can run Auto Levels, Auto Contrast, Auto Color, Auto Sharpen, or any combination of those commands that you like on all the files in your folder. (Unfortunately, you can't batch run the Auto Smart Fix command.) If you don't see the list, click the flippy triangle next to Quick Fix to expand it. If you need a refresher on what each one does, see Chapter 4.

Attaching Labels

The tools in the Labels section let you add captions and copyright notices, which Elements calls *watermarks,* to your images (see Figure 8-13). Watermarks and captions get imprinted right onto the photo itself. The procedure is the same for either, only the content differs. A watermark contains any text you choose, while a caption is limited to your choices from a group of checkboxes.

First, you need to choose whether you want a watermark or a caption (choose from the pull-down menu right below the Label tab). You can't do both at once, so if you want both, add one and then run Process Multiple Files again on the resulting images to add the other.

Watermarks

If you want to create a watermark, you first need to enter some text in the Custom Text box. You can enter any text you want. Then choose the position and appearance of your text as explained later.

Figure 8-13:
Adobe calls the "Happy Trails" custom text in this image a watermark. Elements is very flexible about the fonts and sizes you can choose for a watermark or caption, but you don't get much say in where it goes on your photo if you use Process Multiple Files. For maximum flexibility, use the Text tool as explained in Chapter 10, but you can't batch process using that method.

Text you enter here gets applied to every photo in the batch, so this is a great way to add copyright or contact info that you want on every photo. If you want different text on each photo, check out the Description option for captions, as shown in Figure 8-14.

Figure 8-14:
You just can't beat Process Multiple Files for adding quick copyright information to your photo, although there are other methods that give a more sophisticated look, as described in the tip at the end of this chapter (page 210).

TIP If you want to include the copyright symbol (©), hold Alt while typing 0169 (on the number pad, not the top row of the keyboard). The Mac equivalent is Option-G.

Adding captions

For a caption, you can choose any of the following, separately or in combination:

- **File Name.** You can choose to show the file's name as the caption. If you choose to run the rename option at the same time, you get the new name you're assigning.

- **Description.** Turn this checkbox on to use any text you have entered in the Description section of the File Info dialog box (File → File Info) as your caption. This is your most flexible option for entering text, and the only way to batch different caption text for each photo. Just enter the text for each photo in File → File Info → Description.

- **Date Modified.** This is the date your file was last changed. In practice, that usually means today's date, because you're modifying your file by running Process Multiple Files on it.

Once you've decided what you want your caption to say, you need to make some choices about its position and size. These choices are the same whether you're adding a watermark or a caption, and if you switch from one to the other, your previous choices will appear.

- **Position.** This tells Elements where to put your caption. Your options are Bottom Left, Bottom Right, or Centered. Centered doesn't mean bottom center, incidentally. It puts the text smack in the middle of your image.

- **Font.** From the pull-down menu, choose any font on your system. Chapter 13 has much more information about fonts.

- **Size.** This setting determines how big your type will be. Click the menu next to the two little Ts to choose from several preset sizes, up to 72 point.

- **Opacity.** Use this to adjust how solidly your text prints. Choose 100% for maximum readability or move the slider to the left for watermark type that lets you see the image underneath it.

- **Color.** Use this setting to choose your text color. Click the box to bring up the color picker and make your choice.

TIP If you want to use a logo as a watermark, you can't use the Process Multiple Files tool. But there is a way to apply a logo to a bunch of images. Here's how: Create your logo on a new layer in one of the images. Adjust the opacity with the slider in the Layers palette until you like the results. Save the file. Now you can drag that layer from the Layers palette onto each photo where you need it. You can also do this with Adjustment layers (page 145) to give yourself a sort of batch processing capability for applying the same adjustments to multiple files.

Retouching 102: Fine-Tuning Your Images

Basic edits like exposure fixes and sharpening are fine if all you want to make are simple adjustments. But Elements also gives you the tools to make sophisticated changes that aren't hard to apply, and can make the difference between a ho-hum photo and a fabulous one. This chapter introduces you to some advanced editing maneuvers that will greatly help you either rescue damaged photos or give good ones that little extra zing.

The first part of the chapter shows you how to get rid of blemishes—not only those that affect skin, but also dust, scratches, stains, and other photographic imperfections. There's also information later on in this chapter about some of the more sophisticated digital darkroom techniques you can use to fine-tune your images, like making your colors more vivid or removing all the color from your photo to make it black and white. You'll also learn how to colorize a black and white photo and how to add a pattern to an image.

Fixing Blemishes

It's an imperfect world, but in your photos, it doesn't have to be. Elements gives you some amazing tools for fixing the flaws in your subjects. You can erase crows' feet and blemishes, eliminate power lines in an otherwise perfect view, or even hide objects you wish weren't in your photo. Not only that, but these same tools are great for fixing problems like tears, folds, and stains. With a little effort, you can bring back photos that seem beyond help. Figure 9-1 shows an example of the kind of restoration you can accomplish with a little persistence and Elements 3.

Figure 9-1:
You can do some amazing repair work with Elements if you have the patience—even replacing the almost obliterated face of the grandmother in this old family portrait. It took a heap of cloning and healing to get even this close, but if you keep at it, you can do the kind of work that would have required professional help before Elements.

Elements gives you three main tools for this kind of work:

- **The Spot Healing brush** is the easiest way to repair your photo. Just drag over the area you want to fix. Elements searches the surrounding area and blends that information into the bad spot, making it indistinguishable from the background. It usually works best on small areas, for the reasons explained later.

- **The Healing brush** works similarly to the Spot Healing brush, only you tell the Healing brush the part of your photo to use as a source for the material you want to blend in. This makes it more flexible than the Spot Healing brush, and better suited to large areas, because you don't have to worry about inadvertently dragging in contrasting details that are close to the area you're fixing.

- **The Clone Stamp** offers another way to make repairs. It works like the Healing brush in that you sample a good area and apply it to the area you want to fix. Instead of blending the repair in, the Clone Stamp merely covers the bad area with the replacement. The Clone Stamp is best for situations when you want to completely hide the underlying area, as opposed to letting any of what's already there blend into your repair (which is how things works with the Healing brushes). The Clone Stamp is also your best option when you want to create a realistic copy of detail that's elsewhere in your photo. You might clone over some leaves to fill in a bare branch, or replace a knothole in a fence board with good wood, for instance.

All three tools work similarly: you just drag each tool over the area you want to change. It's as simple as using a brush. In fact, each of these tools requires you to choose a brush, just like the ones you'll learn about in Chapter 11. But brush selection is pretty straightforward; you'll learn in this chapter everything you need to make basic brush choices.

The Spot Healing Brush: Fixing Small Areas

The Spot Healing brush excels at blending any blemish in your photo into the surrounding area. You simply paint over the area you want to repair, and the Spot Healing brush automatically searches the information in the surrounding areas and blends that into the area you're brushing. You don't have to tell the brush where to look for a source. Figure 9-2 shows what a great job the Spot Healing brush can do to make an object look like it was perfect when it was photographed.

Figure 9-2:
The trick to using the Spot Healing Brush is to work in very tiny areas. If you choose too large a brush or drag over too large an area, you're more likely to pick up undesired shades and details from the surrounding area.

Top: The radish in the bottom row has a large gouge in it.

Bottom: By dragging with a brush barely the width of the scar, you can make a truly invisible fix.

The Spot Healing brush's ability to borrow information from surrounding areas is great, but it is also a drawback. The larger the area you drag the brush over, the wider Elements searches for replacement material. So if there's contrasting material too close to the area you're trying to fix, it can unintentionally get pulled into the repair. For instance, if you're trying to fix a spot on an eyelid, you may wind up with some of the color from the eye itself mixed in with your repair.

You get best results from this brush when you choose a brush size that just barely covers the spot you're trying to fix. If you need to drag to fix an oblong area, use a brush the minimum width that covers the flaw. The Spot Healing brush also works much better when there's a large surrounding area that looks the way you want your repaired spot to look.

The Spot Healing Brush has only three settings in the Options bar. From left to right, they are:

- **Brush.** You can use the pull-down menu to choose a different brush style if you prefer (see Chapter 11 for lots more about brushes), but generally, you're best off sticking to the standard brush that Elements starts out with and just changing the size, if necessary.

- **Size.** Use this slider to set the brush size.

- **Proximity.** In this menu, you adjust how the brush works. Proximity tells the Spot Healing brush to search the surrounding area for replacement pixels. Create Texture tells it to blend only from the area you drag it over. Generally speaking, if Proximity doesn't work well, you'll get better results by switching to the regular Healing brush than by choosing Create Texture.

You won't believe how easy it is to fix problem areas with the Spot Healing brush. All you do is:

1. **Activate the Spot Healing brush.**

   Press J and choose the Spot Healing brush in the Options bar, or click the Healing brush icon (the band-aid) in the Toolbox, and choose the Spot Healing brush from the pop-out menu.

2. **Choose a brush size just barely bigger than the flaw.**

   You can do this from the Options bar Size slider or by pressing] (the close bracket key) for a larger brush or [(open bracket key) for a smaller brush.

3. **Click the bad spot.**

   If the brush doesn't quite cover the flaw, drag over the area.

4. **When you release the mouse button, Elements repairs the blemish.**

   You won't see any change to your image while you drag, only after you let go.

Sometimes you get great results with the Spot Healing brush on a larger area if it's surrounded by a large field of good material that's similar in tone to the spot you're trying to fix. Most of the time, though, you're better off with the regular Healing brush for large areas, as well as for flaws whose replacement material isn't right next to the bad spot.

WORKAROUND WORKSHOP

Dust and Scratches

Scratched, dusty prints can create giant headaches when you scan them. As suggested in Chapter 2, cleaning your scanner's glass helps, but lots of photos come with plenty of dust marks already in the print, or in the file itself if the lens of your digital camera was dusty.

A similar problem is caused by *artifacts*, blobbish areas of color caused by JPEG compression. If you take a close look at the sky in a JPEG photo, for instance, you may see that instead of a smooth swathe of blue, you see lots of little distinct clumps of each shade of blue.

The Healing brushes are usually your best first line of defense for fixing these problems, but if the specks are very widespread, Elements offers a couple other options you might want to try.

The first is the Despeckle filter (Filter → Noise → Despeckle), which is sometimes effective for JPEG artifacts. If that doesn't get everything, you can undo it and try the Dust and Scratches filter (Filter → Noise → Dust and Scratches), or the Median Filter (Filter → Noise → Median). The Radius setting for these last two filters tells Elements how far to search for dissimilar pixels for its calculations. Keep that number as low as possible. The downside to the filters in this group is that they smooth things out in a way that can make your image look blurred. Generally, Despeckle is the filter that's least destructive to your image's focus.

The Healing Brush: Fixing Larger Areas

The Healing brush lets you fix much larger areas than you can usually manage with the Spot Healing brush. The main difference between the two tools is that with the regular Healing brush, you choose the area that's going to be blended into the repair. The blending makes your repair look very natural. Figure 9-3 shows what great results you can get with this tool.

The repair material doesn't have to be nearby; in fact, you can sample from a totally different photo if you like. To sample material from another photo, just get both photos arranged on the desktop so that you can easily move the cursor from one to the other.

The basic procedure for using the Healing brush is similar to that for the Spot Healing brush: you drag over the flaw you want to fix. The difference is that with the Healing brush, you first Alt+click (Option-click) where you want Elements to look for replacement pixels.

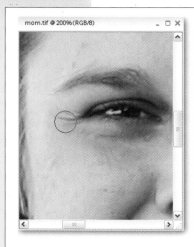 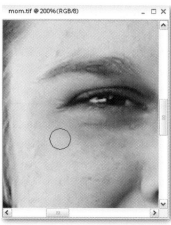

Figure 9-3:
The Healing brush is especially remarkable because it also blends the textures of the areas where you use it.

Left: This photo shows the crows' feet at the corner of the woman's eye.

Right: The Healing Brush eliminates them without creating a phony, airbrushed effect.

The Healing brush offers you several choices in the Options bar:

- **Brush.** Click the brush thumbnail to bring up the Brush Dynamics palette, explained on page 275. This lets you customize the size, shape, and hardness of your brush. But generally, the standard brush works well, so you don't have to change things other than the size here if you don't want to.

- **Mode.** You can choose some blend modes (see page 137) here, but most of the time, you want to choose between the top two options: Normal and Replace. Normal is usually your best choice. Sometimes, though, your replacement pixels may make the area you work on show a visibly different texture than the surrounding area. In that case, choose Replace, which preserves the grain of your photo.

- **Source.** You can choose to sample an area to use as a replacement or you can blend in a pattern. Using the Healing brush with patterns is explained in the upcoming section "Applying Patterns."

- **Pattern thumbnails.** If you chose to use a pattern, this box becomes active. Click it to select the pattern you want to use.

- **Aligned.** If you turn on the Aligned checkbox, Elements keeps sampling new material in your source as you use the tool. The sampling follows the direction of your brush. Even if you let go of the mouse button, Elements continues to sample new material as you continue brushing. If you leave Aligned turned off, all the material comes from the area where you first defined your source point.

  Generally, for both the Healing brush and the Clone Stamp, it's easier to leave Aligned turned off. You can still change your source point by Alt+clicking (Option-clicking) another spot, but you often get better results if you make the decision about when to move on to another location rather than letting Elements decide.

- **Use All Layers.** If you turn this on, Elements samples from all the visible layers (page 135) in the area where you set your source point. Turn it off and Elements samples only the active layer.

It's almost as simple to use the Healing brush as it is to use the Spot Healing brush.

1. **Activate the Healing brush.**

   Press J and choose it from the Options bar, or click the Healing brush icon (the band-aid) in the Toolbox and choose it from the pop-out menu.

2. **Find a good spot you want to sample to use in the repair and Alt+click (Option-click) it.**

   When you click the good spot, your cursor temporarily turns into a circle with cross-hairs in it to indicate that this is the point where Elements will retrieve your repair material from. (If you want to use a source point in a different photo, both the source photo and the one you're repairing must be in the same color mode. (See page 29 for more about color modes.)

3. **Drag over the area you want to repair.**

   You can see where Elements is sampling the repair material from: you'll see a cross marking the sampling point.

4. **When you release the mouse, Elements blends the sampled area into the problem area.**

   Often you don't know how effective you were until Elements is through working its magic, because it takes a few seconds for Elements to finish its calculations and blend in the repair. If you don't like what Elements did, press Ctrl+Z (⌘-Z) to undo and try again.

You can choose to heal on a separate layer. The advantage to doing this is that if you find the end result is a little too much—your granny suddenly looks like a Stepford wife—you can back things off a bit by reducing the opacity of the healed layer to let the original show through. This is a good plan when using the Clone tool, too. Just press Ctrl+Shift+N (⌘-Shift-N) to create a new layer and then turn on "Use all Layers" in the Options bar.

The Clone Stamp

The Clone Stamp is like the Healing brush in some ways. You add material from a source point that you select. The main difference with the Clone Stamp is that it doesn't blend in when the new material is applied. Instead, the Clone Stamp works by covering up the underlying area completely. This makes the Clone Stamp your tool of choice when you don't want to leave any visible trace of what you're repairing. Figure 9-4 shows an example of when cloning is a better choice than healing.

Figure 9-4:
Here's an example of when you'd choose cloning over healing.

Top: This photo has a very distracting Speed Limit sign just above the horse's collar.

Middle: In this photo, the Healing brush didn't do enough to cover up the sign.

Bottom: The Clone Stamp works much better.

The choices you make in the Options bar for the Clone Stamp are very important in getting the best results possible.

- **Brush.** You can use the pull-down menu to select a different brush style (see Chapter 11 for more about brushes), but the standard brush style usually works pretty well. If the soft edges of your cloned areas bother you, you may be tempted to switch to a harder brush. But that usually makes your photo look like you strewed confetti on it, because hard edges don't blend well with what's already in your photo.

- **Size.** Choose a brush that is just big enough to get your sample without picking up a lot of other details that you don't want in your repair. While it may be tempting to clone huge chunks at once to get it done faster, most of the time, you'll do better to use the smallest brush that gets the sample you want.

- **Mode.** You can choose any blend mode (see page 137) for cloning, but Normal is usually your best bet. Other modes can create interesting special effects.

- **Opacity.** Elements automatically uses 100 percent opacity for cloning, but you can reduce this to let some details from your original show through. You have more control if you follow the procedure for cloning on another layer (outlined later) than you do if you adjust your opacity here.

- **Aligned.** This setting works exactly the way it does for the Healing brush (described earlier). Turn it on and Elements keeps sampling at the same distance from your cursor as you clone. Turn it off and you keep putting down the same source material. Figure 9-5 shows an example of when you'd turn on Aligned.

- **Use All Layers.** When you turn this on, Elements samples from all the visible layers in the area where you set your source point. Turn it off and Elements samples only the active layer.

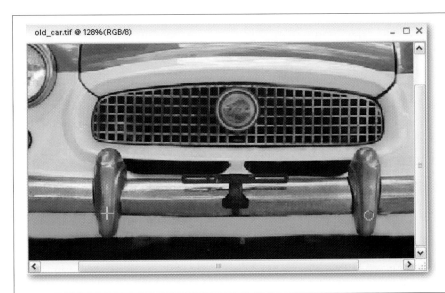

Figure 9-5:
To restore the right upright bumper (which had previously been damaged) the Clone Stamp's align option was used here to pull detail from the left bumper. Leaving the Clone Stamp aligned lets you choose just the details you want for your restoration work, which is especially helpful if the area you're working on is oddly shaped.

Repairing Tears and Stains

With Elements, you can do a great deal to bring damaged old photos back to life. The Healing brush and the Clone Stamp are major players when it comes to restoration work. It can be fiddly work and take some persistence, but you can achieve wonders if you have the patience.

If your photo is missing areas and you're lucky enough to have useable replacement sections elsewhere in your photo, you can use the Move tool to copy the good bits into the problem area. First select the part you want to copy. Then press M to activate the Move tool and Alt+drag (Option-drag) the good piece where you want it. (There's more about the Move tool in Chapter 5.)

You can use the Rotate commands to flip your selection if you need a mirror image. For example, if the left leg of a chair is fine but the right one is missing, try selecting and Alt+dragging (Option-dragging) the left leg with the Move tool. When it's where you want it, go to Image → Rotate → Flip Selection Horizontal to turn the copied left leg into a new right leg.

If you don't need to rotate an object, sometimes you may be able to just increase the Clone Stamp brush size and clone your object where you need a duplicate. Cloning works well only when your background is the same for both areas.

The Clone Stamp shares its space in the Toolbox with the Pattern Stamp, which is explained later. (You can tell which is which because the Pattern Stamp icon has a little checkerboard on it.) Using the Clone Stamp is very much like using the Healing brush. Only the result is different.

1. **Activate the Clone Stamp.**

   Press S and choose it in the Options bar, or click its icon (the rubber stamp) in the Toolbox and choose it from the pop-out menu.

2. **Find the spot in your photo that you want to repair.**

   You may need to zoom way, way in to be able to get a good enough look at what you're doing. See page 60 for how to adjust the view.

3. **Find a good spot to sample as a replacement for the bad area.**

   You want an area that has the same tone as the area you're fixing. The Clone Stamp doesn't do any blending the way the Healing brush does, so tone differences are pretty obvious.

4. **Alt+click (Option-click) the spot you want to clone from.**

   When you click, your cursor turns to a circle with crosshairs in it, indicating that the point it's over is your source point for the repair. Once you're actually working with the Clone Stamp, you see a cross marking the sampling point (instead of the circle and crosshairs you see when you're choosing the source point).

5. **Click the spot you want to cover.**

   Elements puts whatever you just selected down on top of your image, concealing the original. You can drag with the Clone Stamp, but it almost always goes
   into Aligned mode (described earlier) when you do, so often it's preferable to
   use multiple clicks instead for areas that are larger than your sample.

6. **Continue until you've covered the area.**

   With the Clone Stamp, unlike the Healing brush, what you see as you click is
   what you get. Elements doesn't do any further blending or smoothing.

The Clone Stamp is a very powerful tool, but it can be crotchety, too. See the box
"Keeping the Clone Stamp Under Control" for some suggestions on how to make
it behave.

You can clone on a separate layer, just the way you would with the Healing tool.
This lets you adjust the opacity of your repair afterwards. Press Ctrl+Shift+N (⌘-
Shift-N) to create a new layer and then turn on "Use all Layers" in the Options bar.
It's almost always a good idea to clone on a separate layer when you can do so,
since cloning is so much more opaque than healing.

Applying Patterns

Besides applying solid colors to your images, Elements lets you add patterns to
your pictures. You get quite a few patterns with Elements when you buy it, and
you can also download more patterns from online sources (see Chapter 17) or create your own. You can use patterns to add interesting designs to your image, or to
give a more realistic texture to certain repairs.

You can use either the Healing brush or the Pattern Stamp to apply patterns. The
Healing brush has a pattern option in the Options bar. The Pattern Stamp shares
the toolbox slot with the Clone Stamp, and it works very much like the Clone
Stamp, but it puts down a preselected pattern instead of a sampled area.

> **TIP**   There are actually lots of ways to use patterns in Elements, including creating a Fill layer
> that's entirely covered with the pattern of your choice. Fill layers are covered on page 146.

The tool you choose to apply your pattern makes a big difference, as you can see
from Figure 9-6. The next two sections explain how to use both tools.

The Healing Brush

The Healing brush in Pattern mode is great for things like improving the texture of
someone's skin by applying just the skin texture from another photo.

Using patterns with the Healing brush is just as easy and works the same way as
using the brush in normal healing mode: you just drag across the area you want to
fix. The only difference is that you don't have to choose a sampling point, since the

TROUBLESHOOTING MOMENT

Keeping the Clone Stamp Under Control

The clone tool is a great resource, but it definitely has a mind of its own sometimes.

If you suddenly see spots of a different shade appearing as you clone, take a look in the Options bar at the Aligned box. It has a tendency to insist on staying checked and to turn itself back on when you aren't paying attention.

Sometimes the Clone Stamp just won't reset itself when you try to select a new sampling point. If you think about it, it's less surprising that this happens occasionally than that such an amazing tool works as well it does most of the time.

Try clicking the Clone Stamp's icon on the left side of the Options bar and choosing the Reset option, as shown in the illustration. If that doesn't do it, restart the Editor (restart Elements) and delete Elements' preferences file. Here's how: Hold down Ctrl+Alt+Shift (⌘-Option-Shift) immediately after launching Elements. You get a dialog box asking if you want to delete the Elements settings. Say yes. This returns all your Elements settings to where they were the first time you launched the program. (Doing this cures about 90 percent of the problems you may run into in Elements.)

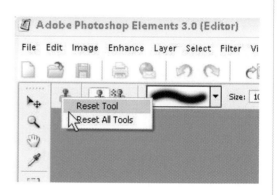

pattern is your source point. When you drag, the pattern you selected blends into your photo.

Click the Pattern button in the Options bar and then choose a pattern from the palette by clicking the pattern thumbnail. There are more pattern libraries available if you click the More button on the Pattern palette, or you can create your own patterns. Figure 9-7 explains how to create custom patterns for use with either the Healing brush or the Pattern Stamp.

> **TIP** You can create some very interesting effects by changing the blend mode (page 137) when using patterns.

The Pattern Stamp

The Pattern Stamp is just like the Clone Stamp, only instead of copying sampled areas, it puts down a predefined pattern that you select from the Pattern palette. The Pattern Stamp is useful when you want to apply a pattern to your image without mixing it in with what's already there. For instance, if you want to see what

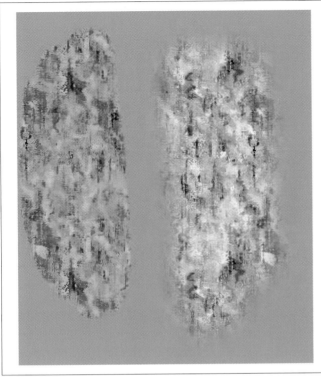

Figure 9-6:
The same pattern applied with the Healing brush (left) and the Pattern Stamp (right.) The Healing brush blends the pattern into the underlying color (and texture, when there is any), while the Pattern Stamp just plunks down the pattern as it appears in the pop-out palette.

your patio would look like if it were a garden instead, you could use the Pattern stamp to paint a lawn and a flower border on a photo of your patio.

To get started, click the pattern thumbnail in the Options bar to open the Pattern palette so you can choose a pattern. Other options for this brush, like the size, hardness, and so on, are the same as for the Clone Stamp. The one difference is the Impressionist option demonstrated in Figure 9-8.

Once you've selected a pattern, just drag in your photo where you want the pattern to appear.

Making Your Colors More Vibrant

Do you drool over the luscious photos in travel magazines, the ones that make it look like the world is full of destinations so vivid they make your regular life seem pretty drab in comparison? What is it about those photos that makes things look so dramatic?

A lot of the time the answer is the *saturation*, or the intensity of the colors. Super-saturated color makes for darned appealing landscape and object photos, regardless of how the real thing may rate on the vividness scale.

Figure 9-7:
You can create your own patterns very easily. Just open an image and make a rectangular selection. Then go to Edit → Define Pattern from Selection. You'll get a pop-up asking you to name the new pattern, and your pattern appears at the bottom of the current pattern palette.

To rename or delete a pattern, just right-click (Control-click) it in the Pattern palette and choose what you want to do. You can download hundreds of different patterns from various online sources. See page 421.

There is a variety of ways to adjust the saturation of your photos. Some cameras offer you settings to help control it. Regardless of how much control you have over saturation in the camera, Elements lets you make all kinds of adjustments to your color saturation. You can manipulate saturation to achieve many different effects. For example, by increasing or decreasing the saturation in a photo, you can shift the perceived focal point, change the mood of the picture, or just make your photo more eye-catching in general.

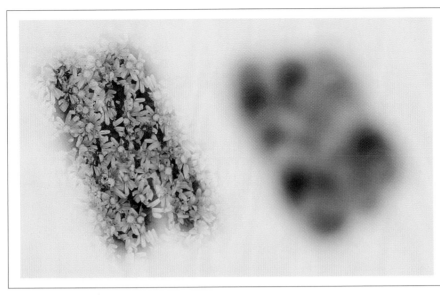

*Figure 9-8:
If you turn on
Impressionist in the
Options bar, your
pattern will be blurred,
giving an effect
vaguely like an
Impresionist painting.
Here, you can see a
pattern put down with
the regular Pattern
Stamp (left) and the
Impressionist stamp
(right).*

It's not necessary to use the entire photo when making a change to the saturation. By increasing the saturation of your subject and decreasing the saturation in the rest of the photo, you can call attention where you want it, even in a crowded picture. Figure 9-9 shows a somewhat exaggerated use of this technique.

It's quite easy to change saturation. You can use either the Hue/Saturation dialog box or the Sponge tool, both of which are explained in the next section. For big areas, or when you want a lot of control, use Hue/Saturation. If you just want to quickly paint a different saturation level (either more or less saturation) on a small spot in your photo, the Sponge tool is faster.

> **NOTE** Many consumer-grade digital cameras are set to crank the saturation of your JPEG photos into the stratosphere. That's great if you love all the color. If you prefer not to live in a Technicolor universe, you may wish to desaturate your photos in Elements to remove some of the excess color.

Using the Hue/Saturation Dialog Box

Hue/Saturation is one of the most popular commands in Elements. If you aren't satisfied with the results of a simple Levels adjustment, you may want to work on the hue or saturation as the next step toward getting really eye-catching color.

Hue simply means the color of your image—whether it is more blue or brown or purple or green. Most people use the saturation adjustments more than the hue controls, but both hue and saturation are controlled from the same dialog box. You can adjust both together or just one.

Figure 9-9:
Top: In this photo, all the little shelfsitter figures are about equal in brightness.

Bottom: To make one figure stand out from the crowd, the figure was selected and the saturation was increased. Meanwhile, the rest of the photo was desaturated.The effect is exaggerated here, but a subtler use of this technique can help call attention to the part of a photo where you want people to focus their attention.

It's possible in Elements to actually change the color of objects in your photos, as you saw in Chapter 4, but you probably want to adjust saturation far more often than you want to shift the hue of a photo.

When you use Hue/Saturation, it's a good idea to make most of your other corrections, like Levels or exposure corrections (see Chapter 7), first. When you're ready to use the Hue/Saturation command:

1. **If you want to adjust only part of your photo, select the area you want.**

   Use whatever selection tools you prefer. (See Chapter 5 for more about making selections.)

2. **Call up the Hue/Saturation Adjustment dialog box.**

Go to Enhance → Adjust Color → Adjust Hue/Saturation or to Layer → "New Adjustment Layer" → Hue/Saturation. As always, if you don't want to make irrevocable changes, use an Adjustment layer instead of working directly on your photo.

3. **Move the sliders until you see what you want.**

   If you want to adjust only saturation, you can probably ignore the Hue slider. (Hue changes the color of your selection.) Move the Saturation slider to the right to increase the amount of saturation (more color) or to the left to decrease it. If necessary, move the Lightness slider to the left to make the color darker or to the right to make the color lighter. Incidentally, you don't have to change all the colors in your photo equally. See Figure 9-10 for how to focus on individual color channels.

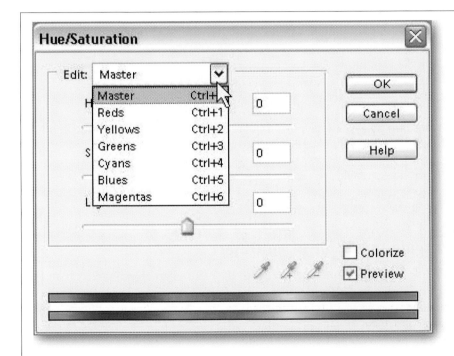

Figure 9-10:
The Hue/Saturation dialog box has a pull-down menu like the Layers palette so you can adjust individual color channels. If only the reds are excessive (a common problem with digital cameras), you can choose to lower the saturation only for the reds without changing the other channels.

NOTE   Generally speaking, if you want to change a pastel to a more intense color, you'll need to reduce the lightness in addition to increasing the saturation—if you don't want your color to look radioactive.

Adjusting Saturation with the Sponge Tool

You can also adjust saturation with the Sponge tool. This is very handy for working on small areas, but all that dragging gets old pretty fast when you're working on a large chunk of your image. For those situations, use Hue/Saturation instead.

Although it's called a sponge, the Sponge tool works like any other brush tool in Elements. Choosing the size and hardness are just the same as choosing them for any other brush (page 270). The Sponge has a couple of unique settings of its own as well:

- **Mode.** Choose here whether to saturate (add color) or desaturate (remove color).

- **Flow.** This governs how intense the effect is. A higher number means more intensity.

To use the Sponge tool, drag over the area you want to change. Figure 9-11 shows an example of the kind of work the Sponge does.

You may want to press Ctrl+J (⌘-J) to create a duplicate layer before you use the Sponge. Then you can always throw out the duplicate layer later on if you change your mind about the changes you made.

1. **Activate the Sponge tool.**

   Click the icon on the toolbar, or press O and choose the Sponge icon. Choose the brush size and the settings you want in the Options bar.

2. **Drag in the area you want to change.**

   If you aren't seeing enough of a difference, up the Flow setting a little. If it's too strong, reduce the number for the Flow.

   TIP If you have a hard time coloring (or decoloring) inside the lines, you can select the area you want before you start sponging. Then the brush won't do anything outside the selection, allowing you to be as sloppy as you like.

Changing the Color of an Object

In Chapter 4, you saw one way to change the color of an object—select it and use the Hue/Saturation sliders in Quick Fix. Elements also gives you some other ways to do this: you can use an Adjustment layer, the Replace Color command, or the Color Replacement tool.

The method you choose depends to some extent on your photo and to some extent on your own preference. Using an Adjustment layer gives you the most flexibility if you want to make other changes later on. Replace Color is the fastest way to change one color that's widely scattered throughout your whole image, and the Color Replacement tool lets you quickly brush a replacement color over the color you want to change. Whichever method you choose, Figure 9-12 shows the kind of complex color change you can make in a jiffy using any one of these methods.

university.tif @ 66.7%(RGB/8)

Figure 9-11:
*Here, the Sponge tool has been
applied to the left side of the window
frame and the roof beside it,
increasing the color saturation in
those areas. Approach the Sponge
tool with some caution. It doesn't
take much to cause degradation in
your image, especially if you have
made many previous adjustments to
it. If you start to see noise (page
313), undo your sponging and try it
again at a reduced setting.*

Using an Adjustment Layer

You can use a Hue/Saturation Adjustment layer to make the same kind of changes
to the color that you saw in Chapter 4. The advantage of the Adjustment layer is
that later on, you can change the settings or the area affected by the layer (as
opposed to changing your whole image). The procedure is exactly the same as that
described in the section "Using the Hue/Saturation Dialog Box," only this time,
you start by selecting the object you want to change.

Figure 9-12:
What if you have a blue and white jug and you want a brown and white one? Just call up Replace Color, and you've got one in a jiffy. Elements gives you several ways to make a complicated color substitution like this one, all of which are covered in this section.

1. **Select the object whose color you want to change.**

   Use any of the Selection tools (Chapter 5). (If you don't make a selection before creating the Adjustment layer, you'll change your entire photo.)

2. **Create a new Hue/Saturation Adjustment layer.**

   Go to Layer → New Adjustment Layer → Hue/Saturation. The new layer affects only the area you selected.

3. **Use the sliders in the dialog box to adjust the color until you see what you want, then click Okay.**

   You need to use the Hue slider to start with. Pick the color you want, and when you've gotten that into the ballpark, use the Saturation and Lightness sliders to adjust the vividness and darkness of the new color.

This method is fine if you have one area of color that's easily selectable. But what if you have a bunch of different areas or you want to change one shade everywhere it appears in your photo? For that, Elements offers the Replace Color command.

Replacing Specific Colors

Take a look at the blue pitcher in Figure 9-12 again. Do you have to tediously select each blue area one by one if you want to make a brown and white jug?

You can do it that way, of course, but an easier way is to use the Replace Color command. It's one of those Elements dialog boxes that look a bit intimidating, but it's a snap to use once you figure it out. Replace Color changes every instance of the color that you select, no matter how many times it appears in your image.

You don't need to start by making a selection when you use Replace Color. As usual, if you want to keep your options for future changes open, make a duplicate layer (Ctrl+J [⌘-J]) for this. When you start, be sure your active layer isn't an Adjustment layer, or Replace Color won't work.

1. **Open the Replace Color dialog box.**

   Go to Enhance → Adjust Color → Replace Color. The Replace Color dialog box
   in Figure 9-13 appears.

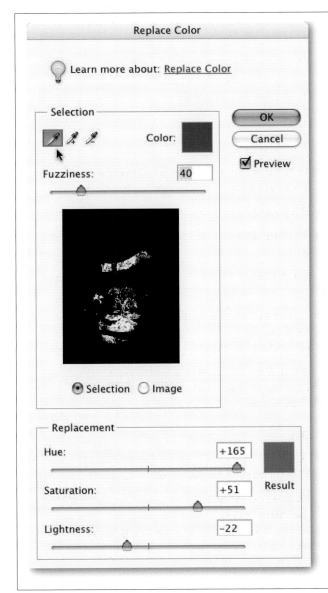

Figure 9-13:
*The funny negative-looking area in the Replace
Color window shows you where the color will be
changed by the sliders, which work the same way
as the Hue/Saturation sliders. You can toggle to a
regular view of your image by clicking the Image
button if you aren't sure you're getting everything.*

2. **Move your cursor over your photo.**

   The cursor changes to an eyedropper. Take a moment to confirm that the left
   eyedropper in the Replace Color dialog box is the active one. That's the one
   without a plus or minus sign.

3. **Click an area of the color you want to replace.**

All the areas of that particular shade are selected, but you won't see the marching ants in your image the way you do with the Selection tools. Figure 9-13 shows how the dialog box tells you what you've selected. If you click more than once with that same eyedropper, you just change your selection instead of adding to it, just the way you would with any of the regular Selection tools (see Chapter 5). To add to your selection, hold down the Shift key and click in your photo again.

Another way to add more shades is to select the middle eyedropper (the one with the plus sign next to it) and click in your photo again. To remove a color, select the right eyedropper (with the minus sign) and click. Alternatively, Alt+click (Option-click) with the first eyedropper, and the shade you click is removed from the selection. If you want to start your selection all over again, Alt+click (Option-click) the Cancel button to turn it to a Reset button.

4. **When you've selected everything you want to change, move the sliders to replace the color.**

The Hue, Saturation, and Lightness sliders work exactly the way they do in Hue/Saturation (explained earlier). Move them and watch the color box in the Replace Color window to see what color you're concocting. If you need to tweak the area of color you're changing, the Fuzziness slider adjusts the range of colors that Color Replacement affects, as shown in Figure 9-14.

5. **Click OK.**

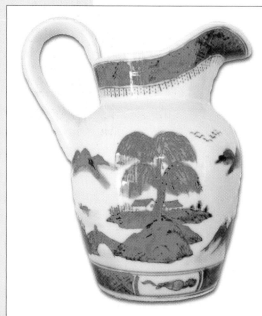

Figure 9-14:
Fuzziness is similar to the Tolerance setting for the Magic Wand (page 108). Take a look at the brown areas of the jug. There's still a lot of blue around them. Set Fuzziness higher (to the right) to include more shades than you've previously been changing (in this figure, making such a change would cause all the blue to get turned to brown). If you find you are picking up little bits of areas you don't want, move Fuzziness to the left to lower it.

TIP   If you want to protect a particular area of your chosen color from being changed, paint a mask on it by using the Selection brush in Mask mode (page 113) before you use the eyedroppers.

Using a Brush to Replace Colors

Elements has had the Replace Color dialog box for a while, but the Color Replacement tool is new in Elements 3. It lets you brush a replacement color onto the area you want to change, without changing any other colors in your photo except the one you target. Figure 9-15 shows how great this tool is for changing hard to isolate areas like feathers.

*Figure 9-15:
Feathers, hair, and fur are usually completely exasperating to try to select. But the Color Replacement tool saves you from having to fool with selections. Just move the crosshairs in the cursor over the area you want to change and click or drag.*

It would have taken hours to get a good selection on this marabou hat, but the Color Replacement tool is smart enough to find all those drifting white areas and change them to aqua- without bleeding the color into other light areas, like the price tag on the adjoining hat.

The Color Replacement tool is actually a subset of the Brush tool. To select it, press B or click the Brush tool. The Color Replacement tool is the choice on the right in the pop-out menu (or you can pick it from the Options bar).

The Options bar settings make a big difference in the way the Color Replacement tool works:

- **Brush Options.** These settings (size, hardness, angle, etc.) work the same way they do for any brush. See Chapter 11 for more information about brushes.

- **Mode.** This is the blend mode the tool uses. Generally you want Color or Hue, although you can get some funky special effects with Saturation.

• **Sampling.** This tells the tool how to look for colors in your image. If you choose Continuous, the brush changes every color that falls under the crosshairs as you move through your photo. Choosing Once means that no matter how far you travel while holding the mouse button, Elements replaces only the color that was under the crosshairs when you first clicked. Background Swatch means that Elements replaces only the color currently featured in the Background color swatch (page 174).

• **Limits.** This setting tells the Color Replacement tool which areas of your photo to look at in its search for color. Contiguous means only areas that touch each other get changed. Discontiguous means the tool changes all the places it finds a color—whether they're touching one another or not.

• **Anti-Aliased.** This setting smoothes the edges of the replacement color. It's best to leave it on.

• **Tolerance.** This is just like the Tolerance setting for the Magic Wand: the higher the number, the more shades of color are affected by the tool. Getting this setting right is the key to getting good results with the Color Replacement tool.

Using the Color Replacement tool is very straightforward:

1. **Pick the color you're going to use as a replacement.**

   Elements uses the current Foreground color as the replacement color. To choose a new Foreground color, click the Foreground color square in the Toolbox and choose a new color from the Color Picker when it appears.

2. **Activate the Color Replacement tool and pick a brush size.**

   See Chapter 11 for help with using brushes. Generally for this tool, you want a fairly large brush, as shown in Figure 9-15.

3. **Click or drag in your photo to change the color.**

   Elements targets the color that is under the crosshairs in the center of the brush.

The Color Replacement tool is great for changing large areas of color to an equivalent tone, but if you want to replace dark red with pale yellow you probably won't like the results. It's not great for colors where the lightness is very different.

> **TIP** You might want to use the Color Replacement tool on a duplicate layer (Ctrl+J [⌘-J]) so that you can adjust the layer opacity to control the effect.

Making Color Photos Black and White

Sometimes you may want to convert your color photos to black and white. If you can't imagine why anyone would willingly do that, consider that in a world crammed full of eye-popping colors, the understatement of black and white really stands out. Also, you may be planning to have something printed where you can't use color illustrations. And of course, for artistic photography, there's still nothing like black and white.

Elements gives you two fundamentally different ways to remove all the color from your image, but they produce quite different results. Figure 9-16 shows you why you need to experiment.

Figure 9-16:
Changing to grayscale can give you very different results depending on the method you use.

Top: Each star in the original has a color value of 250.

Middle: This shows the same photo with the mode converted to grayscale.

Bottom: Using Remove Color causes a very different change.

Remove Color and Hue/Saturation make the same changes to your photo behind the scenes, so the results are pretty much the same with both. Convert Mode can give you quite different results. Here's what you need to know to use each method:

- **Convert Mode.** The simplest solution can be had by going to Image → Mode → Grayscale. This is the most straightforward way, but it's also a bit destructive. Many people prefer to use one of the other methods for important images.

- **Remove Color.** You can also go to Enhance → Adjust Color → Remove Color, or press Ctrl+Shift+U (⌘-Shift-U). This removes the color only from the active layer, though, so if your photo has more than one layer, you need to flatten it (Layer → Flatten Image), or the other layers keep their color.

  Remove Color is really just another way to completely desaturate your photo as you might when using the Hue/Saturation command (page 225). Remove Color is a good method when you might want to recolor part of your photo.

- **Hue/Saturation.** Another solution is to call up the Hue/Saturation dialog box, as explained earlier in the section on Saturation, and move the Saturation slider all the way to the left, or type "−100" into the Saturation box. The advantage to this method is that if you don't care for the shade of gray you get, you can desaturate each color channel separately by using the pull-down menu in the dialog box. This method also lets you tweak your settings a bit to eliminate any color cast you might get from your printer.

TIP   If you're planning to print the results of your conversion, the paper you use can make a big difference in the gray tones you get. If you don't like the results from your usual paper, try a different weight or brand.

OUTSIDE ELEMENTS

Digital Black and White

If you love black and white photography, its current state in the digital world is a good news/bad news situation. The good news is that there are lots of ways to convert your color photos to grayscale. The bad news is that you probably aren't going to be too thrilled when you print the photos out on the average home printer.

For all the wonders of digitizing, there is still nothing that can exactly duplicate the effect of a traditional silver oxide print—although digital printing has made great strides in the past couple of years.

If you want to print black and white photos, you should look into a photo printer that allows you to substitute several shades of gray for your color cartridges. The special inks available are constantly improving, and you can get much better prints now than you could even a year or two ago.

Creating Spot Color

Removing almost all the color from a photo but leaving one or two objects in vivid tones, called spot color, is a very effective artistic device that's long been popular in the print industry. Figure 9-17 shows an example of spot color.

With Elements, creating this kind of effect is as easy as selecting an object. There are all sorts of ways to go about doing this. This section walks you through three of the easiest methods. You can erase your way back to color, use the Remove Color command in conjunction with a selection, or use an Adjustment layer. In learning to use the last method, you'll also learn how to edit the layer mask of an Adjustment layer so that you can change the area the adjustment affects.

The end result looks the same no matter which of these methods you choose. Just select the one you find easiest for the particular photo you want to change.

Erasing Colors from a Duplicate Layer

The simplest way to remove colors from your image is to use the Eraser tool. (See page 291 for more about the different Erasers.) When you use this method, you place a color-free layer over your colored original and erase bits of the top layer to let the color below show through.

1. **Make a duplicate layer.**

   Press Ctrl+J (⌘-J) or go to Layer → Duplicate layer. This is the layer that is going to be black and white.

Figure 9-17:
With Elements, you can easily remove the color from only part of an image.

Top: Here, the photo is a regular color image.

Bottom: In Elements, it's easy to remove the color from the rest of the photo, leaving only the barn in color. This section shows you three easy methods.

2. **Remove the color from the new top layer.**

   Go to Enhance → Adjust Color → Remove Color. (Be sure the top layer is the active one before you do this.) You should now see only a black and white image.

3. **Erase the areas on the top layer where you want to see color.**

   Use the Eraser tool (page 289) to remove parts of the top layer so the colored layer underneath shows through. Be sure that Use All Layers is not turned on. Usually you'll get best results with a fairly soft brush.

If you want to have an image that's mostly colored with only a few black and white areas, reverse the technique—remove the color from the bottom layer and leave the top layer in color. Then erase as described earlier.

When you're finished, you can flatten the layers if you want, but if you keep them separate, you can go back and erase more of the top layer later on if you want. And you'll still have the option of trashing the layer you erased and making a new duplicate of the bottom layer, if you want to start over.

Using Selections and the Remove Color Command

If you don't want to have multiple layers, you can also use the Remove Color command on a selection. (See Chapter 5 for more about making selections.) Just make sure you use this method on a copy or, if you're using Windows, save your image as a version (page 74). You don't want to risk wrecking your original photo.

The procedure for using Replace Color in conjunction with a selection is very simple.

1. **Mask out the area where you want to keep the color in your image.**

   Use the Selection brush in Mask mode (page 113) to paint a mask over the area where you want to keep the color, to protect it from being changed in step 2. In other words, you're going to remove color from everything except where you paint with the Selection brush.

   If you want to keep the color in most of your photo and just remove the color from one or two objects, paint over them with the brush in Selection mode instead of Mask mode.

2. **Remove the color from the selected area.**

   Go to Enhance → Adjust Color → Remove Color, or press Ctrl+Shift+U (⌘-Shift-U). The color disappears from the areas not protected by the mask, but the area under the mask is untouched. (You can also do this step by going to Enhance → Adjust Color → Adjust Hue/Saturation and moving the Saturation slider all the way to the left.)

You should see a photo with color only in the areas that you didn't select. This method is the least flexible. Once you close your image, the change is permanent and not undoable, which is why you don't want to use this method on your original photo.

Using a Layer Mask and the Saturation Slider

If you'd like to keep the option of easily changing your mind about which areas keep the color, it's best to remove the color with a Hue/Saturation Adjustment layer. This is your most flexible choice. Using an Adjustment layer lets you both add and subtract areas of color later if you like.

1. **Select the area where you want to remove the color.**

   Use any Selection tool you like (see Chapter 5 for more about Selection tools). If you think it would be easier to select the area where you want to keep the color, do that, and then press Ctrl+I (⌘-I) to invert your selection so that the area that's going to become grayscale is selected instead.

2. **Create a Hue/Saturation Adjustment layer.**

   Go to Layer → New Adjustment Layer → Hue/Saturation, or click the New Adjustment Layer icon on the Layers palette and choose a Hue/Saturation layer.

3. **In the Hue/Saturation dialog box that appears, remove the color.**

   Move the Saturation slider all the way to the left to remove the color.

Why is this method better? Well, for one thing, you can always discard the Adjustment layer if you change your mind, but that's not all. You can actually edit the Adjustment layer's layer mask (see page 148 for more about what a layer mask is) so that you can change which parts of your photo are in color, even days or weeks later.

Don't want that tree as well as the vine on the house? Or maybe you wish you'd left all the window frames in color? All are easily fixed by editing the layer mask. The next section tells you how.

Editing a layer mask

Elements gives you the ability to make changes to the layer mask of an Adjustment layer any time you want to—as long as the layer hasn't been merged into another layer and the image hasn't been flattened. You might edit your layer mask when you realize your original selection needs some cleaning up, or when you want to make changes to the area the Adjustment layer affects.

> **NOTE**   There's only one tricky thing about editing a layer mask. Remember that masking something means it won't be affected by a change. So the area that shows up in black or red on your layer mask is the area that isn't going to be changed by your adjustment. If you don't see any black or red when you look at a layer mask, the Adjustment layer is going to change your whole photo.

You can work on the mask directly in your photo, or you can make the layer mask visible and work on the mask itself. Here's the simplest way to make changes to the area covered by a layer mask:

1. **Click the layer mask icon for the Adjustment layer you want to edit.**

   It's the right-hand icon on the layer you want to edit (in the Layers palette). If you don't click here first, you'll just be putting regular paint on your photo instead of changing the layer mask.

2. **Paint directly on your image.**

   Use the Brush tool to paint. Paint with black to keep an area from being affected by your adjustment. Paint with white to increase the area affected by the adjustment. In other words, black masks an area, while white increases your selected area.

You can also use the Selection tools (the same way you would on any other selection) to change the mask's area. Just keep in mind that what's selected gets changed by the adjustment, while what's masked doesn't change. See Chapter 5 if you need help making selections. If you watch the layer mask icon in the layers palette, you'll see that it also changes to show where you've painted.

To make a layer mask visible, click it in the Layers palette. Elements gives you a choice of two different ways to see the masked area, as shown in Figure 9-18. You merely Alt+click (Option-click) the right-side thumbnail for the Adjustment layer in the Layers palette, and then you'll see the black layer mask (instead of your photo) in the image window. Add the Shift key when you click to see a red overlay over the photo instead of the black and white view.

The black mask view shows only the mask itself, not your photo beneath it. This is a good choice when you're checking to see how clean the edges of your selection are. If you're adding or subtracting areas of your photo, choose the red overlay view so that you can see the objects in your photo as you paint over them. You can use the method described above to paint in either view.

That's all there is to it, but that's not all you can do to edit a layer mask. You can use shades of gray to adjust the transparency of the mask. If you paint on your mask with gray, you can change the opacity of the changes made by the Adjustment layer. You can let a little color show through the mask, for instance, without letting the full vividness of the color come through. Figure 9-19 shows an example of how you'd use this technique.

The lighter the shade of gray you choose, the more color shows through.

Colorizing a Black and White Photo

So far, you've read about ways to keep color in an image while you make part of it black and white. But what about when you've got a black and white photo to begin with and you want to add color to it? It's very easy to color your black and white photos with Elements. For instance, you can give an old photo the sort of hand-tinted effect you sometimes see in antique prints, as shown in Figure 9-20.

You can easily color things with Elements. Before you start tinting your photo, you should first make any repairs. See the earlier section "Fixing Blemishes" and, for fixes to the exposure, see Chapter 7.

1. **Make sure your photo is in RGB mode.**

   Go to Image → Mode → RGB. Your photo must be in RGB mode or you can't color it. Create a new layer in Color mode.

   Go to Layer → New → Layer and select Color as the layer mode. By choosing Color as your mode, you can paint on the layer and the image details still show through.

Figure 9-18:
Elements not only lets you edit your layer mask, but gives you two different ways to see it.

Top: To see the masked area in black, Alt+click (Option-click) the right thumbnail for the layer in the Layers palette.

Bottom: To see the masked area in red, Alt+Shift+click (Option-Shift-click) the layer's thumbnail.

2. **Paint on the layer.**

   Use the Brush tool (page 270) and choose a color in the Foreground color square (page 174). Keep changing the foreground color as much as you need to. If the coverage is too heavy, in the Options bar, reduce the opacity of the brush.

You can also paint directly on the original layer. But the problem with that is that it's far more difficult to fix things if you make a mistake when you're well into your project. Using the original layer also doesn't give you much of an out if you decide later on that the lip color you painted first doesn't look so great with the skin color you just chose.

Figure 9-19:
By painting with different shades of gray on the layer mask, you can cause the effect of the adjustment to be partially transparent. Here, a fairly light gray was used to paint over the tree so that a little green shows, but it's not the bright, saturated green of the original photo. Only part of the tree was painted to make it easy to see the contrast with what was there before.

POWER USERS' CLINIC

Faking Photoshop

In Chapter 6, you learned about the basics of layer masks and how to use a blank Adjustment layer as a mask by grouping it with the layer you want to mask.

If you're trying to follow a tutorial written for full Photoshop, sometimes you can get closer to the way a layer mask works in full Photoshop by placing your mask underneath the layer you're grouping it with. If you remember, in grouped layers (page 140), it's the bottom layer that calls the shots for things like color and opacity.

If you want to control visibility for parts of the masked layer, if you put the mask layer below it, you can adjust what shows and what's hidden on the real layer, by painting on the layer mask.

Both ways, above and below, have their uses, but they give you control in different ways. If you do a little experimenting, it won't take long to develop a sense for which one you want in a particular situation.

If you use masks a lot, you might want to download add-on tools for Elements that let you paint a mask right on your photo the way you would in Photoshop. (See Chapter 17 for more details about these tools.)

Figure 9-20:
If you decide to color an old black and white or sepia photo, put each color on its own layer. Then later, you can adjust the transparency or change the hue or saturation for one color easily without changing the other colors, too. A very low opacity is enough for really old photos like this one.

SPECIAL EFFECTS

Hints for Coloring Old Photographs

It's easier to put each element of a face that you are going to color—lips, eyes, cheek color, skin—on a separate layer. That way you can change just one color later on without a lot of hassle. You can always merge the layers (Layer → Merge Visible, or Merge Down) later, once you know for sure that you're done.

If you want the effect of a photo that was hand-colored a century ago, paint at less than 100 percent opacity. The tinting on old photos is very transparent.

If you select the area before you paint, you won't have to worry about getting color outside of where you want it, because your paint is confined to your selection.

Skin colors are very hard to create in the color picker. Try sampling skin tones from another photo instead. If it's a family photo, after all, the odds are good that the current generation's basic skin tones are reasonably close to Great-Granddad's.

Tinting an Entire Photo

You can also give an entire photo a single color tint all over, even if the original is a grayscale photo. This can be used to create a variety of different moods.

There are two basic ways to do this. Actually, there are lots more than two, but two should give you the idea. The first method (Layer style) described here is faster, but the second (Colorize) lets you tweak your settings more. Figure 9-21 shows the result of using the Layer style method on a color photo.

For either method, if you want to keep the original color (or lack thereof) in part of your photo, use the Selection brush in Mask mode to mask out the area you don't want to change.

Figure 9-21:
The easiest way to create a monochrome color scheme for your photo is with the Photographic Layer styles, which are explained in Chapter 11. This is the Gray-Green style applied to the original color photo. It removes the existing color and recolors your image in one click. The downside is that you can't edit the color once you're done if you decide you'd rather have orange.

Using a Layer style

Although many people never dig down far enough to find them, Adobe gives you some Photographic Layer styles that make tinting a photo as easy as double-clicking. There's more about Layer styles in general in Chapter 12, but this section tells you all you need to know to use the Photographic styles. It's a very simple procedure.

1. **Create a duplicate layer.**

   Go to Layer → Duplicate Layer or press Ctrl+J (⌘-J). (If you don't create a duplicate layer and your original has only a background layer, you'll get asked to convert it to a layer when you apply the style. Say yes.)

2. **If necessary, change the mode to RGB.**

   Go to Image → Mode → RGB. With this method, it doesn't matter if your original is in color or not. The Layer style gets rid of the original color and tints the photo all at the same time.

3. **Choose a Layer style.**

   Go to the Styles and Effects palette and pick Layer Styles → Photographic Effects. Double-click the style of your choice. You can click around and try different styles to see which you prefer. Undo after each style that you try.

4. **When you see what you like, click OK.**

The drawback to this method is that you can't go back and edit the Photographic Layer styles the way you can edit most other Layer styles. Figure 9-22 explains why.

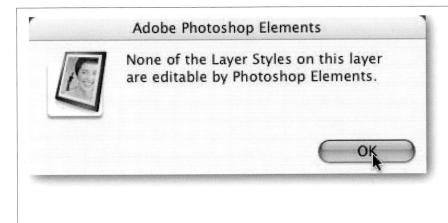

Figure 9-22:
Using the Photographic Layer styles couldn't be simpler, but you have no control over how the effect looks. Also, the Photographic styles can't be edited by double-clicking their icon in the Layers palette the way most styles can. (See Chapter 11 for more about Photographic styles.) That's because they don't contain any of the style elements that you can edit, like Lighting Angle or Drop Shadow Distance.

Using Colorize

You can use the Colorize checkbox in the Hue/Saturation dialog box to add a color tint to a grayscale photo or to change the color of a photo that already has color in it. This method lets you choose any color you like, as opposed to the limited color choices of the Layer styles in the previous section. You can also adjust the intensity of the color with the Saturation slider once you've selected the shade you want.

Figure 9-23 explains how the Colorize setting changes the way the Hue/Saturation command works.

1. **Remove the color from your photo, if necessary.**

   Press Ctrl+Shift+U (⌘-Shift-U) to remove the color.

2. **Make sure your photo is in RGB mode.**

   Go to Image → Mode → RGB.

3. **Colorize your photo on a new layer.**

   Go to Layer → New Adjustment Layer → Hue/Saturation and turn on the Colorize checkbox. When you turn this setting on, your image becomes filled with the foreground color. If you don't like it, that's fine. You're going to change it right now.

Figure 9-23:
If you want to color something that has no color information in it, like a white shirt or a grayscale image, in the Hue/Saturation dialog box, turn on Colorize to add color to the image. If you don't check the Colorize box, you can adjust the hue, saturation, and lightness of white all day long and all you'll do is go from white to gray to black, because there's no color info there for Elements to work on.

4. **Adjust the color until it looks the way you want it to.**

    Move the sliders for Hue, Saturation, and Lightness until you find the look you want, then click Okay. Figure 9-24 shows the results.

If you selected and masked an area, that part should still show the original color.

You can change your mind about the colorizing by double-clicking the left icon on the layer in the Layers palette. That brings up the controls for the Hue/Saturation adjustment again so you can change your settings. And you can also edit the layer mask, as described earlier, if you want to change the area that's affected by the Adjustment layer.

When you're done, if you merge layers, or add a new layer and press Ctrl+Alt+Shift+E (⌘-Option-Shift-E) to produce a new merged layer above the old ones, you can use Levels, Color Variations, and the other color editing tools to tweak the tint effect.

Special Effects

Elements gives you some other useful ways of drastically changing the look of your image. You can apply these as Adjustment layers (Layer → New Adjustment Layer) or by going to Filter → Adjustments. Either way gives you the same options for their settings. You can see them in action in Figure 9-25.

Figure 9-24:
Here's the photo tinted with a purple tone by using the second method (Colorize), which allows you to tweak the results much more. The door was masked out so that it stays in full color.

Figure 9-25:
You can get some interesting special effects with the Adjustment commands, whether you apply them as filters or as Adjustment layers. If you want to use them as filters, it's not a bad idea to start with a duplicate layer.

Top row (left to right): The original photo, Invert, Equalize.

Bottom row: Posterize and Threshold.

In most cases, you use these adjustments as steps along the way in a more complex treatment of your photo, but they can be effective by themselves, too. Here's what each does:

• **Invert** makes your photo look like a negative. It's so useful in doing artistic effects that you can also invert any time in the Editor just by pressing Ctrl+I (⌘-I).

> **NOTE** If you think this sounds like a great way to get your negatives scanned in with a basic flatbed scanner and turned to positive images, sorry, but you need to think again.
>
> Color negatives have an orange mask on them that Elements can't easily undo. You're best off with a dedicated film scanner that's designed to cope with negatives.

• **Equalize** makes the darkest pixel black and the lightest white, and redistributes the brightness values for all the colors in a photo to give them all equal weight. The dialog box lets you choose between simply equalizing your whole photo and equalizing it based on a selection. It doesn't always work, but sometimes Equalize is great for bringing up the brightness level of a dim photo.

• **Posterize** reduces the total number of colors in your photo, giving a less detailed, more poster-like effect. The lower the number you enter in the dialog box, the fewer colors you'll get (thus, the more extreme the result). If you want blocky, poster-like edges in your photo, try Filter → Artistic → Poster Edges instead of or in addition to this.

• **Gradient Map** is pretty complicated. According to Adobe it "maps the gray-scale range of an image to the colors of a specified gradient fill." If you want to know what the heck that means, turn to page 335. Basically, a gradient map lets you apply a gradient based on the light and dark areas of your photo. The gradient colors replace the existing colors in your photo. There's a lot more to it than that, though.

• **Threshold** turns every pixel in your photo to pure white or pure black. You won't find any shades of gray here. Figure 9-26 explains how to adjust the settings for the Threshold command.

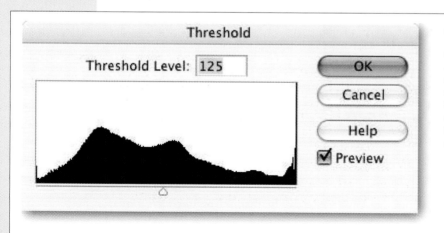

Figure 9-26:
This slider controls the dividing point between black and white pixels in a Threshold adjustment. Slide to the left if you want more white pixels, and to the right for more dark ones.

Creating Panoramas and Transforming Images

Everyone's had the experience of trying to photograph an awesome view—a city skyline or a mountain range, for instance—only to find the whole scene won't fit into one picture, because it's just too wide. Elements, once again, comes to the rescue. With Elements' Photomerge command, you can split any extremely wide view up into several photos and then stitch your pictures together into a panorama that's much larger than any single photo your camera can take. Panoramas can become addicting once you've tried them, and they're a great way to get those wide, wide shots that are beyond the capability of your camera lens.

The general procedure for creating a panorama in Elements is pretty straightforward, but the devil is in the details. In the first part of this chapter, you'll learn how to use the Photomerge command to make panoramas. Since the angle of your image may need a little correcting afterwards, you'll also learn how to use the Elements Transform commands to adjust the images you've created.

You can use Transform in many other situations, too. If you're into photographing buildings (especially tall ones), you'll know that you often you need some kind of perspective correction: a building appears to be leaning backward or sideways because of distortion caused by your camera's lens. The Transform commands are great for straightening things back up.

> **NOTE** Photomerge is great for making larger images by combining photos at their edges. But if you want to combine elements of different photos into one image, like putting a picture of your new girlfriend's face onto a picture of your old girlfriend, page 129 shows you how to do that by putting each element on its own layer.

Creating Panoramas

It's a lot fun to combine your photos into panoramas using the Elements Photomerge command. Your starting point is a group of photos you've taken that can fit together side by side to show a more complete view of your subject in one image. Figure 10-1 shows a partial panorama and the photos that went into it.

Figure 10-1:
With Elements, you can easily stitch together many different shots to make one large image that shows the entire view. Elements easily blended the three photos you see at the top of the figure into the completed panorama you see below them.

Elements can merge together as many photos as you want to include in a panorama. The only real size limitation comes when you want to print out your merges. If you have only letter-sized paper and you create a five-photo horizontal panorama, it's going to be only a couple of inches high, even if you rotate your panorama to print lengthwise. (You can buy printers with attachments that let you print from rolls of paper, so that there's no limit to the longest dimension of your panorama. These printers are very popular with panorama addicts. You can also use an online printing service, like Ofoto.com, to get larger prints than you can make at home. See Chapter 14 for more about how Ofoto works.)

You'll get the best results creating a panorama if you plan ahead when shooting your photos. The pictures should be side by side, of course, and you get much better results if they overlap each other by at least 30 percent. Also, you'll minimize the biggest panorama problem—matching the color of your photos—if you make sure they all have identical exposures. See the box on page 256 for some suggestions.

When you use the Photomerge command, you start by telling Elements which photos to combine, and then you choose your files in the Photomerge's Browse window. When you've got all the photos you want, the actual Photomerge window appears, shown in Figure 10-2. Elements starts things off by doing the heavy lifting of actually merging the photos into one, but you still have to go in and do the clean-up work (trimming, correcting the blending, and so on) if you want stellar results.

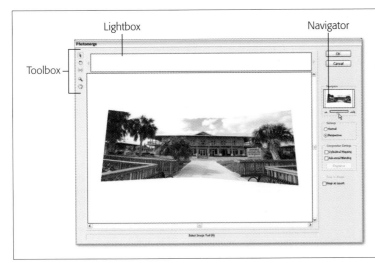

Figure 10-2:
The Elements Photomerge window is your workshop for joining two or more photos into a panorama. Although Elements does a lot of the work automatically, you'll get better results if you go in to tweak things, using the settings on the right side of the window, once Elements has created the basic merge for you.

NOTE   You can also create vertical panoramas—Elements automatically figures out which way your photos fit together.

Selecting Files and Merging Them

The first part of creating a panorama is selecting the photos you want to include. You can save yourself a lot of time and trouble if you go through your photos first, to be sure the color in all the photos matches, before you start your panorama. Figure 10-3 shows why you need to take this step.

When you're ready to create a panorama, just follow these steps:

1. **Go through the photos you want to use and make sure the colors match as closely as possible.**

   Use any of the editing tools in Quick Fix (Chapter 4) or the more advanced options described in Chapter 7 to modify colors and exposure levels. Figure 10-4 demonstrates how to compare the color in your photos as you work.

   TIP   The Browse window doesn't give you thumbnail views—only a list of file names. Make a note of your files' names or rename them so that you'll know which ones are the ones you want.

2. **Start your panorama.**

   To begin a new photomerge, go to File → New → Photomerge Panorama. Mac owners also have an extra option, as shown in Figure 10-5. Wherever you start out from, you see the Photomerge Browse window, which is where you choose the photos you want to combine.

Figure 10-3:
The left version of this three-photo panorama shows the biggest problem most people face when merging images—exposure differences from shot to shot. As you can see from the repaired version on the right, it was necessary to sacrifice some color from the best photo (the top one) to get everything matched up. The Advanced Blending option (page 258) was used to join the bottom two images fairly seamlessly, though. The sky was repaired with a combination of the Clone Stamp (page 217), the Healing brush (page 213), and the Paint Bucket (page 281) tools.

3. **Choose the photos you want to include.**

   Click the Browse button in the window to see a list of the folders and files on your hard drive. Navigate to the one you want and click Choose. If you can't select all the photos at once because they aren't all in the same folder, you can click Browse as many times as you want, and the new files get added to the list in the window.

   On either platform, if you have open photos, they get pre-included in the Browse window. So if you want to merge photos from several different folders, opening all of them is one way to get them into the mix faster than by navigating to each folder separately.

   NOTE   Photomerge copies each file as it adds it to the panorama and doesn't change your originals. You don't need to worry about making copies especially for your panoramas, although paranoid types would say it's always better safe than sorry.

4. **Add more photos if necessary.**

   If you need files from several folders and you didn't get them ahead of time, just keep going back until you've rounded them all up. Just click the Browse button

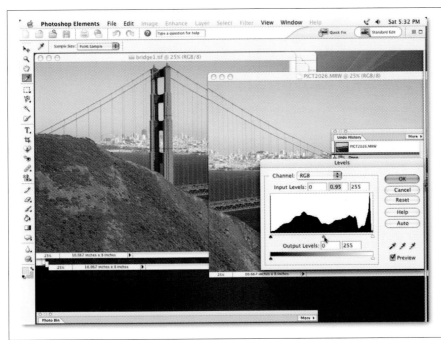

Figure 10-4:
It helps to prepare your photos for merging by adjusting them side by side so that you can compare the colors. Here, a combination of Levels and a little tweaking with the Tint slider (in Quick Fix) gets the photos close enough to get started. You can also get good results sometimes by using Hue/Saturation (page 225) to adjust the individual color channels.

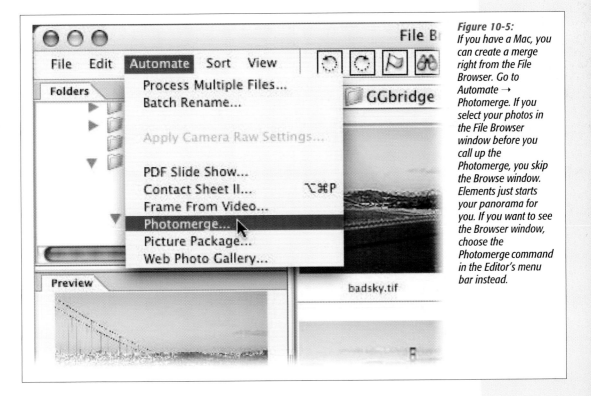

Figure 10-5:
If you have a Mac, you can create a merge right from the File Browser. Go to Automate → Photomerge. If you select your photos in the File Browser window before you call up the Photomerge, you skip the Browse window. Elements just starts your panorama for you. If you want to see the Browser window, choose the Photomerge command in the Editor's menu bar instead.

again. If you inadvertently have more photos than you want, highlight the unwanted photo(s) in the list and click the Remove button.

5. **When you've got all the images you want, click OK.**

If your photos weren't already open, you see them open one by one as Elements starts performing its merge magic. It helps to have the Layers palette (page 126) out where you can see it, since Elements places each merged photo on its own layer before combining them. (If you want your photos to remain on their own layers in the completed panorama, make sure the Keep as Layers checkbox is turned on; this option is explained on page 258). The Undo History palette (page 18) gives you a step by step look at each process Elements goes through to make your panorama.

Elements' first pass isn't always perfect, as you can see in Figure 10-3. The next section explains how to help Elements out when it can't quite figure out how to put things together, and how to improve the look of the combined image.

Adjusting Your Photos

Once your photos appear in the Photomerge window, you see Elements' best-guess effort at combining them. Now your part of the work begins, since you usually need to do a fair bit of tweaking here to get the best results.

Sometimes, for example, as shown in Figure 10-6, Elements just gets confused and combines your photos randomly. In other cases, it just can't figure out where to put a photo at all. When that happens, Elements leaves the photos it can't place up at the top of the window, in the area called the lightbox.

Figure 10-6:
Elements valiantly tries to combine your photos, but sometimes it has trouble lining up images exactly or figuring out how to fit a particular photo into the merge.

Top: Here, Elements guesses more wildly than a 10th-grader on a pop quiz.

Bottom: As you can see in this end result of a five-photo merge, with a little help, Elements can usually do a fine job of combining images—even when it doesn't know where to start.

You can manually drag files into the merge and also reposition photos already in your panorama. Just grab them with the Select Image tool (explained later) and drag them to the correct location in the merge.

If you try to nudge the position of a photo and it keeps jumping away from where you've placed it, turn off "Snap to Image" on the right side of the Photomerge window. Then you should be able to put your photo exactly where you want it. However, Elements isn't doing the figuring for you anymore, so use the Zoom tool to get a good look at the alignment afterwards. You may need to microadjust the photo's exact position.

At the top left of the Photomerge window is a little Toolbox. Some tools are familiar; others are special tools just for panoramas.

- **Select Image.** Use this tool to move individual photos into or out of your merge or to reposition them within it. Press A from the keyboard or click the tool to activate it.

- **Rotate Image.** Elements usually rotates images automatically when merging them, but if it doesn't, or guesses wrong, press R to activate this tool, then click the photo you want to rotate. You see handles on the image, just the way you would with the regular Rotate commands (page 61). Then just grab a corner and turn the photo until it fits in properly. Usually, you won't need to drastically change a photo's orientation, but this tool helps make the small changes often needed to line things up better.

- **Vanishing Point.** To understand what this tool does, think of standing on a long, straight, country road and looking off into the distance. The point at which the two parallel lines of the road seem to converge and meet the horizon is called the vanishing point.

  The Vanishing Point tool in Elements just tells Photomerge where you want that point to be in your finished panorama. Knowing the vanishing point helps Elements figure out the correct perspective. Press V to activate the Vanishing Point tool. Figure 10-7 shows an example of how it can change your results.

- **Zoom tool.** This is the same Zoom tool (page 61) you meet everywhere else in Elements. Click the magnifying glass in the Toolbox or press Z to activate it.

- **Hand tool.** Use the Hand tool (page 63) here when you need to scoot your entire merged image around to see a different part of it. Click the Hand icon in the Toolbox or press H to activate it. When moving an individual photo within your panorama, use the Select Image tool.

You have a few other aids on the right side of the window. Some, like Advanced Blending, adjust the way your photos blend together. Others, like Cylindrical Mapping adjust the cameras's-eye view angle.

IN THE FIELD

Shooting Tips for Good Merges

The most important part of creating an impressive and plausible panorama starts before you even launch Elements. You can save yourself a lot of grief by planning ahead when shooting photos for a panorama.

Most of the time, you know before you shoot that you'll want to try to merge your photos. You don't often say, "Wow, I can't believe I've got seven photos of the Dr. Dre balloon at the Thanksgiving Day parade that just happen to be exactly in line and have a 30 percent overlap between each one! Guess I'll try a merge."

If you know you want to create a panorama, when you're taking pictures, set your camera to be as much in manual mode as possible. The biggest headache in panorama making is trying to get the exposure, color, brightness, and so on to blend seamlessly. Elements is darned good about blending the outlines of the physical objects in your photos. Lock your camera settings so that the exposure of each image is as identical as possible.

Even on small digital cameras that don't have much in the way of manual controls, you may have some kind of panorama setting, like Canon's Stitch Assist mode, that does the same thing.

(To be honest, your camera may make merges itself that work better than what Elements can do, because the camera's doing the image-blending internally. Check out if your model has a panorama feature.)

The more your photos overlap, the better. Elements does what it can with what you give it, but it's really happy if you can arrange a 30 or 40 percent overlap between images.

It's helpful to use a tripod if you have one, and pan heads—tripod heads that let you swivel your camera in an absolutely straight line—were made for panoramas. Actually, as long as your shots aren't wildly out of line, Elements can usually cope. But you may have to do quite a bit of cropping to get even edges on the finished result if you don't use a tripod.

Whether you use a tripod or not, keep the camera level, rather than the horizon, to avoid distortion. In other words, focus your attention more on leveling the body of the camera than what you see through the viewfinder. Use the same focal length for each image, and try not to use the zoom, unless it's manual, so that you can keep it exactly the same for every image.

To control your onscreen view of your panorama, Elements gives you the Navigator in the upper-right corner of the Photomerge window. It works just like the regular Navigator described in Chapter 3. Move the slider to resize the view of your panorama. Drag to the right to zoom in on one area or to the left to shrink the view so that you can see the whole thing at once. If you want to target a particular spot in your merge, drag the red rectangle to control the area that's onscreen.

Fine-Tuning Your Panorama

Once you get all your photos positioned to suit you, you may want to adjust the result to make things look a bit smoother. Elements has several other commands to help you do so.

On the right side of the window, you can see a row of buttons and checkboxes. You'll usually want to try at least a couple of these settings to improve your panorama. The first two—Normal and Perspective—adjust the viewing angle of your panorama. You can choose one or the other, but not both.

Figure 10-7:
You can radically alter the perspective of your panorama by selecting a vanishing point.

Top: Here you see the result of clicking in the center.

Bottom: Here you see the result of clicking on the right hand image. Note that the tool selects only the image, not the actual point—you can click on any photo to put your vanishing point there, but if you subsequently try to tweak it by clicking at a higher or lower point within the same photo, nothing happens.

- **Normal.** This radio button gives you your photomerge as Elements combined it, with no changes to the perspective. If you don't like the way the angles in your panorama look, try clicking Perspective instead.

- **Perspective.** If you click this button, Elements attempts to apply perspective to your panorama to make it look more realistic. Sometimes Elements does a bang-up job, but usually you'll get better results if you help it out by setting a vanishing point, as explained earlier. Sometimes adding cylindrical mapping, explained later, can help. If you still get a totally weird result, go ahead and just create the merge anyway. Then correct the perspective yourself afterward using one of the Transform commands, as explained in the next section.

The Composition settings further down the window aren't mutually exclusive. You can add either of them—Cylindrical Mapping or Advanced Blending—to your panorama if you think it needs their help. Just turn on their checkboxes to use them.

To see what they do to your photo, you need to click the Preview button after turning on their checkboxes (both features are explained in the following list). While you're looking at the preview, you can't make any other changes to your panorama. You have to click "Exit Preview" before you can tweak your panorama any further. You won't see the effect of these settings again until you click OK to tell Elements you're ready for a finished panorama.

NOTE If you use the preview, take a good look at the joins of your merge when Elements is finished. Once in a while it has trouble getting things put back exactly where they were before previewing. In that case, just close the merge without saving and try again.

- **Cylindrical Mapping.** When you apply perspective to your panorama, you may wind up with an image that looks like a giant bow tie. Cylindrical mapping helps put your images back into a more normal perspective by vertically stretching the middle section to make everything the same height. Its called "cylindrical" because it gives an effect like that of looking at a label on a bottle—the middle seems largest, and the image gets smaller as it fades into the distance (on the sides around the back of the bottle). This setting is available only if you select Perspective in the settings above it. If you choose Normal, it's grayed out.

- **Advanced Blending.** It's very rare to get photos with colors that match exactly. Advanced blending tries to smooth out the differences by averaging the color between the photos, and it does help some but usually not enough.

The following two settings really should be at the top of the list, since they're the ones you'd use first when making a panorama.

- **Snap to Image.** Elements automatically places your photos in the panorama exactly where it thinks they go. If you want to override Elements and position your photos yourself, turn off Snap to Image.

- **Keep As Layers.** When you create a panorama, Elements ordinarily combines all your photos into an image that has only one layer in it. If you turn on "Keep as Layers," you get a multi-layered panorama in which each photo is on its own layer (page 123). This makes it a bit easier to go back and apply corrections to one of the photos after the merge, but it also makes for a hugely larger file. Generally, you're better off canceling a merge and working on the photo by itself, then remerging.

Finishing Up: Creating Your Panorama

Once you're happy with your panorama, click the Okay button and wait while Elements puts everything together for you. This may take a while, especially on a memory-challenged computer, so don't worry if it seems like nothing's happening—Elements is calculating like mad.

Usually you have to crop (page 53) your panorama to get rid of the ragged edges, but once you do, it's quite remarkable how much it looks like a single photo. At this point, it is a single image, so you can edit it any of the ways you would edit a normal photo. You need to name and save it, also.

TIP If you want to try out making a panorama, there's a good tutorial in the Help files. Go to Help → Tutorials → "Stitch together a Photomerge Panorama."

Transforming Images

If you ever photograph buildings, you know that it can be tough to do with a fixed-lens digital camera. For example, when you get too close to the building, your lens tends to introduce a certain amount of distortion into the photo. There are special perspective-correcting lenses available, but those won't help if you have a pocket camera (quite aside from their cost, which can be significant).

Fortunately, Elements has a series of Transform commands to help you with some of the more common problems, as shown in Figure 10-8. These commands aren't just for buildings, incidentally, although it's most common to see obvious distortions in architectural photography or photos of room interiors. You can also apply these commands just for fun to create wacky photos or type effects. You can also use these commands on a selection if you make your selection before you begin.

Figure 10-8:
Left: The Transform commands make quick work of straightening up slanting buildings like this one. But if you do lots of architectural photography, you may want to investigate some of the perspective-correcting plug-ins available for Elements.

Right: Here, it took only a dose of Skew and a bit of Distort to pull the building straight and make it tall enough again.

There are several different Transform commands available. Each moves your photo in a different direction. The Free Transform command, described later, includes all the other Transform commands, so you can move things in any direction when you use it.

Skew, Distort, Perspective

Elements gives you four commands to help straighten up the objects in your photos. While they all move your photo in different directions, the way you use them is the same. The Transform commands have the same box-like handles that you see on the Move tool, for example. You choose the command you want, and then the handles appear around your photo. Just drag a handle in the direction you want your photo to move. Figure 10-9 shows how to use the Transform commands.

Figure 10-9:
Here's an example of how you'd use the Skew command to pull a building straight upright. The trick to applying the Transform commands is to make sure you can reach the handles on the corners. It helps to enlarge your image window far beyond the size of the actual image to give yourself room to pull. To do that, just drag the window corner, or better yet, click the large square on the far right of the Shortcuts bar to get into full screen view.

To see the list of Transform commands, go to Image → Transform. The first one, Free Transform, is the most powerful, because it includes all the others. There's more about Free Transform in the next section.

The other Transform commands, which are more specialized, are:

• **Skew** slants an image. If you have a building that looks like it's leaning to the right, you can use Skew to pull it to the left and straighten it back up again.

• **Distort** stretches your photo in the direction you want to pull it. Use it to make buildings (or people) taller and skinnier, or shorter and squatter.

• **Perspective** stretches your photo to make it look like parts are nearer or farther away. For example, if a building in your photo looks like it's leaning away from you, you can use Perspective to pull the top back towards the viewer.

Although Free Transform is the most capable, it can also be trickier to use. You may find it easier to use one of the one-way commands from the previous list so you don't have to worry about inadvertently moving a photo in an unwanted direction.

All the Transform commands, including Free Transform, offer the same settings in the Options bar, which are shown in Figure 10-10.

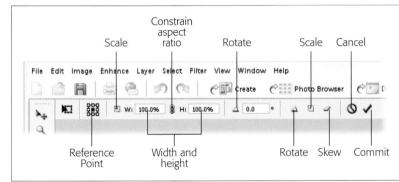

Figure 10-10:
The Options bar for the Transform commands. Scale and Rotate appear twice. The width and height boxes allow you to specify your numbers. Just type them in and then click the Scale icon. If you are scaling to a set size, enter one number and click the Chain icon and your image will be resized with the same proportions.

From left to right, the Option bar settings control:

• **Reference Point Location.** This strange little doodad (shown in Figure 10-11) lets you tell Elements where the fixed point should be when you transform something. It's a miniature cousin of the placement grid you see in the Resize Canvas command (page 72). The reference point starts out in the image's center, but you can tell Elements to move everything using the upper-left corner or the bottom-right corner as the reference point instead. To do that, click the square you want to use as the reference.

• **Scale.** You can resize your image by dragging, or enter a percentage in the width or height box here. Click the Chain icon to keep the original proportions of your image.

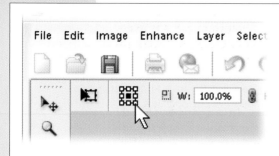

Figure 10-11:
This is where you set the reference point for transformations, which tells Elements the central point for rotations. For eample, if you want your photo to spin around the lower-right corner instead of the center, click the bottom-right square. For the Transform commands, it also tells Elements the point to work from.

- **Rotate.** The box next to the little triangle in the Options bar lets you enter the number of degrees to rotate your image or selection.

- **Rotate.** Click this next triangle and you can grab a corner of your image to make a free rotation (page 51).

  TIP　If you Shift+drag when turning your image, you force it to turn in 15 degree increments.

- **Scale.** Click here if you want to resize your image by dragging—as opposed to entering numbers in the Scale boxes to the left of the Options bar.

- **Skew.** Click here and you can pull a corner of your image to the left or right, the way you do with the Skew command.

- **Cancel.** Click the No symbol to cancel your transformation.

- **Commit.** Click the checkmark to accept your transformation. Pressing Enter/Return does the same thing.

In most cases, you can transform your object without much reference to these settings, except for the Cancel/Commit buttons. The easiest way to transform your photo is to grab a corner and drag. Here's how you might proceed:

1. **Position your image to give yourself room to work.**

   You need to position your photo so that you have room to drag the handles far beyond its edges. Figure 10-9 is a good example of an image that's sufficiently expanded to make lots of transformations.

2. **Choose how you want to transform your image.**

   Go to Image → Transform and select the command you want. It's not always apparent which is best for a given photo, so you may want to try all three in turn. You can always change your mind and undo your changes by pressing Escape before you accept a change, or undo using Ctrl+Z (⌘-Z) once the change has been made.

Transform commands can be applied only to layers, so if your image has only a background layer, the first thing Elements does when you choose one is to ask you convert it to a regular layer. Just say yes and go on. Once the Transform command is active, you see the handles around your image.

3. **Transform your image.**

   Grab a handle and pull in the direction you want the image to move. You can switch to another handle to pull in a different direction, too. If you decide you made a mistake, just press the Escape key (Esc) to return to your original photo.

4. **When you're happy with how your photo looks, accept the change.**

   Click the Commit button (the checkmark) in the Options bar, or press Enter/Return. Click the Cancel button instead if you decide not to apply your transformation to your photo.

Free Transform

Free Transform combines all the other Transform commands and lets you warp your image in many different ways. If you aren't sure what you need to do, Free Transform is a good choice, because it combines all the other Transform commands into one.

You use Free Transform exactly the way you use the other Transform tools, following the steps listed earlier. The difference is that with Free Transform, you can pull in any direction, using keystroke combinations to tell Elements which kind of transformation you want to apply. Each particular transformation, listed as follows, does exactly the same thing it would if you selected that transformation from the Image → Transform menu:

- **Distort.** To make your photo taller or shorter, Ctrl+drag (⌘-drag) any handle. You should see a gray arrowhead for your cursor.

- **Skew.** To make your photo lean to the left or right, Ctrl+Shift+drag (⌘-Shift-drag) a handle in the middle of a side. You should see the gray arrow with a tiny double-arrow attached to it.

- **Perspective.** To correct the way an object appears so that it leans away from you or towards you, press Ctrl+Alt+Shift (⌘-Option-Shift) and drag a corner. You see the same gray arrowhead that you see when you're distorting.

The Free Transform command is the most powerful of all the transformation commands, but when you're pulling in several different directions, it can be tricky to keep your photo from warping. Consequently, some people prefer to use the simpler Transform commands and apply multiple transformations instead.

Barreling and Pinching

The Transform commands are great when you need to pull your image in one dimension only, but they're not much help if your image suffers from the bowed appearance that comes from barrel (outward) or pinch (inward) distortion:

- **Barrel distortion.** When you shoot up close with your lens wide open, you may see that vertical lines in your photo balloon outwards, as shown in the extreme example in Figure 10-12.

- **Pinch distortion.** The opposite of barreling, where the subject looks slightly squeezed. It happens at the opposite end of the focal length scale, but fortunately isn't usually a big problem for digital cameras.

Figure 10-12:
This photo shows a dramatic example of barrel distortion. Note how the wall with the clock on it bends outward in the middle. (This is a crop, so you are seeing only one quarter of the barreling—without the corresponding bowing of the lower half or the other side of the complete image.)

Adobe suggests going to Filter → Distort → Pinch to correct barrel distortion and Filter → Distort → Spherize for pinch distortion. These filters (see Chapter 12 for more about filters) work fairly well, but since the preview window is so small, it can be tricky to use them.

For either filter, try a setting of 5 percent to start with, and keep undoing and redoing by using Ctrl+Z (⌘-Z). You could also choose a very low number, like 1 percent, and keep applying the filter by pressing Ctrl+F (⌘-F) until you've reduced the distortion enough.

Many people prefer third-party solutions like the free PTlens plug-in, which is part of Panotools panorama-stitching software. You can download this free for Windows from *http://panotools.sourceforge.net/*. There is a version for Mac OS X, called PTMac, available from *www.kekus.com*, but it's shareware, not freeware.

Both Web sites also feature panorama software that may interest you if you find you want more than Photomerge can do, like a 360 degree panorama, for example. There are many other panorama creation programs available for both platforms, and you might find you prefer them because most are more automatic than the Elements version.

Part Four: Artistic Elements

4

Drawing with Brushes, Shapes, and Other Tools

If you're not of the artistic persuasion, you may feel tempted to skip this chapter. After all, you probably just want to fix and enhance your photos. What do you care about brush technique? Surprisingly enough, you should care quite a lot. In Elements, the idea of a brush extends to a great many things you might not expect. Brushes aren't just for painting a moustache and horns on a picture of someone you don't like, or for blackening your sister's teeth in that old school photo.

Many tools in Elements use brushes to apply their effects. So far, you've already run into the Selection brush, the Clone Stamp, and the Color Replacement tool, to name just a few. And even with the Brush tool, you can paint with lots of things besides color—like lights or shadows, for example. In Elements, when you want to apply an effect in a precise manner, you're often going to use some sort of brush to do it.

If you are used to working with real brushes, their digital cousins can take some getting used to, but there are many serious artists now who paint primarily in Photoshop. With Elements, you now have access to most of the same tools as in Photoshop, if not quite all the settings available for each tool. Figure 11-1 shows an example of the detailed work you can do with Elements and some artistic ability.

This chapter explains how to use the Brush tool, some of the other brush-like tools (like the Erasers), and how to draw shapes even if you can't hold a pencil steady. You also get some practical applications for your new skills, like dodging and burning your photos to enhance them, and a super-easy way to create sophisticated artistic crops for your photos.

Figure 11-1:
*This complex drawing by artist
Jodi Frye was done entirely in
Elements. If you learn to wield
all the drawing power in
Elements, you can create
amazingly detailed artwork.
Jodi has a gallery of many more
Elements drawings in a wide
variety of styles at www.
frontiernet.net/~jlfrye/
Jodi_Frye.*

Picking and Using a Basic Brush

If you look at the Toolbox, you'll see the Brush tool icon just below the Eraser.
(Don't confuse it with the Selection brush, which is up above the Type tool.) Click
the Brush tool's icon or press B to activate it.

The Brush is one of the tools that include a hidden drawer—you can choose
between the Brush, the Impressionist brush, and the Color Replacement brush.

You can read about the Impressionist brush later in this chapter, and about the Color Replacement brush on page 233. This section is about the regular Brush tool.

If you look at the Options bar (Figure 11-2), you can see that the Brush offers you a lot of opportunity for customizing the tool.

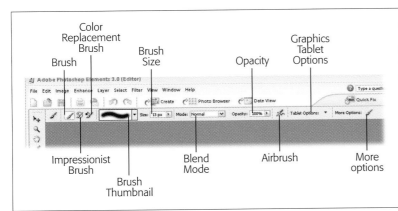

Figure 11-2:
These are the Options bar settings for the Brush tool. By changing these settings and the hidden settings—revealed when you click the More Options button—you can dramatically alter the behavior of any brush.

Here's a quick rundown (from left to right) of the available Brush options:

- **Brush, Impressionist brush, or Color Replacement tool.** Click any of these three icons to activate the particular brush tool you want. The Impressionist brush applies a painting style effect. The Color Replacement tool lets you brush in a replacement color for any particular color in your image.

- **The Brushstroke thumbnail.** The Options bar displays a thumbnail of the stroke you'd get with the current brush. Click the brushstroke thumbnail to see the Brush palette. Elements gives you a bunch of basic brush collections, which you can view and select here. You can also download many more from various Web sites. (See Chapter 17 for more about where to look for brushes to add to Elements.)

  If you click the pull-down menu, you'll see that you get more than just hard or soft brushes of various sizes (see Figure 11-3). You also get special brushes for drop shadows, brushes that are sensitive to pen pressure if you're using a graphics tablet (although they also work if you're using the mouse—you just don't have as many options), and brushes that paint shapes and designs.

  NOTE One very cool feature of the brushes in Elements is that any changes you make to a brush are shown in the little brushstroke thumbnail in the Brush palette.

- **Size.** This pull-down menu lets you adjust the size of your brush—anywhere from one pixel up to sizes that may be too big to fit on your monitor. Or you can just type in a size. Figure 11-4 shows you an easy way to adjust brush size using your mouse. You can also press the close bracket key (]) to quickly increase brush size or the open bracket key ([) to decrease it as you're working.

Figure 11-3:
Elements gives you a pretty good list of different brushes to choose from, or you can add your own. You can make brushes, too, as explained on page 276.

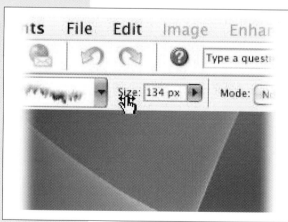

Figure 11-4:
Clicking on pull-down menus to choose your brush size is so last-version. In Elements 3, you don't need to open pull-down menus like this one to adjust their contents. Just move your cursor under the word "size," and your cursor changes into a hand-with-double-headed-arrow. Now you can "scrub" back and forth right on the Options bar to make the changes—left for smaller, right for larger. This trick also works anywhere in Elements you see a numerical pop-out slider (as in the Layer palette's Opacity menu, for example).

- **Mode.** Choices in this pull-down menu determine your blend mode. The modes determine how the brush color interacts with what's in your image. For example, Normal simply paints the current foreground color (more about all the Mode choices later).

- **Opacity.** Opacity controls how thoroughly your brushing covers what's beneath it. You can use the pull-down menu's slider or type in any number you like, from 1 to 100. 100 percent gets you total coverage.

- **Airbrush.** Clicking the little pen-like brush just to the right of the Opacity control lets you use the brush as an airbrush. Figure 11-5 shows you how this works.

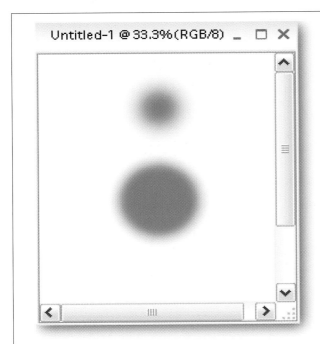

Figure 11-5:
As with real airbrushes, Elements' airbrush option causes Elements to continue to "spray" paint as long as you hold down the mouse cursor, regardless of whether the mouse is moving or not.

Top: This shows the effect of one click with the brush in Regular mode.

Bottom: This shows the effect of the same brush in Airbrush mode. Notice how far the color has spread out beyond the actual brush cursor when using the airbrush. Not every brush offers this option.

- **Tablet Options.** If you use a graphics tablet, you can use these settings to tell Elements which settings should respond to the pressure of your stroke. There's more about graphics tablets in Chapter 17.

- **More Options.** Clicking this icon gets you the Brush Dynamics palette, which gives you oodles of ways to customize your brush, which are covered in the next section. If you're using your brush for artistic purposes, you should familiarize yourself with these settings, since this is where you can set a chiseled stroke or a fade, for example.

To actually use the Brush, you enter your settings—make sure you've selected the color you want in the Foreground color square (page 174)—and then just drag across your image wherever you want to paint.

> **TIP**   If you ever want to return a brush to its original settings, click the Brush button on the far-left side of the Options bar, then click Reset Tool from the pop-up menu.

One of the biggest differences between drawing on a computer and drawing with a real brush is that, on a computer, it doesn't matter how hard you press the mouse. But if you've got a graphics tablet, an electronic pad that causes your pen movements to appear instantly onscreen, you can replicate real-world brushing, including pressure effects. Chapter 17 tells you everything you need to know about using a graphics tablet.

> **NOTE** If you're used to painting with long, sweeping strokes, keep in mind that in Elements, that technique can be frustrating. That's because when you undo a mistake (by pressing Ctrl+Z [⌘-Z]), Elements undoes everything you've done while you've been holding down the mouse button.
>
> In tricky spots, you can save yourself some aggravation by using shorter strokes so you don't have to lose that whole long curve you painstakingly worked on just because you wobbled a bit at the end. (The Eraser tool [page 289] can be handy in these situations, too, for tidying up.)

TROUBLESHOOTING MOMENT

What Happened to My Cursor?

One thing that drives newcomers to Elements nuts is having the Brush cursor change from a circle to little crosshairs, seemingly spontaneously. This is one of those "It's not a bug; it's a feature" situations. Many tools in Elements offer you the option of what is called the precise cursor, shown in the illustration. There are situations where you might prefer to see those little crosshairs so that you can tell exactly where you're working.

You toggle the precise cursor by pressing the Caps Lock key. So if you hit that key by accident, you may find yourself in precise cursor mode with no idea of how you got there. Just press it again to turn it off.

There's one other way you may wind up with the precise cursor, and this time you have no choice in the matter. It happens when your image is so small in proportion to the cursor that Elements must display the crosshairs to show the brush in the right scale for your image. Zooming the view larger usually gets your regular cursor back, unless you're working with a 1-pixel brush, which always uses crosshairs.

There's another wrinkle to the mysterious cursor problem. Your cursor may look like a tiny icon instead of the brush circle. Once again, this is a preference. Go to Edit → Preferences → Display and Cursors → Painting Cursors → Brush Size (Photoshop Elements → Preferences → Display and Cursors → Painting Cursors → Brush Size) to get back the normal brush. This preference window also lets you turn off the specialized cursors for tools like the Lasso tools. To do so, in the Other Cursors box, choose Standard.

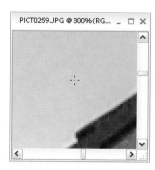

> **TIP** To draw or paint a straight line, hold down the Shift key while your draw or paint. If you click where you want your line to start, and press and hold Shift, and then click at the end point, Elements draws a straight line between those two points. It's important to click first, then press Shift, or you may draw lines where you don't want them.

Modifying Your Brush

When you click the More Options button in the Options bar, you'll see a palette that lets you customize the brush in a number of ways. Its official name is the Brush Dynamics palette. You'll also run into a version of this palette for some of the other brush-like tools, like the Healing brush.

The Brush Dynamics palette options let you change the way your brush behaves in a number of sophisticated and fun ways. Mastering these settings goes a long way toward getting artistic results in Elements.

- **Spacing** controls how far apart the brush marks get put down. A lower number makes them close together, a higher number farther apart, as shown in Figure 11-6.

Figure 11-6:
The same brush stroke with the spacing set at 5 percent, 75 percent, and 150 percent (respectively, from top to bottom). You may have been wondering why some of the brush thumbnails look like long caterpillars, when the brush should paint an object, like a star or leaf. The reason? Cramped spacing: the thumbnail shows the spacing as Elements originally sets it. Widen the spacing to see separate objects instead of a clump.

- **Fade** controls how fast the brush stroke fades out—just the way a real one does when you run out of paint. Think of the numbers as sort of "how many steps" it would take to run out of paint. A lower number means it fades out very fast (very few steps) while a higher one means the fade happens later (more steps). You can pick a number up to 9999, so with a little fiddling, you should be able to get just what you want.

   If the brush isn't fading fast enough, decrease the number. If it fades too fast, increase it. A smaller brush usually needs a higher number than a larger brush would. You may find that you need to set the spacing up into the 20s or higher to make fading show any visible effect.

- **Hue Jitter** controls how fast the brush switches between the background and foreground colors. Some brushes, especially the ones that you'd use to paint objects like leaves, automatically vary the color for a more interesting or realistic effect. The higher the number here, the faster the color moves from foreground to background color. A lower number means the brush takes a longer distance to get from one color to the other. Brushes that acknowledge hue jitter don't put down only the two colors, but a range of hues in between. Not all brushes respond to this setting, but for the ones that do, it's a pretty cool feature. Figure 11-7 shows you how it works.

- **Hardness** controls whether the brush edge is sharp or fuzzy. This setting isn't available with all brush types, but when it is, you can choose any value between zero and 100 percent.

Figure 11-7:
Top: A brushstroke with no hue jitter.

Middle: The same brushstroke with a medium hue jitter value.

*Bottom: The same brushstroke with a high hue jitter value. The foreground/
background colors here are red and blue. Notice how the brush automatically
does a little shading, even without allowing for jitter. It takes a fairly high number
to get all the way to blue in a stroke of this length.*

- **Scatter** means just what it says—how far the marks get distributed in your stroke. If scatter is very low, you get a dense, line-like stroke, whereas a higher value gives an effect more like random spots.

- **Angle and Roundness.** If you've ever painted with a real brush, you should understand these two right away. They let you create a more chiseled edge to your brush and also rotate it so that it's not always painting with the edge facing the same direction. Painters don't use only round brushes, and you don't have to in Elements, either.

  There are some brushes in the libraries that aren't round, like the calligraphy and chalk brushes. But you can adjust the roundness of any brush to make it more suitable for chiseled strokes. See Figure 11-8.

There's also a checkbox ("Keep these settings for all brushes") you can turn on if you want to keep the same settings for all your brushes.

Saving Modified Brush Settings

If you modify a brush and you like the result, you can save it as a custom brush. You can alter any of the existing brushes and save the result—a great feature if you're working on a project that's going to last a while and you don't want to have to keep modifying the settings again and again. Or maybe you just want to be able to use both the original brush and your redesigned one. Either way, to create your own brush, just:

1. **Choose a brush to modify.**

   Select a brush in the Brush palette. You can customize any of the brushes.

2. **Make the changes you want.**

   Change the brush settings until you get what you're after. Watch the brush thumbnail in the Options bar as you go. It changes to reflect your new settings.

3. **Tell Elements you want to keep the new brush.**

   Click the arrow in the upper-right corner of the brush thumbnails palette and choose "Save Brush." Elements asks you to name it. You don't absolutely have to, but naming brushes makes them easier to keep track of.

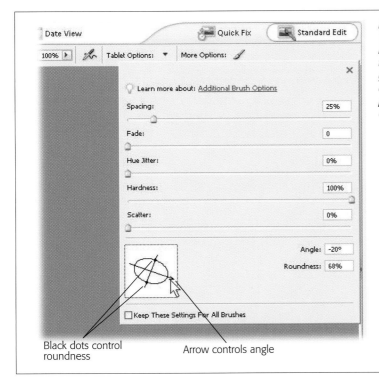

Figure 11-8:
To adjust the angle and roundness of a brush, you push the black dots to make the brush rounder or narrower, then grab the arrow and spin the brush to the angle you want. You can also type a percentage directly into either the Angle or Roundness box.

Black dots control roundness

Arrow controls angle

4. **Click OK.**

The brush shows up in the bottom of your list of brushes.

Deleting brushes is pretty straightforward. You can select the brush in the Brush palette and then choose Delete Brush from the pop-out menu. Or you can Alt+click (Option-click) the brush thumbnail. The cursor will change to a pair of scissors when you hold down the key. Clicking with the scissors deletes the brush.

You can also make a selection from an image and save it as a brush, if you like (the next section shows you how). Just remember, though, that brushes by definition don't have color, so you save only the shape of your selection, not the full coloring of it. The color you get is whichever color you choose to apply. If you want to save a full color sample, try saving your sample as a pattern (page 221) or a texture (page 464) or just use the clone stamp repeatedly instead.

The Specialty Brushes

So far you've been reading about brushes that behave pretty much as brushes do in the real world—they paint a stripe of something, whether color, light, or even transparency.

But in the digital world, a brush doesn't have to be just a brush. With some of the brushes included in Elements, you can paint stars, flowers, disembodied eyeballs, gravel, or even rubber ducks with just one swipe of the brush, as shown in Figure 11-9.

Figure 11-9:
You can digitally doodle using the Elements brushes even if you can't draw a straight line. Everything in this lovely drawing was done with brushes included with Elements. The leaves were painted with a brush that paints leaves, the yellow ducks come from a brush that paints rubber ducks, and so on.

If you click the arrow next to the brush thumbnail in the Options bar, you'll see the list of brushes in the current category and a pull-down menu that lets you investigate the other brush sets you got with Elements. The brushes used in Figure 11-9, for example, came from several different categories, but you have all of them if you have Elements. Some brushes are sensitive to your pen pressure if you're using a graphics tablet (page 419).

The Specialty brushes respond very readily to changes in the Brush Dynamics settings (covered earlier in this chapter). Your choices there can make a huge difference in the effect you get—whether you're painting swathes of smooth grass, like a lawn, or scattered sprigs of dune grass, for instance. You get the exact same list of choices described in the previous section on the Brush Dynamics palette: spacing, fade, hue jitter, etc.

> **TIP** If you've tried some of the special effects brushes and found the results rather anemic, you can always go back once you've painted and punch up the color with a Multiply layer (page 155), just as you would do for an overexposed photo.

Making a Custom Brush

You can turn any picture, or selection within a picture, into a brush that paints the shape you've selected. Figure 11-10 shows what a wreath looks—and behaves like—when it's been turned into a brush.

Figure 11-10:
Top: If you want to make a brush to draw holiday wreaths, just select a wreath in a photo and save it as a brush.

Bottom: You can paint better than you thought! Notice, too, that some of the ragged edges of the wreath were left out to improve the shape of the brush.

It's surprisingly easy to create a custom brush from any object you have a picture of.

1. **Open a photo or drawing that includes what you want to use as a brush.**

   You can choose an area as large as 2,500 pixels square. (Remember, you can resize your selection once it's a brush, just the way you can resize any other brush, so don't worry if it's a big area.)

2. **Select the object or region you want.**

Use any of the Selection tools. It's a good idea to check your selection with the Selection brush in Mask mode as a last step (page 113). That's because any stray areas you included by mistake get painted down with each stroke—just as if you wanted them to be there.

3. **Create your brush.**

Go to Edit → Define Brush from Selection. You see a dialog box showing the shape and asking you to name your new brush. Check the thumbnail to be sure it's exactly what you had in mind. If not, click Cancel and try again. If you like what you've got, click Okay.

The new brush shows up at the bottom of your Default list of brushes. If you want to get rid of it, highlight the thumbnail in the brush thumbnails, click the arrow on the right side of the palette, and go to "Delete Brush."

The Impressionist Brush

When you paint with the Impressionist brush, you blur and blend the edges of the objects in your photo, just like an Impressionist painting. At least that's what's supposed to happen. This brush can be very tricky to control, but you can get some very interesting effects, especially if you paint with it on a duplicate layer and play with the Opacity control (page 272). Usually you want a very low opacity with this brush, or some of the curlier styles will make your image look like it's made from poodle hair.

The Impressionist brush has most of the same options as the regular Brush, but if you click the More Options button, you'll see three new choices:

- **Style** determines what kind of brushstroke effect you want to create.
- **Area** tells Elements the size and number of brushstrokes.
- **Tolerance** is how similar in color pixels have to be before they're affected by the brush.

If you really want to create a hand-painted look, you might prefer the brushstroke filters (Filter → Brush Strokes). Chapter 12 explains how to use them. The Impressionist brush is really not the best tool for true Impressionist effects, although its blurring qualities can sometimes be useful, because it covers large areas faster than the Blur tool.

The Pencil Tool

The Pencil tool is basically just another brush, although it has its own icon, just above the Eraser in the Toolbox. Click it or press N to activate the Pencil.

It has many of the same setting options as the Brush—like size, mode, and opacity—but it offers only hard-edged brushes. In other words, you can't draw fuzzy lines with the pencil, not even the kind of lines you'd sketch with a soft pencil. The Pencil's lines are always very well defined.

You use the Pencil tool the same way you use any other brush. The big difference is the Auto Erase option (the checkbox is located in the Options bar). Auto Erase makes the Pencil paint with the background color over areas that contain the foreground color. But if you start dragging in an area that doesn't contain the foreground color, it paints with the foreground color instead. This is really confusing until you try it, but then it's pretty easy to understand. Take a look at Figure 11-11 for some help in understanding what's going on, or better yet, create a blank document and try it yourself.

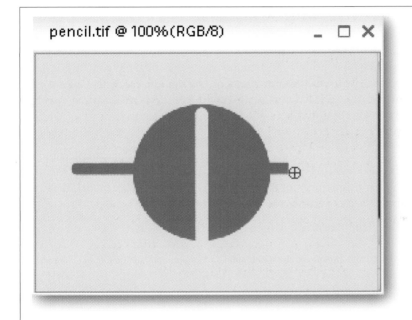

Figure 11-11:
The slightly confusing Auto Erase option, used to create two lines: a horizontal one consisting of the foreground color (blue) and a vertical one consisting of the background color (pink).

The horizontal line was drawn by starting with the cursor in the background (thus, the pencil erased the pink, leaving a blue line across the circle). On the other hand, the pink line was drawn by starting inside the blue circle, causing the background color to be exposed.

The Paint Bucket

When you want to fill a large area with color in a hurry, the Paint Bucket's the tool for you. It's right below the Brush tool in the Toolbox. If you click it or press K to activate it, then click in your image, the entire available area (either your whole image, or the current selection) gets flooded with color. It works something like the Magic Wand: just as the Magic Wand selects the color you click, the Paint Bucket fills only the color you click.

Use this tool to change the color of a solid layer with one click. Most of the Options bar settings for the Paint Bucket are probably familiar:

- **Fill.** Choose to fill the area with the foreground color (page 174) or a pattern. You can choose from any of the existing patterns (listed in the Pattern drop-down menu on the Options bar). Or you can create your own, just as you would with the Pattern Stamp (see page 222).

- **Mode.** Use the Paint Bucket in any blend mode, as explained earlier in this chapter on page 281.

- **Opacity.** 100 percent opacity gives you total coverage; nothing shows through the paint you put down. Lower the percentage for a more transparent effect.

- **Tolerance.** This setting works the same way it does for the Magic Wand (page 108). The higher the number, the more shades the paint fills.

- **Anti-aliased.** This setting smoothes the edges of the fill. Leave it turned on unless you have a specific reason not to.

- **Contiguous.** This is another old familiar from the Magic Wand. If you leave Contiguous on, you change only areas of the chosen color that touch each other. Turn it off, and all areas of the color you click get changed, whether they're contiguous or not.

- **Use All Layers.** Fills any pixels that meet your criteria, no matter what layer they're on. To keep out just one layer, click the Eyeball icon on the Layers palette to hide the layer you want to exclude. Turn it back on by clicking the same spot again after using the Paint Bucket. Don't forget that you can lock the transparent parts of layers in the Layers palette. (See page 136.)

You can undo a Paint Bucket fill with the usual Ctrl+Z (⌘-Z).

> **TIP**   You can sometimes improve blown out skies by using the Eyedropper (page 177) to select an appropriate shade of blue from another photo, then filling the blown-out areas of your sky using the Paint Bucket at a very low opacity.

Dodging and Burning

Like Unsharp Mask, dodging and burning are old darkroom techniques to enhance photos and emphasize particular areas. Dodging lightens shadows and brings out the details hidden in them, and burning darkens highlights, bringing out their details. Both tools live with the Sponge tool in the Toolbox, so you may have run into them while you were using the Sponge.

You may think that since you have the Shadows/Highlights command, you don't have any need for these tools. But they still serve a useful purpose, because they let you make selective changes, rather than affecting the entire image the way Shadows/Highlights does. Figure 11-12 gives an example of when you might need to work on a particular area.

clapping.tif @ 100%(Layer 1, RGB/8)

Figure 11-12:
Although the overall shadow/highlight balance of this photo is about right, the detail in the face of this little concert-goer is obscured by backlighting and by her father's shadow. Careful dodging and burning can really improve these problems, as you can see in Figure 11-13.

Skillful use of dodging and burning can greatly enhance the effectiveness of your photo, although it helps to have an artistic eye to spot what you want to emphasize and what you want to downplay.

Both the Dodge and Burn tools are really variants of the Brush tool, except that they don't apply color directly—they just affect the colors that are already present in your photo. Adobe refers to these two as the "toning tools."

One caution about these tools, though—unless you use them on a duplicate layer, you can't undo the effect once you close your photo. So you need to be careful how you use them. Actually, many people prefer to dodge and burn using the method described in the section "Blend Modes," rather than with the actual Dodge and Burn tools.

Dodging

The Dodge tool is used to lighten areas of your image and to bring out details that may be hidden in shadows. It's a good idea to create a separate layer (Layer → Duplicate Layer or Ctrl+J [⌘-J]) when you use this tool, to preserve your image if you go overboard. Be sure you're applying the Dodge tool to a layer that has something in it, or nothing happens.

1. **Activate the Dodge tool.**

   Click the Sponge tool in the Toolbox and choose the Dodge tool (the lollipop-like paddle) from the pop-out menu, or press O and click the Dodge tool in the Options bar. You'll see the usual brush options, but with one difference: a choice of whether the tool should work on highlights, midtones, or shadows.

2. **Drag over the area you want to change.**

   Choose a very low opacity for these tools and drag more than once to get a more realistic result (see Figure 11-13). After you're done, if you think the Dodge tool's effect is still too strong, you can always reduce the opacity of the layer in the Layers palette.

Dodging can be used to create highlights or to even out areas that have been too deeply shadowed.

Burning

The Burn tool does exactly the opposite of what the Dodge tool does. It darkens and can be used to make highlights show more details. Of course, there have to be some details there for the tool to work. If your photo's highlights are blown out (see page 157), you won't get any results no matter how much you apply the tool.

The Burn tool is applied exactly the same way the Dodge tool is, and most of the time, you'll probably want to use these tools in combination. They work best for subtle changes. Applying them too vigorously gives an obviously faked look to your photo. But careful use can help draw attention to specific parts of your photo.

> **TIP** You can switch between the Dodge and Burn tools by pressing the O key until the tool you want is highlighted in the Options bar. (The Sponge tool is between them.)

Blending and Smudging

In Elements, you can control how the color you add to your image blends with the colors that are already there. This section takes a look at blending in two different ways—using the Smudge tool to literally mix elements of your image together, and using blend modes to determine how the colors you paint change what's already in your image. Blend modes are almost limitless in how you can use them to manipulate your images.

Figure 11-13:
Figure 11-12 after the Dodge and Burn tools. The girl's features are much easier to see, but if you look closely, you can see that the colors in her face are a bit flat. See the figure in the box on page 287 to compare a different method for selectively adjusting highlights and shadows. Both solutions have advantages and disadvantages. Things are deliberately a bit too strong in both figures to show you the perils of getting over-zealous with either method.

Blend Modes

Blend modes control how the color you add when you paint reacts with the pixels in your image—whether you just add color (Normal mode), make the existing color darker (Multiply mode), or change the saturation (Saturation mode).

Many uses for the blend modes are more advanced and beyond the scope of this book (the book would be well over a thousand pages long). But Figure 11-14 shows a few examples of how simply changing the brush blend mode can radically change your result.

Blend modes can be combined together in ways that create results that even Elements pros can't always predict, though, so experimenting is the best way to learn about them. Also, many of the more advanced books on Elements include projects that require using the different modes.

Figure 11-14:
This photo shows the effect of some of the different blend modes when used with the Brush tool. The same color was used for every one of the vertical stripes—you can see how different the result is from just changing the mode. From left to right, the modes are: Normal, Color Burn, Color Dodge, Vivid Light, Difference, and Saturation.

Blend modes are grouped according to the effects that they have. The top group includes what you might call painting modes, followed by modes for darkening, lightening, adjusting light, special effects modes, and adjusting color.

It's also important to be aware that the modes work quite differently with layers than with tools. In other words, painting with a brush in Dissolve mode is going to produce an effect quite different than creating a layer in Dissolve mode and painting on it, as shown in Figure 11-15.

Modes are really cool and very useful once you get used to using them, but if you are just starting out in Elements, there's no need to worry about them right away.

> **TIP**   Elements 3 includes a new blend mode: Hard Mix. It produces a sort of posterization of the colors in your image, reducing everything to white, black, green, red, blue, yellow, cyan, or magenta.

The Smudge Tool

The Smudge tool does just what its name says. You can use it to smear the colors in your image, just as if you had rubbed them with your finger. You can even "finger paint" with the Smudge tool, if you feel the call of your inner fifth grader. Adobe describes the effect of the Smudge tool as being "like a finger dragged through wet paint." A warning—if you have a slow computer, there can be quite a bit of lag time between when you apply the Smudge tool and when the effect actually shows up. This makes it tricky to control, because you need to resist the temptation to keep going over the area until you see results.

Blend Modes Instead of Dodge and Burn

You can do a lot in Elements without ever getting down and dirty with blend modes, but there are a lot of things you can do more effectively and easily if you take the time to familiarize yourself with them. For instance, you might prefer the effect you get using a layer in Overlay mode to that of the Dodge and Burn tools. The nice thing about using a layer is that you can always trash the layer if you decide you don't like your changes. If you've applied the Dodge tool, say, by clicking it 87 times, then you're pretty much stuck with what you've done.

To adjust a photo using an Overlay blend mode layer instead of the Dodge and Burn tools, you'd first make basic adjustments like Levels or Shadows/Highlights. Then, when you're ready to fine-tune your photo by painting over the details you want to enhance, here're the steps you'd follow:

1. Create a new layer.

   Go to Layer → New → Layer or press Ctrl+Shift+N (⌘-Shift-N).

2. Before you dismiss the New Layer dialog box, choose the Overlay blend mode for your new layer.

   Select Overlay in the Layer mode menu and turn on the box that says "Fill with Overlay-neutral color (50% gray)." You won't see anything happen yet.

3. Set the foreground and background colors to their original settings.

   Press D to set the colors in the Foreground/Background squares to black and white.

4. Activate the Brush tool.

   Choose a brush (set to Normal mode) and set the opacity very low, maybe 17 percent or so. You'll need to experiment a bit to see how low a setting is low enough.

5. Paint on the areas you want to adjust.

   Paint with white to bring up the detail in dark areas and with black to darken overly light areas. (Remember that you can switch colors by pressing X.) The detail on your photo comes up just like magic.

This is just one example of what you can do with modes, and the figure shows how it compares with using the Dodge and Burn tools. The color isn't grayish—as dodging made it—but the contrast where shadowed areas meet bright ones still needs some work. It has the added advantage of being adjustable by changing the opacity of the overlay layer

.

PICT0259.JPG @ 33.3%(Layer 1, RGB/8)

Figure 11-15:
Blend modes behave differently when used in layers than they do when you use a tool in the same mode. Both these strokes were done using Dissolve mode in pure black at 100 percent opacity. The difference is that the top stroke is painted with the Brush tool in Dissolve mode while the bottom one is a brush stroke in normal mode on a Dissolve layer.

The Smudge tool hides under the Blur tool in the Toolbox. Click the Blur tool and, from the pop-out menu, choose the Smudge tool (its icon is a finger, painting), or press R and keep pressing it till the Smudge tool's icon is active.

The Smudge tool offers mostly the same settings as a regular brush, including the Use All Layers option (page 217), with two differences, Strength and Finger Painting:

- **Strength.** This setting means just what it says—it controls how hard the tool smudges the colors together. A higher number results in more blending.

- **Finger Painting.** Turning on this box makes the Smudge tool smear the foreground color at the start of each stroke. Otherwise, it uses the color that's under the cursor at the start of each stroke. Figure 11-16 helps you understand the difference.

Once you've chosen your settings, smudge away.

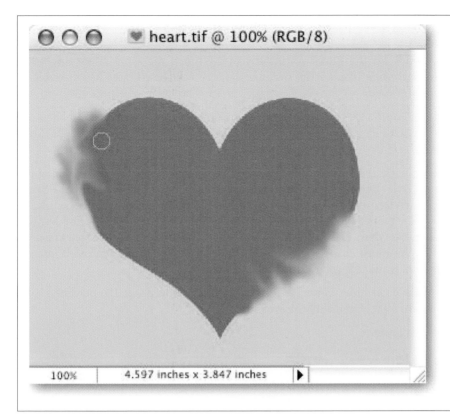

Figure 11-16:
The Smudge tool smears colors together. The stroke on the left was done with the Finger Painting checkbox turned on, which lets you introduce a bit of the foreground color (green, in this case) into the beginning of each stroke. This is very useful for shading or when you need to mix in just a touch of another color. The smudging on the right was done with Finger Painting off, so it uses only the colors that are already in your image.

NOTE   When using the Smudge tool, you only see results where two colors come together. It blends together the pixel colors where edges meet. If you use Smudge in the middle of an area of solid color, nothing happens.

The Eraser Tool

Everyone makes mistakes sometimes. Adobe has thoughtfully included three different mistake-fixers. If you click and hold the Eraser's icon in the Toolbox, you'll see the Eraser, the Magic Eraser, and the Background Eraser. You'll probably use all three Erasers at one time or another. You can also activate the Eraser by pressing E and then clicking the one you want in the Options bar.

Using the Eraser

The Eraser is basically just another kind of brush tool, only instead of adding color to your image, it removes color from the pixels. How it works varies a little, depending on where you use it.

If you use the Eraser on a regular layer, it replaces the color with transparency. On a background layer, or one in which transparency is locked, it replaces whatever color is there with the background color (see Chapter 6 for more about how layers work).

The settings for the Eraser are mostly pretty much the same as for any other brush—including brush style, size, and opacity—but the Eraser has a couple of options of its own:

- **Mode.** For the Eraser, Mode doesn't have anything to do with blend modes, but rather tells Elements the shape of the eraser you want to work with. Your choices are Brush, Pencil, and Block.

  You can see the difference in how the Eraser is going to work by watching the brush style preview in the Options bar as you change Modes. Picking the Brush or Pencil lets you use the Eraser as you would those tools—in other words, by choosing a brush you can choose any brush you like. The Brush option lets you make soft-edged erasures, while Pencil mode makes only hard-edged erasures. Choosing Block changes the cursor to a square, so that you can use it just the way you would a regular artist's erasing block—sort of.

- **Opacity** determines how much of the color is removed—at 100 percent, it's all gone (or all replaced with the background).

To use the Eraser:

1. **Activate the Eraser.**

   Click the Eraser tool in the Toolbox or press E. The tool looks like an eraser, so it's easy to find.

2. **Choose your settings.**

   Select the kind of Eraser you want, select a mode, and then choose the eraser's size and opacity.

   These choices work the same way they do for regular brushes, except for Mode, as noted earlier. The next two sections tell you all about the Magic Eraser and the Background Eraser.

3. **Drag anywhere in your image to remove what you don't want.**

   You may need to change the size of the Eraser a few times. It's usually easiest to use a small eraser (or the Background Eraser as explained later) to accurately clear around the edges of the object you want to keep, as shown in Figure 11-17. Then you can use a larger brush to get rid of the remaining chunks, once you don't have to worry about accidentally going into the area you want to keep.

   TIP   You can use a selection to limit where the Eraser operates.

It can be tedious to erase around a long outline or to remove entire backgrounds, so Elements has two other kinds of Erasers for those situations.

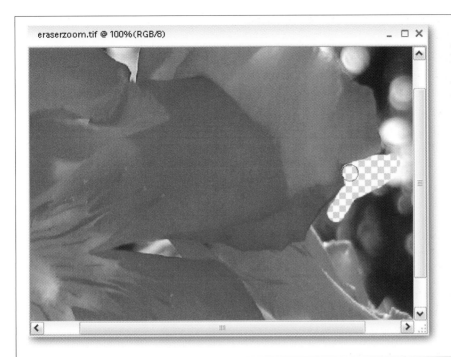

Figure 11-17:
Accurate erasing
around an object
usually means
zooming way, way in
so that you can control
which pixels the Eraser
is changing.

The Magic Eraser

Once you try it, you are likely to wonder why the heck Adobe gave this pedestrian tool such an intriguing name. What's so magic about the Magic Eraser?

Well, not much, really. It's a "Magic" Eraser as in the "Magic" Wand, because it works very much like the Magic Wand tool (page 108). You use it to select pixels of a single color or range (depending on the tolerance settings). It even has the same little sparklies as the Magic Wand does in its icon to remind you of the relationship.

The problem, as Figure 11-18 shows you, is that the Magic Eraser is not as clean in its work as the other erasers. Still, it can be a big help in eliminating large chunks of solid color.

It's usually best to use the Magic Eraser in combination with at least one of the other erasers if you're looking to achieve really clean results.

The Background Eraser

Lots of people think this eraser deserves the name "Magic" much more than the Magic Eraser does. The Background Eraser is a tremendous help when you want to remove all the background around an object. For example, say you've got a photo of a football and you want to quickly remove the ball from the background.

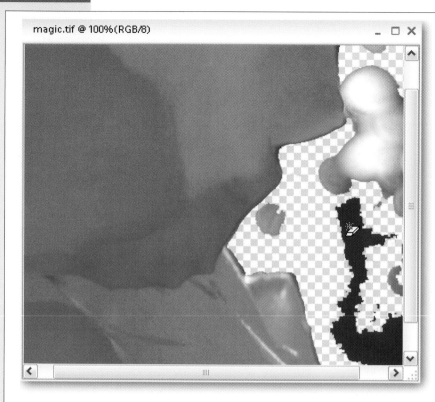

magic.tif @ 100%(RGB/8)

Figure 11-18:
This figure shows a close-up look at the Magic Eraser at work on the flower petals from Figure 11-17. One click of the Magic Eraser got rid of a bunch of the background, and setting the Tolerance higher would've gotten even more. But if you look closely, you can see the disadvantage of the Magic Eraser— the edges of the flowers are fringed with dark ragged areas it didn't eliminate.

The Background Eraser erases all the pixels under the brush (but outside the edges of the object) and renders the area it's used on transparent, even if it's a background layer. (If you click with it on a background layer, your computer may hesitate initially, because it's busy transforming your background to a regular layer.) Here's how to use it:

1. **Select the Background Eraser.**

   Either go to the Toolbox, click the Eraser icon, and then select it from the popout menu, or press E and click its icon in the Options bar. It's the eraser with a pair of scissors next to it.

2. **In the Options bar, choose a brush size.**

   The cursor turns to a circle with crosshairs in it. These crosshairs are important. They are the Background Eraser's "hotspot." Any color that you drag them over is turned to transparency. The circle size changes depending on how large a brush you've chosen, but the crosshairs stay the same size. As you can see in Figure 11-19, with a large brush, there may be a lot of space around the crosshairs, so it's easy to remove big chunks of the background at once, since everything in the circle is going to get eliminated.

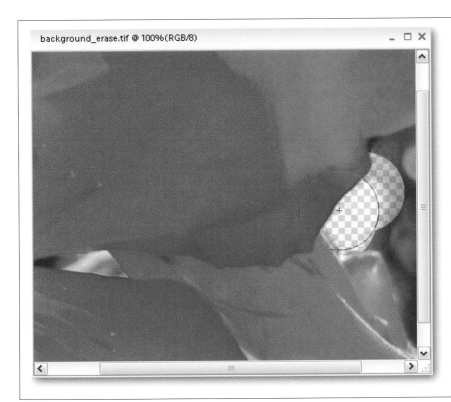

Figure 11-19:
The Background Eraser does a very careful job of separating the flowers from their background. Just be sure to keep the little crosshairs outside the color you want to keep. Here, because the crosshairs are outside the petals, only the background is getting removed. But if you moved the crosshairs into the flower, you'd be biting chunks out of it with the tool.

3. **Drag in your photo.**

   Move around the edge of the object you want to keep, being very careful not to let the crosshairs move into the object, or else you'll start erasing that, too. If you make a mistake, just use Ctrl+Z (⌘-Z) to undo your actions.

If you want to remove the background from around an object, you might find it most effective to start with the Background Eraser around the edge of your object. Then, use the other Erasers to clean up afterward. The advantage to working this way is that you don't have to clean up junk left over from the Magic Eraser. It's also easier to maneuver the Background Eraser than the regular Eraser, especially if you don't have a graphics tablet.

Drawing with Shapes

Wow, so many brush options and Adobe still isn't done—there's yet another way to draw things in Elements. Elements includes a Shape tool, which lets you draw geometrically perfect shapes, regardless of your artistic ability. And not just simple shapes like circles and rectangles. You can draw animals, plants, starbursts, picture frames—all sorts of things, as shown in Figure 11-20. This tool should appeal to anyone whose grade school masterpieces always seemed to get put up on the wall behind the piano somewhere.

Figure 11-20:
Here are just a few of the shapes that you can draw with Elements, even if you have no artistic ability. These objects can be made to look much more impressive when you gussy them up with Layer styles (page 322) and filters (page 306).

Turning yourself into an artist by using the Elements' Shape tool is easy. Just follow these steps:

1. **Open an image or create a new one.**

   You can add shapes to any file that you can open in Elements.

2. **Activate the Shape tool.**

   Click the Shape tool in the Toolbox, or press U. The Shape tool is sometimes a little confusing to newcomers to Elements, because the icon reflects the shape that's currently active—so you may see a rectangle, a polygon, or a line, for instance. The little cartoon speech balloon of the Custom Shape tool is the icon Elements initially presents you with.

3. **Select the kind of shape you want to draw.**

   Click the shape you want in the Options bar. You can choose a rectangle, a rounded rectangle, an ellipse, a polygon, a line, or a custom shape. (If you choose the Custom shape, you have many different shapes to choose from.) All the shapes, and their accompanying options, are described in the following sections.

4. **Adjust your settings in the Options bar.**

   Choose a color by clicking the color square in the Options bar or use the foreground color (page 174). If you click the Options bar color square itself, you see the Color Picker (page 175). If you click the arrow to the right of the square, you get the Color Swatches palette instead (page 180).

   If you have special requirements, like a rectangle that's exactly 1"×2", click the arrow next to the shape thumbnail for the Shape Options palette, and enter the size of your shape.

There's also an Options bar setting that lets you apply a layer style (see page 322) as you draw your shape. Just click the drop-down arrow on the right side of the Style box and choose the style you want from the popout palette. To go back to drawing without a style, choose the rectangle with the diagonal red line through it.

5. **Drag in your image to draw the shape.**

Notice that how you drag the cursor affects the final appearance of the shape. The way you drag determines the proportions of your figure. If you're drawing a fish, you can drag so that it's long and skinny or short and fat. Even with practice, it may take a couple of tries to get exactly the proportions you want.

TIP   If you're trying to create copies of a particular shape, use the Shape Selection tool, described later, to create copies of the first shape.

The Shape tool automatically puts each shape on its own layer. If you don't want to do that, or you need to control how shapes interact, you can use the squares in the middle of the Options bar. They're the same as the ones for managing selections (page 107). Use them to add more than one shape to a layer, subtract a shape from a shape, keep only the area where shapes intersect, or exclude the areas where they intersect.

You can also turn any shape from a vector image (infinitely resizable) into a raster image (pixels) by clicking the Simplify button in the Options bar. The box "Rasterizing Vector Shapes" tells you everything you need to know about the difference between vector and raster images.

TIP   If you want to draw multiple shapes on one layer, click the "Add to Shape" rectangle in the Options bar. Then, everything you do is on the same layer. Shapes don't have to touch or overlap to use this option.

The following sections describe all of the main shape categories and their special settings.

Rectangle and Rounded Rectangle

The Rectangle and the Rounded Rectangle tools work pretty much the same way and are very popular for creating Web page buttons. They both have Shape options settings in the Options bar for:

• **Unconstrained.** Choose this to draw a rectangle of whatever dimensions you want. How you drag determines the proportions of your shape.

• **Square.** To draw a square instead of a rectangle, click this radio button before you start, or just hold down the Shift key as you drag.

- **Fixed Size.** This makes Elements draw your shape the size you specify. Just enter the dimensions you want in inches, pixels, or centimeters.

- **Proportional.** Use this if you know the proportions you want your rectangle to have, but not the exact size. Just type in the proportions. So if you enter a length of 2 and a height of 1, no matter where you drag, the shape is always twice as long as it is high.

- **From Center.** This lets you draw your shape from its center instead of from a corner. It's useful when you know exactly where you want the shape but aren't sure exactly how big it needs to be.

- **Snap to Pixels.** This setting makes sure that the edge of your rectangle falls exactly on the edge of a pixel. You'll get crisper looking edges with it turned on. It's available only for the Rectangle and Rounded Rectangle tools.

Most of the Shape tools have similar options. The Rounded Rectangle has one option of its own, though: Radius. This is the amount, in pixels, that the corners are rounded off. A higher number means more rounding.

Ellipse

The Ellipse has the same Shape Options as the Rectangle tool. The only difference is that you can opt for a circle instead of a square. The Shift key constrains the Ellipse to a circle.

Polygon

You can draw any kind of polygon using this tool. You set the number of sides yourself in the Options bar.

The shape options in the Options bar pull-down menu are a bit different for this tool:

- **Radius.** This sets the distance from the center to the outermost points.

- **Smooth Corners.** If you don't want sharp edges at the corners, choose Smooth Corners.

- **Star.** This setting inverts the angles to create a star-like shape, as shown in Figure 11-21.

- **Indent Sides by.** If you're drawing a star, this sets how much (in percent) you want the sides to indent.

- **Smooth Indent.** Use this if you don't want sharp angles on your star.

Figure 11-21:
Top: A hexagon.

Bottom: Checking the Star option inverts the angles on a polygon, so that instead of drawing a hexagon, you create a star.

Line Tool

Use this tool for drawing straight lines and arrows. Specify the weight (the width) of the line in pixels in the Options bar. If you want an arrowhead on your line, the Shape options give you some settings for adding one to your line as you draw:

- **Start/End.** Do you want the arrowhead at the start or the end of the line you draw? Tell Elements your preference with this setting.

- **Width and Length.** This determines how wide and how long you want the arrowhead to be. The measurement unit is the percentage of the line width, so if you enter a number lower than 100, your arrowhead is narrower than the line it's attached to. You can pick values between 10 percent and 1,000 percent.

- **Concavity.** Use this setting if you want the sides of the arrowhead indented. The number determines the amount of curvature on the widest part of the arrowhead. See Figure 11-22. Pick a setting between –50 percent and +50 percent.

TIP   There are also arrows available in the Custom Shape tool if you want something fancier.

The Custom Shape Tool

The Custom Shape lets you draw a huge variety of different objects. Its icon is the little cartoon talk bubble shape in the Toolbox. Click it or press U to activate the Custom Shape tool. With this tool, you can draw a wealth of different shapes, as you can see from Figure 11-23.

Once the Custom Shape tool is active, if you look in the Options bar, you see a little window labeled Shape with the arrow for a pull-down menu next to it. Click this arrow to bring up the Elements Shape Picker.

There are a variety of different shapes in the Default group but if you click the arrow at the upper-right corner of the window, you get a menu giving you a great many more choices. If you want to be able to scroll through all of them, just choose "All Elements Shapes."

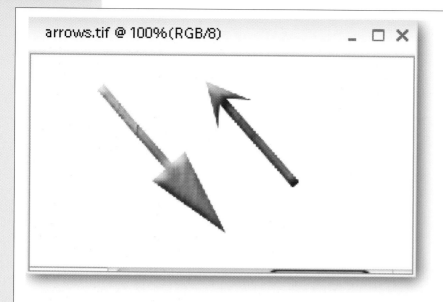

arrows.tif @ 100%(RGB/8)

Figure 11-22:
Two arrows drawn with the Line tool. The left arrow has no concavity; the right one has concavity set to 50 percent. Incidentally, both arrows have Layer styles applied to them so they aren't so flat looking. You can read more about how to do that in the next chapter.

Rasterizing Vector Shapes

Back in Chapter 3, you read about how the majority of your images (definitely your photos) are just a bunch of pixels to Elements. These are known as raster images. The shapes you draw with the Shape tools work a little differently. They're called vector images.

A vector image is made up of a set of directions, specifying what kind of geometric shapes should be drawn. The advantage of vector images is that you can size them way up or down without producing the kind of pixelation you see when you resize a raster image too much.

Your shape keeps its vector characteristics until you simplify the layer that it's on. Simplifying, also called rasterizing, just means that Elements turns your shape into regular pixels. Once you simplify, you have the same limitations on resizing as you do for a regular photo. For example, you can make your image smaller, but you can't make it larger than 100 percent without losing quality. Sooner or later, you'll want to transform your vector image to a regular raster image so that you can do certain things to it, like adding filters or effects.

If you try to do something that requires simplifying a layer, Elements generally asks you to do so, via a pop-up dialog box. To rasterize your shape, just click Okay, or click the Simplify button in the Options bar. Remember that once you've rasterized a shape, if you try to resize, you won't get the nice, clean unpixelated results that you got when it was a vector image. If you need to resize a shape, it's easiest to start over with a new shape—if that's feasible (which is yet another good reason to use layers).

Also, it may puzzle you that, where at one time you were able to change the color of an existing shape by clicking the color box, now, all of a sudden, the shape totally ignores what you do in the Options bar. That's because you simplified the shape layer. Simplifying always affects the entire layer—everything on it is simplified, or nothing is. Once your shape is simplified, you have to make a selection and change the color the way you would on any detail in a photo.

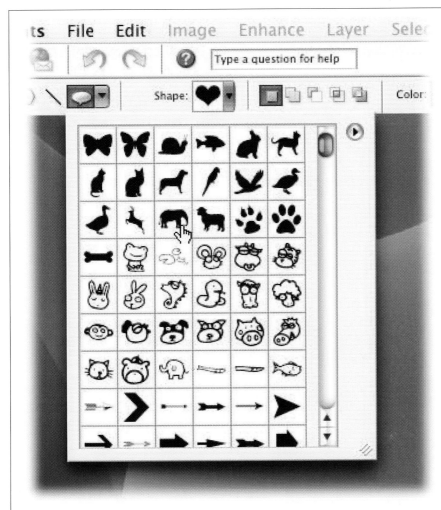

Figure 11-23:
This is just a small part of the shape library you can choose from in the Shape Picker. You can download more custom shapes and add them to C:\ Program files\Adobe Photoshop Elements 3\ Presets\Custom shapes (Applications → Adobe Photoshop Elements 3 → Presets → Custom Shapes). Look for the file extension .csh when you want shapes that you can add to your library. Downloaded shapes that you add show up as drawing options when you click the More button on the Shapes palette.

NOTE   There's a copyright symbol available in the custom shapes if you prefer not to use text to create one.

The Custom shape also has a few optional settings, like the other Shape tools. They are:

- **Unconstrained.** You control the proportions of your shape by the way you drag.

- **Defined Proportions.** The shape always has the proportions the designer gave it when it was created.

- **Defined Size.** The shape is always the size it was originally created to be—dragging won't make it bigger or smaller. It just plinks out at a fixed size that you can't control, except by resizing after the fact.

• **Fixed Size.** You enter the dimensions you want, in inches, pixels, or centimeters.

• **From Center.** You start drawing in the center of the object.

The Shape Selection Tool

The arrow in the Options bar just to the left of the Rectangle tool is the Shape Selection tool. This is a special kind of Move tool (page 119) that works only on shapes that haven't been simplified yet, as explained in Figure 11-24.

It may seem unnecessary, but if you are working with shapes, it saves a lot of time not to have to keep switching tools when you want to move one shape.

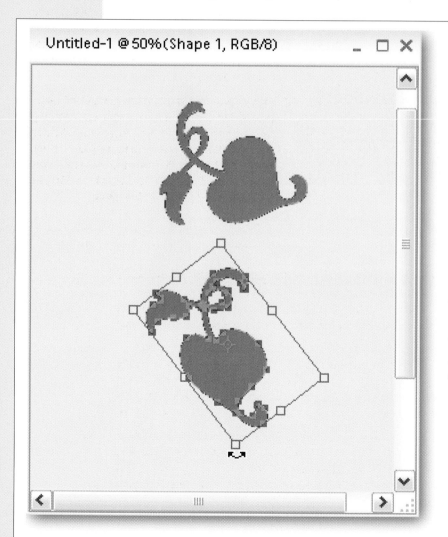

Untitled-1 @ 50%(Shape 1, RGB/8)

Figure 11-24:
The Shape Selection tool gives you the same kind of bounding box as the Move tool and it works the same way, but only on shapes that have not been simplified yet. You can apply transformations like skewing and rotating, too, when the Shape Selection tool is active.

Once you've simplified a shape layer, you need the regular Move tool to move it around. You can always use the Move tool, even on shapes where you can use the Shape Selection tool. But the Shape Selection tool works only on shapes that haven't been simplified yet.

Click the Shape Selection tool and then move your shape. Your shape doesn't have to be on the active layer. You can also use the Shape Selection tool to combine multiple shapes into one by clicking the Combine button.

The Shape Selection tool works just like the Move tool. You can drag to move, hold down Alt (Option) to copy (instead of moving) the original shape, drag the handles to resize the shape, and so on.

WORKAROUND WORKSHOP

Drawing Outlines and Borders

If you've played around at all with the Shape tool, you may have noticed that you can't draw shapes that are just outlines (i.e., that aren't filled with color). No matter what you do, your shape is a solid block.

Even if you haven't ever touched the Shape tool you may be wondering how the heck to get a simple plain colored border around a photo.

The easiest way to create an outline is to make a selection using the Marquee tool or other selection tools and then select Edit → Stroke (Outline) Selection. The Stroke dialog box pops up and lets you enter the width of the line in pixels and choose a color.

You'll also see choices for Location, which tell Elements where you want the line—around the inside edge of the selection, centered on the edge of the selection, or around the outside. If you're bordering an entire photo, don't choose Outside, or the border won't show, because it's off the edge of your image.

You can choose a blend mode if you like and set the opacity. Using a mode can give you a more subtle edge than a normal stroke does. The Transparency setting just ensures that any transparent areas in your layer stay transparent. When you're finished adjusting the settings in the Stroke dialog box, click OK, turn off your Marquee, and you've got yourself an outlined shape.

The Cookie Cutter

The Cookie Cutter is new in Elements 3, and at first glance, you may think it's a pretty silly tool. But it's actually one of the more interesting new features. It creates the same shapes as the Custom Shape tool, but you use it on a photo to crop it to the shape you chose. Want a heart-shaped portrait of your sweetie? The Cookie Cutter is your tool.

If you are not into that sort of thing, don't go away, because hidden away in the shapes library are some of the most sophisticated artistic crop shapes you can find. You can use them to get the kinds of effects that people pay commercial artists big bucks to create—like creating abstract crops that give a jagged or worn edge to your photo (an effect that's great for contemporary effects).

You can also combine the result with a stroked edge as explained in the box "Drawing Outlines and Borders," and maybe even a Layer style (page 322). Even without any additional frills, your photo's shape will appear more interesting, as shown in Figure 11-25.

Figure 11-25:
A quick drag with the Cookie Cutter is all it took to create the bottom graphic from the top photo. If you want to create custom album or scrapbook pages, you can rotate or skew your crops before you commit them. See page 259 for how to rotate and skew your images.

You use the Cookie Cutter just the way you use the Custom Shape tool, but you use it on a photo.

1. **Activate the Cookie Cutter tool.**

   Click the Cookie Cutter in the Toolbox (the icon looks like a heart), or press Q.

2. **Select the shape you want your photo to be.**

   Choose a shape from the Shapes palette by clicking the downward arrow next to the shape display in the Options bar. You have access to all the Custom Shapes, but pay special attention to the Crop Shapes category. Click the More button on the Shape Picker to see all the shape categories it contains, or choose "All Elements Shapes."

3. **Adjust your settings, if necessary.**

You have the same Shape Options described earlier for the Custom Shapes, so you can set a fixed size or constrain proportions if you want. Click the Shape Options button to see your choices.

You can choose to feather the edge of your shape, too. Just enter the amount in pixels. (See page 106 for more about feathering.) The other option, Crop, crops the edges of your photo so they're just large enough to contain the shape.

4. **Drag in your photo.**

A mask appears over your photo, and you see only the area that will still be there once you crop, surrounded by transparency.

5. **Adjust your crop if necessary.**

You can reposition the shape mask or drag the corners to resize it. Although the cropped areas disappear, they'll reappear as you reposition the mask if you move it so that they are included again.

Once you've created the shape, you'll see the Transform options in the Options bar until you commit your shape (which means that you can skew or distort it if you want). You can drag the mask around to reposition it if you'd like, or Shift+drag a corner to resize it without altering the proportions. It may take a little maneuvering to get exactly the parts of your photo that you want inside the crop.

6. **When you've gotten everything lined up the way you want, click the Commit button in the Options bar or just press Enter (Return).**

If you don't like the results, click the Cancel button on the Options bar, or press Escape. Once you've made your crop, you can use Ctrl+Z (⌘-Z) if you want to undo it to try something else.

TIP   The Cookie Cutter replaces the areas it removes with transparency. If the transparency checkerboard makes it too hard for you to get a clear look at what you've done, temporarily create a new white layer beneath the cropped layer. You can delete it once you're sure you're happy with your crop.

Filters, Effects, Layer Styles, and Gradients

There's a popular saying among artistic types who use software in their studios: *tools don't equal talent.* And it's true: no mere program is going to turn a klutz into a Klimt. But Elements has a few special tools—*filters, effects,* and *Layer styles*—that can sure help you fool a lot of people into thinking you're a better artist than you actually are. It's amazing what a difference you can make to the appearance of any image with only a couple of clicks.

Filters are an automated way to change the appearance of your image. You can use filters for enhancing and correcting your image, but Elements also gives you a bunch of other filters that are great for unleashing all your artistic impulses, as shown in Figure 12-1.

Most filters have settings that you can adjust to control how the filter changes your photo. Because you get nearly a hundred different filters with Elements, there isn't room in this chapter to cover each filter individually, but you'll learn the basics of applying filters and you'll get in-depth coverage of some of the filters you're most likely to use frequently.

Effects are like little macros or scripts, designed to make very elaborate changes to your image, like creating a three-dimensional frame around it, or adding a layer of realistic wood or brick. They're very easy to apply—you just double-click a button—but tweaking their settings is not as easy to do as it is with filters, since effects are programmed to make very specific changes.

Layer styles change the appearance of just one layer of your photo. They're very popular for creating impressive-looking text, but you also can apply them to objects and shapes. Some Layer styles produce results similar to what you might

Figure 12-1:
Elements filters let you add all sorts of different artistic effects to your photos.

Top: These figures show how you can change a photo to resemble a colored steel engraving.

Bottom: These figures show how you can create a watercolor look. For both images, several filters were applied to build up the effect.

get from one of the effects, but Layer styles and effects are very different under the hood in what happens to your photo when you apply them. Most Layer styles include settings you can easily modify.

You can combine filters, effects, and Layer styles on one image if you like. And you may spend hours trying different groupings, because it's addicting to watch the often unpredictable results you get when you mix them up.

The last section of this chapter focuses on *gradients*. A gradient is a rainbow-like range of color that you can use to color in an object or a background. But that's not all gradients are good for. You can also use gradients and *gradient maps*—gradients that get distributed according to the brightness values in your photo—for very precise retouching effects.

Using Filters

Filters make it possible for you to change the content of your photos in very complex ways, and using them is as easy as double-clicking a button. Elements gives you a huge number of filters, which are grouped in categories to help you choose the one that does what you need. This section offers a quick tour through the filter categories as well as some information about using a few of the most popular filters, like the Noise and Blur filters.

To make it easy to apply filters, Elements presents all your filters in a few different places: the Filter menu, where you choose them from the list that appears, and the Styles and Effects palette. There's also a Filter Gallery, a new feature that makes it very easy to get a good idea of how your photo will look when you apply your filter of choice. The next part of this section explains how to use all three methods.

Applying Filters

Using Elements' filters is really easy. You can choose to apply any filter from either the Filter menu or the Styles and Effects palette. Every filter is listed in both places. In the Filter menu, you choose your filter by name from the list. In the palette, thumbnail images give you a preview of what the filters do. The filters do exactly the same thing no matter which way you choose them.

With Elements 3, you also get the Filter Gallery, a great new invention that gives you a good preview of what a filter looks like when applied to your image. Some filters automatically open the Filter Gallery when you choose them from the menu or the palette. Or you can call up the Gallery itself (without first choosing a filter) by going to Filter → Filter Gallery. Not every filter can be applied from the Gallery—only some of the filters with adjustable settings.

> **TIP** Elements makes it easy to apply the same filter repeatedly. Press the Ctrl+F (⌘-F) keyboard shortcut, and Elements applies the last filter you used, with whatever setting you last used. The top listing in the Filter menu also always features the last filter used (selecting it works the same way as the keyboard shortcut: you get the same settings you just used).

Filter menu

If you find it easiest to search out your chosen filter by looking at a text list, this is the method you'll probably want to use. The filters are grouped into 14 main categories, with many individual filters in each group. There's a divider below the bottom category ("Other"). When you first install Elements, the Digimarc filter is the only filter below this line, but other filters you download or purchase will appear here, too.

When you choose a filter from the list, one of three things happens:

- **Elements applies the filter automatically.** This happens if the filter's name in the list doesn't have an ellipsis (…) after it. Just look at the result in your photo and undo it (Ctrl+Z [⌘-Z]) if you don't like its effect. If you do like it, you don't have to do anything else.

- **You see a dialog box.** The Elements filters that have adjustable settings have an ellipsis (…) after their names. Some of them (mostly correctional filters) open a dialog box where you can tweak the settings. Set everything as you want it, watching the small preview in the dialog box to see what you're doing. Then click OK.

- **You see the Filter Gallery.** Some of the more artistic, adjustable filters call up the Filter Gallery so that you can get a nice large preview of what you're doing and also so you can rearrange the order of multiple filters before applying them. Applying filters from the Gallery is explained later.

Regardless of how you've applied the filter, once you're done, you can always undo it (Ctrl+Z [⌘-Z]) if you're not happy with the effect. If you like it, there's no need to do anything else, except of course to eventually save your image.

> **TIP** Since there's no way to undo filters after you've closed your image, many people apply filters to a duplicate layer. Press Ctrl+J (⌘-J) to create a duplicate layer.

Styles and Effects palette

If you're more comfortable with visual clues when choosing a filter, you can also find any filter in the Styles and Effects palette, which is, logically enough, also where you apply effects. The advantage of the Styles and Effects palette is shown in Figure 12-2.

The Styles and Effects palette is usually one of the three palettes in the Palette bin the first time you launch Elements. If it's not there waiting for you, go to Window → Styles and Effects to call it up. You'll see a little pull-down menu on the left side. Choose Filters there, and then you can use the menu on the right to limit your viewing options to filters in any particular category, if you like. The categories are the same ones you see in the Filter menu.

To apply a filter from the palette, double-click its thumbnail. If the filter has settings, you get the same dialog box or Filter Gallery you'd see if you'd applied the filter from the Filter menu, as described earlier.

One small drawback to applying filters from the palette is that you can't tell from the thumbnail whether a filter is one that applies automatically. There's no clue like the ellipsis (…) to tell you which group a filter falls into.

Filter Gallery

The Filter Gallery, shown in Figure 12-3, is a great new feature in Elements 3. It gives you a much larger preview window, a look at all the little green apple thumbnails so you have a visual guide to what your filter will do, and most importantly, it lets you apply filters like layers—you can stack them up and change the order in which they're applied to your image. Changing the order of filters can make some big differences in how they affect your image. You get very different results if you apply Ink Outlines *after* the Sprayed Strokes filter than you do if you apply Ink Outlines first, for example. The Gallery lets you play around and experiment to see which order gets you the exact look you want. The layer-like behavior of the filters in the gallery is only for previewing, though. They don't end up as real layers.

The Gallery is more for artistic filters than for corrective filters. You can't apply the Sharpening or Noise filters from the Gallery, for instance. All the Gallery filters are in the artistic, brush stroke, distort, sketch, stylize, and texture categories. (See the next section for an overview of all the filter categories Elements offers.)

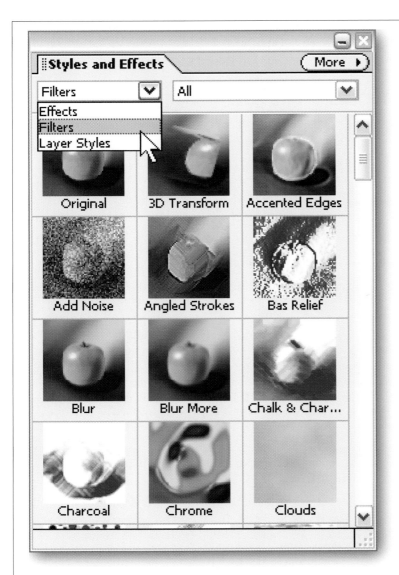

Figure 12-2:
The Styles and Effects palette gives you a preview of what every filter looks like when applied to the same photo of a green apple. If you know what you want a filter to do but don't know what name to look for, scrolling through these thumbnail images should help you find the one you want.

To apply a filter from the palette, double-click the thumbnail, or click the thumbnail once and then choose Apply from the palette's More menu. Or you can right-click (Control-click) and, from the pop-up menu, choose Apply.

The Filter Gallery is divided into three panes. On the left side is a preview of what your image will look like when you apply the filter. The center holds the thumbnails for the different filters, and the right side contains the settings for the currently chosen filter. At the bottom of the settings pane are your filter layers. You can see what filters you've applied, and add or subtract layers and rearrange their order here.

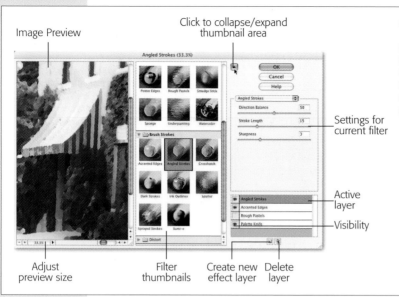

Image Preview

Click to collapse/expand thumbnail area

Angled Strokes (33.3%)

Settings for current filter

Active layer

Visibility

Adjust preview size

Filter thumbnails

Create new effect layer

Delete layer

Figure 12-3:
The Filter Gallery. If you want a larger preview, you can click the arrow that the cursor is over in the figure to collapse the thumbnails and regain that entire section for preview space.

NOTE   Filter layers work something like regular layers (Chapter 6) with one important difference: your filter layers are what you might call "working" layers. In other words, you only have separate filter layers until you click OK. Then all your chosen filters get applied to your image at once. You can't close your photo and come back later and still expect to see the filters as individual, changeable layers after you've actually applied the filters. And most importantly, your filters become part of the layer you apply them to. You aren't creating a new permanent layer when you use the Filter Gallery.

In addition to letting you adjust the settings for a given filter, the Filter Gallery lets you perform a few other tricks:

- **Adjust the preview of your image.** In the lower-left corner of the Gallery, directly click the percentage listing or click the arrow next to it for a list of preset sizes to choose from. You can also click the plus and minus arrows to zoom the view in or out. Easier still, use the Ctrl+= (⌘-=) and Ctrl+– (⌘--) shortcuts to zoom in and out from the keyboard.

- **Choose a new filter.** Just click a filter's thumbnail once and you get the settings for the new filter and the preview image updates right away—usually (see the box on page 312).

- **Add a new filter layer.** You can stack up filters in layers in the Filter Gallery the way you would layers in the Layers palette. Each time you click the New Filter Layer icon (see Figure 12-4), you add another filter layer to the ones you already have.

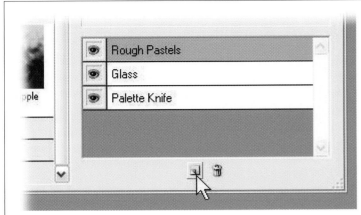

Figure 12-4:
If you've used layers before (see Chapter 6), these little icons should look familiar. In the Filter Gallery, they make new filter layers instead of regular layers. Click the square to add a new filter layer to your image. The Eye icons turn visibility on and off just as they do in the Layers palette. It's true that the filters preview in layers, but they don't show up as real layers in the Layers palette-only in the Filter Gallery.

- **Change the position of filter layers.** Just drag them up and down in the stack like regular layers to changer the order in which they'll get applied to your image.

- **Hide filter layers.** Click the eye next to a filter layer at the bottom of the palette to turn off visibility, just like in the Layers palette.

- **Delete filter layers.** Highlight any filter layer by clicking it, then click the Trash icon to delete it.

- **Change the content of a layer.** You can change what kind of filter is in a particular layer. For instance, if you applied, say, the Smudge Stick and you like all your other changes, but wish you had used the Glass filter instead, you don't have to delete the Smudge Stick layer. Instead, just highlight the Smudge layer and click the Glass filter button to change the layer's contents.

NOTE   Ctrl+F (⌘-F) reapplies all the filters that were in your last gallery set if you press it again after using the Filter Gallery.

Filter Categories

Elements divides the filters into categories to help make it easier for you to track down the filter you want. Some of the categories, like Distort, contain filters that vary hugely in what they do to your photo. Other categories, like the Brush Stroke filters, contain filters are all pretty obviously related to one another. Here's a quick breakdown of the categories:

- **Adjustments.** These filters apply some photographic, stylistic, and artistic changes to your photo. Most of the adjustments are explained in Chapter 8, which is also where you can find more information on Photo Filters (see page 201).

- **Artistic.** This is a huge group of filters that do everything from making your photo look like it was cut from paper (Cutout) to making it look like a quick

UNDER THE HOOD

Filter Performance Hints

If Elements could speak, it might say, "Easy for *you*," when it comes to filters and effects. Although you don't have to do much to apply them, Elements has a huge amount of work to do on its end. If your computer is slow or memory-challenged, it can take a long time to apply filters and even to update the preview. You can speed things up by applying filters to a selection. Filters that have their own dialog boxes (as opposed to the Filter Gallery) will show a flashing line under the size percentage below the preview area to indicate the progress they're making. A few other filter-related tips are worth remembering:

- Filters won't do anything if they don't have pixels to work on, so be sure you're targeting a layer with something in it and not an Adjustment layer.

- If you apply a filter to a selection, you'll usually want to feather the edges a fair amount to help the filter edges blend into the rest of your photo.

- Alt+click (Option-click) the Cancel button to turn it to a Reset button. Clicking Cancel makes the window goes away, while Reset lets you start over without having to call up the filter again.

- If your filters are grayed out in the Filter menu, check to be sure you're not in 16-bit mode (page 199) or in grayscale, bitmapped, or index color (all these color modes are explained on page 29).

sketch (Rough Pastels). You generally get the best effects with these filters by using multiple filters or applying the same one multiple times.

- **Blur.** The blur filters let you soften the focus of your photo and add artistic effects. They're explained later.

- **Brush Strokes.** These filters apply brush stroke effects to your photo to give it a hand-painted look.

- **Distort.** These filters warp your image in a great variety of ways. The Liquify filter is the most powerful, and it's explained in the next chapter on page 352.

- **Noise.** Use these filters to add or remove grain from your image. They're explained later.

- **Pixelate.** The Pixelate filters break your image up in different ways, making it show the dot pattern of a magazine halftone, or the fragmented look you see on television where they're concealing someone's identity.

    NOTE The Color Halftone filter makes your photo look like a *halftone*, a one-color image whose pixels simulate the shades of gray you see in a black and white photo. It's not the same as true halftone screening, which is not available in Elements. If your printer needs a halftone, you need to either get Photoshop or ask the printer to do the conversion for you.

- **Render.** This group includes a pretty diverse bunch of filters that let you do things like create a lens-flare effect (Lens Flare), transform a flat object so it looks three dimensional (3D Transform), and make fibers (Fibers) or clouds

(Clouds). The Lighting Effects filter, a powerful but confusing filter that's like a whole program in itself, helps you change the way lighting appears in your image. For a full rundown on what this filter does, as well as how to use it, check out the "Missing CD" page at *www.missingmanuals.com*.

- **Sharpen.** These filters give your photo an impression of improved focus. They're explained on page 182.

- **Sketch.** These filters not only make your photo look like it was drawn with different instruments (like charcoal, chalk, and crayon)—you can also make your photo look like it was embossed in wet plaster, photocopied, or stamped with a rubber stamp.

- **Stylize.** These filters create special effects by increasing the contrast in your photo and displacing pixels. You can make your photo look radioactive, reduce it to outlines, or make it look like it's moving fast with the Wind filter (explained later).

- **Texture.** These filters change the surface of your photo to look like it was made from another material. Use them to create a crackled finish (the Craquelere filter), stained glass (Stained Glass), or a mosaic effect (Mosaic Tiles).

- **Video.** These filters are for use in creating and editing images for videos.

- **Other.** This is a group of fairly technical filters that you can highly customize. The High Pass filter is explained on page 185. You can use Offset to shift an image or a layer a little bit.

- **Digimarc.** Use this filter to check for Digimarc watermarks in photos. Digimarc is a company that lets subscribers enter their information in a database so that anyone who gets one of their photos can find out who the copyright holder is.

You can find a number of filter plug-ins online, ranging from free to very expensive. Chapter 17 gives you some suggestions for places to start looking. It's important to note that filters are platform-specific: Windows plug-ins won't work on Macs, and vice versa. Once you've installed new filters, you access them at the bottom of the list in the Filter menu.

Useful Filter Solutions

This section shows you how to use some of the most popular and useful filters to correct your photos and create a few special effects. You'll learn how to modify the graininess of your photos to create an aged effect or smooth out a repair job. And you'll also see how to blur your photos to create a soft-focus effect, or to make your subjects look like they're moving.

Removing noise: getting rid of graininess

Noise, the appearance of undesired graininess in an image, is a big problem with many digital cameras, especially those with small sensors and high megapixel counts. It's rare to find a fixed-lens camera with more than 5 megapixels that doesn't have some trouble with noise, especially in underexposed areas. If you shoot using the RAW format, you can correct a fair amount of noise right in the RAW Converter (page 189). But the RAW Converter won't help if you're shooting JPEGs. And even RAW files may need further noise reduction once you've edited your photo after converting it.

Elements includes the Reduce Noise filter, which is designed specifically to help you get rid of noise in your photos. To get to it, go to Filter → Noise → Reduce Noise. You get a dialog box with a preview window on the left side and settings adjustments on the right. To use the filter, first use the controls below the preview to set the view to at least 100 percent, or preferably even higher. It's important to be able to see the pixels in your photo so that you can see how the filter is changing them as you adjust the settings.

You get three settings, each of which you control by using a slider:

- **Strength** controls the overall impact of the filter. This setting controls the same kind of noise as the Luminance Smoothing setting in the RAW converter (page 199). The stronger you set it, the greater the risk of softening your photo.

- **Preserve Details.** Using noise reduction can soften the appearance of your photo. This setting tells Elements how much care to take to preserve the details of your image.

- **Reduce Color Noise.** This setting adjusts uneven distribution of color in your image. You can set this slider pretty high without a negative impact on your photo.

For each setting, move the slider to the right if you want more and to the left if you want less, while watching the effect in the preview window. You might notice a little lag time before the preview updates. When you see what you want, click Okay to apply the filter.

The Elements 3 noise reduction filter does a fine job on areas with a small amount of noise, like the skies in many JPEG photos. But if your camera has major noise problems, you may find you still need third-party noise reduction software.

The two most popular programs are probably Noise Ninja (*www.picturecode.com*) and Neat Image (*www.neatimage.com*). Both have demo versions you can download to try out the programs. Both are available for Mac and Windows computers. If you search with Google for "noise reduction software," you'll get a variety of other options as well.

Adding noise: smoothing out repair jobs

Elements also gives you a filter for *creating* noise. Why do that when most of the time you try so hard to get rid of noise? One reason is when you're trying to age the appearance of your photo. If you want to make a photo look like it came from an old newspaper, for instance, you'd add some noise.

The other most common use for noise is to help make repaired spots blend in with the rest of an image. If you've altered part of a photo in Elements, especially by painting on it, the odds are that the repaired area is going to be perfectly smooth. That's great if the rest of the photo is noise free. But if the rest of the photo is a little noisy, that smooth patch is going to stand out like a sore thumb. Add a bit of noise to make it blend in better with the rest of the photo, as shown in Figure 12-5.

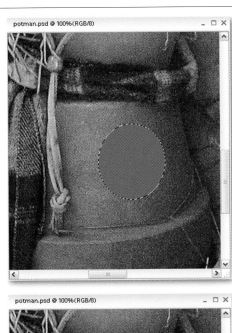

Figure 12-5:
Top: If you use the Average blur filter on this noisy photo, the blended area sticks out like a sore thumb.

Bottom: If you add some noise, the changes you've made are less noticeable.

To add noise to a photo, start by selecting the area where you want to add the noise (if you don't want to change your whole photo). Using a duplicate layer (Ctrl+J [⌘+J]) for the noise is a safe step, since you can always undo your changes if you've got them on a layer.

1. **Call up the Add Noise filter.**

   Go to Filter → Noise → Add Noise to bring up the dialog box with the settings for the filter.

2. **Adjust the settings to your liking.**

   The settings are explained in the following list. Use the preview window in the dialog box to check how the changes are affecting your photo.

3. **When you're satisfied, click OK.**

You have three options in the Add Noise dialog box:

- **Amount.** This controls how heavy the noise is going to be. Just drag the slider to the right for more noise or to the left for less. You can also type in a number. A higher percentage means more noise.

- **Uniform or Gaussian.** These buttons let you control how the noise gets distributed through your image. Uniform is just what it says—the same all over. Gaussian means that the noise will be distributed to produce a more speckled effect.

   If you're adding noise to duplicate existing noise in a grainy photo, you'll probably want a Gaussian distribution. For an old newspaper photo look, try Uniform. In either case, experiment until you get what you want.

- **Monochromatic.** This setting limits noise to the colors already existing in your photo. Take a look at the middle image in Figure 12-6 and notice how many more colors you can see inside the noise, compared to the solid red of the original. The noise was applied with the Monochromatic setting turned off.

Noise can also help you when you want to apply special effects to blocks of solid color, as shown in Figure 12-6.

Figure 12-6:
Filters can really spruce up solid objects.

Top: An unfiltered solid red heart.

Middle: This image has noise added to it.

Bottom: The Angled Strokes filter gives this image a hand-painted look.

Gaussian Blur: drawing attention to a foreground object

The Gaussian Blur filter lets you control how much your image is blurred. When you use the Gaussian Blur, you have to set the *radius,* which controls how much you want the filter to blur things. A higher radius produces more blurring; a preview window shows you what you're doing.

The Gaussian blur is probably the most frequently used of the Blur filters. Besides blurring large areas of your photo, like the background in the bottom photo in Figure 12-7, a Gaussian Blur at a very low setting can be used to soften lines—very useful when you're trying to achieve a sketched effect.

Figure 12-7:
Top: This photo could use some help from the Blur filters. The hawk is hard to distinguish from the rest of the photo; blurring helps center the focus on the hawk.

Bottom: With a Gaussian Blur filter applied to the background, the hawk becomes the clear focal point of the photo.

Radial Blur: producing a sense of motion

As you can see in Figure 12-8, the Radial blur really produces a sense of motion. It has two available styles: Zoom, which is designed to give the effect of a camera zooming in, and Spin, which produces a circular effect around your designated center point.

Figure 12-8:
A Radial Blur applied in Zoom mode. As you can see, this filter can produce an almost vertiginous sense of motion. If you don't want to give people motion sickness, go easy on the Amount setting.

The Radial Blur dialog box may look a bit complicated, but it's really not. Unfortunately, you don't get a preview with this filter, because it drains so much processor power. That's why you have a choice between Draft, Good, and Best Quality. Use Draft for a quick look at roughly what you'll get. Then, most of the time, choose Good for the final version. There's not much difference between Good and Best except on large images, so don't feel that you must choose Best for the final version all the time.

Once you've chosen your method (Zoom or Spin), then set the amount, which controls the intensity of the blur that's applied. Next, click inside the Blur Center box to identify the point where you want the blur to center, as shown in Figure 12-9. Finally, click OK when you're finished.

> **NOTE** If you want to create a soft-focus effect, you can sort of manage with the Blur filters or the Impressionist brush. But a much better option is the free Dreamy FX filter from Dreamsuite (*www.autofx.com/freeplugins/dreamy7.html*). They also have a much better mosaic filter than the one included in Elements, and it's free, too (*www.autofx.com/freeplugins/mosaic2.htm*).

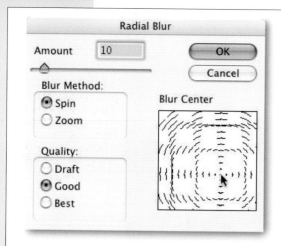

Figure 12-9:
The Blur Center box lets you identify the center point of the Radial Blur's effect (whether you've chosen Zoom or Spin mode). Drag the ripple drawing inside the box in any direction; here, the center point has been moved just to the right and down from its original position in the center of the box.

Adding Effects

Like filters, effects give you loads of ways to really change the appearance of your photo—from adding green slime textures to adding classy picture frames. Although you apply effects with a simple double-click, these clicks actually trigger a sequence of changes that Elements applies to your image. Some of the effects involve many complex steps, although you can't always see every step happening onscreen. Sometimes you can see how busy Elements is, though. Try one of the three-dimensional frame effects, and you'll see Elements scurry around, doing things like adding canvas, cropping, or trimming.

> **NOTE** You can't usually customize or change an effect's settings. Effects are typically an all-or-nothing deal. For example, if you use the Wood Frame effect, you either take the wood frame Elements wants to apply to your image, or you don't. No need to ask if you can adjust the wood grain finish. You can't.

You apply effects from the Styles and Effects palette (choose Window → Styles and Effects; then from the palette's left side pull-down menu, select Effects).

As with filters, the effects are grouped into categories—frames, image effects, textures, and text effects. Just as with filters, use the right menu on the Styles and Effects palette to see all your choices, or those from only one category. The thumbnail images give you a preview of what the effect will do to your image.

> **NOTE** Effects don't get their own menu the way filters do.

To apply an effect, double-click its thumbnail in the Styles and Effects palette. That's all there is to it. If you don't like the result, press Ctrl+Z (⌘-Z) to undo it, but there's not much you can tweak in the effects, although some aspects of some effects (like shadows in some of the frame effects) can be adjusted by going to Layer → Layer Style → Scale Effects. Figure 12-10 shows the Vignette Frame effect.

Figure 12-10:
Effects let you apply super simple frames. Here, an oval selection was made around the house, and then the Vignette Frame effect was applied, followed by the Wild Frame.

NOTE You can't apply an effect or a Layer style to a background layer. Double-click your background layer in the Layers palette to convert it to a regular layer first.

Here're a few other effects-related tips to help you get the most out of these nifty-but-quirky features:

- Most effects flatten (page 145) or simplify (page 298) your image. Therefore, it's usually best to make a copy of your image, or wait until you're done making all your other edits, before applying an effect.

- Some effects create additional layers: check the Layers palette once you're done applying them. You may want to flatten your image to reduce the file size before printing or storing it.

- Text effects are also popular. (Chapter 13 has lots more information about creating and modifying text.) Keep in mind that when you apply a text effect, the text gets simplified (page 298), which means you can't edit the individual words; they're all now just a bunch of pixels. Therefore, make sure you're happy with the size, font, and spelling of your text before you apply an effect to it.

Layer Styles

Like filters and effects, Layer styles let you transform objects by giving them new characteristics, like Drop Shadows, for instance. Layer styles are especially useful for modifying individual objects, like text and buttons, because you can edit the text and change the button's shape even *after* you've applied the Layer style.

Layer styles, as their name suggests, work on the contents of one layer—rather than on your whole image. That's important. A Layer style affects the *entire* contents of a layer. If you want to apply a Layer style to just one object in your picture, select the object and put it on a layer of its own (Layer → New → Layer via Copy or New → Layer via Cut). Figure 12-11 shows what you can do with Layer styles.

Figure 12-11:
Layer styles are great for making fancy buttons for Web sites. Changing this plain black Custom Shape was as simple as clicking the Sunset Sky Layer style (in Complex Styles), adding a bevel, and then making the bevel bigger. (Keep reading to learn how to edit Layer styles.)

Layer styles don't change your image as drastically as effects do. If you apply a Text Layer style, for instance, you can still edit the text or change the font, because Layer styles don't simplify your text the way effects do.

You apply Layer styles from the Styles and Effects palette (Window → Styles and Effects). From the palette's left-side pull-down menu, choose Layer Styles. Then from the menu on the right, choose a Layer style category. Finally, select the layer you want to modify (by highlighting it in the Layers palette) and then click the Layer style you want to use. The box on page 324 shows you how to modify any style's settings.

> **NOTE** Some tools, like the Text tool (covered in Chapter 13), have an Options bar box that lets you choose a Layer style.

Here's a quick rundown of the choices available in each Layer style category:

- **Bevels.** Bevels give objects a more three-dimensional look by making them appear raised from the page or embossed into it. Figure 12-12 shows an example of how combining a bevel and a drop shadow can add a lot of dimension to even a simple shape.

- **Drop Shadows.** This category adds shadows that make your object look like it's floating above the page.

Figure 12-12:
Here's the heart image from earlier in this chapter. Adding a bevel and a drop shadow gives it much more dimension and depth.

TIP Adding a drop shadow to an entire photo requires adding canvas (see page 72) to give the shadow someplace to fall. The easiest way to add a drop shadow around an entire photo is to use the Drop Shadow effect from the Frame effects, rather than using a Layer style.

- **Inner Glows.** Adding an Inner Glow adds light around the inside edge of your object.

- **Inner Shadows.** Inner Shadows give your image a hollow or recessed effect by casting a shadow within the object, rather than outside it the way drop shadows do.

- **Outer Glows.** Outer Glows create the same kind of glows that Inner Glows do, only they go around the outer edge of your image.

- **Visibility.** These styles change the opacity and visibility of your layer. Use them to create a ghosted effect—or when you're applying multiple Layer styles and you want to use the outlined shape of an object without having the object itself visible.

- **Complex.** This category includes a variety of elaborate Layer styles that let you make an object look like it's made from metal, cactus, painted, and several other styles. These are particularly useful for applying to type.

- **Glass Buttons.** These styles are supposed to make objects look like glass buttons, but many people think they look more like plastic. They are useful for creating Web page buttons.

- **Image effects.** This group gives you a wealth of ways to transform your photo, including fading it and making it look like the pieces of a puzzle or a tile mosaic.

- **Patterns.** These styles apply an overall pattern to your image. Want to make something look like it's made from metal or dried mud, or to fill in a dull background with a really vivid pattern? You'll find lots of choices here.

- **Photographic effects.** This group includes several favorite traditional photographic techniques. You can add a quick Sepia effect or add a variety of monochrome effects to a photo.

- **Wow Chrome, Neon, Plastic Styles.** Use these styles to make an object look like it's made from shiny chrome, outlined in neon, or made from plastic.

> **NOTE** Layer styles must be applied to a regular layer, so if you try to apply one to a background layer, you'll be asked to convert it to a regular layer before the style will apply itself.

To remove a Layer style, right-click (Control-click) the layer in the Layers palette and choose Remove Style, or go to Layer → Layer Style → Clear Layer Style. These commands are all-or-nothing: if your layer has multiple styles, they all go away at once. To remove one style at a time, use the Undo History palette.

> **TIP** If you want to see what your image looks like without the styles you've applied to it, go to Layer → Layer Style → Hide Effects.

You can download hundreds of additional Layer styles from the Internet (see Chapter 17 for tips on where to look). It's easy to get addicted to collecting Layer styles, because they're so much fun to use.

POWER USERS' CLINIC

Editing Layer Styles

Once you've applied a Layer style, you can edit it as much as you want. Just double-click the Layer Styles icon in the Layers Palette (it looks like a fancy cursive F) or select Layer → Layer Style → Style Settings.

Once the Style Settings dialog box appears, you can edit a shadow direction, its distance, any inner or outer glows, and the height of bevels.

Not all options will be available for every effect. For instance, if you don't have any Inner Glow, the Inner Glow option will be grayed out.

For drop shadows, once the Style Settings dialog box is open you can drag the shadow around, right in your image window, until it's positioned where you want it.

The changes you make affect the style as you're currently applying it—there's no way to change the standard settings for each style.

Applying Gradients

You may have noticed that a few of the Layer styles fade out a color at the edges. In fact, Elements lets you fade colors in many different ways by using *gradients,* in which colors blend and fade in almost any way you can imagine. You can use gradients to create anything from a multicolored rainbow extravaganza to a single color that fades away into transparency. Figure 12-13 shows you a few examples of what you can do with gradients. The only limit is your imagination.

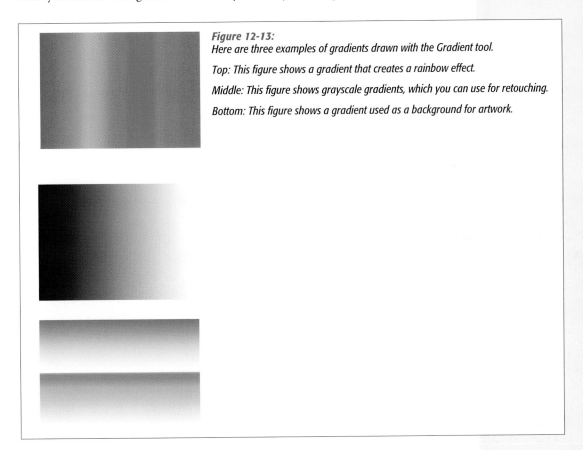

Figure 12-13:
Here are three examples of gradients drawn with the Gradient tool.

Top: This figure shows a gradient that creates a rainbow effect.

Middle: This figure shows grayscale gradients, which you can use for retouching.

Bottom: This figure shows a gradient used as a background for artwork.

You can apply gradients directly to your image using the Gradient tool, or you can create *Gradient Fill layers,* which are entire layers filled with—you guessed it—gradients. You can even edit gradients and create new ones using the Gradient Editor. Finally, there's a special kind of gradient called a *gradient map* that lets you replace the colors in your image with the colors from a gradient. This section covers the basics of using all these tools and methods.

The Gradient Tool

If you want to apply a gradient to a particular object in your image, the Gradient tool is the fastest way to do it. The Gradient tool may seem complicated when you first see it, but it's actually pretty easy to use. Start by activating the Gradient tool in the Toolbox (the black and white rainbow) or by pressing G. Figure 12-14 shows the Gradient tool's Options bar.

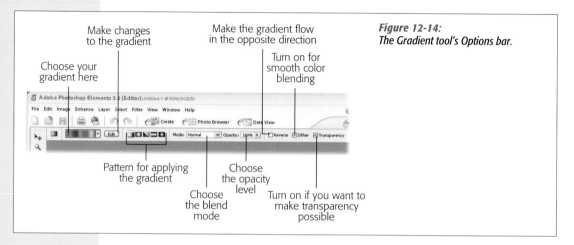

Make changes to the gradient

Make the gradient flow in the opposite direction

Figure 12-14:
The Gradient tool's Options bar.

Choose your gradient here

Turn on for smooth color blending

Pattern for applying the gradient

Choose the opacity level

Choose the blend mode

Turn on if you want to make transparency possible

Using the Gradient tool is as easy as dragging. You click where you want the gradient to begin and then drag to the point where you want it to stop. When you click to set the boundaries of the gradient, you set only the edges of the color transition—but the gradient still covers the entire available space. For example, say you're using a yellow-to-white gradient.

If you click to end the gradient one-third of the way into your photo, the color stops transitioning at that point, but the remaining two-thirds of your photo will be covered with white. Drag the gradient within a selection marquee if you want to apply the gradient to a limited area only.

> **TIP** The Gradient tool puts the gradient on the same layer as the image you apply it to, which means that it's hard to change anything about your gradient after it's applied. If you think you might want to change your gradient, use the Gradient Fill layer, described later.

Some gradients use your chosen foreground and background colors as the two colors that generate the gradient. But Elements also offers a number of preset gradients, which are gradients in different color schemes that Adobe has created for you.

Click the arrow to the right of the gradient thumbnail in the Options bar, and you'll see a little palette of different gradients, some of which use your selected colors and others that are preset with their own color scheme. The gradients are grouped into categories; you can only work with the gradients in one category at a time.

Click the More arrow on the upper-right corner of the gradient thumbnails pop-out menu to see all the available gradient categories. Choose one, and the available gradients change to reflect those in the new category.

You can also download gradients from the Internet and add them to your library, or you can create your own gradients from scratch. (See Chapter 17 for some ideas about where to look for new gradients.) Creating and editing gradients is explained later, in the section about the Gradient Editor.

You can customize your gradient in several ways, even without using the Gradient Editor. When the Gradient tool is active, you see several choices in the Options bar:

- **Gradient.** Click the arrow to the right of the thumbnail to choose a different gradient than the one displayed.

- **Edit.** Click this button to bring up the Gradient Editor (explained later).

- **Gradient types.** Use this setting to determine the way the colors flow in your gradient. Click a thumbnail to choose how the gradient will be applied. From left to right, your choices are: Linear (in a straight line), Radial (a sunburst effect), Angle (a counterclockwise sweep around the starting point), Reflected (from the center out to each edge in a mirror image), and Diamond. Figure 12-15 shows what each one looks like.

- **Mode.** You can apply a gradient in any blend mode. (See page 137.)

- **Opacity.** If you want your image to be visible through the gradient, reduce the opacity here.

- **Reverse.** This setting changes the direction in which the colors are applied so that instead of yellow to blue from left to right, you get blue to yellow, for instance.

- **Dither.** Checking this box makes the edges of the color transitions blend together.

- **Transparency.** If you want to shade to transparency anywhere in your gradient, you need to turn this on.

Using the Gradient tool

To apply a gradient with the Gradient tool, first make a selection if you don't want to see the gradient in your whole image. Then:

1. **Choose the colors you want to use for your gradient.**

   Click the Foreground/Background color squares to choose colors. (Some gradient choices ignore these colors.)

2. **Activate the Gradient tool.**

   Click it in the Toolbox or press G.

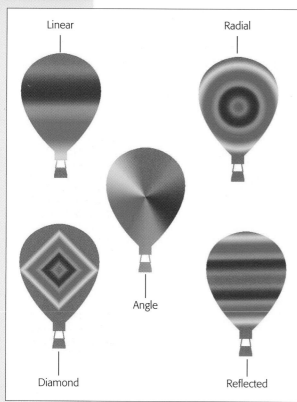

Linear

Radial

Figure 12-15:
The same gradient pattern applied using the different gradient types: Linear, Radial, Angle, Reflected, and Diamond.

Angle

Diamond

Reflected

3. **Select a gradient.**

   Go to the Options bar and click the Gradient thumbnail and choose the gradient you want. Then make any changes to the Options bar settings.

4. **Apply your gradient.**

   Drag in your image from the starting point to the ending point of where the gradient should run. If you're using a linear gradient, you can make the gradient run vertically by dragging up and down. You can make it go left to right by dragging sideways. For Radial, Reflection, and Diamond gradients, try dragging from the center of your image to one edge. If you don't like your results, Ctrl+Z (⌘-Z) to undo it. Once you like the gradient, you don't need to do anything special to accept it, except of course to save your image before you close it.

Gradient Fill Layer

You can also apply your gradient using a special fill layer. Most of the time, this is a better choice than the Gradient tool, especially if you want to be able to make changes to your gradient later on.

To create a Gradient Fill layer, go to Layer → New Fill Layer → Gradient. The New Layer dialog box (page 130) appears, which lets you set the opacity for the layer and choose a blend mode (page 137), if you like. Once you click Okay, the new layer immediately fills with the currently selected gradient, and the dialog box shown in Figure 12-16 pops up. You can change many of the settings for your gradient here or choose a different gradient.

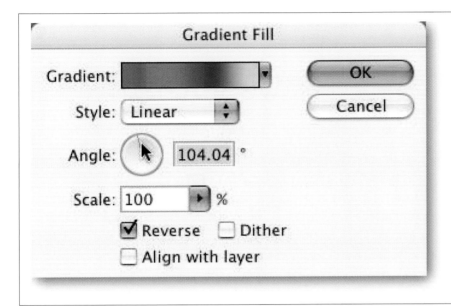

Figure 12-16:
The Gradient Fill dialog box gives you access to most of the same settings you find in the Options bar for the Gradient tool. The major difference is that in the fill layer, you set the direction of your gradient by typing in a number for the angle or by changing the direction of the line as shown here. You don't get a chance to set the direction by dragging, as you do with the Gradient tool.

The settings in the Gradient Fill dialog box are the same as those in the Options bar for the Gradient tool:

- **Gradient.** To choose a different gradient, click the arrow next to the thumbnail for the Gradient palette. To choose from a different gradient category, click the arrow on the palette and choose the category you want.

- **Style.** You get the same choices you do for the tool (for example Linear, Diamond, and so on). In this case, you only see the name of the style. Choose a different style and it previews in the layer itself.

- **Angle.** This controls the direction the colors will run in. Enter a number in degrees or spin the line in the circle to change the direction of the flow.

- **Scale.** This setting determines how large your gradient is relative to the layer. 100 percent means they're the same size. If you choose 150 percent, for example, the gradient exceeds the size of your layer, which means you'll see only a portion of the gradient in the layer. For example, if you had a black-to-white gradient, you'd see only shades of gray in your image. If you turn off "Align with Layer," you can adjust the location of the gradient relative to your image. Just drag the gradient in your image.

- **Reverse.** Turn this on to make colors flow in the opposite direction.

- **Dither.** Use this setting to create smooth color transitions.

- **Align with Layer.** This setting keeps the gradient in line with the layer. Turn it off, and you can pull the gradient around in your image to place it exactly where you want it.

When you've gotten the gradient looking the way you like, click OK to create your layer. You can edit it later by double-clicking the left icon for the layer in the Layers palette.

Editing a Gradient

The Elements Gradient Editor lets you create gradients that include any color combination you like. You can even make gradients in which the color fades to transparency, or you can modify existing gradients. For instance, you can easily make a two-color gradient where the fade is very one-sided, if you want a large plain area where you can put text (the plain area helps keep the text readable).

The Gradient Editor isn't the easiest tool in the world to use. This section will give you the basics you need to get started. Then, like much of Elements, a little bit of playing around with it will help you understand how the Gradient Editor works.

The Gradient tool must be active to launch the Gradient Editor. Click the Edit button in the Options bar to see the Gradient Editor (see Figure 12-17).

The Gradient Editor opens showing the currently selected gradient. You can choose a different gradient by picking from the thumbnails at the top of the Gradient Editor window, or by clicking the arrow to the right and choosing a new category from the list. You'll learn how to save your gradients later in the chapter.

Using the Gradient Editor

To get started using the Gradient Editor, first choose your gradient's type and smoothness settings:

- **Gradient Type.** Your choices are Solid or Noise. Solid gradients are the most common types of gradient; they let you create transitions between solid blocks of color. Noise gradients, which are covered later in this section, produce bands of color, as you might see in a spectrometer.

- **Smoothness.** This setting controls how even the transition appears between colors.

Most of the work you'll do in the Gradient Editor takes place in the *Gradient bar,* the long colored bar where your chosen gradient is displayed. The little boxes (also called *stops*) and diamonds surrounding the Gradient bar let you control the color and transparency of your gradient.

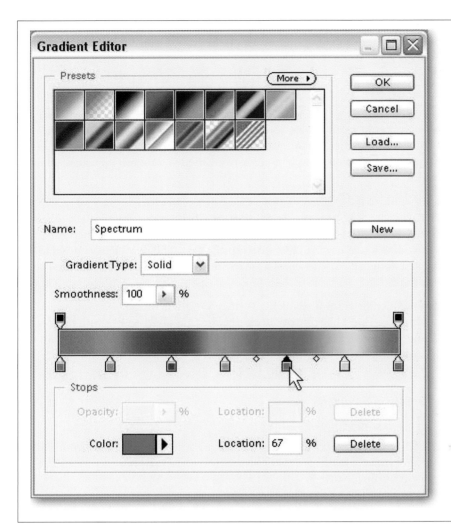

Figure 12-17:
The powerful and complex Gradient Editor.

For now, you only care about the stops *beneath* the Gradient bar. Each is a Color Stop; it represents where a particular color falls in the gradient. You always need at least two Color Stops in a gradient.

If you click a stop, the pointed end turns black, letting you know that it's the active stop. Anything you do at this point is going to affect the area governed by that stop. You can slide the stops around to change where the colors change in your gradients. The Color Stops let you customize your gradient in lots of different ways. Using them, you can:

• **Change where the color transitions.** Click a Color Stop, and you see a tiny diamond appear under the bar. The diamond is the midpoint of the color change. Diamonds always appear between two Color Stops. You can drag the diamond in either direction to skew the color range between two Color Stops so that it more heavily represents one color over another. Wherever you place the diamond tells Elements the point at which the color change should be half completed.

- **Change one of the colors in the gradient.** Click any Color Stop and then click the color-picking window (at the bottom of the Gradient Editor, in the Stops section) to bring up the Color Picker (page 175). Choose a new color, and the gradient automatically alters to reflect your change. You can also pick a new color by moving your cursor over the Gradient bar. The cursor turns to an eyedropper that lets you sample a color from the bar or from anywhere in your image.

- **Add a color to the gradient.** Click a Color Stop, then click again (not in the bar, but anywhere just beneath it) to indicate where you want the new color to appear. You see a new Color Stop where you clicked. Next, click the color-picking window to choose the color you want to add. The new color appears in the gradient at the new stop. Repeat as many times as you want, adding a new color each time.

- **Remove a color from a gradient.** If there's a gradient that's *almost* what you want but you don't like one of the colors, you don't have to live with it. You can remove a color by clicking its stop to make it the active color. Then click the Delete button to remove that color. The Delete button is grayed out if no Color Stop is active.

Transparency in gradients

You can also use the Gradient Editor to adjust the transparency in a gradient. Elements gives you nearly unlimited control over the transparency in your gradients and over the opacity of any color at any point in the gradient. Adjusting opacity in the Gradient Editor works very much like using the Color Stops to edit the colors. Instead of Color Stops, you use Opacity Stops.

> **NOTE**   Transparency is particularly nice in images for Web use, but remember that you need to save in a format that supports transparency, like GIF, or you lose the transparency. If you save your file as a JPEG, the transparent areas will become opaque white. See Chapter 15 for more about file formats for the Web.

The Opacity Stops are the little boxes *above* the Gradient bar. You can move an Opacity Stop to wherever you want and then adjust the transparency by using the settings in the Stops section of the Gradient Editor. Click the Gradient bar wherever you want to add more Opacity Stops (click above the Gradient bar, rather than in it). The more Opacity Stops your Gradient bar has, the more points at which you can adjust your gradient's opacity.

Here's how to add an Opacity Stop and then adjust its opacity setting:

1. **Click one of the existing Opacity Stops.**

   If the little square on the stop is dark, it means the stop is completely opaque. A white square is totally transparent. The new stop will have the same opacity as the stop you click, but you can adjust the new stop once you've created it.

2. **Add a stop.**

   Click anywhere along the Gradient bar where you want to add a stop. If you want your gradient to be precisely positioned, you can enter numbers (indicating percent) in the Location box below the gradient bar. For example, 50 percent positions a stop at the midpoint of the Gradient bar.

3. **Adjust the new stop's opacity.**

   Go to the Opacity box below the Gradient bar and either enter a percentage or click the arrow to the right of the number and move the slider to change the opacity setting. If you want to get rid of a stop, click its tab and press Delete.

By adding stops, you can make your gradient fade in and out, as shown in the background of Figure 12-18. This is a simple vertical one-color to transparent linear gradient that's been edited so that it fades in and out a few times.

Figure 12-18:
You can make a gradient fade in and out like this background by adding more Opacity stops and reducing the opacity level of each stop.

Creating noise gradients

Elements also lets you create what Adobe calls *noise gradients*. A noise gradient isn't speckled (as you might expect if you're thinking of camera noise). Instead, noise gradients randomly distribute their colors within the range you specify, giving a banded or spectrometer-like effect to the gradient. The effect can be interesting, but noise gradients can be a bit unpredictable. The noisier a gradient is, the more banding of the colors you'll see, and the greater the number of random colors.

You can create a noise gradient by clicking the More button on the Options bar gradient pop-out menu and selecting Noise Samples in the pop-out list of categories. Or you can click the Edit button to bring up the Gradient Editor and choose Noise as your Gradient Type.

Noise gradients have some special settings of their own in the Gradient Editor:

- **Roughness** controls the percent of noise in the gradient (see Figure 12-19).

Figure 12-19:
The amount of noise in a gradient can make quite a difference in the effect you get.

The top figure shows a Solid gradient. Below that is a gradient with the same colors and 50 percent noise. At bottom is a gradient with the same colors and 90 percent noise.

- **Color Model** determines which color mode you work in, RGB or HSB. RGB gives you red, blue, and green color sliders, while HSB lets you set hue, saturation, and brightness.

- **Restrict Colors.** If you want to keep your colors from getting too saturated, turn on this checkbox.

- **Add Transparency** puts random amounts of transparency into your gradient. Keep clicking the Randomize button until you see an effect you like.

Saving Gradients

After all that work, you'll probably want to save your gradient so you can use it again. To save a gradient, you have two options:

- **Click the New button in the Editor.** Enter a name for your new gradient in the Name box. Your gradient gets added to the current category. Elements creates a new preset gradient for you that's now available in the Gradient thumbnails.

- **Click Save.** The Save dialog box appears, and Elements asks you to name the gradient. You'll save the new gradients in a special Gradients folder, which Elements automatically takes you to in the Save dialog box. When you want to use the gradient again, click Load and then select it from the list of gradients that appear.

  TIP You can also save and load gradients from the More menu on the Options bar gradient pop-out menu.

Gradient Maps

Gradient Maps let you use gradients in nonlinear ways. In other words, instead of a rainbow that shades from one direction to another, in a gradient map, the gradient colors are substituted for the existing colors in your image. Gradient maps can be used for funky special effects or for serious photo corrections.

What Elements does when you create a Gradient Map is map the brightness values of your image to a gradient (light to dark) and then replace the existing colors with the gradient you choose, using the lightness values as a guide for which color goes where.

That may sound complicated, but if you try it, you'll quickly see what's going on. Take a look at Figure 12-20, for instance. Applying a gradient map dramatically livens up this really dull photo, but that's not all gradient maps are good for. Gradients and gradient maps can also be valuable tools for straight retouching. See the box on page 337 for how to use gradients to fix the color in your photo.

Figure 12-20:
Left: A pedestrian shot with a totally blown-out sky.

Right: The shot becomes something altogether different when you apply a gradient map adjustment.

You can apply a gradient map directly to your image by going to Filter → Adjustments → Gradient Map. But most times, it's preferable to use a Gradient Map Adjustment layer, because it's easier to edit after you've created the layer. Here's how:

1. **Create a Gradient Map Adjustment layer.**

   Go to Layer → New Adjustment Layer → Gradient Map. You see the dialog box shown in Figure 12-21.

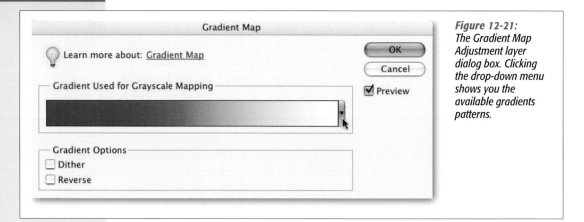

Figure 12-21:
The Gradient Map Adjustment layer dialog box. Clicking the drop-down menu shows you the available gradients patterns.

2. **Choose a gradient.**

   You'll see a grayscale gradient in the dialog box. That's the map of the lightness/darkness values that Elements has made for your image. If you want your image to show color, you need to choose a color gradient. Click the arrow at the right of the Gradient bar and choose a color gradient.

   The Dither setting adds a little random noise to make smoother transitions. The Reverse setting switches the direction the gradient is applied to the map. For example, if you chose a red to green gradient, reversing it would put green where it would have previously put red, and vice versa. It's worth giving this a try—you can get some very interesting effects.

3. **Click OK when you are satisfied with the result.**

   Elements automatically replaces the colors in your image with the equivalent values from the gradient you chose.

Remember, too, that you don't have to use your gradient in Normal mode. You can use any blend mode (page 137). You can spend hours playing around with the different effects you can get with the gradient map. Other filters and adjustments can produce very unexpected results when used with it.

> **TIP** Try Equalizing your image (Image → Adjustments → Equalize) after applying a gradient map adjustment. The colors can shift quite dramatically. Equalize is a good thing to try if you find that your gradient map makes your image look dull or dingy. You may need to merge the layers (see page 142) to get this to work though, since you can't equalize an Adjustment layer. (See page 248 for more about the Equalize command.)

Using Gradients for Color Correction

If your only interest in Elements is enhancing and correcting your photos, you may think that all this gradient business is a big waste of time. But keep in mind that gradients and gradient maps aren't just for introducing lurid colors into your photos. They can be powerful tools to help you with correcting your photographs.

For instance, say you've got a photo where one side is much darker than the other. You might want to apply an Adjustment layer so it affects only the dark side of the image.

You can do this by grouping a black to white or transparent gradient layer beneath the Adjustment layer (see page 140). Or you can bring up the layer mask of the Adjustment layer (see page 229) and apply your gradient directly to the mask.

You can use a Gradient Map layer the same way, although you may have to use the Gradient Editor to change the distribution of the light and dark values to get the best effect.

Type in Elements

If you want to add text to your photos, Elements makes it easy. You can quickly create all kinds of fancy text to use on greeting cards, as newsletter headlines, or as graphics for Web pages.

Elements gives you lots of ways to jazz up your text: you can apply Layer styles, effects, and gradients, or you can warp your type into psychedelic shapes. And the Type Mask tools let you fill individual letters with the contents of a photo. Best of all, most type tools let you change your text with only a few button clicks (see Figure 13-1). By the time you finish this chapter, you'll have learned about all the ways that Elements can add pizzaz to your text.

Adding Type to an Image

It's a cinch to add text to an image in Elements. Just select the Type tool, choose your font, and type away. The Type tool has a Toolbox icon that's easy to recognize—a capital T. There are actually four different type tools, all of which are hidden behind the Toolbox icon's pop-out menu: the Horizontal Type tool, the Vertical Type tool, the Horizontal Type Mask, and the Vertical Type Mask.

You'll learn about the Type Mask tools later in this chapter. To get started, you'll focus on the regular Horizontal and Vertical Type tools. As their names imply, the Horizontal Type tool lets you enter type that runs left to right, while the Vertical Type tool is for creating type that runs down the page instead of across it.

When you use the Type tools, Elements automatically puts your text on its own layer. This makes it easy to throw out your text and start over again later.

Happy Birthday

Happy Birthday

Figure 13-1:
With Elements, you can take basic type and turn it into the same kind of snazzy headline type you see on greeting cards and magazine covers. It took only a couple of clicks to turn the plain black type in the top figure to the extravaganza below.

TROUBLESHOOTING MOMENT

Why Does the Type Tool Turn My Photo Red?

If your image gets covered with an ugly orange-red film every time you click it with the Type tool, you've got one of the Type Masks turned on. (Type Masks are useful when you want to create text that's cut from an image. They're covered later in this chapter.)

To switch over to the regular Type tools, click the Type tool icon in the Elements Toolbox. Use the pop-out menu to select either of the regular Type tools (horizontal or vertical). Or you can click the correct icon in the Options bar.

Type Options

Whether you select the Horizontal or Vertical Type tool, the first thing you're going to want to do is take a look at the many settings available in the Options bar (Figure 13-2). These choices let you control pretty much every aspect of your type, including font selection, font color, and alignment.

Your choices from left to right are:

- **Tool Selection.** These buttons select which Type tool you want to use. From left to right, your choices are the Horizontal Type tool, the Vertical Type tool, the Horizontal Type Mask, and the Vertical Type Mask. Once you select one tool and click in your image, the other tools disappear. Go to the Toolbox icon's pop-out menu to change your tool selection.

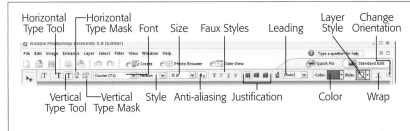

Horizontal Type Tool | Horizontal Type Mask | Font | Size | Faux Styles | Leading | Layer Style | Change Orientation

Vertical Type Tool | Vertical Type Mask | Style | Anti-aliasing | Justification | Color | Wrap

Figure 13-2:
The Type Options bar lets you control lots of different settings, most of which are pretty standard, like the font you want to use and the size of the letters. It's the choices toward the right end—like Warping and Layer style—where the fun begins.

NOTE If you choose the Vertical Type tool, your columns of type run from right to left instead of left to right. If you want vertical type columns to run left to right, you need to put each column on its own layer and position them manually.

- **Style.** Here's where you select the styles available for your font, like Medium, Bold, or Italic.

- **Font.** Choose your font, listed here by name. Elements uses the fonts installed on your computer.

- **Point Size.** This is where you choose how big your type should be. Text is traditionally measured in *points*. You can choose from the list of preset sizes in the pull-down menu or just type in the size you want. You aren't limited to the sizes shown in the menu—you can type in any number you want. See the box on page 345 for help understanding the relationship between points and actual size in Elements.

  If points make you nervous, you can change the type measurement unit to millimeters or pixels, or picas in Edit → Preferences → Units and Rulers (Photoshop Elements → Preferences → Units and Rulers).

- **Anti-aliasing.** This setting smoothes the edges of your type. Turn it on or off by clicking the little square with "a a" on it. Anti-aliasing is explained later, but usually you want it turned on.

- **Faux Styles.** Faux as in "fake." If your chosen font doesn't have a Bold, Italic, Underline, or Strikethrough version, you can tell Elements to simulate it here by clicking the appropriate icon. (This option is not available for some fonts.)

- **Justification.** These buttons tell Elements how to align your text, just like in your word processor. If you enter multiple lines of type, here's where you tell Elements whether you want it lined up left, right, or centered (for horizontal type). If you select the Vertical Type tool, you see squares of type that are aligned top, bottom, or middle. Choose the icon that shows the alignment you want.

- **Leading.** This setting controls the amount of spacing between the lines of type, measured in points. For horizontal type, leading is the difference between the baselines (the bottom of the letters) on each line. For vertical type, leading is the distance from the center of one column to the center of the column next to it. Figure 13-3 demonstrates what a difference leading can make to the appearance of your text. The first setting you'll always see is Auto, which is Elements' guess about what looks best. You can change leading by choosing a number from the list or entering the amount you want (in points).

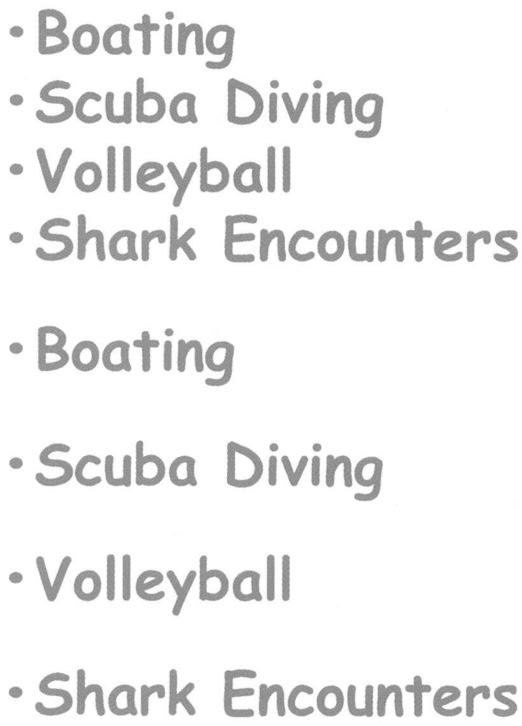

Figure 13-3:
Leading is the space between lines of type.

Top: Here, you can see a list with Auto leading.

Bottom: Here's one with the leading number set much higher.If you change the leading of vertical type, you change the space between the vertical columns of type, rather than the space between letters in an individual column. See the box "Using Asian Text Options to Control Text Spacing" on page 347 for how to tighten up the space between letters that are stacked vertically.

- **Color.** Click this square to set your text's color. When you've made your selection, the Foreground color square also changes to show the new color. Click the arrow to the right of the Options bar square to bring up the Color Swatches instead (page 180) of the Color Picker.

  NOTE When the Type tool cursor is active in your image, you can't use the keyboard commands to reset Elements' standard colors (black and white) or to switch them. You'll need to click the relevant buttons in the Toolbox instead. (See page 174 for how to use the Toolbox's color-picking squares.)

- **Layer Style.** You can choose to apply a Layer style (page 322) to your text as you type it. Just click the box and choose a style from the pop-out palette. If you've chosen a style and you want to revert to no style, choose the white rectangle with a red line through it from the pop-out palette.

- **Warp.** The little T over a curved line hides a multitude of options for distorting your type in lots of interesting ways. There's more about this option in the section "Warping Type."

- **Orientation.** This button changes your text from horizontal to vertical, or vice versa (you first need to type some text for this option to become active). You can also change type orientation by going to Layer → Type → Horizontal or Vertical.

These two choices don't show up till you've actually typed something:

- **Cancel.** When you add type to your image, the text automatically gets placed on its own layer. Click this button to delete this newly created text layer. This Cancel button works only if you click it before you *commit* your text (explained in the next bullet point). To delete text after you've committed it, drag its layer to the Trash in the Layers palette.

- **Commit.** Click the checkmark after you type on your image to tell Elements that yes, you want the text to remain as it appears. Committing your type gives you access to the other tools again.

If you see either of these buttons, you haven't committed your type, and many menu selections and other tools won't be available until you do. When you see the Cancel and Commit buttons in the Options bar, you are in what Elements calls "Edit mode," where you can make changes to your type, but most of the rest of Elements isn't available to you. Just click Commit or Cancel to get the rest of the program options back.

Creating Text

Now that you're familiar with the choices you've got in the Options bar, you're ready to start adding text to your image. You can add type to an existing image, or start by creating a new file (if you want to create type to use as a graphic by itself). To use either the Horizontal or Vertical Type tools, just follow these steps:

1. **Activate the Type tool.**

   Click the tool in the Toolbox or press T, then select the Horizontal Type tool or the Vertical Type tool from the pop-out menu.

2. **Modify any settings you want to change on the Options bar.**

   See the list in the previous section for a run-down of your choices. You can make changes after you enter your type, too, so your choices aren't set in stone yet. Elements lets your type remain editable until you simplify the layer. (See page 144 for more about what simplifying a layer means.)

3. **Enter your text.**

   Click in your image where you'd like your text to go and then begin typing. The Type tools automatically create a new layer for your text. If you're using the Horizontal Type tool, the horizontal line you see is the baseline your letters sit on. If you're typing vertically, the vertical part of the cursor is the centerline of your character.

Type the way you would in a word processor, using the Enter (Return) key to create a new line. Elements doesn't *wrap* type (i.e., automatically adjust it to fit a given space), so you need to make your returns manually.

As noted earlier, if you want to use the Vertical Type tool, you can't make the columns of type run left to right. If you need multiple vertical columns of English language text, enter one column and then click the Commit button. Then start over again for the next column, so that each column is on its own layer.

4. **Use the Move tool if you don't like where the text is positioned.**

   Sometimes the text isn't placed exactly where you want it. The Move tool helps you reposition your text. If you need to move vertical type columns, wait until you've committed the type to rearrange the columns.

5. **If you like what you see, click the checkmark in the Options bar to commit the type.**

   When you commit your type, you tell Elements that you accept what you've created. The Type tool cursor is no longer active in your photo once you commit. If, on the other hand, you don't like what you typed, click the Cancel button in the Options bar, and the whole type layer goes away.

Once you've entered type, you can modify it using most of Elements editing tools—you can add Layer styles (page 322), move it with the Move tool, rotate it, make color adjustments, and so on.

> **NOTE** If you try to paste text into Elements by copying it from your word processor, the results are unpredictable. Sometimes it's fine, but you may find it comes in as one endlessly long line of text. If that happens, it's easier to type your text in Elements from scratch than to try to reformat the text.

Editing Type

In Elements, you can change your text after you've entered it, just like in a word processor. Elements lets you change not only words, but the font and its size, too, even if you've applied lots of Layer styles (see Figure 13-4). You modify text by highlighting it and making the correction or changing your settings in the Options bar.

> **TIP** Elements gives you a quick way to preview what your text will look like in other fonts. First, select the text and then click in the Font box in the Options bar. In Windows, you can use your mouse's scroll wheel (or up and down arrow keys) to run down the font list. You'll see your words appear in each font as you go down the list. On a Mac, you can do the same thing by clicking in the Font box, and using the arrow keys to run through the list of fonts. (You can use either the up and down arrows or the left and right arrows.)

TROUBLESHOOTING MOMENT

How Resolution Affects Font Size

It's easy enough to pick the font size in the Text tool's Option's bar. But you may find that what you thought would be big, bold, headline-sized type is almost invisible on your image because it looks tiny. What gives?

In Elements, the actual size of text in your image is tied to the resolution of your image. So if you thought that choosing 72-point type would give you a headline that's an inch high, it will, but only if the *resolution* of your file is also 72 pixels per inch (ppi). The more you increase the resolution, the smaller that same type is going to be. If you double the resolution to 144 ppi, your text prints half an inch high. If you triple it to 216 ppi, it's a third of an inch high.

If you're working with high-resolution images, you have to increase the size of your fonts to allow for the extra pixel packing that comes from increased resolution.

It's not uncommon to have to choose sizes that are much higher than anything listed in the size menu in the Options bar. Don't be afraid of really big sizes if you need them—just keep entering larger numbers in the size box until the text looks right in proportion to your image.

Another thing that sometimes causes confusion is that you have to remember that Elements is creating the type based on the actual size of your image, not the view size. People often try to put very small type on a very big image and wonder why it looks so bad. If you aren't sure about the actual size of your document, try going to View → Print Size before typing. This view offers only an approximation, but it will help you get a better idea of what your text will look like.

You can make all these changes as long as you don't *simplify* your type. Simplifying is the process of changing text from an easily editable vector shape to a rasterized graphic. In this respect, text works just like the shapes you learned about in Chapter 11: once you simplify text, Elements doesn't see it as text anymore, just as a bunch of regular pixels.

You can either choose to simplify text yourself (by selecting Layer → Simplify Layer), or you can wait for Elements to prompt you to simplify, which it will do when you try to do things like apply a filter or add an effect to your type.

> **TIP**   Some text effects automatically simplify your text without asking first. So make sure you've made all the edits you want to your text before using these effects.

Smoothing type: antialiasing

Antialiasing smoothes the edges of your type. It gets rid of the "jaggies" by blending the edge pixels on letters to make the outline look even, as shown in Figure 13-5. In Chapter 5, you read about antialiasing for graphics, and antialiasing has a similar effect on type.

Elements always starts you off with antialiasing turned on, and 99 percent of the time you'll want to keep it on. The main reason you might want to turn it off is to avoid *fringing*—a line of unwanted pixels that make it look like the text was cut out from an image with a colored background.

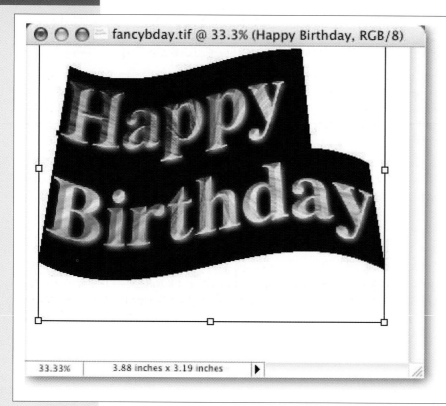

Figure 13-4:
If you change your mind about what you want to say, no problem. Here, the text from Figure 13-1 is highlighted so that the words can be changed. The best part is that you can change the text to say anything, and all the formatting stays exactly the same. You can't do this after you simplify a type layer, though.

Figure 13-5:
The same letters with and without antialiasing. If you look at the letters on the right, you can see how the edges are much more jagged and rough-looking compared to the letters on the left.

You turn antialiasing off and on by clicking the Anti-aliasing button (the two Ts) in the Options bar. The button is dark when antialiasing is on. In Elements 3, you can also turn antialiasing off and on by going to Layers → Type → Anti-Alias Off or Anti-Alias On. Once you simplify type, you can't change the antialiasing setting for the type.

> **TIP** If you're seeing really jagged type even with antialiasing turned on, check your resolution. Type often looks poor at low resolution settings—just as photos do. See page 64 for more about resolution.

Using Asian Text Options to Control Text Spacing

Getting letters spaced correctly when using the Vertical Type tool can be tough. Elements lets you set the *leading,* but with vertical type, your leading setting affects the spacing between *columns* of letters, not the spacing of the letters within a column.

Also, sometimes you might want to adjust the spacing between letters written in horizontal text. Elements lets you make either of these fixes, but you need to use the Asian Text Options, even if you're writing in English.

To get started, go to Edit → Preferences → General (Photoshop Elements → Preferences → General) and put a check next to "Show Asian Text Options." Then, the next time you click in an image with the Type tool, you'll see an Asian character in the Options bar, just to the left of the Cancel button.

Click the symbol for a pop-out menu with three options: tate-chuu-yoko, mojikumi, and a pull-down menu with percentages on it. You want the pull-down menu, which is for *tsume.* Tsume reduces the amount of space around the characters or letters you apply it to.

To apply tsume, just highlight the characters you want to change and select a percentage from the pull-down menu. The higher the percentage, the tighter the spacing becomes.

You can select a single letter or a whole word for tsume. Since it reduces the space all the way around each letter you apply it to, you can use it for either vertical or horizontal text, although for horizontal type, you'd be most likely to use it to tidy up the spacing of just one or two letters. For vertical type, tsume is a great way to tighten up the vertical spacing of your text.

Warping Type

With Elements, you can warp the shape of your type in all sorts of fun ways. You can make it wave like a flag, bulge out, twist like a fish, arc up or down, and lots more. These complex effects are really easy, too, and you can still edit the type once you've applied the effects. Figure 13-6 shows just a few examples of what you can do. If you add a Layer style (explained later), warps are even more effective.

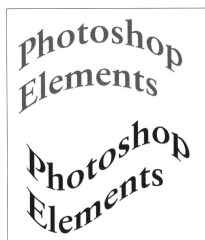

Figure 13-6:
Elements gives you oodles of ways to warp your type. Here are just a few of the basic warps, applied using their standard settings. Clockwise from the upper left: Arch, Inflate, Arc Upper, and Flag. You can tweak these effects endlessly using the sliders in the Warp dialog box.

To warp your type, follow these steps:

1. **Enter the text you want.**

   Use the Move tool (page 119) to reposition your text if necessary.

2. **Select the text you want to warp.**

   Make sure the Text layer is the active layer or you won't be able to select what you typed.

3. **Click the Create Warped Text button in the Options bar.**

   It's the T with a curved line under it. The Warp Text dialog box, shown in Figure 13-7, appears.

4. **Tell Elements how to warp your text.**

   Select a warp style from the pull-down list. Next, make any changes you want to the sliders or the horizontal/vertical orientation of the warp. Tweaking these settings can radically alter the effect. Push the sliders around to experiment. You can preview the results right in your image. Your choices are described in more detail in the next section.

5. **When you come up with something you like, click OK.**

   TIP   You can't warp type that has the Faux Bold style applied to it. Elements reminds you if you forget and try to do so.

Elements gives you lots of different warp styles to choose from, and you can customize the look of each style by using the settings in the Warp Text dialog box, described in the next section.

The Warp Text dialog box

The little dialog box that comes up when you click the Create Warped Text button is pretty straightforward. Your setting choices are:

- **Warp Style.** This is where you choose your warp style: Arc, Flag, and so on. These choices are in the pull-down menu. To help you choose a style, Elements gives you thumbnail icons demonstrating the general shape of each warp.

- **Horizontal/Vertical.** These radio buttons control the orientation of the warping. Most of the time, you'll want to leave the button the same as the text's orientation, but you can get interesting effects by warping the opposite way.

   A vertical warp on horizontal text gives more of a perspective effect, like the text is moving towards you or away from you. You can get some very funky effects by putting a horizontal warp on vertical text.

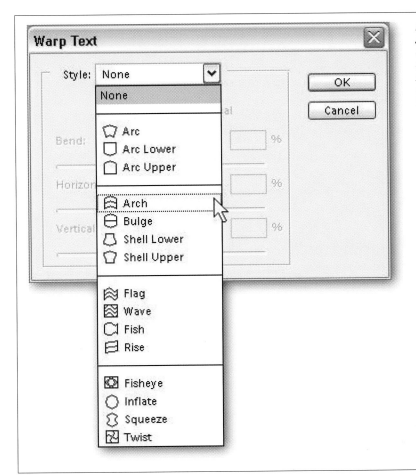

- **Bend.** This is where you tell Elements how much of an arc you want. If you want to change the arc from Element's standard setting, type a percentage in the box or just move the slider until you get what you want. A higher positive percentage makes a bigger warp. A negative number makes your text warp in the opposite direction. For example, if you want an inverted arc, choose the Arc style and move the slider into the negative region.

- **Horizontal/Vertical Distortion.** These settings control how much your text warps in the horizontal or vertical plane. Moving the sliders gives you a very high degree of control over just how and where your text warps. They work pretty much the same way as the Bend setting—type a negative or positive percentage or move the sliders.

The best way to find the look you want is to experiment. It's lots of fun, especially if you apply a Layer style first to give your type a three-dimensional look before warping it.

TIP Many of the Warps look best on two lines of type, so that the lines bend in opposite directions. However, you can also get very interesting effects by putting two lines of type on separate layers and applying a different warp to each.

To edit your warp after it's done, double-click the Warp thumbnail icon in the Layers palette. Doing that automatically makes the text layer active and highlights the text. Then, click the Warp icon in the Options bar again. The Warp dialog box opens and shows your current settings. Make any changes you want or set the style to None to get rid of it.

NOTE There are helpful step-by-step instructions for warping text in the How To palette. Go to Window → How To if the palette isn't already in the Palette bin, and click the flippy triangle next to "Working with Text." Then choose "Warping Text."

Adding Special Effects

Besides warping your type, you can apply all kinds of Layer styles, filters, and effects to give your text a more elaborate appearance (see Figure 13-8). You can change your text's color, make it look three-dimensional, add brushstrokes for a painted effect, and so on. (There's more about Layer styles, filters, and effects in Chapter 12.)

Figure 13-8:
It took only two clicks to go from plain type to the figure shown here. The first click applied a Wow Plastic Layer style (located at the bottom of the Layer Styles palette). The next click applied the Water Reflection effect (located in the Text Effects in the Styles and Effects palette).

Elements gives you lots of different ways to add special effects to your text. The following sections show you three of the most interesting: applying the Text effects, using a gradient to make rainbow-colored type, and using the Liquify filter to warp your text in truly odd ways.

NOTE Layer styles must be applied *before* simplifying, while filters and effects can't be applied *without* simplifying. You can apply all three kinds of changes to the same text, but you need to keep these restrictions in mind and plan out your order of operations accordingly.

Text Effects

The Styles and Effects palette's pull-down menu contains an entire category dedicated to special Text effects. You can emboss your type into a photo, give it a reflection as shown in Figure 13-8, make it look like wood or brushed metal, and on and on. You apply Text effects just the way you would apply any other effect—make the type layer active and double-click the effect you want.

If you already have Layer styles on your text, it's hard to predict how much the effects will respect the Layer styles. Some effects build onto the changes you've previously made with Layer styles; others undo anything you've done before. Experimenting is the best way to find out what happens when you combine Layer styles and effects.

> **TIP**   If you choose the "Clear Emboss" effect on a white background, your text looks kind of like the Beatles' White Album cover—nothing but a blank white page. Try using this effect where there's color or a pattern.

Type Gradients

If you want to create type that's filled with a gradient pattern—rainbow colored type, in other words—it's probably easiest to start with a Type Mask, as explained later. But if you already have some existing text, as long as it's not yet simplified, you can easily fill it with a gradient for a rainbow effect.

> **TIP**   A heavier, chunky font shows off your rainbow better than a thin, spidery one.

Filling text with a gradient is easy. First, make sure you've got some text in your image, then follow these steps:

1. **Create a new layer for your gradient. Make sure it's adjacent to your text layer.**

    You're going to group the two layers, which is why they need to be next to each other. To create the new layer, press Ctrl+Shift+N (⌘-Shift-N) or go to Layer → New → Layer. Look at the Layers palette to be sure the new layer is the active layer. Click it if it isn't.

2. **Make a rectangular selection around your type.**

    Use the Rectangular Marquee tool. (See page 102 for more about using the Marquee tools.)

3. **Activate the Gradient tool.**

    Click the Gradient tool in the Toolbox and choose a gradient style in the Options bar. (See page 325 for more about how to select, modify, and apply gradients.)

4. **Fill the selection with the gradient.**

Drag across the selection to fill it with the gradient. Your text disappears, because the gradient covers everything. That's fine for the moment. You're going to fix that in the next step.

5. **Group the gradient with the text layer.**

Go to Layer → Group with Previous. The gradient now is visible only within the outline of your type. You can drag the gradient layer around within the outline of the type to change which part of the gradient appears in the text. When you like what you see, you're done.

> **TIP**   You can get rainbow effects even more easily by using some of the Layer styles, such as the Angled Spectrum pattern (found in the Patterns category of the Styles and Effects palette). Several other patterns give a gradient-like effect and so do a few of the Complex Layer styles.

Applying the Liquify Filter to Type

The Warp Text button in the Options bar (explained earlier, on page 347) gives you lots of ways to reshape your type. But there's an even more powerful way to warp type: the Liquify filter (see Figure 13-9).

Figure 13-9:
The Liquify filter can reshape text in many different ways, including adding a flame-like effect (shown here), making letters twirl around on themselves, or making text undulate like it's under water.

> **NOTE**   You can actually use the Liquify filter to warp anything in an image—not just text. Use it to alter objects in photographs and drawings, for example. Fix someone's nose, make your brother look like E.T., give a scene a watery reflection, and so on.

To use the Liquify filter, you first need to simplify the layer your text is on (Layer → Simplify Layer). (Remember, your text can't be edited once you simplify it.) Then, call up the Liquify filter dialog box by going to Filter → Distort → Liquify. You can also get to it by double-clicking the Liquify filter thumbnail in the Distort section of the Styles and Effects palette.

You see yet another large Elements dialog box. Like most of them, it's fairly straightforward once you learn your way around it. In the upper-left corner of the Liquify dialog box is a little Toolbox with some very special tools in it (see Figure 13-10).

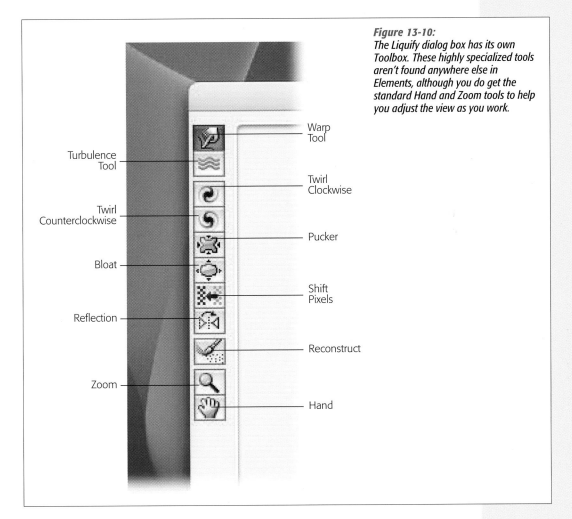

Figure 13-10:
The Liquify dialog box has its own Toolbox. These highly specialized tools aren't found anywhere else in Elements, although you do get the standard Hand and Zoom tools to help you adjust the view as you work.

From top to bottom they are:

- **Warp tool.** This lets you push the pixels of your image in whichever direction you want, although it usually takes a fair amount of coaxing to create much of an effect.

- **Turbulence tool.** You can use the Turbulence tool to create clouds and waves. This tool is very dependent on the Turbulent Jitter setting on the right side of the window (explained later). A higher number creates a smoother effect.

- **Twirl Clockwise.** Hold this tool down on your image, and the pixels under your cursor spin in a clockwise direction. The longer you apply this tool, the more extreme the spin effect.

- **Twirl Counterclockwise.** This is the opposite of the Twirl Clockwise tool. It makes the pixels under the cursor spin counterclockwise.

- **Pucker.** This tool makes the pixels under the cursor move toward the center of the brush.

- **Bloat.** This tool is the opposite of the Pucker tool. It makes pixels move *away* from the center of the brush.

- **Shift Pixels.** The pixels you drag this tool over move perpendicularly in relation to the direction of your stroke. For example, if you drag from the top of an image in a straight line down, the pixels you pass over will move to the right. Alt+drag (Option-drag) to change the direction of the shift.

- **Reflection.** Drag to create a reflection of the area the tool passes over. Overlapping strokes create a watery effect.

- **Reconstruct.** Pass this wonderful tool over areas where you've gone too far, and you selectively return them to their original condition without wrecking the rest of your changes.

- **Zoom and Hand tools.** These are the same Zoom (page 61) and Hand (page 63) tools you find elsewhere in Elements.

Your image appears in the preview window in the center of the dialog box. You can adjust the view with the Zoom tool or by using the magnification menu in the lower-left corner of the image area.

> **TIP** It often helps to zoom in very closely when using the Liquify filter. If you've added text to a large image, select the text with the Marquee tool before activating the Liquify filter. Then you'll see only the selected area in the filter preview, which makes it easier to get a high zoom level.

At the right side of the dialog box are the Tool Options settings:

- **Size.** This controls the size of the brush. You can enter a number as low as 1 pixel or as large as 600 in the space provided.

- **Pressure.** This is how much the brush affects the pixels you drag over. The range is from one to 100. The higher the pressure, the stronger the effect of the brush. If you're using a graphics tablet, turn on "Stylus Pressure" so that the harder you press, the more effect you get.

- **Turbulent Jitter.** This controls how smooth your changes look. The higher the number, the smoother the effect you get from your changes.

To use the filter, just pick your tool, modify your Tool Options (if you want), and then drag across your image. This is a very processor-intense filter, so there may be a fair amount of lag time before you see results, especially if your computer is slow. Give the filter time to work.

There's a Revert button, which returns your image to its original condition before you started using the Liquify filter. You can also Alt+click (Option-click) the Cancel button to turn it to a Reset button (which resets the tool settings as well as your photo). When you like what you see in the preview, click Okay and wait a few seconds while Elements applies your transformations. Then you're done.

Type Masks: Setting an Image in Type

So far in this chapter, you've been reading about how to create regular type and how to glam it up by applying Layer styles and effects. But in Elements, you can also create type by filling letters with the contents of a photo, as shown in Figure 13-11.

Figure 13-11:
By using the Type Mask tools, you can create type that's made from an image. You can also use the Type Mask tools to emboss type into your photo. See Figure 13-13.

The Type Mask tools work by making a selection the shape of your letters. Essentially, you're creating a kind of stencil that you'll place on top of your image.

Once you've used the Type Mask to create your text-shaped selections, you can perform all sorts of neat modifications to your text. You can emboss type into your image (which makes it looks like it's been stamped into your image); you can apply a stroke to the outline of your text (useful if your font doesn't have a built-in outline option); or you can copy and move your text to another document entirely.

Using the Type Mask Tools

Working with the Type Mask tools is pretty easy. The following steps show you how to create a Type Mask and lay it over an image so that the letters you create are filled with whatever's in your image:

1. **Select an image that you want to use to create the text.**

2. **Activate the Type Mask tool.**

   Click the Type tool in the Toolbox or press T. Select the Type Mask tool you want—horizontal or vertical. (Use the pop-out menu or click the icon in the Options bar.) The Type Mask tools behave just like the regular Type tools—a horizontal mask goes across the page, a vertical mask, up and down.

3. **Click your image and start typing.**

   When you click, a red film covers your entire image. The red indicates the area that *won't* be part of your letters. By typing, you're going to cut a visible selection through the red area. When you type, instead of creating regular type, you're creating a type-shaped selection. You can see the shape of the selection as you go.

   TIP   It's important to choose a very blocky font for the type mask, since you can't see much of the image if you use thin or small type.

   It's hard to reposition your words once you've committed them, so take a good look at what you've got. While the mask is active, you can move the mask by dragging it, as explained in Figure 13-12.

Figure 13-12:
Once you've activated the Type Mask tool and clicked on your image, you'll see a red mask appear across your picture. As you start typing, your text appears, as seen here. To move a selection made with the Type Mask tool, hold down Ctrl (⌘), and you can easily drag your selection around in your image as long as you haven't committed it yet.

4. **Don't click the Commit button till you are satisfied with what you have.**

   Once you click the Commit button (the checkmark icon on the right side of the Options bar), you can't alter your type as easily as you can with the regular Type tool. That's because the regular tools create their own layers, while the Type Mask tools just create selections. Once you commit, your type is just like any other selection—Elements doesn't see it as type anymore, so you can no longer change the size by highlighting the text and picking a different size, for example.

5. **When you're happy with your selection, finish by clicking the Commit button.**

   Once you click the Commit button, you see the outline of your type as an active selection. You can move the selection outline by nudging it with the arrow keys.

6. **Remove the non-text portion of your image.**

   Go to Select → Inverse and press Backspace/Delete to remove the rest of the image. Alternatively, you could copy and paste the selection into another document.

Figure 13-13 shows the effect of pressing Ctrl+J (⌘-J) and placing a Type Mask selection on a duplicate layer of its own and then adding Layer styles to the new layer.

Creating Outlined Type

If the font you're using doesn't come with a built-in outline style, there's no quick option for creating outlined type in Elements (the way you can in a Microsoft Word, for example). By using the Type Mask tools, though, you can create outlined text quite easily.

To make a text outline like the one shown in Figure 13-14:

1. **Open your image or create a new one (if you just want the type by itself).**

2. **Activate the Type Mask tool of your choice.**

   Click the Type tool or press T. Then select either of the Type Mask tools.

3. **Choose your font and size.**

   Use the settings in the Options bar. This is another effect that works better with a fairly heavy font rather than a slender one. Bold fonts also work well here, rather than regular fonts.

4. **Enter your type.**

   Type in your image where you want the text to go. If you want to warp your type, do it now, before you commit the type.

5. **Click the Commit button.**

   Be sure you like what you've got before you do, because once you commit the text, it changes to a selection that's hard to edit.

Figure 13-13:
By copying text to another layer, you can bevel or emboss it into your photo. Notice that this photo shows what you need to watch out for—the G is really hard to see, because it blends right into the image. You may need to place your text a few times before you get it positioned correctly. Or you could also add a colored outline to make it stand out more, as described in the "Creating Outlined Type" section.

Figure 13-14:
By using the Type Mask tools, you can create outline type almost as quickly as ordinary type.

6. **Add a stroke to your outline.**

Be sure the type selection is active, then go to Edit → Stroke (Outline) Selection. Choose a line width in pixels and the color you want, then click Okay. Your selection is now a linear outline of the text you typed.

Part Five:
Sharing Your Images

5

Printing Your Photos

Now that you've gone to so much trouble making your photos look terrific, you'll probably want to share them with other people. The next three chapters look at the many different options Elements gives you for sharing your photos with the world at large.

This chapter covers the traditional method—printing your photos. You can print your photos at home on an inkjet printer, take them to a printing kiosk at a local store, or use an online printing service. Adobe makes it especially easy to use Ofoto, their online printing partner. And you're not limited to merely ordinary prints these days. You can create hardcover books, calendars, album pages, and greeting cards, too.

> **NOTE** Printing is one area where the differences between the Windows and Mac versions of Elements start to become apparent. This chapter points out any big differences as they come up.

Getting Ready to Print

Whether you're going to print at home or send your photos out, you need to make sure your image file is setup to give you good-looking prints.

The first thing to check is your photo's resolution, which controls the number of pixels in your image. If you don't have enough pixels in your photo, you're not going to get a good print. 300 pixels per inch (ppi) is usually considered optimum, and a quality print needs a resolution of at least 150 ppi to avoid the grainy look you see in low-resolution photos (see page 64 for more on setting your photo's resolution).

NOTE   Be sure you set your resolution to a whole number—decimals tend to cause black lines on your prints. In other words, 247 ppi is fine, but you may have problems if the ppi is 247.32.

If you're printing on photo paper or sending your photos out for printing, check to be sure that your photos are cropped to a standard paper size. (See page 53 for more about cropping.) And if you're printing at home, the paper you print on makes a big difference in the color and quality of your output. You'll get the best results if you use your printer manufacturer's recommended paper and ink.

Using a Photo Processing Service

You don't even need to own a printer to print your photos. There's no shortage of companies hoping you'll choose them for the privilege of printing out your photos. You can order prints online or use a print kiosk at a local store. Elements makes it very easy to prepare your photos for printing either way. Just save your photos in a compatible file format (see page 75 for more about picking different file formats). The JPEG format is usually your best bet, but always check with the service you plan to use to see if they have any special requirements.

If you plan to physically take your photos in for printing (as opposed to ordering them online), burn the photos to a CD and take that in. You'll have fewer problems than you would if you try to copy your edited photos back on to your camera's memory card.

NOTE   If you have a Mac, don't burn your CD in iPhoto. iPhoto makes CDs using a proprietary format that photo-printing kiosks can't read. Instead, export your photos from iPhoto to the desktop and burn from the Finder to create a disc that anyone can read.

Ordering Prints from Within Elements (Windows Only)

Adobe has partnered with Kodak's online photo-printing service, Ofoto.com, which makes it easy to upload photos directly from the Organizer. You can share photos with other Ofoto.com account holders (creating an account is free), or order prints or books. (There are many other online printing services that you can also use, but the process isn't integrated right into Elements the way it is with Ofoto.)

The first time you click the Organizer's Print shortcut and choose "Order Prints," the Organizer displays an Ofoto.com window, which asks you to set up an Ofoto account if you don't already have one. An easy-to-follow wizard appears to help you set up your account. (If you already have an Ofoto account, you just log in.)

Then you tell Ofoto how many prints you want of each photo you've selected and which sizes they should be. You confirm your order, and in a few days, your prints arrive in the mail. The entire process is very easy, and the pricing is competitive with most drugstore photo printing.

To get started, you first need to make sure Elements has the latest software for connecting to Ofoto. To check for recent updates, in the Organizer, go to Edit → Preferences → Services. In the Available Services section, select Print (in the first pulldown menu) and "Adobe Photoshop Services, provided by Ofoto" (in the second menu). Then click the Refresh button.

> **TIP** While you're in the Services window, you might also want to click "Update Creations" to get any new layouts for the Create projects. Several designs have been added since Elements 3 first came out.

Once you've created your Ofoto account and you're ready to order prints:

1. **In the Organizer, select the photos you want to print.**

   If the photos you want are scattered around, you may find it easier to make a temporary collection (see page 37 for how to create a collection) so that you can easily see them all once. Alternatively, you can also just Ctrl+click to select the photos you want.

2. **Connect to Ofoto.com.**

   Go to File → Order Prints, or in the Shortcuts bar, click the Printer icon and then choose Order prints. If you're not already online, Elements brings up an Internet connection window. Click okay, and Elements connects you to the Ofoto Web site.

3. **Log in to your Ofoto account.**

   Enter your name and password.

4. **Order your prints.**

   Select the size and number of prints for each photo, then enter your shipping information. You'll receive an envelope of prints in the mail in a few days. The only difference between online prints and film prints is that the envelope contains a contact sheet (a page of thumbnail-sized photos), instead of negatives. (You still have your "negatives," which are your original files.)

Elements makes ordering prints from Ofoto very convenient. Of course, you can use Ofoto without the Organizer, and you can use other online print services like Shutterfly (*www.shutterfly.com*) if you like. The real advantage of ordering from Elements is the convenience of being able to work right from the Organizer.

> **NOTE** Mac owners can order prints and books from Ofoto by using iPhoto. If you don't use iPhoto, you can download Ofoto Express for Mac (*www.ofoto.com/DownloadClient.jsp*), which helps you upload your photos to Ofoto's Web site.

Printing from the Editor

If you want to do your own printing, you can print directly from the Elements Editor. If you're a Mac owner, this is where you'll do your printing, although most of this section applies to both platforms equally. If you've got the Windows version of Elements, you can only print one photo at a time from the Editor, but it's convenient not having to run back to the Organizer every time you want to print a photo. (Printing multiple photos, like contact sheets, is handled by the Organizer, which is explained later.)

Before you actually print your photos, for best results, you need to check the settings in two windows—the Page Setup dialog box, and the Elements Print Preview Window.

Page Setup

The Page Setup window is the same for all the programs you have on your computer. It's where you set your page size and orientation and tell the computer which printer you're using, if you have more than one printer.

Whether you're using Windows or a Mac, you get to Page Setup by going to File → Page Setup. You can also press Ctrl+Shift+P (⌘-Shift-P) or click the Page Setup button on the Elements Print Preview window (explained later).

In Page Setup, start by choosing the correct printer. In Windows, click the Printer button to choose a printer. On a Mac, choose it from the pull-down menu. This setting is important for getting your margins exactly right. Next, in the main Page Setup window, choose the paper size you want and the orientation (portrait or landscape). When you've selected these settings, you're ready to go to the Elements Print Preview dialog box.

Print Preview

Print Preview is your control center for printing from Elements. It offers you a great many ways to tweak your prints, from simply positioning your photo correctly to making very sophisticated color adjustments.

Press Ctrl+P (⌘-P) in the Editor to call up the Print Preview window. For simple printing, just make sure the photo is properly positioned on the page and click Print. If you're lucky, you'll get a perfect looking print. If you don't like the color, the next section on color management explains your options.

Don't be intimidated by the Print Preview window, which is shown in Figure 14-1. You probably won't need all the settings every time you print, but each setting comes in handy sooner or later.

On the left side of the Print Preview window is a thumbnail showing the location where your photo will print. Normally, Elements shows a *bounding box,* the black outline with handles on the corners indicating the edges of your photo. Don't worry, the bounding box itself doesn't print along with your photo. The box just

Figure 14-1:
The Editor's Print
Preview dialog box is
identical for Mac and
Windows except for
the button in the
upper-right corner. On
the Mac, shown here,
the button says "Print
Layouts" and clicking
it brings up the Picture
Package window (see
below). In Windows,
the button's label is
"Print Multiple
Images." Clicking it
sends you to the
Organizer print dialog
box, discussed in the
next section. Turning
off the "Center Image"
checkbox lets you
drag your photo
around manually, so
you can position it
wherever you like
(assuming you've got
room on your paper).

gives you a way to move and resize your image by dragging the handles. If seeing the bounding box bothers you, get rid of it by turning off the Show Bounding Box checkbox.

The familiar Elements Rotate symbols appear below the right corner of the image window. Use these if you need to change the orientation of your photo.

If you want to print only part of a photo, Figure 14-2 shows how to print a selected area of a picture. Your selection must be a plain rectangle or square without any feathering (see page 106), or Elements won't print it.

You can resize your photo in Print Preview in several ways:

- **Print Size menu.** Choose any print size from the list or enter a Custom Size. "Fit On Page" changes the size of your image, if necessary, to fit the size of the paper you're using.

- **Scaled Print Size.** Resize your photo by a certain percent or by entering new dimensions here. (If you want a custom size, you can just enter the size here. You don't have to change the Print Size pull-down menu, too.)

- **Bounding Box.** You can also use the bounding box to change the size of your image. Hold Shift (to keep the proportions the same) and drag a box (on any of the bounding box's corners) to make your image larger or smaller.

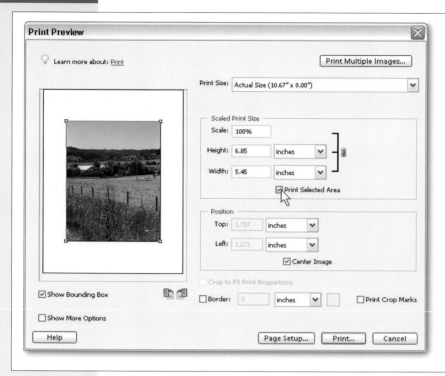

Print Preview

Learn more about: Print

Print Multiple Images...

Print Size: Actual Size (10.67" x 8.00")

Scaled Print Size
Scale: 100%
Height: 6.85 — inches
Width: 5.45 — inches
☑ Print Selected Area

Position
Top: 1.787 — inches
Left: 1.273 — inches
☑ Center Image

Crop to Fit Print Proportions

☑ Show Bounding Box
☐ Border: 0 — inches
☐ Print Crop Marks

☐ Show More Options

Help
Page Setup... Print... Cancel

Figure 14-2:
If you don't want to print your entire photo, you don't actually have to crop it before printing it. You can select the area you want and then turn on "Print selected area." The rest of your photo vanishes, and you see only the part you selected. You can treat the selection like an entire image—move it, resize it, put a border around it, and so on.

- **Crop to Fit Print Proportions.** If your image has a different aspect ratio than the paper you're printing on, and you're feeling lazy, turn this checkbox on, and Elements crops your print for you.

You need to be cautious about resizing in Print Preview, though. Elements resamples your image (see page 71) to make it fit the size you choose. Don't go larger than 100 percent, or the quality of your photo starts to deteriorate and you'll get a warning from Elements (see Figure 14-3).

The other settings in the main part of the Print Preview window are:

- **Position.** This tells Elements where to put your photo on the page. Elements starts you out with the "Center Image" checkbox turned on. You need to turn it off before you can reposition your image. To change the location of your photo, either drag its thumbnail or type the amount of offset you want in the boxes provided. (Top controls how far your image is from the top of the page; Left controls the distance from the left edge of the page.)

- **Border.** If you want to add a border to your photo, turn on the Border checkbox and enter the size you want for your border (in inches, millimeters, or points). Elements shrinks your photo to accommodate the border. Then click the white square to bring up the Elements Color Picker (see page 175) so that you can choose a color for your border.

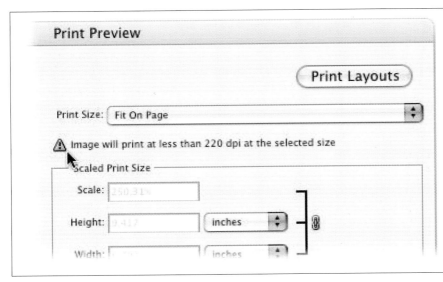

Figure 14-3:
If your resizing activities are going to reduce your photo's resolution below 220 ppi, Elements warns you about the result. Generally, it's better to do most resizing, especially any resizing upward, before you get to Print Preview. Enlarging your photo in Print Preview can make for grainy, poor-quality prints.

- **Print Crop Marks.** This setting, found to the right of the Border settings, lets you print guidelines in the margins of your photo to make it easier to trim it exactly. Crop marks are primarily useful for trimming bordered photos so that the borders are exactly even.

There are two more basic settings that don't appear until you turn on "Show More Options," which is just above the Help button. When you turn on "Show More Options," the Print Preview window expands and you see:

- **Label.** Directly under the "Show More Options" box are the label settings. You can print the file name or caption on your photo by turning on the relevant checkbox. The thumbnail window shows you where your text gets printed.

- **Invert Image.** This setting horizontally reverses your image. Use it when printing transfers for projects like t-shirts. It's located on the lower-right side of the Print Preview window.

The other settings that appear when you expand the window are advanced color settings. They're explained in the next section.

> **NOTE** Print Preview is not *color managed*, which means that what you see in the window is not meant to show you the exact colors you'll get when you print. Instead, you're just looking at the position of your photo.

More printing options—color management

Elements gives you several advanced color-related settings in the Print Preview window. If you're content with the way your prints look without adjusting these settings, just be happy and ignore them. But if you don't like the color you're getting from Elements, you need to turn on "Show More Options" at the bottom of the Print Preview window, which expands to show you these new options.

If you remember from Chapter 7, Elements is a *color-managed* program, which means it tries to coordinate the color settings used by a wide variety of devices and programs: your photo (which may retain color settings applied by your camera), your monitor, your Elements settings, and your printer. Sometimes you need to step in and help Elements decide which settings are best, since different devices can have different interpretations of what individual colors look like.

The most important choice you need to make is whether you want Elements or your printer to manage your photo's color settings. (It's possible to let both Elements *and* your printer have a say in color management, but that almost always mucks things up.) You make your decision in the Color Management section of the Print Preview dialog box, where you'll see three settings:

- **Source Space.** This shows you which, if any, color space your file is tagged with (for example, sRGB or Adobe RGB). You don't actually choose a setting here; instead, this line tells you the color space associated with your file. See page 162 for more about color spaces.

- **Print Space.** This is where you decide whether Elements or your printer handles color management. If you choose Same as Source, you're letting your printer take over the color management duties. Or you can let Elements take over by assigning one of the many profiles shown in the list.

- **Intent.** Intent tells Elements what to do if your photo contains colors that fall outside the range of the print space you're using. Your choices are explained in the box "What's Your Intent?" If you choose Same as Source as your print space, this setting is not available.

The easiest way to set up color management, and a good way to start, is to choose Same as Source for the Print Space setting. This means that Elements just hands your photo over to your printer and lets your printer take care of the color management duties. Then all you need to do is select the proper paper profile and settings for your printer.

Selecting a paper profile sounds complicated, but it's usually as simple as choosing, say, "Photo Paper Plus Glossy" from the list of options in your *printer driver*, the utility program that lets you control your printer's settings. In Windows, you'll find these options in Page Setup → Printer → Properties. On a Mac, you'll find them in Copies and Pages in the OS X Print dialog box. The exact wording differs from brand to brand, but Figure 14-4 shows a popular printer's settings.

> **TIP** If your camera takes photos in sRGB and you've been editing them in No Color Management or Limited Color Management, don't alter your workflow by choosing Adobe RGB for the output. Your colors may shift drastically.

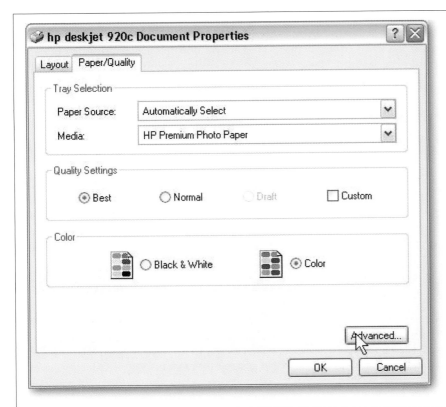

Figure 14-4:
Even a basic model like this older HP inkjet printer includes some options for color management, if you feel you need them. Clicking the Advanced button calls up another window that shows your color management options. Most of the time, just selecting the right settings in Elements' Print Preview window and choosing the correct paper type will give you good prints. Most modern printer drivers automatically choose the correct ink setting for the paper you've chosen. Don't override these settings unless you've got a good reason.

UNDER THE HOOD

What's Your Intent?

The Intent setting in Elements Print Preview window is the most confusing of the color management options for most people. Here are the basics of what you need to know to choose a setting. Sometimes your photo may contain colors that fall outside the boundaries of the print space you're using. Intent just tells Elements what to do if that happens. You have four choices:

- **Perceptual** tells Elements to preserve the relationship between the colors in your image—even if that means Elements has to do some visible color shifting to make all the colors fit.

- **Relative Colorimetric** tries to preserve the colors in both the source and the output space by shifting things to the closest matching color in the printer profile's space. This is Elements' standard setting, and it's usually what you want, because it keeps your colors as close as possible to what you see on your screen.

- **Saturation** makes colors very vivid but not necessarily very accurate. This setting is more for special effects than for regular photo printing.

- **Absolute Colorimetric** lets you simulate another printer and paper. This setting is for specialized proofing situations.

There are limitless variations on how you can use the color settings in Elements, and you may need to experiment a bit to find what works best for you. See the box "Economical Print Experiments" for advice on how to cheaply test out a bunch of different print settings. If you go looking around for more information, you'll find that this is a very controversial subject. Everyone has a different approach that is the "right" one. In fact, there are innumerable ways that may all lead to good results.

Economical Print Experiments

If you've just gone out and bought top-quality photo paper, you may be suffering from a bit of sticker shock and perhaps even thinking, "Oh yeah, great. Now I'm supposed to use this stuff up experimenting? At that price?"

The good news is, while you will have to bite the bullet and sacrifice a sheet or two, you don't need to waste the whole box. Instead, try this: make a small selection somewhere in a photo you want to print, press Ctrl+C (⌘-C) and go to File → New from Clipboard. You get a new file with only a small piece of your photo in it.

This is your test print. In Print Preview, turn off the Center Image checkbox and drag your small photo to the upper-left corner of the page. Run the page through your printer using Elements' standard settings. If your print looks good, you're ready to print the whole photo.

On the other hand, if you don't like the result, press Ctrl+P (⌘-P) to bring up Print Preview again. This time, move your test strip over to the right a little bit. Change your settings (keeping note of the changes you've made) and print again on the same piece of paper. Your new test prints out beside the first strip. Keep moving the test area around on the page, and you can try out quite a few different combinations of settings, all on the same sheet of paper.

Printing from the Organizer (Windows)

Elements also lets you print from the Organizer if you're using Windows. The Organizer gives you many more output options than the Editor, including printing several photos on one page. You can create contact sheets of thumbnails, picture packages (like you'd order from a professional photographer), and labels. You can also easily add all kinds of fancy borders to your photos in the Organizer.

The Print Selected Photos dialog box is the Organizer's print control center. Press Ctrl+P or click Print shortcut → Print to bring it up (see Figure 14-5).

Print Selected Photos has a strip down the left side of the window that displays the thumbnails of the photos you've selected for printing. You can add or remove photos here by using the buttons at the bottom of the page. Click Add to bring up a window where you can search for additional photos, or highlight a photo's thumbnail and click the Trash icon to remove it.

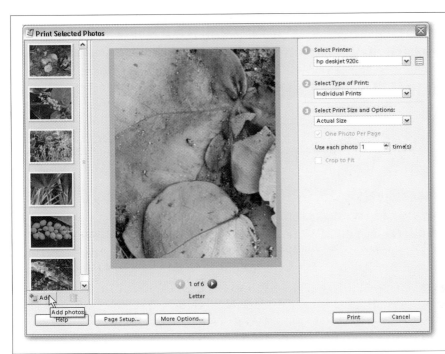

There's a preview window in the center of the dialog box, and the right side of the dialog box gives you a few easy-to-understand options to choose from:

- **Select Printer.** Choose the printer you want to use if you have more than one printer. The little icon to the right of the printer name is a shortcut to your printer preferences.

- **Select Type of Print.** You can choose to make individual prints, a contact sheet, a picture package of multiple photos, or pick from a few different label styles. The next sections explain how to use the multiple print options.

- **Select Print Size and Options.** This is where you select the size of your prints and how many times you want to use each photo, if you're printing multiple images. For example, you can choose to print one photo four times or four different photos one time each. If you turn on the One Photo Per Page checkbox, each image prints out on a separate page if you're printing picture packages. Crop to Fit tells Elements to perform any cropping necessary (if you want to decide where to crop your photos, use the cropping tools you learned about on page 53).

    NOTE   The size options you see are dependent on the page size you selected in Print Setup. So if you see only letter-sized options and you want, say, A4, check to be sure you've chosen A4 as your paper size.

Click "More Options" at the bottom of the Print Selected Photos window, and you'll get the same options for captions, inverting, and color management that you get in the Editor. When you're ready to print, enter your settings and click Print.

Printing Multiple Images (Windows)

The Organizer really shines when it comes to printing more than one photo at once. You can print a contact sheet that shows small thumbnails of many images. You can also choose to create a picture package that features multiple pictures in multiple sizes. Finally, you can choose from a limited selection of label sizes.

Contact Sheets

Contact sheets show thumbnail views of multiple images on a single page. They're great for creating a visual reference guide to the photos you've archived onto a CD. You might print a contact sheet of all the photos on a memory card as soon as you download the photos to your computer, even before editing them (see Figure 14-6).

Figure 14-6:
An Elements contact sheet. The Columns menu, in the Select a Layout section, lets you decide how many columns appear on your contact sheet.

To print a contact sheet, in the Print Selected Photos dialog box, go to Select Type of Print and choose Contact Sheet. Your options immediately change to show "Select a Layout," and you can use the following settings to customize your contact sheet:

- **Columns.** Here's where you decide how many vertical rows of photos to have on a page. Choose up to nine columns per page. The more columns you have, the smaller your thumbnails are. Even if you have only one image currently chosen, increasing the number of columns shrinks the thumbnail size.

- **Add a Text Label.** If you want a caption on each image, you can choose the Date, Time, and/or Filename here.

- **Page Numbers.** You can add page numbers if you're printing multiple pages. If all your photos fit on one page, this choice is grayed out.

You can add and remove images as explained earlier. When you like your layout, click Print.

Picture Package

Elements' Picture Package tool lets you print several images on one sheet. You can print a package that's one photo printed repeatedly, or create a package that includes multiple photos.

To get started, press Ctrl+P, and the Print Selected Photos dialog box appears. Go to Select Type of Print and choose Picture Package. Next, under Select a Layout, choose which composition style you want. Then choose a frame, if you'd like one, by picking from the Select a Frame drop-down menu. Add photos to your package by clicking on the Add button in the lower-left corner of the dialog box. Figure 14-7 shows you how to change the layout of your photos once they're on the page. When you've got your package arranged as you want it, click Print.

Labels

You can also print your photos on sticky labels from the Organizer. Elements gives you choices based on the popular Avery brand label sizes. You can use other brands, too, but you just have to figure out which labels correlate to the Avery sizes listed.

You get a choice of four Avery label sizes, as shown in Figure 14-8. If you print labels from the Organizer, print a test copy on regular paper first and check the alignment of the labels and your paper. If necessary, use the Offset boxes to adjust the location of the labels on the sheet.

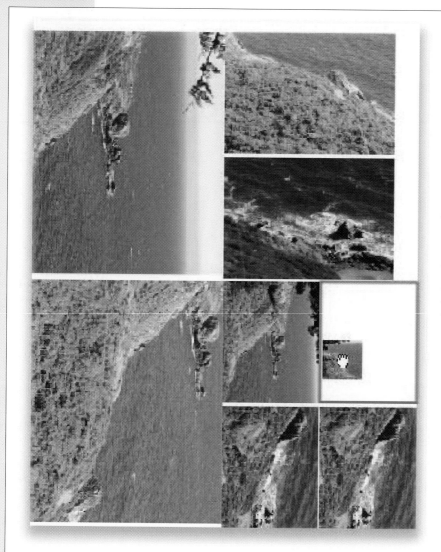

Figure 14-7:
*Reorganizing your
package is drag-and-
drop easy. If you have
empty space in your
layout and you want
to fill it, just drag a
thumbnail to the slot
where you want it.
Here you see a photo
being dragged into an
empty part of the
layout.*

*Changing the size of a
photo is easy. Just
drag it from the box
it's currently in to a
different-sized box. To
remove a photo from
the package, highlight
it on the left side of the
main window and click
the Trash can icon.*

WORKAROUND WORKSHOP

Creating Your Own Package

Whether you're using Windows or a Mac, you may prefer to set up your own layout for printing multiple photos on one page. You can make your own picture package from scratch, and it's not hard to do.

1. Save all the photos you want to use at the same resolution.

2. Create a new document (Ctrl+N (⌘-N) or File → New). Make sure it's the size you want your complete package to be. Also make sure it has the same resolution as your photos. (See page 64 for more about setting a file's resolution.) You can also save time by choosing the 8-1/2" x 11" preset size from the New file menu. That's already set to 300 ppi.

3. Drag each photo into your new document. Do this from the Layers palette (see page 126). Then position the photos as you wish. You can use the Move tool or scale to resize them (see page 119).

4. When you have all your photos positioned and sized to suit you, save the combined file and print it. You can create a smaller file by flattening the layers first (Layer → Flatten Image). Flatten only if you don't think you'll want to tweak your layout later on.

You can also create new layouts for yourself in the Organizer. Go to *C:\Program files\Adobe\Photoshop Elements 3.0\shared_assets\layouts*. Choose the layout that's closest to what you want and duplicate it. Then open it in a text editor and make the changes you want. (The layouts aren't easy to figure out, but fortunately, there's a read-me file that explains what to do. You'll find it in *C:\Program files\Adobe\Photoshop Elements 3.0\shared_assets\layouts_readmes*) When you're done, save the altered text file under a new name back into the same folder.

The Mac version of Elements makes it easier to edit the existing layouts, as explained later.

Figure 14-8:
Elements lets you add fancy borders to your Avery labels. The labels shown here are the smallest size (2.25" x 3").

Printing Multiple Images (Mac Only)

If you have a Mac, consider yourself lucky. You have many more options for printing multiple photos than your Windows counterparts do. Elements makes it very easy to create and customize contact sheets containing many small thumbnails on one page. You can also print Picture Packages with several differently sized photos on one page, and you can easily edit these picture package layouts to get exactly the arrangement you want.

Contact Sheet II

Contact sheets show many small thumbnails of different photos. You can use a contact sheet to keep track of the photos on a CD or as a record of all the images in one shooting session, for example. The Contact Sheet II included in Elements makes it a snap to create a contact sheet that's laid out exactly the way you want it to look.

To create a contact sheet, press ⌘-Option-P, or select the images you want in the File Browser, and then go to Automate → Contact Sheet II. You can also start by going to File → Contact Sheet II. In either case, you get the window shown in Figure 14-9.

You get quite a few choices if you'd like to customize your contact sheet page layout:

- **Source Images.** This is where you pick the photos you want to include. You can choose from any open files or from files you selected in the File Browser (page 39).

- **Document.** This is where you select the overall settings for your page. Set the page size in inches, centimeters, or pixels. Then enter a resolution and choose between RGB color and grayscale for your color mode (see page 29). Choosing the "Flatten all layers" setting doesn't affect your originals—it just produces a contact sheet in which text and images are on the same layer. Usually you'd leave "Flatten all layers" turned on to create efficient file sizes.

- **Thumbnails.** These settings let you determine how the thumbnails get laid out. Choose whether you want your pictures to go across or down the page (as they're being laid out), how many rows and columns you'd like, whether to let Elements figure out the spacing between thumbnails or whether to choose this spacing yourself. "Rotate for Best Fit" turns the thumbnails so they fit on the paper most efficiently. If you don't like having photos improperly oriented, turn this checkbox off.

- **Use Filename as Caption.** Choose this setting if you want to see the name of each photo appear as a caption. Your font choices are Helvetica, Times, and Courier. Getting the font size right may take a little experimenting.

When you've chosen your images and like the layout, click Okay. The contact sheet is pretty processor intensive, so it may take a while to complete your contact sheet.

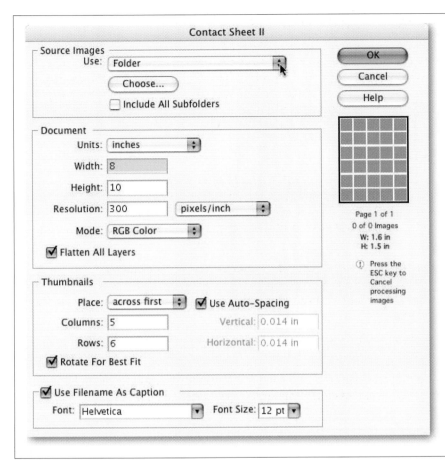

Figure 14-9:
You can customize the Mac contact sheet much more than the Windows Organizer version, including settings like the amount of space between your thumbnails. As you make changes to your settings, the layout thumbnail on the right changes to reflect your choices.

You can press the Escape key if you can't wait for Elements to finish it. Once you've created your contact sheet, you can save it or print it the way you would any other .psd file.

Picture Package

The Mac version of Elements also makes it very easy to print a group of pictures, called a Picture Package, on one page. You can make a picture package that features one photo printed several times in different sizes, or create a picture package that includes more than one photo.

To create a picture package, in the Print Preview dialog box, click the "Print Layouts" button, or choose File → Picture Package. You'll see the dialog box shown in Figure 14-10.

There are a lot of choices in the Mac picture package dialog box:

Figure 14-10:
To add a new photo or replace an existing photo, click any box in the layout and choose the replacement photo from the Open dialog box that appears. (The Mac picture package doesn't let you drag files around the way the Windows version does.)

- **Source Images.** Choose from the Use drop-down menu to select the pictures you want to appear in your package. If you choose lots of files, Elements uses as many pages as necessary to fit them all in.

- **Document.** This is where you pick the overall settings for your package. You can set the page size (8"×10", 11"×16", or 11"×17"), the layout (how many photos appear on one page and their sizes), resolution, and whether you want RGB color or Grayscale. Flatten layers works the same way as it does for the contact sheet.

    NOTE For some silly reason, the resolution defaults to 72 pixels per inch (ppi). If you don't increase it to around 180 ppi or higher, your photos are probably going to print badly—all pixelated and blurry. It's best to use 300 ppi if you can. See page 64 for more about resolution.

- **Label.** This is where you can choose to have text appear on your photos. If you don't want any text, leave it at None. If you want text, you can use the file name, copyright, description, credit, or title from the file's metadata settings (page 39). There's a box to enter custom text as well. The other options are for the text itself: font (same choices as the contact sheet), size, color, opacity, and position. Click the color box to bring up the Color Picker (see page 175) if you don't want black text.

    You can also rotate the text so that if your photos are printing sideways, the text still prints right side up on the photo. You can use the Opacity and Position settings to create a watermark, as explained on page 208.

When you've gotten everything arranged as you want it, click Okay and watch while Elements creates your picture package. When the picture package is complete, you can print it or save it like any photo.

Customizing the picture package

You're not limited to the picture package layouts that Elements gives you. You can customize a layout in all sorts of different ways and then save it to use again, if you like. Start by choosing the preset layout that's closest to what you want. Click the Edit Layout button in the Picture Package window, and the dialog box shown in Figure 14-11 appears.

*Figure 14-11:
There are lots of ways to customize a Picture Package layout. Enter numbers on the left side of the page or just click an image (Elements calls them zones here) to bring up handles.*

Resizing is just like using the Move tool— you can drag or resize a zone, or Option-click it for a pop-up menu that includes some standard sizes. You can also delete a zone by clicking it and then clicking the "Delete Zone" button. If you want to set things up from scratch, click "Delete All."

You can choose a preset page size or type in a custom page size in inches, centimeters, millimeters, or pixels. You can also change the size and location of the images in your package. Adobe calls the space for an image a *zone*. The boxes where you can type in custom sizes are grayed out until you select a zone in the window. If you click a zone and then click Add Zone, Elements creates an additional zone instead of replacing the one you clicked.

If there's no space left that's big enough for the new zone, Elements just dumps the new zone on top of the existing layout and leaves you to sort things out (which you can do by deleting an existing zone to make room for the new zone).

"Snap to Grid" helps you line your zones up neatly. When you've customized your layout to suit you, name the new layout and click Save. Make sure you're saving to the folder Adobe Photoshop Elements 3 → Presets → Layouts so that Elements can find your new package again. In the future, the new layout will show up in your list of preset layouts under the name you've given it.

Creating Projects (Windows Only)

If you're using Windows, the Elements Organizer makes it a snap to create photo books, album pages, greeting cards, and calendars. You use the Create options in the Organizer for these fun projects. (There are other Create projects, too, like slideshows and Web Galleries, which are discussed in Chapters 15 and 16.) You can choose to print or email your project when you've completed it.

> **TIP** Mac folks, you can create similar projects in iPhoto or perform a Google search for templates you can download and use in Elements.
>
> On both platforms, if you bought a boxed copy of Elements (as opposed to getting it bundled with a camera or scanner), you received a folder of extra backgrounds, frames, and album page layouts, which are located on the installation CD inside the Goodies folder (look in a folder called Art).

All Elements Create projects use easy-to-follow wizards, which launch from the Creation Setup window (see Figure 14-12).

Figure 14-12:
Elements' Create projects are very easy to put together. Just follow the steps as Elements leads you through them. On the start page, shown here, the small icons above the OK button indicate the different ways you can share your completed project. Hover your mouse over each icon for details about each option.

You can get started on any of the Create projects from either the Editor or the Organizer.

1. **Start by calling up the Create wizard.**

   Click the Create button on the Shortcuts bar in either the Editor or the Organizer. In the Organizer, you can also go to File → New → Creation. The Creation Setup window appears.

2. **Choose the type of project you want to create.**

   Select a project from the list on the left side of the window, then click OK.

3. **Choose how you want your finished project to look.**

   In "Step 1: Creation Setup," select a design (called a *template*) from the list available, then choose your options at the bottom of the window. Your exact choices vary, depending on the template you choose. Usually you can choose the number of photos per page, and whether to include page numbers or captions. Some templates also let you choose to add additional text in the form of headers (text above your photo) or captions (which appear below your photo). When you've made your choices, click OK.

4. **Choose the photos you want to use.**

   In "Step 2: Arrange Your Photos," you can choose the photos you want (if you didn't already have some photos selected when you started your project). Drag photos to change their order, or add or delete photos by using the buttons at the top of the page.

   "Use Photo Again" places a duplicate of an image you've already used once in your project into the list again. You'd use this option when making a calendar where you want more than one month to show the same photo, for example.

5. **When you're satisfied with the number of photos and the order they're in, click OK to move to "Step 3: Customize."**

   You now see a preview of your project. Figure 14-13 shows how to add text, if your project gives you the option to do so. You can change the font, size, and justification for multiple lines of text, but the starting options are usually pretty effective, too. Use the pull-down menu above the image to navigate to the different pages of your project if it has more than one page.

   When you've got your text entered, click OK to move to step 4.

6. **In "Step 4: Save," name your project and save it.**

   You have the option of using the title you chose as the name. Just check the box. You can also choose to have the photos you've used appear the Photo Browser when you finish. Do this if you want to create another project with the same photos. Once you save, you move on to step 5.

Figure 14-13:
With any of the print projects, you can add text by double-clicking wherever you see a box like this one. You can resize the text boxes by dragging the handles, or you can move your text by dragging it. If you discover you made a typo, just double-click the text again to edit it. If you don't enter any text, the placeholder text that says, "Double-Click to Add Text" doesn't print. You just won't get any text.

7. **In "Step 5: Share," choose what you want to do with your project.**

   You can choose to create a .pdf file, email your creation (see Figure 14-14), or print it out. If you created something like a photo book that can be printed by Ofoto.com, the Order Online button is active. Otherwise, it's grayed out.

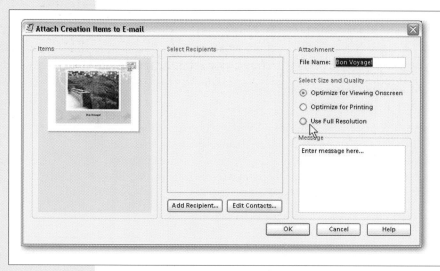

Figure 14-14:
When you choose to email a Create project, you can format it in a number of different ways including: optimized for onscreen viewing, ready for printing by the recipient, or at full resolution.

At any time, you can back up to a previous step or cancel your project altogether by using the buttons at the bottom of the window. Your completed creation gets added to the Organizer. You can see a list of all your stored Create projects by going to File → Open Creation.

Here are a few notes about each project type:

- **Photo books and album pages.** You can order hardbound photo books through Ofoto.com (page 362). In the template list, the styles you can order online are clearly marked. When you order your book, check the pull-down menu on the Order page to see the different cover types—they make quite a difference in the cost of the book.

  The Title photo appears through a cutout in the cover (see Figure 14-15). Books can be up to 80 pages long, depending on the style you select. If you have less than 20 pages of photos, you get nagged all along the way to add more, but you can order a book with blank pages at the end if you want to. You can add text to pages in the form of headers (text above the photo) and captions (text below the photo) except in the full-bleed book, where the photos take up the entire page.

  NOTE If you choose to include captions in a Create project, Elements starts out by using whatever is in the photo's caption field in the photo's Properties dialog box (page 39). You can alter the text just for the project by double-clicking the Caption field in the project and entering the new text, but it won't change the original photo's caption in the Organizer.

Figure 14-15:
When you create a photo book, the portion of your title photo that will appear on the cover is marked when you reach step 3. If it's not the area you want, just drag the photo to reposition it. So, for example, in this image, the cover would feature the dark blue square on the left, rather than the light blue areas.

Double-Click to Insert Title

Books and album pages give you the option of setting a pattern for the number of photos on succeeding pages so that every page isn't identical. In the menu for "Number of Photos Per Page," there are sequences at the bottom of the list that let you set the pattern you want, like a page with one photo followed by a page with two.

NOTE The album page layouts in Create always position your photos in landscape orientation. If you want portrait orientation, you can't use the Create wizard.

• **Cards and Postcards** each come with their own wizards, although they're both very similar. Both options let you use only one photo, which makes it a little confusing when you pass through "Step 2: Arrange Your Photos." This just gives you the option of starting a card and then choosing a photo, or changing your mind about which photo you want to include. If you select more than one photo, only the first gets used.

Both cards and postcards show your entire photo with a light mask over the portion that will be cropped away in the completed project. You can drag the photo around a bit if you need to reposition it on the page. Cards have space for text inside them, so don't forget to use the menu to write something if you don't want the inside to be left blank.

NOTE Cards and postcards depend on the paper size you chose in Page Setup for the size of the final output.

• **Wall Calendars.** You can choose from a number of different styles. Most styles suggest that you use 13 images, which puts a separate image on the title page. If you want to use a photo you're also using for one of the month pages, just select it and then click "Use Photo Again" and drag the duplicate to the first position.

Elements and the Web

Printing your photos is great, but it costs money, takes time, and doesn't do much to instantly impress friends with your newfound photo prowess. Fortunately, Elements comes packed with tools that make it easy to not only email your photos, but also to post them on the Web.

Once you get the hang of sharing your photos online, Elements is ready for all your digital sharing needs. This version of Elements lets you send your photos to cellphones, Palm-based handhelds, and even to your television set. In this chapter, you'll learn how to email your photos, and how to prepare them for use as Web site graphics. You can also create elaborate slideshows and mini Web sites featuring your pictures, which you'll learn about in Chapter 16.

Image Formats and the Web

Back in the Web's early days, making your graphic files small was important, because most Internet connections were about as quick as camels. Nowadays, file size isn't as important; your main obligation when creating graphics for the Web is ensuring they're compatible with the Web browsers people use to view your Web pages. That means you'll probably want to use either of the two most popular image formats, JPEG or GIF:

- Use the **JPEG** (Joint Photographic Experts' Group) format for images with lots of detail and where you need smooth color transitions. For example, photos are almost always posted on the Web as JPEGs.

NOTE   JPEGs can't have transparent areas, although there is a workaround for that: fill the background around your image with the same color as the Web page you want to post it on. The background blends into the Web page, giving the impression that your object is surrounded by transparency.

- **GIFs** (Graphics Interchange Format) are great for images with limited numbers of colors, like corporate logos and headlines. Text looks much sharper in the GIF format than it does as a JPEG. GIFs also allow you to keep transparency as part of your image.

- The **PNG** (Portable Network Graphic) format is another Web graphics format that was created to overcome some of the disadvantages of JPEGs and GIFs. (PNG files have .png at the end of their file names.) There's a lot to like about PNG files. They can include transparent areas, and the format reduces the file size of photographs without the loss of data that happens with JPEG files. The big drawback to PNG files is that only newer Web browsers deal with them very well. Older versions of Internet Explorer are notorious for not supporting the PNG format, so if you've got potential viewers with ancient computers, you probably won't want to use PNG.

Elements makes it easy to save your images in any of these formats. You do so by using the Save for Web dialog box, which is covered in the next section.

Saving Images for the Web or Email

If you plan to email your photos or put them up on your Web site, Save for Web is a terrific tool that takes any open image and saves it in a Web friendly format; it also gives you lots of options to help achieve maximum image quality while keeping file size to a minimum. The goal of Save for Web is to create as small a file as you can without compromising the image's onscreen quality.

Save for Web creates smaller JPEG files than you get by merely using Save As, because it strips out the EXIF data, the information about your camera (see page 39). To get started with Save for Web, go to File → Save for Web or press Ctrl+Alt+Shift+Save (⌘-Option-Shift-Save). The dialog box shown in Figure 15-1 appears.

The most important point to remember when saving images for the Web is that the resolution (measured in pixels per inch, or ppi) is completely irrelevant. All you care about are the image's pixel dimensions, e.g., 400×600. If you have a photo that you've optimized for print, you'll almost certainly need to drastically downsize it. This is easy to do in Save for Web.

There are a lot of useful tools in Save for Web. In the top left corner is a Toolbox, featuring the Hand, Zoom, and Eyedropper tools, with a color square below the Eyedropper. The Hand and Zoom work the same way they do elsewhere in Elements.

Figure 15-1:
*The Save for Web
dialog box makes it
easy to get the exact
image size and quality
you want. The left
preview shows your
original image (the
size changes, if you
resize, but the quality
always reflects the
image's original state).
The right preview
shows both changes to
image size and quality.*

Below each image preview, you'll see the file size and the estimated download time, which you can adjust (by modifying your assumptions about your recipients Internet connection speed, as explained in Figure 15-2). You can also adjust the zoom percentage (using the Zoom menu at the bottom of the window), but usually you'll want to stick to 100 percent, because that's the size your image will be on the Web.

In the upper-right corner of the window are your file format and quality choices. What you see varies a bit depending on which format you've chosen. Below that are your options for resizing your image. If you want to create animated GIFs, those tiny moving images you see on Web pages, you set up the animation at the bottom of the settings panel. How to create animated GIFs is explained later.

Using Save for Web

When you're ready to use Save for Web, follow these steps:

1. **Launch the Save for Web dialog box.**

   Go to File → Save for Web or press Ctrl+Alt+Shift+S (⌘-Option-Shift-S). The Save for Web dialog box appears.

2. **Choose the format and quality settings you want for your Web image.**

   Your choices are explained in the following section.

Click to change download assumptions

Figure 15-2:
The Save for Web window gives you an estimate of how long it's going to take to download your image. If you want to change the download assumptions (for example, the speed of the Internet connection), go to the upper-right corner of the preview area and click the arrow button for the pop-out list shown here.

3. **If necessary, resize your image so that it fits onscreen without having to scroll.**

   If you want to make sure that anyone can see the whole image (no matter how small the monitor), enter 650 pixels or less for the longest side of your photo in the New Size area. (650 pixels is about the largest size that can fit on small monitors without scrolling, but if you're sending to someone with an older monitor you may want to stay below 500 pixels.) As long as Constrain Proportions is turned on, you don't have to enter the dimension for the other side. You can also resize your image by entering a percent (for example, entering 90 shrinks your image by 10 percent). When you're finished entering the new dimensions, click Apply.

4. **Check your results.**

   Look at the file size again to see if it's small enough and take a close look at the image quality in the preview area. Use Elements file size optimization feature, if necessary, as explained in Figure 15-3. You can also preview your image in your actual Web browser (see the section "Previewing Images and Adjusting Color" on page 391).

5. **When everything looks good, click OK.**

   You're asked to name the new file and choose a location to save it in.

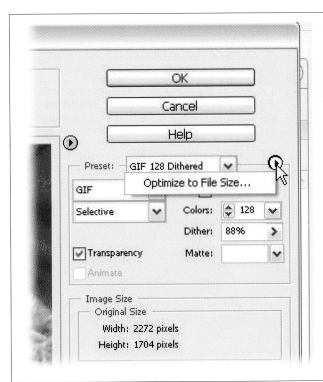

Figure 15-3:
*When you click the triangle next to the Preset menu,
Elements gives you a dialog box that lets you enter
a desired file size. Use K (kilobytes) and MB
(megabytes) as your units of measurement. Once
you've entered your numbers, click OK. Elements
reduces your image to the size you requested.*

Save for Web file format options

One way to reduce your file size is to reduce the physical size, as explained in step
3. But you can also make your file smaller by adjusting the quality settings. Your
quality options vary depending on which format you're using.

- **JPEG.** Elements offers you a variety of basic quality settings for your JPEGs:
  Low, Medium, High, Very High, and Maximum. You can further adjust the
  quality by entering a number in the Quality box on the right. A higher number
  means higher quality. Generally, Medium is often enough if you're saving for
  Web use. If you use Save for Web to make JPEG files for printing, you'll want
  Maximum.

  If you turn on the Progressive checkbox, your JPEG loads from the top down.
  This was popular for large files when everyone had slow dial-up connections,
  but it does make a slightly larger file, so it's not as popular today. The ICC profile checkbox lets you keep any color space profile embedded in your image.
  (See page 162 for more about color profiles.) Matte lets you set the color of any
  area that is transparent in your original (see Figure 15-4). If you don't set a
  matte color, you get white.

Figure 15-4:
The JPEG format doesn't preserve transparent areas when you save your image. But Elements helps you simulate transparency by letting you choose a matte color, which replaces the transparency. When you choose a matte color that's identical to your Web page's background, you create a transparent effect. Elements gives you three ways to select your color: click the arrow on the right side of the matte box, sample a color from your image with the eyedropper tool, or click the color square in the matte box to call up the Color Picker. (See page 175 for more about using the Color Picker.) The black matte around this lizard will blend into the black background of the page it goes on.

- **GIF.** GIFs get smaller the fewer colors they contain. Elements GIF format names tell you the number of colors that will be in your GIF. For example, when you see GIF-128, GIF-32, and so on, the number is the number of colors in the GIF. You can also use the colors box to set your own number of colors. Use the arrows on the left edge of the box to scroll to the number you want, or just type it into the box.

  If you turn on Interlacing, your image will download in multiple passes (sort of like an image that's slowly coming into focus). With today's computers, interlacing isn't as useful as it used to be on slower machines. If you want to keep transparent areas transparent, leave Transparency turned on. If you don't want transparency, you can choose a matte color the way you do for a JPEG. If you created a GIF you plan to animate, turn on Animate (see page 392).

  Dithering is an important setting. The GIF format works by compressing and flattening large areas of colors. If you choose dithering, Elements blends existing colors to make it look like there are more colors than there actually are in your GIF. For instance, Elements might mix red and blue pixels in an area to create purple. You can choose how much dither you want. Sometimes you don't want any dithering—it depends on the image.

- **PNG-8.** PNG-8 is the more basic of your PNG choices in Elements, and you get pretty much the same options as you do for a GIF.

  Both PNG-8 and GIF also give you advanced options for how to display colors (generating the color lookup table if you're a Web design maven). You can totally forget this option even exists, but if you're curious, these are your choices: Selective, the standard setting, favors broad areas of color and keeps to Web Safe colors; Perceptual favors colors the human eye is more sensitive to; Adaptive samples colors from the spectrum appearing most commonly in the image; and Restrictive keeps everything within the old 216-color Web palette.

- **PNG-24.** This is the more advanced level of PNG, which lets you use transparency. Your save options are the same as those for JPEG files.

TIP The Elements Color Picker lets you limit your choices to "Web Safe Colors," but do you need to stick to this limited color palette for Web graphics? Not really. You need to be seriously concerned about keeping to Web-safe colors only if you know the majority of people looking at your image will be using very old Web browsers. All modern Web browsers have been able to cope with a normal color range for several years now.

Getting colors to display consistently in all browsers is another kettle of fish entirely. See the next section, "Previewing Images and Adjusting Color."

Previewing Images and Adjusting Color

Elements gives you a few different ways to preview how your image will look in a Web browser. You can start by looking at your image in any Web browser you've got on your computer (see Figure 15-5).

To add a new browser, click the Preview In drop-down list and choose Edit List. Then, in the dialog box that appears, click Add Browser and navigate to the one you want. If you want to have all your browsers listed, just click "Find All." From now on you can pick any browser from the list. When you do, Elements launches the browser with your image in it.

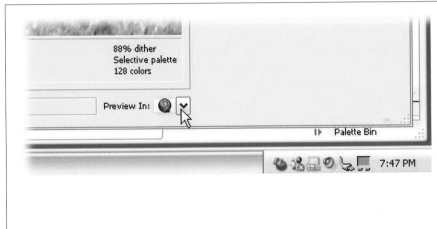

Figure 15-5:
To preview your image in a Web browser, click the Preview In icon to launch your computer's standard Web browser, or click the arrow and choose a browser from the list. The icon you see may vary, because Elements uses your particular browser's icon (or the last browser you used for previewing in Elements).

NOTE The Web browser Opera appears in the browser list, since Elements Help runs on a highly customized version of Opera (which gets added to your computer when you install Elements).

If you want to get a very rough idea of how your image might look on other people's monitors, click the arrow that's just above the upper-right corner of the right preview window. Above the modem specifications, you see a list of color options:

- **Uncompensated Color** shows colors the way they normally appear on your monitor. This setting makes no adjustment to the color. It's what you usually see.

- **Standard Windows Color** shows colors the way they should look on an average Windows monitor.

- **Standard Macintosh Color** shows colors the way they should look on an average Mac monitor.

- **Use Document Profile.** If you kept the ICC profile, this setting tries to match how your image will look as a result of that.

These are all only rough approximations. You've only got to take a stroll down the monitor aisle at your local electronics chain to see what a wacky bunch of color variations are possible. You really can't control how other people are going to see your image unless you go to their homes and adjust their monitors for them.

> **NOTE**   Changing any of these color options affects only the way the image displays on your monitor; it doesn't change anything in the image itself.

Creating Animated GIFs

Elements makes it easy to create *animated GIFs,* those little animated illustrations that make Web pages look annoyingly jumbled or delightfully active, depending on your tastes. If you've ever seen a strip of movie film or the cells for a cartoon, Elements does something similar with these specialized GIFs.

Animated GIFs are made in layers. (If you download an animated GIF and open it up in Elements, it appears as a multi-layered image.) When you create an animated GIF, you make a new layer for each frame. Save for Web creates the actual animation, which you can preview in a Web browser.

> **NOTE**   It's a shame that you can't easily animate a JPEG the way you can a GIF. Most elaborate Web animations involving photographs are done with Flash, which is another program altogether.

Probably the best way to learn how to create an animated GIF is to make one. Here's a little tutorial on making twinkling stars.

Before you start, set your background color to black and your foreground color to some shade of yellow. (See page 174 if you need help setting your foreground/background colors.)

1. **Create a new document.**

    Press Ctrl+N (⌘-N). Set the size to 200 pixels by 200 pixels, choose RGB for the Color mode, and choose Background Color for your Background Contents.

2. **Activate the Custom Shape Tool.**

   From the Shapes palette (in the Options bar), click the triangle inside the blue circle and then select Nature. Choose the Sun 2 shape, which is in the top row, in the second box from the left side.

3. **Draw some stars.**

   Draw one yellow star, then click the "add to shape area" square in the Options bar before drawing four or five more stars (this puts all the stars on the same layer, which is important, since then you won't have a bunch of layers to merge).

4. **Merge the star layer and the background layer.**

   Choose Layer → Merge Down. You now have one layer containing yellow stars on a black background, like the bottom layer shown in Figure 15-6.

5. **Duplicate the layer.**

   Choose Layer → Duplicate Layer. You now have two identical layers.

6. **Rotate the top layer 90 degrees.**

   Click any other tool in the Toolbox and then go to Image → Rotate → Layer 90° Left (if the Move Custom Shape tool is active, the Rotate command doesn't work). You should now have two layers with stars in different places on each one, which is why you did the rotation.

7. **Animate your GIF.**

   Go to File → Save for Web and turn on the Animation checkbox. (Select GIF as your Save format if Elements didn't already do so for you—you won't see the Animation checkbox for other formats.) You can adjust the time between slides if you want. Leave Looping turned on. That makes the animation repeat over and over. If you turn off Looping, your animation plays once and stops.

8. **Preview your animation.**

   You can use the arrows in the animation controls to step through your animation one frame at a time, but for a more realistic preview, view the image in a Web browser (explained in the previous section). The stars should twinkle. Well, okay, they flash off and on. Think of twinkling lights. Save your animation, if you like, by clicking OK.

Emailing Your Photos

Elements makes it easy to email your photos. With just a few button clicks, Elements preps your image, fires up your email program, and attaches your image to an outgoing email. Of course, you can email your images yourself (without Elements' help), and you might prefer that method since you get more freedom to specify settings like file size. When you email images from within Elements, the

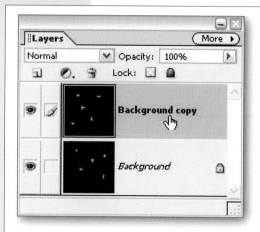

Figure 15-6:
There are only two frames in this animated GIF, which makes for a pretty crude animation. The more frames you have, the smoother the animation, but more frames makes a bigger file. On a tiny image like this one, size doesn't matter, but with a larger image your file can get huge pretty fast.

ON THE WEB

Creating Web Buttons

Elements makes it really easy to create buttons to use on Web pages. Here's what you need to do:

1. Set the Foreground color square to the color you want to use and use the Shape tool to draw the shape you want. (It helps to choose "Actual Pixels" for your view size when doing Web work, because that gives you the same size you'll see in a Web browser.)

2. Apply one or more Layer styles (page 322) to make your button look more three-dimensional. Bevels, some of the Complex Layer styles, or the Wow Layer styles are all popular choices.

3. Add any necessary text using the Type tool (page 339). You may want to apply a Layer style to the text, too.

4. Save as a GIF.

---

program controls the size of the files you can send. The email options on the Mac version are pretty basic; in Windows, the Organizer gives you a lot of fancy templates for creating specially designed email.

Emailing Images (for Macs)

To email a photo from the Mac version of Elements, just go to File → Attach to Email. If your image is particularly large, or isn't a JPEG file, Elements presents you with a dialog box that offers to convert your image to a JPEG file and resize it (see Figure 15-7).

Elements then launches whatever program you regularly use for email. Your photo appears as an attachment. Just address the message, add whatever text you want in the body of the email, and click Send.

Elements won't let you attach more than one photo at a time to each message. If you want to send more than one photo, or you prefer to resize your photos your-

Figure 15-7:
Click Auto Convert if
you want Elements to
resize your image.
Clicking Send As Is—
you guessed it—sends
your file without
changing it.

self, you can always do it the old-fashioned way: launch your email program, click the Attachments button, and navigate to the file you want.

Emailing Images (for Windows)

The Organizer gives you an almost bewildering array of formatting choices for emailing your photos. You can send pre-arranged groups of photos, frame your photos, change the background color, and so on. There's one big annoyance when you send from the Organizer, though: you get an ad for Elements in every message you send from Elements.

> **TIP**   Don't want to be in the advertising business? To get rid of the Adobe ad at the bottom of your messages, highlight it in the message and press Backspace, or if you want to eliminate it from all your Elements emails, go to *C:\Program Files\Adobe\Photoshop Elements 3.0\shared_assets\ locales\en_us\email\signatures*. Open the files you find there in a text editor and remove the advertising lines. From now on, your mail is ad free.

To use the Elements email features, go to File → Attach to E-Mail (in the Editor or Organizer), or in the Organizer, click the Share button on the shortcuts bar and choose E-mail (or press Ctrl+Shift+E).

Even if you start from the Editor, you get bounced over to the Organizer to set up and send your message. Wherever you start from, you'll see the window shown in Figure 15-8.

Next, decide whether you want to enter an email address now. You can:

- **Do nothing.** Wait till Elements is through, then type the address in the completed email before you send it.

- **Add Recipient.** Click this button and enter a name and email address. Elements offers to keep a *contact list,* a list of people you regularly send emails to. For future emails, you can just select names from the list. There's more about the contact book in the box on the following page.

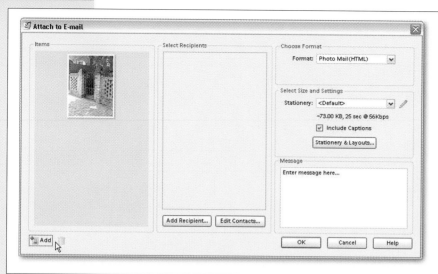

Figure 15-8:
The setup window for emailing from the Organizer is pretty easy to use. You can start with one photo or a selected group. To send more photos, click the Add button at the bottom of the window, navigate to the one(s) you want, and click OK. Remove photos you don't want by highlighting them and clicking Delete.

ORGANIZATION STATION

The Contact Book

The Organizer makes it easy to call up the addresses of people you regularly email by keeping a Contact Book. Any time you click Add Recipient in the E-mail window you get the option to add the address to the Contact Book. You can also get to the contact book by going to Edit → Contact Book in the Photo Browser or Date View.

Once you've got the Contact Book open, to add an address, just click the New Contact button. Then you can enter a name, email address, phone number, and other contact info. To edit or delete a contact, just highlight it in the list and click the relevant button.

You can also create groups of names in the Contact book, for times when you want to send the same photo to several people at once. To do this, click New Group, enter a name for the group, and then select an entry or entries in the Contact Book and click "Add." The name goes into the Members list. To remove a name from the group, highlight it in the Members list and click Remove.

You might find the Contact Book is a great feature; you might ignore it altogether. The choice is yours.

- **Use the Contact Book.** Elements can keep a list of all the addresses of people you normally send photos to.

The next important decision you have to make is what kind of email you'd like to send:

- **HTML (Photo Mail).** Elements lets you send emails formatted in HTML, the language used to create Web pages. This option gives you all kinds of fancy design choices; your photo gets embedded in the body of the email.

  The catch is that the recipient has to be using a mail program that understands HTML mail. Most newer email programs are fine with this type of email, but if you're mailing to someone using AOL 4, for instance, your picture is not going

---

to appear correctly. (Even if a mail program allows HTML mail, if your recipient has that option turned off, it's not going to be smooth sailing.) The next section gives you more information about Elements' HTML mail options.

- **Simple Slide Show.** This option creates a basic PDF format slideshow of all your images. All you have to do is name your slideshow. There's more about slideshows in Chapter 16.

- **Individual Attachments.** This is your most traditional choice. Selecting this sends each photo as a standard email attachment. The Convert Photos to JPEGs option automatically changes your files to JPEGs if they aren't already in that format. If they are, the option is grayed out.

HTML mail options

Elements also gives you a ton of options for gussying up your photos if you choose HTML (Photo Mail). When you send HTML mail, your message gets formatted using a *template,* a stationery design in which your photo appears.

Once you select HTML (Photo Mail), you see the chosen template listed under "Select Size and Settings," along with the file size. You also see the estimated download time (for an ordinary dial-up modem) to help you determine if your email is reasonably sized. You can choose whether to display captions, and below that, you can click "Stationery and Layouts" to choose different backgrounds and to customize what you've chosen.

When you click Stationery and Layouts, a wizard presents a long list of stationery theme categories with several choices in each. The preview window updates to show each one as you click it. When you find a style you like, click Next Step to go to the Customize window.

In the Customize window, you can change the size of your photo(s) if you wish. If you're mailing more than one photo, you have a choice of several different page layouts. Below the layouts, you can choose a typeface (from a list of five common fonts). Click the box to the right of the font name to choose a Web-safe color for the text. If you've chosen a frame style that leaves empty space around the photo, you can customize the background color of your email. When you've adjusted everything to your liking, click Done. Click Cancel if you don't want to send the email after all.

When you click Done, Elements takes you back to the main E-mail window. You won't see your completed formatting until you click OK in the main window. Then Elements creates your ready-to-send mail. You can make any changes to the message and address just as you would to any other email. And you send it off like any other email, too.

PDF slideshows

You can also email a group of your photos as a slideshow. Elements uses the popular PDF format, which lets your recipients page through each slide. They just launch the slideshow and view the photos one by one. You can create a PDF slideshow from the Create wizard (see page 408), or you can make a slideshow right in the E-mail window.

To do so, just select your photos as described earlier, then choose "Simple Slide Show (PDF)" as your format in the E-mail dialog box. You get offered a choice of sizes, including "Leave as Is." Name the slideshow and click OK. Elements generates a standard email message with the slideshow as a PDF attachment. Your recipient needs to have a PDF-viewing program like Adobe Reader or Mac Preview.

Sending Photos to Other Gear (Windows)

Now that practically everyone has a cellphone with a camera and a viewing screen, Adobe has kept pace by making it easy for you to send your photos to cellphones and Palm-based computers. You can even send your photos to your TiVo. If you live the high-tech lifestyle, Elements gives you several ways to get your photos to and from your gear:

- **Send to Cellphone.** If you and your friends like to look at tiny pictures on tiny screens, you can send photos directly to a cellphone. Go to Share → Send E-Mail to Mobile Phone, and you see the dialog box shown in Figure 15-9.

Figure 15-9:
The window for emailing to a cellphone is very similar to the regular email window. The big difference is that your size choices are very limited. The Contact Book displays any numbers you've entered as mobile phone numbers; otherwise, entering addresses is exactly the same as for regular email.

- **Get photos from Cellphone.** If you have a camera phone and you'd like to import the photos into Elements, go to File → Get Photos → from Mobile Phone or press Ctrl+Shift+M. In Edit → Preferences → Mobile Phone, you can specify a download folder and also designate it as a watched folder (see page 24 for more about watched folders).

- **Palm OS.** You can send photos to a Palm handheld running Palm OS 4.0 or higher. The recipient needs Adobe Reader 3.0 for Palm OS. When you first go to Share → Send to Palm OS Handheld, Elements offers to download the latest version for you.

- **TiVo.** If you'd like to view your photos via your TiVo, go to Share → Publish to TiVo DVR This won't work unless your TiVo is currently connected and available.

ON THE WEB

Sharing Photos Online

The Organizer lets you post photos at Ofoto.com (page 362) so that your friends can view them. Your friends can order prints directly from Ofoto, using their own accounts (which are free to set up).

To upload a photo, just select it in the Organizer and then select Share → Share Online, and log into your Ofoto account. (Creating an Ofoto account is covered on page 362.) You can also select and upload more than one photo at a time.

Another photo-sharing alternative is *www.pixentral.com.* There you can upload any image in JPEG, GIF, or PNG format, as long as it's less than 2 MB in size.

Just click Choose File and select your file. That's it. No registration, no need to provide any personal information or sign up for anything.

Once your photo shows up, you copy the link to the photo and email that to your friends. They click it or paste it into their Web browsers. Nobody can see the photo unless you send them the link. After 30 days, if no one's viewed your photo, it disappears from the site.

Pixentral is free, but they do accept donations. Other popular photo-hosting sites include *www.pbase.com* (the granddaddy of them all, but not free), *www. smugmug.com,* and *www.flickr.com.*

Web Photo Galleries and Slideshows

Last chapter, you learned how to email your photos. But what if you've got legions of friends? Do you have to email your pictures to everyone? Not with Elements, which also lets you create Web Photo Galleries, collections of ready-made Web pages featuring all the photos you want to show off. Elements can also help you put together digital slideshows, complete with fancy between-photo transitions and even audio.

Other programs offer more sophisticated options for both galleries and slideshows, but Elements gives you some basic tools that are simple to use.

> **NOTE** For all the projects in this chapter, you need to finish any editing, cropping, or enhancing of your photos before you begin. Once your pictures are in the gallery or slideshow, you can't edit them there.

Web Photo Galleries

A Web Photo Gallery is a great way to share a group of photos with your friends. When you create a Web Gallery, Elements whips up a collection of Web pages, which you can then post on a Web site, if you have one. You give the URL (the Web site address) to your friends and they use a browser to visit your site and see your photos.

Maybe you want to show everyone the pictures of your son's graduation or your daughter's motocross championship. By setting up a Web Photo Gallery, you can let everyone see your photos, attractively arranged, while saving them the trouble of downloading every single photo or waiting for you to remember to get some extra prints made. Figure 16-1 shows one of the galleries you can create with Elements.

Figure 16-1:
Just choose the photos and the style you want and Elements creates a Web Photo Gallery for you. Some gallery styles, like this one, are modern and rather spare. Others are more traditional looking. This style lets viewers click the thumbnails at the bottom of the window to move from picture to picture. Some styles use forward and back arrows instead of the thumbnails.

Creating a Web Photo Gallery is pretty simple. You choose the photos and the gallery style you want, and then Elements does all the work: it takes care of writing all the HTML, the language used to create Web pages, and it also creates any thumbnail images, if your gallery style uses them.

When Elements is done, it saves all the necessary files in a folder which you then need to upload to your Web site. Most Internet service providers (ISPs) give you a reasonable amount of Web server space. If you look on your ISP's Web site, you'll probably find a help page explaining how to upload files to any Web space that's allotted to you.

NOTE Elements' Web Photo Galleries don't let you include audio or video—just still photos.

Creating a Web Photo Gallery (in Windows)

In Windows, you create your Web Photo Gallery from the Organizer. Begin by selecting the photos you want to include. It's important to select your photos first, because otherwise, the Organizer includes all the photos in the Photo Browser. Do any editing to your photos and rotate them, if necessary, before you get started creating a gallery.

Then choose either of the following options:

• Go to File → New → Creation.

• Click the Create button in the Shortcuts bar.

In either case, choose Web Photo Gallery from the first screen of the Create wizard, and then click OK. The window shown in Figure 16-2 appears. This is where you create your gallery.

Figure 16-2:
To rearrange the photos in your gallery, just drag them so they appear in the order you want. To add photos, click the Add button and choose the image(s) you want. To remove a photo, select it, then click Remove.

Your photos appear down the left side of the window, pretty much as they do in all the Create projects. This time, they're numbered in the order in which they'll appear in your slideshow. At the top of the main part of the window, you see a preview of the currently selected style. You get a choice of many different styles, making it easy to find just the look you want. Some styles are very modern and minimalist while others are more traditional. Click the Gallery Style pull-down menu and select other styles to see a small preview of each style.

> **TIP** In all the Create projects, don't hesitate to investigate style options that have titles that don't sound appealing to you. There's often quite a difference between the look of a style and its title.

Once you've chosen your gallery style, you need to make some choices in the tabs below the style preview. Which options are available depends on the gallery style you've chosen. Some styles let you customize many aspects of the design, while others offer few options.

Here are the options for each tab. For most gallery styles, at least some of the options are grayed out.

- **Banner.** This is where you name your gallery. The name shows up right on the page in some gallery styles and in the top bar of the browser window for all styles. Some styles let you enter a subtitle as well. All the styles let you enter an email address that appears as a link in the gallery (making it easy for people to contact you). Some styles also let you choose the fonts and color for the text, but these choices are grayed out for most styles.

  TIP Unless you think you don't get enough spam, don't enter an email address in standard form, like hlector@quietlambs.net. There are Web-trawling robots endlessly searching the Web for readable addresses. Instead, try something like hlectorATquietlambs.net and explain to your friends how to replace the AT with @.

- **Thumbnail.** The galleries include thumbnails of all the pictures in the gallery. For some styles, you navigate through the pictures by clicking on the thumbnails, while other galleries display thumbnails only on the main page. This tab lets you choose how large your thumbnails should be. For some styles, you can choose how you want your thumbnails labeled and the font and size of the labels.

- **Large Photos.** These are the options for displaying the main images in your gallery. Choices range from small to extra-large. Elements automatically resizes your photos for optimum Web viewing, unless you turn off Resize Photos.

  You also get to choose your image quality setting. Medium is fine for general use. If you want the large photos to have captions, this tab is where you can choose to show the file name, caption, and/or date. You can also choose the font and size for your captions here.

- **Custom Colors.** This option is grayed out for some styles. For many styles, like the Museum design, you can choose your own colors for text and links.

Once you've made your selections, you need to enter a name (enter the name in the Site Folder box). Then select a destination folder where Elements can publish and save the files it's created. Elements starts you out by proposing a location; click Browse to pick a different location. After you click Save, you'll see a window similar to the one shown in Figure 16-3.

The Web Photo Gallery Browser lets you preview your gallery to get an idea of what it will look like when it's on your Web site. If you like what you see, you're all set. If you want to change something about your gallery, the easiest way is to start over, using the same name you just entered. When you do that, Elements warns

Figure 16-3:
Elements for Windows contains its own preview window for your gallery, shown here.

you that you're going to overwrite all the existing files, and that's just what you want to do (since you'll create a new set of files to replace the files you previously created).

> **TIP** To find out the file size of your Web Photo Gallery, right-click the folder containing it and choose Properties.

OUTSIDE ELEMENTS

Email a Web Photo Gallery

The Web Photo Galleries aren't really meant to be emailed, but you can do so if the resulting folder isn't too large. The recipient needs to be a little computer-savvy, too, because you can't just double-click a Web Photo Gallery and expect to see it open.

But if you've got a friend who's familiar with the basics of opening Web files, here's what you need to do. When you send your Web Photo Gallery, send the entire folder that has the name you chose when you created it. You must include all the contents—there's nothing superfluous in there. Everything is needed for the gallery to work.

To view a Web Photo Gallery in any Web browser, first launch the browser, or open a new browser window if you're already online. Then go to File → Open and navigate to the gallery folder. One file in there is called index. html. Open that file, and your gallery displays in the browser. This works for any operating system, so you don't need to worry about whether your friends are using PCs or Macs

---

TIP   If you're familiar with HTML, you can edit your completed gallery if you like. Navigate to the folder you've created and find the file you want to change. Open it up in a text editor or HTML editor, make your changes, and save the file. Make sure to save the file in its previous location and also make sure you haven't changed the file name or its extension.

Creating a Web Photo Gallery (on the Mac)

Mac owners get the same Web Photo Gallery that's included in Photoshop CS, which is somewhat more robust than the Organizer Web Photo Gallery. To start, you can go to File → Create Web Photo Gallery or to File Browser → Automate → Web Photo Gallery. You then see the window shown in Figure 16-4.

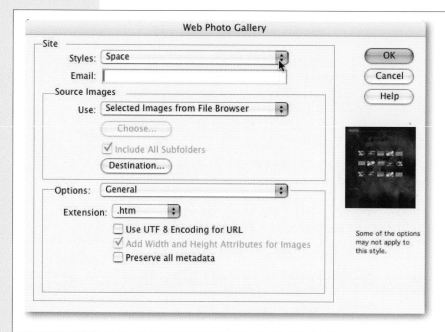

Figure 16-4:
The Mac Web Photo Gallery window doesn't give you an option to add photos individually. You need to either open all the photos you want to include so that they're all in the Photo bin, or put them together into a folder to simplify the process before you start.

The window gives you a long list of choices for customizing your gallery:

- **Style** lets you choose the gallery design you want to use. There's a preview of the selected style on the right side of the window so you can see what you're choosing. The designs offer the same navigation options available in the Windows version: some have a strip of thumbnails across the bottom of every page, others use arrows for navigation.

- **Email.** Enter an address here if you want to include an email address on your Web Gallery.

- **Source Images.** This is where you tell Elements which photos to use in your gallery. You can choose from open files, files preselected in the File Browser, or a folder. If you choose Folder, the Browse button becomes active and you can navigate to the folder you want. You can also choose to include the images in any subfolders.

- **Destination.** Tell Elements where you want your gallery to be created. You have to select a folder that Elements can put your gallery into. It's best to create a new folder for this purpose, since you don't want other files getting mixed up with your gallery when you upload it. To create a new folder, click Destination, and navigate to where you want the folder to be. Then click the New Folder button on the bottom-left corner of the dialog box.

The Options section is where you customize the style you've chosen. The Options pull-down menu gives you several choices:

- **General.** You can choose here whether to use .htm or .html as your extension. (Don't change it unless you know you need to.) If you like, you can opt for UTF 8 encoding, which is more reliable for Asian languages but not supported by all browsers. You can also choose to add width and height attributes to the HTML code Elements creates for faster downloading. Finally, you can opt to preserve the metadata in the files (page 39 has more about metadata).

- **Banner.** Here's where you tell Elements the name you want to use for your site. It appears as a headline across the home page. You can also include the photographer's name and contact info (this can include street address, phone number, and email) and the date (today's date, unless you change it). You can also choose the font used to display this information. The font size setting is for the main banner only. The sizes are relative, not point sizes, so 5 is larger than 3.

    NOTE If you don't delete or change the existing banner text, your gallery appears with the site name "Adobe Web Photo Gallery."

- **Large Images.** These are the settings for your gallery photos. Turning on the Add Numeric Links checkbox adds numbers to each image to help you keep track of where they are in a large gallery. You can also set the size of your photos and the image quality (see page 386 for more about image quality options).

    The Quality box and slider both do exactly the same thing. A higher quality creates bigger files. For some designs, you can set the size of the border around each image. Your title options may include: the file name, title, description, copyright, or credits from the metadata. You don't have access to all these choices in most of the styles. Font sets the font for displaying this data.

- **Thumbnails.** The Web Photo Galleries all include thumbnails of your images. For some styles, you can set how many rows and columns of thumbnails are displayed, as well as choosing their size. You may have the same choices for borders, titles, and fonts that you do for the large images, depending on the gallery style.

- **Custom Colors.** Some gallery styles let you choose link colors, text colors, custom background colors, or banner colors. For most gallery styles, at least a few of the choices will be grayed out.

- **Security** is a feature unique to the Mac version. You can add copyright information to your images. You can choose the font, size, color, opacity, and positioning if you decide to include copyright information.

Once you've made all your choices, click OK, and Elements creates your Web Photo Gallery. Then Elements launches Safari (or whatever your standard Web browser is) so you can preview the site. If you don't like what you've got, the easiest thing is to start over. Be careful about re-using the same folder, though, because Elements doesn't always neatly overwrite your previous files. You may get some leftovers from your first try, so create a new folder just to be safe.

> **TIP** The HTML code produced by the Web Photo Gallery sometimes produces pages that render incorrectly in browsers other than Internet Explorer. If you know how to edit HTML, you can clean up the code yourself.

You can also edit the gallery styles. To edit the styles, go to Applications → Adobe Photoshop Elements 3 → Presets → Web Photo Gallery and open the style you want in an HTML editor or text editor. Make your changes and save the edited file back to the same place. You can duplicate styles and have multiple versions of a style as long as you put them all into the correct folder and give each a different name.

To email your gallery, see the box on page 405.

Slideshows

Elements makes it easy to create very slick little slideshows—some even with music and fancy transitions between the images—that you can play on your PC or send to your friends. In Elements 3, there's a difference between the Windows slideshows, one of which can include sound, and the Mac version, which makes a PDF slideshow that can have transitions but not sound. (PDF is Adobe's Portable Document format.) Each version is explained separately in the following sections.

Creating Windows Slideshows

In Elements for Windows, you have a choice of two kinds of slideshows: a simple PDF slideshow and a much fancier Custom slideshow that you burn to a VCD (video CD format). There are advantages and drawbacks for each.

Simple PDF slideshow

The easiest way to create a PDF slideshow in Windows is to use the slideshow option in the E-mail window. Start by selecting the photos you want to include in the Organizer, then choose File → Attach to E-mail. You can also create a PDF slideshow by clicking the Create button in the Options bar. Go to Create → Slide-show → Simple Slideshow. This option works pretty much the same way as the E-mail window, but you get more control over your slideshow. Once you click OK, the window shown in Figure 16-5 appears.

Figure 16-5:
The thumbnail images you see here are just for your convenience while creating your slideshow—the finished version doesn't include thumbnail navigation. To change the order of your photos, just drag the thumbnails into the order in which you want them to appear. Use the Add Photos button to find additional images, or highlight a photo and click Remove Photo to remove it. If you want to use a photo more than once in your slideshow, highlight the photo you want, then click "Use Photo Again." Elements makes a copy that you can drag to the place in the thumbnails where you want it to appear.

The settings in the PDF slideshow creation dialog box are:

- **Photos and thumbnails.** This is where you see the photos you've chosen for your slideshow. Use the Add Photos button to find more photos if you need them. To remove a photo, select the photo, then click Delete Photo.

- **Transition** controls how the slideshow moves from one photo to the next. You can leave it set at Random, the factory setting, and Elements gives you a different transition between each photo, or you can choose one transition style to use for all your photos. You can't designate different transitions between each slide with this slideshow the way you can with the Custom slideshow (covered in the next section).

- **Duration.** This sets how long each photo stays onscreen before the next one replaces it.

- **Loop.** If you turn on "Loop after last page," your slideshow repeats endlessly until you stop it.

- **View slideshow after saving.** Leave this on, and Elements launches Adobe Reader (your PDF viewing program) so you can watch your show.

- **Photo Size.** If you're burning the show to a CD, you can safely leave it at Original and let your friends see your pictures at their actual size. If you want to email it, you may want to choose smaller-sized photos. If you choose a size other than Original, you can also choose an image-quality setting. For CD, you want High. For sending by email, Medium works well.

When you're all set, click Save, name your slideshow in the Save dialog box, and choose where to save it. Unless you turned off the preview function, Elements now launches Adobe Reader and displays your show in a full-screen view. If you want to stop it, or when it's done, click Escape to return to your normal Windows layout. You can then go to Share → E-mail to send your slideshow, or you can burn it to a CD the way you would any other file.

The advantage of the PDF slideshow is that almost anyone can view it. The recipient just needs to have a program that can open PDF files, like the free Adobe Reader.

> **TIP** When the PDF slideshow is ready, it politely announces that it has successfully created itself. You have to dismiss the announcement window before the slideshow plays.

Custom slideshow

The Custom slideshows let you add audio and special transitions between your slides. You can then either save the slideshow or burn it onto a video CD (VCD) that's designed to play in a regular DVD player. The idea is that you give these VCDs to your friends and then they can pop them into a DVD player, even if they don't have computers.

Unfortunately, VCDs don't always work the way they're supposed to. Before you jump in and start playing Cecil B. DeMille, there's one thing you should know about the Custom slideshow. It looks great, sounds great, and plays great on your computer, but it's often a dog on opening night. In other words, once you burn your slideshow in the VCD format it may look terrible. The additional bad news is that the poor quality doesn't matter too much, because many people are going to have trouble playing the VCD anyway. (This is a just a problem inherent with the VCD format—it's not the fault of Elements.)

It's a great pity, really, but the compression your slideshow undergoes in the VCD creation process squishes out an awful lot of the data. When what's left gets stretched to full-screen view, the results often appear pixelated and blocky-looking.

Worse, to view your VCD, your friends need a DVD player that can play the very latest Windows Media formats, since that's the file type Elements creates when it makes VCDs. Bottom line: give the Custom slideshow a simple test run with one or two photos before you spend a lot of time with it. If your friends can't see your show or you don't like the quality (which you can't adjust), there's not much point in investing hours in using it.

If you're still up for creating a Custom slideshow, here's a quick rundown of how to do it. (It's a darn shame that this feature is so pesky, because this thing is absolutely crammed with really cool features. Hopefully, Adobe will get it fixed in Elements 4.)

First, from the Organizer, select the images you want to include. Then click Create, choose Slide Show, and pick Custom Slide Show. The Elements Slide Show Editor launches (see Figure 16-6).

Figure 16-6:
The Elements Slide Show Editor is jam packed with options. Adobe has included lots of ways to customize your slideshow, such as adding transitions between slides and songs to accompany your show.

Across the top of the Slide Show Editor window, you see the following menu items:

- **File.** The menu choices here let you save your slideshow (either as a .wmv file or as a VCD), switch to full-screen preview mode, or you can quit the Slide Show Editor.

- **Edit.** Among your choices here: you can add or edit audio, undo and redo, and delete or duplicate frames. You can also set your slideshow preferences here (see Figure 16-7). Probably the most important option in this menu is Change Background Color, which lets you select a new background color for your slides.

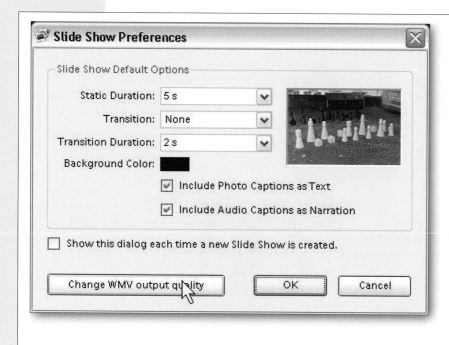

Figure 16-7:
You can set the slide duration and text color for all your slideshows in the Slideshow Preferences window. It's also a great place to try out transitions. If you want to see how a particular transition looks, select it from the Transition list. You'll see it play in the little preview area on the right. If you choose a transition here, it gets automatically applied to every slide, but you can still override this manually for individual slides by clicking in the slideshow's timeline and choosing a different one.

TIP   If you have a memory-challenged computer, using the Undo command in the Edit menu can be faster than dragging in the thumbnail timeline.

- **Add.** The choices in this menu let you add photos, blank slides, text, and audio.

- **Transitions.** The Custom Slideshow lets you add cool transitions between your slides. If you select a transition from the timeline at the bottom of the Slideshow Editor (see Figure 16-8), you can apply it here to all your slides, or clear the transition from one slide, or from all slides.

NOTE   If you're wondering about why you'd want to add a blank slide, you can use these with text added to them to create title screens and credits.

Once your photos are in the order you want them, click in the timeline to set the duration for each slide, as well as the transitions between them. You can also add audio, which is explained in the next section. When you've got everything set, press F11 or the Full-Screen Preview button (in the upper-right corner of the window) to watch your show. If you like it, click the Save shortcut. If you don't like it,

Figure 16-8:
The timeline at the bottom of the Slideshow Editor shows thumbnails of each image and includes a space to set the duration and transition between each slide. As shown here, you get quite a list of transitions, along with thumbnails to help you remember what each one does.

click the Close button on the main Slideshow window and say No when asked if you want to save your slideshow.

You must save and name your slideshow before you can make a VCD from it. If you choose the VCD option in the File menu, you get reminded to save your slideshow first. You can burn a VCD directly from the File menu in the Slideshow window, or after you've saved your slideshow, you can go to Create → VCD with Menus. If you make your VCD from the Create wizard, you can burn multiple slideshows onto one CD, if there's room.

Audio for slideshows

Elements makes it easy to add music to a Custom slideshow. To do so, just click the Add Audio bar at the very bottom of the Slide Show Editor window. (The bar always looks like it's grayed out, but it works.) After you click the bar, a window appears that lets you find the audio files you want to use in your slideshow. (Elements supplies you with a few sample audio files, so you always have music available, even if you don't have any audio files on your PC.)

The title and length of the song display at the bottom of the Slide Show Editor. If you click "Fit Slides to Audio," Elements automatically figures out the timing so that your slideshow is exactly as long as your song.

You can also include an audio caption for a particular slide in your show. If you used your camera's audio feature to record notes when you took the shot, click the Microphone icon in the shortcuts bar. The Edit Narration window appears. Your pre-recorded audio caption is one of the options in the dialog box. If you want to add a fresh recording click "Edit Audio Caption" (see Figure 16-9).

Figure 16-9:
You can record an audio caption for a photo right in Elements if your computer has the requisite hardware, like a soundcard and microphone.

Click the red Record button the same way you would on a tape recorder, and start talking. Click the Stop button when you're done. Use the controls to play it back. You can record over and over again until you get something you want to save. When you close the window, Elements asks if you want to save the caption.

You can also add an audio caption to any file in the Photo Browser by right-clicking an image and selecting Show Properties. Then choose General. Click the audio icon at the bottom of the window to bring up this same dialog box.

PDF Slideshows for the Mac

For Macs, there's only one slideshow option, a PDF slideshow. (PDF is Adobe's Portable Document format.) Elements helps you makes a good quality slideshow very easily, but it doesn't allow you to add any audio. You need to use iPhoto, iMovie, iDVD, or another program if you want to make a slideshow with a soundtrack.

The PDF slideshow is the same one included with Photoshop CS. To call it up, go to File → Automation Tools → PDF Slide Show, or in the File Browser, go to Automate → PDF Slide Show. The PDF Slide Show window, shown in Figure 16-10, appears.

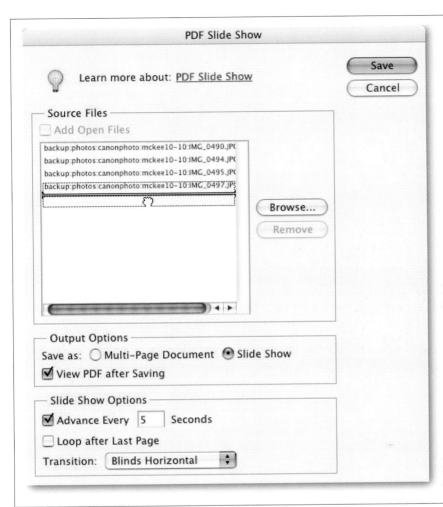

Figure 16-10:
As you add files, they appear in the Source Files window. Note that you get the file path with the file name at the end instead of a visual preview. If your photos are buried deep in many layers of folders, the file path is so long you won't see the actual name of your image. To get around this, try putting all your photos for the slideshow into a folder on your desktop. Once you've gotten all your photos into the list, just drag to change their order if you need to. The top image appears first.

If you've selected files in the File Browser, they're already listed in the Source Files window when it opens. To add additional photos, click the Browse button and navigate to the ones you want. To remove a photo, highlight its name, and click Remove. You can also choose to add all your open files, if you want. This option is grayed out if no photos are open.

Your other options are:

- **Output.** You can choose to create a slideshow or a multi-page PDF with one photo per page. If you want to see your slideshow when it's done, leave "View PDF after saving" turned on.

  NOTE You need Adobe Reader to view the slideshow as a slideshow. If you open your slideshow in Preview, you'll just get a multi-page PDF that won't play.

- **Slideshow Options.** This section becomes active when you click the PDF Slideshow button. You can set how long each slide should appear onscreen, whether to loop back from the end to the beginning for continuous play, and what transition, if any, to use between the slides.

Once you've chosen your options, click Save to create the slideshow. Elements asks you to name the file, and then you see the PDF options dialog box. You have one main choice to make in the PDF Options dialog box. Choose between:

- **Zip.** This choice creates a Zip format file. (Zip is a popular format for compressing files.)

- **JPEG.** Choose this to apply JPEG compression to your images. If you choose JPEG, you have the same quality choices you get in Save for Web (see page 387). As always, the higher the quality, the larger the file size.

There are two other checkboxes at the bottom of the window:

- **Save Transparency.** If you need transparency for any of your images, turn this on.

- **Image Interpolation.** This setting lets other programs that might need to resample the file interpolate while they resample. You can ignore it completely.

Click Okay, and Adobe Reader launches and plays your slideshow. Press Escape when the show is done, or when you want to stop previewing it.

WORKAROUND WORKSHOP

Other Options

There's no question that while the slideshow options in Elements are handy, they're not the best out there by a long shot. On both platforms, there are lots of other programs that do a better job. If you need to create elaborate slideshows with audio, check out some of the Flash-based programs, like SWF 'n Slide from Vertical Moon (*www.verticalmoon.com*), which is available for both Mac and Windows. For Windows, ProShow Gold from Photodex (*www.photodex.com*) is very popular.

Macs have the iLife applications: iPhoto, iMovie, iDVD, and GarageBand (for soundtracks), but there are many more elaborate programs available as well. Elements guru and teacher Ray Robillard has prepared a very comprehensive tutorial on how to create slideshows using iPhoto, iMovie, and iDVD. You can download it at *http://homepage.mac.com/carbmac/FileSharing8.html*.

And if you don't like the Elements Web Galleries, JAlbum (*www.datadosen.se*) is a popular free alternative for both Windows and Mac.

6

Part Six:
Additional Elements

Chapter 17: Beyond the Basics

Beyond the Basics

So far, everything in this book has been about what you can do with Elements right out of the box. But like many things digital, there's a thriving cottage industry devoted to souping up Elements. You can add new brush shapes, wild Layer styles, and fancy filters. Best of all, a lot of what's out there is free. And many of the tools are especially designed to make Elements behave more like Photoshop.

This chapter looks at some of these extras, how to manage the stuff you collect, and how to know when you really do need the full version of Photoshop instead. You'll also learn about the many resources available for expanding your knowledge of Elements beyond this book.

Graphics Tablets

Probably the most popular Elements accessory is a *graphics tablet,* which lets you draw and paint with a pen-like stylus instead of a mouse. If trying to use the Lasso tool with a mouse makes you feel like you're trying to write on a mirror with a bar of soap, a graphics tablet is for you. Figure 17-1 shows a graphics tablet in use.

> **NOTE**   There are very deluxe tablets that act as a monitor and let you work directly on your image. But you need to budget a few thousand dollars for that kind of convenience.

Most tablets work like the one shown in Figure 17-1. You use the special pen on the tablet just as you would a mouse on a mouse pad; any changes you make appear right on your monitor.

Figure 17-1:
A Wacom Graphire tablet in action. This tablet is 6" x 8"–a bit larger than the smallest size availabe (4" x 5"). The working area is inside the rectangle on the tablet surface. For basic photo retouching, a small size is usually fine once you get used to it. If you want to do more drawing and you generally use sweeping strokes when you draw, you may want a larger tablet.

For most people, it's much easier to control fine motions using a tablet's pen compared to a mouse. Moreover, when you use a tablet, many of the brushes and tools in Elements are *pressure sensitive*—the harder you press, the darker and wider the line becomes. This lets you create much more realistic paint strokes, as shown in Figure 17-2.

In the Elements Brush tool, there are Tablet Options next to the Airbrush setting in the Options bar. Many brushes and tools are automatically pressure sensitive when you hook up a tablet. You can also choose whether to let the pressure control the size, opacity, roundness, hue jitter, and scatter for your brushes. (See Chapter 11 for more about Brush settings.)

With a tablet, you can also create hand-drawn line art—even if you don't have an artistic bone in your body—by placing a picture of what you want to draw on the surface of the tablet and tracing the outline. Also, if you find constant mousing troublesome, you may have fewer hand problems when using a tablet's pen. Most tablets also come with a wireless mouse, which you can use on the surface of the tablet, or you can use your regular mouse the way you always do.

Tablet prices start at less than a hundred dollars these days, a big drop from what they used to cost. There are many models of tablets, and the features vary widely.

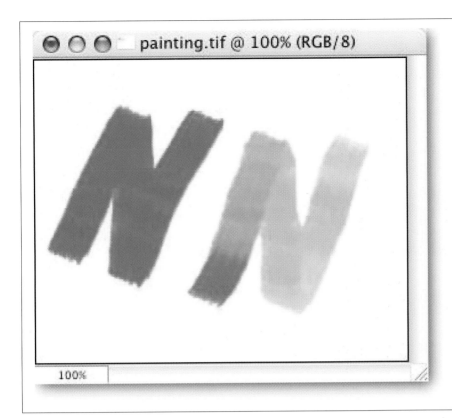

Figure 17-2:
Two almost identical paint strokes, starting with fairly hard pressure and then lightening up. Both were made using the identical brush and color in Elements. The only difference is that the stroke on the left was drawn with a mouse, and the one on the right came from a tablet. You can see what a difference the pressure sensitivity makes.

Sophisticated tablets offer multiple levels of sensitivity and respond when you change the angle at which you hold the stylus.

Wacom, one of the big tablet manufacturers, has some pretty nifty tablet demos on their European Web site (*www.wacom-europe.com/uk/use-it/demos/index.asp*). You can't actually simulate what it's like to use a tablet, but the animations give you a good idea of what your life would be like if you went the tablet route.

Free Stuff from the Internet

You have to spend some money if you want a graphics tablet, but there's a ton of free stuff—tutorials, brushes, textures, and Layer styles, for example—available online that you can add to Elements. Most of these add-ons will say they work with Photoshop, but since Elements is based on Photoshop, you can use most of them in Elements, too.

Here are some popular places to go treasure hunting:

- **Adobe Studio Exchange** (*http://share.studio.adobe.com*). On Adobe's own Web site, you can find hundreds and hundreds of downloads, including more Layer styles than you could ever use, brushes, textures, and custom shapes (to use with Shape tool). They're all free, but you do have to register. This site is one of the best resources anywhere for extra stuff. About 99 percent of the items listed are made specifically for Photoshop, but Photoshop's brushes, swatches, textures, shapes, and Layer styles work with Elements, too.

- **Creative Mac** (*www.creativemac.com*). Windows owners, don't let the name put you off. Almost everything on this site works on both platforms. Here you'll find many great tutorials and a wonderful source for specialty brushes, especially for tricky things like hair and skin.

- **MyJanee** (*www.myjanee.com*). Lots of tutorials and free downloads here.

- **Sue Chastain** (*www.graphicssoft.about.com*). This is another Web site with lots of downloads and many tutorials.

There are many, many other Web sites. Just enter what you're looking for as your Google search term, and you're bound to see many choices.

> **NOTE** A word of warning: before setting off on your search, make sure you have a good pop-up window blocker for your Web browser. And if you use Windows, be sure you have good antivirus software installed as well as detectors for adware and spyware.

If you're willing to pay a little bit, you've got even more choices. You can find everything from more elaborate ways to sharpen your photos to really cool collections of special edges and visual effects. Prices range from donationware (you pay if you like it) to some quite expensive and sophisticated plug-ins that cost hundreds of dollars. There are also books you can buy, like the *Wow!* series (Peachpit Press), which have very little text, but just illustrations of the styles available on the included CD.

With so many goodies available, it's easy to find yourself overwhelmed trying to keep track of everything you've added to Elements. Your best bet is to make backup copies of anything you download so you'll have it if you ever need to reinstall Elements.

Elements also includes a Preset Manager (Figure 17-3) that can help manage certain kinds of downloads. Go to Edit → Preset Manager to launch it.

> **NOTE** Windows plug-ins don't work on the Mac, and vice versa (many plug-ins offer two versions, one for each platform).
>
> Elements 3 is based on Photoshop CS, so CS downloads are compatible. Things designed for older versions of Photoshop or Elements usually work with newer versions, but not the other way around. So a brush made for Photoshop CS works in Elements 3 but not Elements 2.

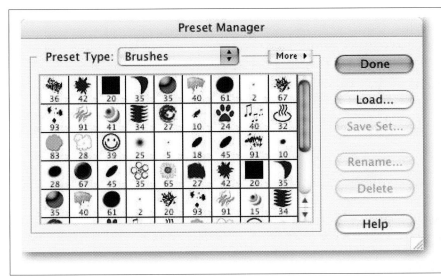

Figure 17-3:
The Elements Preset Manager offers a place to see all your brushes, swatches, gradients, and patterns in one place. You can use it to switch which groups are loaded, to add or remove items, and so on—the same way you do in the main brush window.

Making Elements More Like Photoshop

There are a few important tools in Photoshop that Elements lacks. But the good news is that you can download add-ons for Elements that give you access to some of Photoshop's most important features. Because Elements is based on Photoshop, there are a lot of Photoshop features still in Element's underlying programming code. All that Adobe did was leave out a way to get to them. Consequently, several people have developed add-ons for Elements that let you use these features, although in a limited way.

Grant Dixon has created a free set of tools for Elements which you can download at *www.cavesofice.org/~grant/Challenge/Tools/index.html*. Figure 17-4 shows you just how many powerful tools you get for free. And Richard Lynch's *Hidden Power of Photoshop Elements* books (*www.hiddenelements.com*) include a CD with similar tools and several additional ones. The book is not an easy read, but you'll learn a lot about the advanced capabilities of Elements, and the tools are definitely worth the investment if you're serious about Elements. With these two add-ons, you can go a very long way toward regaining some of Photoshop's special talents.

Here are some of the tools you can add to Elements from either the Dixon or the Lynch site:

- **Curves.** Despite its name, curves is not a drawing tool. Instead, the curves command is similar to levels (page 163), but with many more points of correction. Curves lets you make more sophisticated adjustments to color and brightness. These tools don't let you edit a curve the way Photoshop does. You have to trash the curves layer and make a new one, but this is still a very important retouching tool.

Figure 17-4:
*Grant Dixon's Elements tools include curves, layer
masks, and several advanced color tools. You'll find the
installation instructions on the "Missing CD" page at
www.missingmanuals.com.*

- **Layer Masks.** If you try to do tutorials or projects written for Photoshop, you constantly get told to edit the layer mask. In full Photoshop, you can just paint a mask right onto a layer—sort of the way you make a selection with the Selection brush. These add-ons let you do this without using the cumbersome workaround described in Chapter 6.

- **Channel Mixer.** These tools let you edit the color values for each channel in a way that isn't possible with Levels.

Another big difference between Elements and Photoshop is *Actions.* Actions are something like macros, in which Photoshop follows a script and carries out several actions quickly. The effects in Elements are really actions, but you can't write your own.

In Photoshop, you can record your own actions, and there are many, many actions available for download from the resources listed in this chapter and from *www. atncentral.com.* The great news about Elements 3 is that, while it can't record actions, it can run them. You'll find directions for installing action files in Elements on the "Missing CD" page at *www.missingmanuals.com.* Not all actions work in Elements. If an action has a step that requires a process that Elements can't do, or that is handled differently in Elements, the action won't run unless someone rewrites it for Elements. However, many actions written for Photoshop will work if you don't mind the extra hassle of installing them in Elements. For any given action, the best way to find out whether it works is to try it.

When You Really Need Photoshop

You can do an enormous amount with just Elements, but some people do need the full version of Photoshop. While the Elements add-ons help a lot, in most cases, they're not as full-featured as what you get with Photoshop. If you need the ability to write your own actions, or if you need to work extensively in CMYK mode, you need Photoshop.

CMYK mode is the color mode used for commercial printing. If you send a file to a print shop, they usually tell you it needs to be a CMYK file. You can't convert files to CMYK in Elements, although Richard Lynch's tools include a workaround for this. However, it's much more complex than doing it in full Photoshop. If you need CMYK files on a regular basis, it's worth the extra price of Photoshop to avoid the aggravation. If you only occasionally need CMYK, you might just ask your printer. Usually most print shops are willing to convert the file for you for an additional charge.

In Photoshop you get more of everything: more choices, more tools, more settings, more types of adjustment layers, and so on.

Beyond This Book

You can do thousands of interesting things with Elements that are beyond the scope of this book. Your bookstore has dozens of titles on Elements and Photoshop, and a lot of things are common to both programs. There are all kinds of specialized books on everything from color management to making selections to scrapbooking.

In addition, there are hundreds tutorial sites on the Web. Besides those mentioned earlier in the chapter, other popular sites include:

- **Adobe** (*http://www.adobe.com/education/training/photoshop_elements/main.html*). Plenty of free online training for Elements here.

- **Jay Arraich** (*http://arraich.com/elements/psE_intro.htm*). Much Elements information, both basic and advanced, from a longtime Photoshop guru.

Two important resources that have all kinds of interesting information are:

- **Elements Challenge pages** (*www.cavesofice.org/~grant/Challenge/*). Maintained by Grant Dixon, this site offers you a chance to try your Elements skills with a different Elements challenge every week. Anyone is welcome to participate, no matter what your skill level. If you feel intimidated by some of the entries, don't be. Everyone started off as a beginner. There's also a links page with many tutorial and download sites.

- **Photoshop Elements User** (*www.photoshopelementsuser.com/*). This is the Web site for a subscriber-only print newsletter, but it also includes some free online video tutorials, a forum, and a good collection of links. This is the first publication especially for Elements.

If you search Google, you're sure to find a tutorial for any project you might have in mind, although many of them are written for full Photoshop. In most cases, they can be adapted to Elements. If you get stuck or you need help with any other aspect of Elements, there's a very active online community that's sure to have an answer for you. Besides the sites already mentioned, try:

- **Adobe Support forum** (*www.adobe.com/forums*). Scroll down the page to find the Elements User-to-User forum. Lots of helpful and friendly people here. It's your best bet for getting answers without calling Adobe support.

- **Digital Photography Review** (*www.dpreview.com*). You'll find many camera-specific forums on this site. You can also get a lot of Elements answers in the Retouching forum if you specify in your question that you've got Elements rather than Photoshop.

- **Retouch pro** (*www.retouchpro.com/forums*). The forums here cover all kinds of retouching and artistic uses of Elements and Photoshop.

- **Adobe Photoshop Elements Alliance** (*www.elementsusers.com*) Another forum strictly for Photoshop Elements.

There's no question about it: Once you get familiar with Elements, it's addicting! Lots of other folks have found out how much fun this program is, and you shouldn't have any trouble finding the answer to any question you might have.

The only limit to what you can do with Elements is your imagination. Enjoy!

Part Seven:
Appendixes

7

The Organizer, Menu by Menu

This appendix gives you a quick tour of the main menus in the Organizer, which is found only in the Windows version of Elements. The Organizer has two main windows: Photo Browser and Date View. Both offer the same menu choices—everything listed here is available in either window. There are keyboard shortcuts and buttons in the Organizer windows that give you access to many of these menu items. When there's an alternate method, it's listed in the text.

In addition to the main menus discussed here, the Organizer is chock full of contextual menus. You can right-click almost anywhere in the Organizer, and you'll get a menu with several options specific to the object you clicked. Click a tag, for instance, and you get a menu that includes choices for editing the tag or changing it to a category.

File Menu

This menu is where you import photos, start new projects, manage your catalogs, and export your photos. It's also where you quit the Organizer when you're done.

Get Photos

This is where you import photos into the Organizer. You can tell Elements to find and import photos from:

- **A camera or card reader** (or press Ctrl+G)

- **A scanner** (or press Ctrl+V)

- **Files and folders** (or press Ctrl+Shift+G)

- **Mobile phones** (or press Ctrl+Shift+M)

- **An online sharing service** (like Ofoto.com). See page 399 for more about online sharing.

Get by Searching tells Elements to search your entire drive for photos. You can also tell Elements to import photos from a PhotoDeluxe album or an ActiveShare album (two older programs' album formats).

New

You can choose to create a new blank file that will appear in the Editor. (The Organizer itself doesn't create blank files.) You can also copy a photo in the Organizer (Ctrl+C) and choose to start a new Editor file by copying your photo from the Clipboard (the invisible file that stores what you copy until you paste it somewhere).

You can also select "Create…" to bring up the Create wizard (see Chapter 14). If you know the kind of project you want, you can go directly to its wizard. You can choose to make a:

- **Slideshow** (see page 408)

- **Video CD** (see page 410; you need to create a slideshow before you can use this menu item)

- **Card** (see page 384)

- **Calendar** (see page 384)

- **Album page** (see page 383)

- **Photo book** (see page 383)

Browse Folders in Editor

This command switches you to the Editor's File Browser (see page 39). Use the File Browser when you want to visually search for photos that aren't in the Organizer.

Open Recently Edited File in Editor

Choose a recent file from the list, and the Organizer opens it in the Editor so you can work on it there.

Open Creation

Any Create project that you've already made (see page 380) appears when you choose this menu item. If you develop lots of Create projects, this is the way to see a list of all your projects so you can decide which to open for editing or sharing.

Catalog

This is where you manage your catalogs (see page 30) if you have more than one. A window opens where you can choose a catalog to open or recover from a list of your existing catalogs. You can also create a new catalog.

Burn

If you want to burn a photo or a group of photos to a CD, choose this command. It actually sends you to the same wizard you use to back up your entire catalog, so you can do either activity from this command. Chapter 3 has more information about backing up your files.

Backup

It's wise to keep a good backup of your catalog; this command makes it easy to do so. It calls up the same wizard you get when using the Burn command. You can choose to back up your entire catalog or just a few photos. See page 79 for detailed directions on using Backup.

Restore

Choose this to replace your catalog with an archived version, if you accidentally delete photos or otherwise run into trouble with the current version. Restore is also a good maintenance tool. If your catalog mysteriously balloons to a huge file size, Restore can usually compress it to bring it back down to a reasonable size. You might want to run Restore every couple of weeks as part of your maintenance routine.

Duplicate

Highlight a photo or a Create project and choose this menu item (or press Ctrl+Shift+D) to make a duplicate.

Reconnect

Sometimes your Organizer catalog (page 30) can't find a file when you ask for it. Usually this happens when you move or rename a file using a method outside of Elements (like Windows Explorer). This command tells the Organizer to find the file again. You can choose to reconnect:

- **Missing File.** Choose this to reconnect one file.
- **All Files.** The Organizer searches for all the files it can't find.

Watch Folders

Use this command if you regularly import photos into certain folders. Elements monitors the folders you choose and checks for new graphics stored inside them. You can tell Elements to automatically place any photos it finds into your catalog, if you want. If you prefer, Elements can just notify you that it found new files and let you decide what to do with them.

Rename

If you want the Organizer to be able to keep track of your photos, you need to move and rename them from within Elements. If you want to change the name of a photo, choose this menu item or press Ctrl+Shift+N.

Write Tag Info to Files

Normally your Organizer tags exist only in your catalog's database. If you want to make the tag information part of the photo file itself (the way keywords are in Photoshop CS or in the Mac version of Elements), choose this menu item. Elements writes your tags into the file's metadata (see page 39).

Move

If you want the Organizer to keep track of your photos, you must move them within Elements once they're in your catalog. To move a photo, choose this menu item and then select a destination in the window that appears. You can also move files by dragging them if you go to View → Arrangement → Folder Location. You'll see a new pane on the left of the Photo browser with a schematic view of the folder structure of your hard drive (just like you see elsewhere in Windows). You can drag your photos into the folders you want.

Export

If you want to export a group of photos for use by another application, this is one way to do it. Choose Export from the menu, and you get a dialog box where you can choose the destination of your files and rename them if you like. You can also choose to convert the exported files to a different format. Your choices are JPG, PSD, TIFF, or PNG. This is a useful feature if you need to create JPEGs for printing at a store kiosk, for example.

Attach to E-Mail

This brings up the Organizer's email window, which is described in detail in Chapter 15.

Page Setup

This calls up your system's regular Page Setup window, where you choose the page size and the orientation of your document and the printer you plan to use. There's more about printing from the Organizer in Chapter 14. Pressing Ctrl+Shift+P also brings up the Page Setup window.

Print

Choose this command, and you get the Organizer's Print Selected Photos window, which is discussed in detail in Chapter 14. You can also press Ctrl+P.

Order Prints

This is your portal to connecting to Ofoto.com to order prints or photo books. See Chapter 14 for how to order prints online from the Organizer.

Exit

You can close the Organizer here or by pressing Ctrl+Q. The Editor doesn't quit along with the Organizer. If the Editor is also running, you must exit it separately.

Edit

This menu contains choices that let you make changes to your files. It's also where you can access your Elements preferences to change their settings.

Undo

You can undo your last action in the Organizer by selecting Undo or by pressing Ctrl+Z.

Redo

If you undo something and then change your mind, redo it here or press Ctrl+Y.

Copy

To copy something to the Clipboard, highlight it and select this menu item or press Ctrl+C.

Select All

Choose this to select all the photos in a window, or press Ctrl+A.

Deselect All

To clear all selections, choose this or press Ctrl+Alt+A.

Delete from Catalog

This removes a photo from the catalog database. You can also press Delete to do the same thing. If you want to remove the photo from your hard drive as well, the dialog box that appears gives you the option to do so.

Rotate 90° Left

To rotate a photo 90 degrees to the left, select it, then choose this menu item or just press Ctrl+the left arrow key.

Rotate 90° Right

To rotate a photo 90 degrees to the right, select it, then choose this menu item or just press Ctrl+the right arrow key.

Auto Smart Fix

To instantly apply the Auto Smart Fix command to your photo, choose this item or press Ctrl+Shift+I. See page 88 for more about Auto Smart Fix.

Edit 3GPP Movie

This is where you can edit movies to send to wireless devices, like cellphones, that also have the ability to play video. Your movie must be in 3GPP or MPEG-4 format. Select this menu item for a window with your editing controls.

Auto Fix Window

This selection launches an Organizer window containing several quick one-button photo fixes. See page 98.

Go to Quick Fix

Choose this item to go to the Organizer's Quick Fix Window (see Chapter 4).

Go to Standard Edit

Choose this item to go to the Editor. You can also press Ctrl+I.

Adjust Date and Time

If you want to adjust a file's date and time settings, select this item. You get three choices:

- **Change to a specified date and time.** This lets you adjust the date and time manually.

- **Change to match the file's date and time.** This changes the time and date to reflect the last time you modified the file.

- **Shift by a set number of hours (time zone adjust).** This lets you change the date and time of a selected group of photos. Any changes you make get made to all the photos you've selected. For example, if you elect to move the time back three hours (via the Time Zone Adjust dialog box), all your selected photos have their times moved back three hours.

Add Caption

To add a caption to an image, choose this menu item or press Ctrl+Shift+T.

Update Thumbnail

If an image thumbnail stops displaying correctly or doesn't show the correct image, choose this menu item or press Ctrl+Shift+U.

Set as Desktop Wallpaper

To use one of your photos as wallpaper for your desktop, just click its thumbnail in the Photo Browser, then choose this menu item or press Ctrl+Shift+W.

Stack

This is where you create and manage photo stacks. Stacks are groups of photos that you want to store together. Only the top photo shows in the Photo Browser until you expand the stack. Stacks can be made from unrelated photos, unlike version sets (see later). Your options here are:

- **Create Stack.** Highlight your photos and choose this menu item to put them into a stack. You can also press Ctrl+Alt+S.

- **Unstack** modifies a selected photo stack so that the photos it includes are no longer joined together.

- **Reveal Photos in Stack.** Choose this or press Ctrl+Alt+R to see all the photos in a stack.

- **Flatten Stack** reduces your stack to the visible photo, eliminating the hidden photos.

- **Remove Photo from Stack.** Use this to remove a single photo from a stack.

- **Set as Top Photo.** Highlight a photo and choose this to send that photo to the top of the stack. From now on, it becomes the visible photo.

Version Set

This is where you manage your version sets. When you make changes to a photo in the Editor, you have the option of creating a *version set*. In a version set, each time you save your photo, Elements saves it as a copy with a new name, i.e., a different version. In this way, you can save many files containing your changes and go back to any one at any time. Your options here are:

- **Reveal Photos in Version Set.** Choose this to see all your versions at once.

- **Flatten Version Set.** Use this to reduce a version set to one photo, the top one.

- **Revert to Original.** This takes your photo back to the state it was in when you first brought it into the Organizer

- **Set as Top Photo.** Highlight a photo and choose this option to send that photo to the top of the stack. From now on, it becomes the visible photo.

Color Settings

This is where you can set your color space. See page 162 for more about color spaces. You can also press Ctrl+Alt+G to bring up Elements color settings.

Contact Book

If you've created a contact book of email addresses (to use when sending your photos from Elements) you can access or edit it here. See page 396.

Preferences

This is where you can make changes to your Organizer settings for getting and saving photos; connecting to cameras, scanners, or mobile phones; emailing; editing; and creating tags, collections, and calendars. It's also where you start when you're getting set up to order prints from Ofoto.com (see page 362). You can also get to the Editor's preferences from this menu.

Find

This menu is really the heart of the Organizer in some ways. You can search for your photos in many different ways from this menu.

Set Date Range

Choose this menu item, and a dialog box appears that lets you specify start and end dates. The Organizer shows all the photos that fall in the date range you specify. You can also press Ctrl+Alt+F.

Clear Date Range

After you've searched for a date range, choose this menu item to return to your complete catalog in the Photo Browser, or press Ctrl+Shift+F.

By Caption or Note

When you choose this item, you get a dialog box in which you can search for any text in your captions or notes. It doesn't have to be the entire caption. The Organizer finds all the photos with those words in either field. You can also press Ctrl+Shift+J.

By Filename

Enter part of a file name and the Organizer finds the file for you. Ctrl+Shift+K also brings up the same window.

By History

Choose to find your file based on any of the following factors:

- **Imported On** is the date you brought your file into the Organizer.

- **Received from.** You can use this if you've received photos from a member of a group in your Contact Book. (See page 396.)

- **E-mailed to.** You can search by the names of people you've emailed your photos to, but only if you sent the messages from the Organizer.

- **Printed On.** Search for the photos you printed on a certain date.

- **Ordered Online.** Search for the photos you've ordered from Ofoto.com.

- **Shared Online.** Search for the photos you've shared at Ofoto.com (see page 362).

- **Used in Creations.** Search for all the photos you've used in your Create projects.

- **Used in Web Photo Galleries.** Search for all the photos you've used in a Web Photo Gallery (see page 401).

By Media Type

The Organizer doesn't organize only still photos. You can also use it to keep track of movies and audio files. Here, you can search for all the files of a particular type:

- **Photos.** Find still photos (press Alt+1).

- **Video.** Find video clips (press Alt+2).

- **Audio.** Find your audio files (press Alt+3).

- **Creations.** Find all your Create projects (press Alt+4).

- **Find items with audio captions.** If you've recorded captions for any of your photos (see page 413), you can search for them by choosing this menu item (or by pressing Alt+5).

Items with Unknown Date and Time

Choose this menu item if you want to find any photos that haven't been properly tagged with the date and time. You can also press Ctrl+Shift+X.

By Color Similarity with Selected Photo(s)

This is a very cool feature. If you want to find photos that have colors and tones that are similar to a particular photo (or group of photos), select the photo(s) you want to match, then choose this item. Elements ranks all your photos by color. The closest matches appear at the top of the list.

Untagged Items

To find photos that you haven't tagged yet, choose this menu item or press Ctrl+Shift+Q.

Items Not in Any Collection

Choose this menu item to find all the photos you haven't used in collections yet.

View

This menu lets you control how your photos are presented in the Organizer. It also includes two very cool ways to look through a group of photos or compare photos.

Photo Review

This is one of the best features in the Organizer. Choose it or press F11, and you get a full-screen slideshow of your photos. There's a small control strip to help you navigate through them. It's a great way to check through a group of newly imported photos.

> **TIP**   Since the Windows version of Elements 3 doesn't really give you a true full-screen view of your photo in the Editor (there are always toolbars hanging around) many people like to switch back to the Organizer and press F11 to get a really good full-screen look.

Photo Compare

This is similar to Photo Review in that you get a full-screen view. But in Photo Compare, you get to see any two photos of your choice side by side. It's great for choosing which photos you want to keep or print. You can also get to Photo Compare by pressing F12.

Refresh

If you need to refresh the view, choose this menu item or press F5.

Go To

When you're looking through photos, use this to go:

- **Backward** (press Alt+left arrow)
- **Forward** (press Alt+right arrow).

Arrangement

This is an important menu item. It tells the Organizer how you want to see the photos in the Photo Browser. You can choose to arrange your photos by:

- Date (Newest First)
- Date (Oldest First)
- Import Batch
- Folder Location
- Color Similarity
- Collection Order
- Stack Order
- Version Set Order

Media Types

Choose this item to bring up a window where you can choose what kinds of media the Organizer displays. Your choices are photos, videos, audio, and creations. Just turn on the ones you want and turn off the ones you don't.

Details

When Details is turned on, you see the information about your photos in the Photo Browser window, like the date and the tag icons. Turn Details off to see just the thumbnails with no other information.

Timeline

When Timeline is turned on, you see the Timeline above the Image Well (see page 33). To hide the Timeline, turn it off here.

Collapse All Tags

Choose this item to collapse all the tags in the Organize bin, leaving only their categories showing. You can also press Ctrl+Alt+T.

Expand All Tags

Choose this item to see the list of all your tags expanded in the Organize bin so that every tag is visible. You can also press Ctrl+Alt+X.

Collapse All Collections

Choosing this option collapses, on the Collections tab, all collections, leaving only collection *groups* visible.

Expand All Collections

Choosing this option expands, on the Collections tab, all collections so that you can see every collection in the list.

Expand All Stacks

To see every photo in every stack, choose this menu item or press Ctrl+Alt+V.

Window

This menu is where you choose which parts of the Organizer are visible. Most of the items are grouped in pairs, because you must choose one or the other. For instance, you have to choose between Photo Browser and Date View for the main Organizer window.

Photo Browser

If you want to see the Photo Browser window, you can choose it here or click the button on the Shortcuts bar.

Date View

Date View displays your photos on a calendar. You can switch to Date View here or click it in the Shortcuts bar.

Organize Bin

The Organize bin at the right of the Photo Browser displays your tag and collections information. You can turn it on and off here, to hide or reveal it.

Tags

To see the Tags tab in the Organize bin, turn it on here, or turn it off to switch to the Collections tab. (You can also just click the tabs themselves in the Organize bin.)

Collections

To see the Collections tab in the Organize bin, turn it on here, or turn it off to switch to the Tags tab. (You can also just click the tabs themselves in the Organize bin.)

Properties

To see the Properties window for a photo, highlight it and then choose this menu item or press Alt+Enter.

Dock Properties in Organize Bin

If you use the Properties window so much that you'd like to keep it around, choose this to send it to live in the Organize bin where you can always see it.

Welcome

Choose this to bring up the Elements Welcome window that you see when the program first launches. If you've chosen to always start in the Organizer and you want to change it, call up the Welcome window here and then make your change at the bottom of the window.

Help

This menu is where you find the Elements Help files and tutorials, as well as information about the program itself.

Help

You can call up the Elements Help application here, or press F1. Or click the Help button in the menu bar.

About Photoshop Elements

Choose this to see a scrolling window with information about the version of Elements you've got. You'll also see a very long list of patents and credits—an impressive testimony to the complexity of the engineering that went into Elements.

Glossary of Terms

The Elements Help files include a glossary of terms relating to digital imaging. If you're wondering what a term means, this menu item takes you to the glossary index so you can look it up.

Tutorials

The Elements Help files include some excellent tutorials. Choose this item to see a list of them.

System Info

Choose this for a window showing information about Elements itself and also about your Windows operating system. If you can't remember which service pack you have, for instance, you can check here. There's also information about some important plug-ins. If you're not sure whether you have QuickTime, for example, that information is here, too.

Online Support

Choose this option, and Elements launches your Web browser and attempts to go to Adobe's support Web site. If you're not connected to the Internet when you select this, Elements also launches an Internet connection window.

Registration

If you didn't register Elements with Adobe the first time you used the program, you can choose this to bring up the registration window again.

Photoshop Elements Online

This takes you to the main product page for Photoshop Elements on Adobe's Web site. Like the online support link, Elements launches your browser and offers to connect to the Internet if you're not already online when you chose this menu item.

The Editor, Menu by Menu

The Editor's menus are far more complex than the menus in the Windows Organizer. Both Standard Edit and Quick Fix have the same menus, although most choices are grayed out when you're in Quick Fix mode. If you need a menu item that's unavailable in Quick Fix, just switch back to the Standard Editor to use it.

There are a fair number of differences in the menu choices between the Windows and Mac versions of Elements. You'll see those noted as they come up. Also, several of the menus in Elements are dynamic; they change quite a bit to reflect the choices currently applicable to your image. That means the choices you see in this appendix are only representative of those you might see. The Layer menu, for instance, offers you very different options depending on the current state of your image and which layer is active.

Photoshop Elements (Mac Only)

This menu contains items that relate to the entire Elements program. It's where you find information about Elements, make your preference choices, hide Elements, and quit the program. (The blue Apple menu is OS X–related. Nothing in that menu pertains exclusively to Elements.)

About Photoshop Elements

Choose this and you'll get a window showing which version of Elements you're using. Option-click the menu for a window full of scrolling information about the people who created Elements and the many, many patents involved in the creation of this program. Keep holding Option while the window scrolls, and you'll find out what Adobe thinks of you. Click the window again to close it.

About Plug-In

This contains a pop-out list of all the plug-ins in your copy of Elements. The program comes with a huge number of plug-ins—you don't have to do anything to make them work—they're all preinstalled. Choose a particular plug-in from the list to see information about it.

Color Settings

This is where you choose your color space for Elements (see page 162). You can also press Shift-⌘-K.

Preferences

This menu gives you access to the many Elements settings you can customize. The preference screens available from this menu are:

- **General** (you can also press ⌘-K to go to this screen)
- **Saving Files**
- **Display and Cursors**
- **Transparency**
- **Units and Rulers**
- **Grid**
- **Plug-ins and Scratch Disks**
- **Memory and Image Cache**
- **File Browser**

Services

This is your connection to the various Mac OS X application services, like Grab (for making Screen Captures), Stickies (for making virtual sticky notes), and so on.

Hide Photoshop Elements

To hide Elements, choose this menu item or press ⌘-Control-H. You can also hide Elements by clicking the desktop, but this doesn't hide any open images, only the Elements menus, toolbars, and palettes. To hide image windows as well, use the keystroke command.

Hide Others

To hide any other open programs, choose this or press Option-⌘-H.

Show All

Choose this to make all your open programs visible.

Quit Photoshop Elements

To quit Elements, choose this, or press ⌘-Q.

File Menu (Windows and Mac)

The File menu commands let you create, import, browse, save, and print files.

New

Choose this menu item if you want to start a new file in Elements. You can choose from:

- **A blank file.** Press Ctrl+N (⌘-N).
- **Image from Clipboard.** This automatically pastes anything you've copied into a new file.
- **Creation** (Windows only). Choose this to go the Create wizard (see page 380).
- **Photomerge Panorama.** See Chapter 10 for more about how to combine your photos into panoramas.

Open

Choose this menu item or press Ctrl+O (⌘-O) to open an existing file.

Open As (Windows Only)

This menu option (or Alt+Ctrl+O) lets you choose the format for a file as you open it.

Browse Folders

Use this menu command or press Shift+Ctrl+O (Shift-⌘-O) to bring up the Editor's File Browser, which is explained on page 39.

Open Recently Edited File

This menu item contains a pop-out list of the most recent files you've had open in Elements.

Duplicate

When you need to make a copy of your photo, choose this.

Close

To close the active image window, choose this or press Ctrl+W (⌘-W).

Close All

To close all your open image windows, choose this or press Shift+Ctrl+W (Option-⌘-W).

Save

To save your work, choose this menu item or press Ctrl+S (⌘-S).

Save As

To save your image under another file name or in a different format, choose this item or press Shift+Ctrl+S (Shift-⌘-S).

Save for Web

To save an image so that it's optimized for use on the Internet, choose this menu item or press Alt+Shift+Ctrl+S (Option-Shift-⌘-S) to bring up the Save for Web window, explained on page 386.

Attach to E-Mail

For Windows, this menu choice launches the Organizer's E-mail window. (See page 393.) On a Mac, it launches your regular email program and creates a message with your file as an attachment.

Create Web Photo Gallery (Mac Only)

On a Mac, you start a Web Photo Gallery either from this menu or from the Automate menu in the File Browser. See Chapter 15 for more about Web Galleries.

File Info

Choose this menu item or press Alt+Ctrl+I (Option-⌘-I) to bring up the File Info window, which displays information about your image.

Place

Use this command to place a PDF, Adobe Illustrator, or EPS file into an image as a new layer. If the artwork is larger than the image you place it in, Elements automatically makes it small enough to fit.

Organize Open Files (Windows Only)

Choose this menu option to add the files you have open in the Editor to the Organizer.

Process Multiple Files

This is where you batch process your files to rename them, change their format, add copyright information, and so on (see page 203 for everything that Elements lets you do to groups of files). Mac owners also have this command in the File Browser's Automate menu.

Import

This is where you bring certain file formats into Elements. It's also where you can connect to external devices like scanners. (They'll show up in this menu if you install their drivers.) Your basic choices before you connect or install anything are:

- **Anti-aliased PICT** (Mac only)
- **PDF Image**
- **PICT Resource** (Mac only)
- **Frame from Video**
- **WIA Support** (Windows only)

Export

This command is always grayed out. That's normal. Adobe left it in for the benefit of any third-party plug-ins that might need it to be there. But you don't need it in Elements to use the program's standard tools and commands. (The Windows Organizer contains an active Export command.)

Automation Tools

This menu item gives you other choices for working with PDF files.

- **PDF Slideshow** (Mac only). You start creating a slideshow here or from the File Browser's Automate menu.
- **Multi-Page PDF to PSD.** This command extracts the graphics from a PDF file.

Page Setup

This calls up your system's regular Page Setup window, where you choose the page size and the orientation of your document and select the printer you plan to use. There's more about printing from the Organizer in Chapter 14. Pressing Shift+Ctrl+P (Shift-⌘-P) also brings up the Page Setup window.

Print

Choose this command, and you get the Print Preview window, which is discussed in detail in Chapter 14. You can also press Ctrl+P (⌘-P).

Contact Sheet II (Mac Only)

Create a contact sheet containing small thumbnails of many photos here or from the File Browser's Automate menu. See page 376 for more information on how this works.

Picture Package (Mac Only)

Combine multiple photos on one page here or from the File Browser's Automate menu. See page 373 for more on how this works.

Print Multiple Photos (Windows Only)

Choose this command, and you get the Organizer's "Print Selected Photos" window, which is discussed in detail in Chapter 14. You can also press Alt+Ctrl+P.

Order Prints (Windows Only)

This is your portal to connecting to Ofoto.com to order prints or photo books. See Chapter 14 for how to order prints online from the Organizer.

Exit (Windows Only)

You can close the Editor here or by pressing Ctrl+Q. The Organizer doesn't quit along with the Editor. If the Organizer is also running, you must exit it separately.

Edit Menu

This menu contains choices that let you make changes to your files. It's also where you can access your Elements preferences to change their settings if you use Windows.

Undo

You can back out of your last action by selecting Undo or by pressing Ctrl+Z (⌘-Z). You can keep applying this command to undo as many steps as you've set in the Undo History palette preferences (Edit → Preferences → General → History States [Photoshop Elements → Preferences → General → History States]).

Redo

If you undo something and then change your mind again, redo it here or press Ctrl+Y (⌘-Y).

Revert to Saved

Choose this command to return your image to the state it was in the last time you saved it.

Cut

To remove something from your image and store it on the Clipboard (so that you can paste it into another file), choose this or press Ctrl+X (⌘-X).

Copy

To copy something to the Clipboard, highlight it and select this menu item or press Ctrl+C (⌘-C). This command only copies the top layer in a file with layers. To copy all the layers in your selected area, use Copy Merged instead.

Copy Merged

This copies all the layers in the selected area to the Clipboard. You an also press Shift+Ctrl+C (Shift-⌘-C).

Paste

Use this command or press Ctrl+V (⌘-V) to add whatever you've cut or copied into an image.

Paste Into Selection

This is a special command for pasting something within the confines of an existing selection. See page 104 for more on how this command works. Choose Paste Into Selection here or by pressing Shift+Ctrl+V (Shift-⌘-V).

Delete

This command removes what you've selected without copying it to the Clipboard—it's just gone. You can also press Backspace (Delete).

Fill, Fill Layer, Fill Selection

Use this to add a Fill layer to your image. When you have no image open, this menu item reads Fill and is grayed out. Open a photo and you see Fill Layer, which lets you create a new Fill layer (see page 145). If you make a selection in your image, it changes to Fill Selection. Your Fill layer options are a bit different using this item compared to creating a Fill layer from the Layer menu or in the Layers palette. You can't choose to create a Gradient Fill layer here, for instance.

Stroke (Outline) Selection

This command lets you place a colored border around the edges of a selection.

Define Brush, Define Brush from Selection

If you want to create a custom brush from your photo or from an area of your photo, choose this command. The process is explained in detail on page 278.

Define Pattern, Define Pattern from Selection

This command creates a pattern from your image or selection. See page 221 for more about patterns.

Clear

Use these commands to permanently remove information from: the Undo History, Clipboard Contents, or All (both of them). If you have a corrupt image in the Clipboard (or one that's too large), it may cause Elements to slow way down or quit on you. Once in a while, the Clipboard may get stuck, too—you try to copy and paste an item but still get whatever you copied previously. Clear fixes all these problems.

Color Settings (Windows Only)

This is where you choose your color space for Elements. You can also press Shift+Ctrl+K. See page 162 for more about color spaces.

File Association (Windows Only)

This menu item brings up a window where you can choose which file types open automatically in Elements. Or you can set a file to open in a different program instead of Elements.

Preset Manager

This is where you access the Elements Preset Manager, a window that helps you manage your brushes, swatches, gradients, and patterns. See page 422 for more on how the Preset Manager works.

Preferences (Windows Only)

This menu gives you access to the many Elements settings you can customize. The preference screens available from this menu are:

- **General** (you can also press Ctrl+K to go to this screen)
- **Saving Files**
- **Display and Cursors**
- **Transparency**
- **Units and Rulers**
- **Grid**
- **Plug-ins and Scratch Disks**
- **Memory and Image Cache**
- **File Browser**

Image

The Image menu lets you make changes to your image. Here you can rotate it, change its shape, crop or resize it, or change the color mode.

Rotate

These commands let you change the orientation of your image. The first group of choices applies to your whole image. The Rotate commands are explained on page 49. Your options are:

- 90° Left
- 90° Right
- 180°
- Custom
- Flip Horizontal
- Flip Vertical

The next group does the same thing but on a layer or selection. The menu choices change depending on whether you have an active selection in your image. If you have a selection, you'll see Selection instead of Layer.

- Free Rotate Layer
- Layer 90° Left
- Layer 90° Right
- Layer 180°
- Flip Layer Horizontal
- Flip Layer Vertical

Finally you can choose to:

- Straighten and Crop Image
- Straighten Image

These last two commands are mostly for use with scanned images.

Transform

The Transform commands let you change the shape of your image by pulling it in different directions. They're explained in detail in Chapter 10. Your choices are:

- **Free Transform** incorporates all the other three commands. You can also press Ctrl+T (⌘-T).
- **Skew** slants an image.
- **Distort** stretches your photo in the direction you want to pull it.
- **Perspective** stretches your photo to make it look like parts are nearer or farther away.

Crop

Choosing this command crops your image to the area you've selected. See page 53.

Divide Scanned Photos

You can create a group scan by placing several photos on your scanner glass at once, then choose this command. Elements then cuts your photos apart and straightens and crops each individual photo. See page 47 for more about how this works.

Resize

Here is where you change the actual size of your image (as opposed to changing the size of the view on your screen). Resizing is explained in Chapter 3. Your choices are:

- **Image Size** (see page 64).

- **Canvas Size** (see page 72).

- **Reveal All**, which is available only for certain PSD files. Some versions of Photoshop hide the area outside a selection when you use the Crop tool. If you have one of these images, the command becomes active. You use it to see the area that was hidden by the crop.

- **Scale** (see page 261).

Mode

This is where you can change the color mode for your image. See page 29. Your mode choices are:

- **Bitmap**

- **Grayscale**

- **Indexed Color**

- **RGB Color**

There are two other commands in this menu:

- **Convert to 8-bit** reduces images from 16-bit color to 8-bit (see page 199).

- **Color Table** shows you the color table (the colors of your image shown as swatches) for an Indexed Color image.

Enhance

This menu contains the commands you use to adjust the color and lighting of your images. The top part of the menu contains the commands that apply automatically, and the bottom half includes the changes you can adjust.

Auto Smart Fix

This adjusts lighting and color at the same time. See page 88. You can also apply it by pressing Alt+Ctrl+M (Option-⌘-M).

Auto Levels

Auto Levels adjusts the individual color channels of your image. See page 91. You can also apply it by pressing Shift+Ctrl+L (Shift-⌘-L).

Auto Contrast

Auto Contrast adjusts the brightness and darkness of your image without changing the colors. It's explained on page 92. To apply this command from the keyboard, press Alt+Shift+Ctrl+L (Alt-Shift-⌘-L).

Auto Color Correction

This adjusts your color something like the way Levels does, but it looks at different information in your photo to make its decisions. You can also apply it by pressing Shift+Ctrl+B (Shift-⌘-B).

Adjust Smart Fix

This is the same as the Auto Smart Fix, but you get a slider to adjust the degree of change it makes to your photo. Call up the Adjust Smart Fix dialog box from the keyboard by pressing Shift+Ctrl+M (Shift-⌘-M).

Adjust Lighting

The commands under this menu item adjust the light and dark values in your photos. Your choices are:

- **Shadows/Highlights.** (See page 156.)

- **Brightness/Contrast.**

- **Levels.** You can also press Ctrl+L (⌘-L) to bring up the Levels dialog box. See page 168.

Adjust Color

These settings adjust the colors in your image. You can change a color, replace a color, remove a color cast, remove all the color from your image, or color a black and white photo. Choose from:

- **Remove Color Cast.** (See page 172.)

- **Adjust Hue/Saturation.** (See page 225.) You can also press Ctrl+U (⌘-U) to bring up the Hue/Saturation dialog box.

- **Remove Color.** (See page 235.) Pressing Shift+Ctrl+U (Shift-⌘-U) also removes color.

- **Replace Color.** (See page 230.)

- **Color Variations.** (See page 172.)

Layer

The Layer menu contains commands for creating and managing Layers. (Chapter 6 is all about Layers.) This is the most dynamic menu in Elements—what you see at the bottom of the menu changes very much depending on the layers you've got and the characteristics of the active layer. This is a basic rundown of the main menu options you'll usually see if your open image has only a background layer. (Some choices are visible but grayed out). The choices for merging and combining layers change the most as your layers change.

New

This is where you create new, regular (as opposed to Adjustment) layers. You can create a new:

- **Layer.** Press Shift+Ctrl+N (Shift-⌘-N) to do this from the keyboard.

- **Layer from Background.**

- **Layer via Copy.** Ctrl+J (⌘-J) is the keyboard equivalent.

- **Layer via Cut.** Press Shift+Ctrl+J (Shift-⌘-J) to do this from the keyboard.

If your image doesn't currently have a background layer you also see Background from Layer.

Duplicate Layer

This command makes a duplicate of the active layer. As long as you don't have a selection, you can also use Ctrl+J (⌘-J) to do the same thing.

Delete Layer

If you want to eliminate a layer, click it in the Layers palette to make it the active layer and choose this command.

Rename Layer

Choose this to rename a layer. You can also double-click the layer's name in the Layers palette.

Layer Style

If a layer has a Layer style applied to it (see page 322), you can adjust it here:

- **Style Settings** brings up the dialog box where you can adjust some of the settings of a Layer style. Double-clicking the Layer style icon in the Layers palette brings up the same dialog box.

- **Copy Layer Style** lets you copy any styles applied to a layer to the Clipboard so you can apply them to another image or layer.

- **Paste Layer Style** applies your copied style to a new layer, even in a new image.

- **Clear Layer Style** removes all the styles applied to a layer.

- **Hide All Effects** hides all the styles applied to a layer so that you can see what your image looks like without them.

- **Scale Effects** lets you adjust the size of certain aspects of Layer styles.

New Fill Layer

This creates a layer that's filled with a color or pattern. You can also do this from the Layers palette by clicking the Create Adjustment layer icon. You can choose a layer that's filled with:

- **Solid Color**

- **Gradient** (see page 325)

- **Pattern** (see page 221)

New Adjustment Layer

This command creates a new Adjustment layer. Adjustment layers are explained on page 145. The types of layers you can create are:

- **Levels** (page 163)

- **Brightness/Contrast**

- **Hue/Saturation** (page 225)

- **Gradient Map** (page 335)

- **Photo Filter** (page 201)

- **Invert** (page 248)

- **Threshold** (page 248)

- **Posterize** (page 248)

Change Layer Content

For Adjustment and Fill layers, you can change the type of layer you've got, as long as you haven't flattened your layers. For example, you could change a Levels layer into a Hue/Saturation layer. You can also change an Adjustment layer to a Fill layer, and vice versa. The choices include all the layers listed in the two previous sections.

Layer Content Options

This brings up the dialog box for an Adjustment or Fill layer. You can also double click the left icon for the layer in the Layers palette.

Type

This gives you ways to modify a Type layer, as long as it hasn't been simplified. You can choose:

- **Horizontal.** Change vertical type to horizontal type.

- **Vertical.** Change horizontal type to vertical type.

- **Anti-aliasing Off.** Antialiasing is explained on page 345.

- **Anti-aliasing On.**

- **Warp Text.** (See page 347.)

- **Update All Text Layers.**

- **Replace All Missing Fonts.** If your image is missing fonts, this command replaces them, but you can't choose the replacement. It's usually just as easy to replace fonts by highlighting the text and selecting a new font in the Options bar.

Simplify

This rasterizes your layer, turning the layer content from a vector to pixels. See page 298 for more about the difference between vectors and pixels.

Group with Previous

This command links two layers together in such a way that the bottom layer determines the opacity of the upper layer. See page 140. The keyboard command is Ctrl+G (⌘-G).

Ungroup

This command returns grouped layers to being two unrelated layers. The keyboard command is Shift+Ctrl+G (Shift-⌘-G).

Arrange

Use these commands to change the order of layers in the layers stack, or just drag them in the Layers palette. See page 138. (Front is the top of the stack, and back is directly above the background layer.)

- **Bring to Front.** Press Shift+Ctrl+] (Shift-⌘-]).

- **Bring Forward.** Press Ctrl+] (⌘-]).

- **Send Backward.** Press Ctrl+[(⌘-[).

- **Send to Back.** Press Shift+Ctrl+[(Shift-⌘-[).

Merge Layers

This command combines multiple layers into one layer. The keyboard command is Ctrl+E (⌘-E). You may also see Merge Down, which merges a layer with the layer immediately beneath it, or Merge Clipping Mask, which merges grouped layers.

Merge Visible

This merges all the visible layers into one layer. To do this from the keyboard, press Shift+Ctrl+E (Shift-⌘-E).

Flatten Image

This command merges all the layers into one background layer.

Select

This menu lets you make, modify, and save selections in your image. See Chapter 5 for more about selections.

All

This selects your entire image. Press Ctrl+A (⌘-A) to do the same thing.

Deselect

This removes all selections from your image. From the keyboard, press Ctrl+D (⌘-D).

Reselect

If you apply the Deselect command, but then want your selection back again, choose this or press Shift+Ctrl+D (Shift-⌘-D).

Inverse

Choosing this command switches the selected and unselected areas of your image. The area that wasn't previously selected is now selected, and the previously selected area is now unselected. The keyboard command is Shift+Ctrl+I (Shift-⌘-I).

Feather

Feathering blurs the edges of a selection. See page 106. Pressing Alt+Ctrl+D (Option-⌘-D) brings up the same dialog box.

Modify

These commands let you change the size or edges of your selection. They're all explained in Chapter 5.

- **Border** selects the edge of your selection (page 117).
- **Smooth** rounds the corners of rectangular selections (page 117).
- **Expand** moves the edge of your selection outward (page 117).
- **Contract** moves the edge of your selection inward (page 117).

Grow

This expands your selection to include more contiguous areas of similar color. See page 117.

Similar

This also expands your selection to include more areas of similar color, but Similar doesn't restrict the growth areas to only contiguous areas the way Grow does.

Load Selection

If you have saved a selection, choose this command to use it again.

Save Selection

If you wish to save a selection so that you can use it another time without recreating it, use this command. See page 121.

Delete Selection

Use this command to permanently remove a saved selection.

Filter

Filters let you change the appearance of your image in all sorts of ways. There are some filters that are mostly for correcting and improving your photos and others that create artistic effects. There are a lot of filters in Elements, and in this menu, they're grouped into categories to make it easier to find one that does exactly what you want. You can also apply filters from the Styles and Effects palette. There's more about using filters in Chapter 12. Every image responds to filters differently, so the descriptions here are a very rough guide.

Reapply Last Filter

The top item in this menu always features the last filter you've applied. Choose the filter here to use it again with the exact same settings you previously used. If you want to change the settings, you need to choose the filter from its regular place in the list of filters. You can also press Ctrl+F (⌘-F) to reapply the last filter.

Filter Gallery

The Filter Gallery lets you try the effects of different filters, rearrange them, and preview what they'll look like in your photo.

Adjustments

The filters in this category are primarily, but not exclusively, for correcting and enhancing photos. These filters are discussed in Chapter 9, unless otherwise noted.

- Equalize
- Gradient Map (see page 335)
- Invert (or Ctrl+I [⌘-I])
- Posterize
- Threshold
- Photo Filter (see page 201)

Artistic

These filters let you apply a wide variety of artistic effects to your image, ranging from a watercolor effect to making it look like it was sketched with pastels.

- **Colored Pencil** makes your photo look like it was sketched with a colored pencil on a solid colored background.
- **Cutout** makes your image look like it was cut from pieces of paper.
- **Dry Brush** makes your photo look it was painted using dry brush technique.
- **Film Grain** adds grain to make your photo look like old film.
- **Fresco** makes your photo look like it was painted quickly in a dabbing style.

- **Neon Glow** adds vivid color to your image while softening the details.

- **Paint Daubs** gives your photo a painted look.

- **Palette Knife** makes your photo look like you painted it using a palette knife, i.e., a thin layer of paint revealing the canvas beneath.

- **Plastic Wrap** makes your image look like it's covered in plastic.

- **Poster Edges** gives your image accented, dark edges while reducing the number of colors in the rest of the photo.

- **Rough Pastels** makes your image look like it was quickly sketched with pastels.

- **Smudge Stick** uses short diagonal strokes that soften the image by smearing the detail.

- **Sponge** paints with highly textured areas of contrasting color like you'd get by sponging on color.

- **Underpainting** makes your image look like it's painted on a textured background.

- **Watercolor** simplifies the details in your image the way they would be if you were creating a watercolor painting.

Blur

These filters soften and blur your images. Page 318 tells you all about how to use them.

- Average

- Blur

- Blur More

- Gaussian Blur

- Motion Blur

- Radial Blur

- Smart Blur

Brush Stroke

These filters give your image a hand-painted look.

- **Accented Edges** emphasizes the edges of objects as though they were drawn in black ink or white chalk.

- **Angled Strokes** creates diagonal brush strokes that all run in the same direction.

- **Crosshatch** creates diagonal brush strokes that crisscross.

- **Dark Strokes** paints dark areas of your image with short, tight, dark strokes, and light areas with long, white strokes.

- **Ink Outlines** makes your image look like it was drawn with fine ink lines.

- **Spatter** gives the effect you'd get from a spatter airbrush.

- **Sprayed Strokes** paints your image with diagonal, sprayed strokes in its dominant colors.

- **Sumi-e** gives the effect of drawing with a wet brush full of black ink, in a Japanese-influenced style.

Distort

These filters warp your image in a variety of different ways.

- **Diffuse Glow** makes your image look as though you're viewing it through a soft diffusion filter.

- **Displace** lets you create a map to tell Elements how to distort your image.

- **Glass** makes your image look like you're viewing it through different kinds of glass.

- **Liquify.** (See page 352.)

- **Ocean Ripple** gives an underwater effect by adding ripples to your image.

- **Pinch.** (See page 264.)

- **Polar Coordinates** lets you create what is called a cylinder anamorphosis. That's the kind of distortion where a distorted image looks normal when you see it in a mirrored cylinder.

- **Ripple** creates a pattern like ripples on the surface of water.

- **Shear** distorts your image along a curve.

- **Spherize.** (See page 264.)

- **Twirl** spins your photo, rotating a selection more in the center than at the edge, producing a twirled pattern.

- **Wave** creates a rippled pattern but with more control than the Ripple filter gives you.

- **Zigzag** creates a bent, zigzagging effect that's stronger in the center of the area you apply the filter to.

Noise

You can use these filters to add *noise* (grain) to your photos or remove noise from them. They're discussed on page 313.

- **Add Noise**
- **Despeckle**
- **Dust & Scratches**
- **Median**
- **Reduce Noise**

Pixelate

These filters break up the appearance of your photo into spots or blocks of various kinds.

- **Color Halftone** adds the kind of dotted pattern you see in commercially printed color.
- **Crystallize** breaks your image into polygonal blocks of color.
- **Facet** reduces your image to blocks of solid color.
- **Fragment** makes your image look blurry and offset.
- **Mezzotint** creates an effect something like that of a mezzotint engraving.
- **Mosaic** breaks your image down to square blocks of color.
- **Pointillize** creates a pointillist effect by making your photo look like it's made of many dots of color.

Render

This is a diverse but powerful group of filters that transform your photo in many ways.

- **3-D Transform** can be used to make you image look like it's on a cube, cylinder, or sphere.
- **Clouds** covers your image with clouds using the foreground/background colors.
- **Difference Clouds** also creates clouds, but the first time you apply it to an image, portions of the image are inverted.
- **Fibers** creates an effect like spun and woven fibers.
- **Lens Flare** creates starry bright spots like you'd get from a camera lens flare.
- **Lighting Effects** is a powerful and complex filter for changing the light in your photo.
- **Texture Fill** lets you use a grayscale image as a texture for your photo.

Sharpen

These filters make your photo appear to be in better focus. They are discussed in Chapter 7.

- Sharpen
- Sharpen Edges
- Sharpen More
- Unsharp Mask

Sketch

This is another group of artistic filters. Most of them make your image look like it was drawn with a pencil or graphics pen.

- **Bas Relief** gives your photo a slightly raised appearance, as though it's carved in low relief.
- **Chalk & Charcoal** makes your photo look like it was sketched with a combination of chalk and charcoal.
- **Charcoal** gives a smudgy effect to your image, like a charcoal drawing.
- **Chrome** is supposed to make your image look like polished chrome, but you might prefer the Wow chrome Layer styles in the Styles and Effects palette.
- **Conté Crayon** makes your image look like it was drawn with conté crayons using the foreground/background colors.
- **Graphic Pen** makes the details in your image look like they were drawn with a fine pen using the foreground color, with the background color for the paper color.
- **Halftone Pattern** gives the dotted effect of a halftone screen, like you see in printed illustrations.
- **Note Paper** makes your image look like it's on handmade paper. The background color shows through in spots in dark areas.
- **Photocopy** makes your photo look like a Xerox copy.
- **Plaster** makes your image look like it was molded in wet plaster.
- **Reticulation** creates an effect you might get from film emulsion—dark areas clump and brighter areas appear more lightly grained.
- **Stamp** makes your image look like it was stamped with a rubber stamp.
- **Torn Edges** makes your photo look it's made from torn pieces of paper.
- **Water Paper** makes your photo look like it was painted on wet paper, making the colors run together.

Stylize

These filters create special effects by displacing the pixels in your image or increasing contrast.

- **Diffuse** makes your photo less focused by shuffling the pixels according to the settings you choose.

- **Emboss** makes objects in your image appear stamped or raised.

- **Extrude** gives a 3-D effect by pushing some of the pixels in your image up, something like toothpaste squeezed from a tube.

- **Find Edges** emphasizes the edges of your image against a white background.

- **Glowing Edges** adds a neon-like glow to the edges in your photo.

- **Solarize** produces an effect like what you'd get by briefly exposing a photo print to light while you're developing it. It combines a negative and a positive image.

- **Tiles** breaks your image up into individual tiles. You can choose how much to offset them.

- **Trace Contour** outlines areas where there are major transitions in brightness. The result is supposed to be something like a contour map.

- **Wind** makes your image appear windblown.

Texture

These filters change the surface of your photo to look like it was made from another material.

- **Craquelure** produces a surface effect like cracked plaster.

- **Grain** adds different kinds of graininess to your photo.

- **Mosaic Tiles** is supposed to make your photo look like it's made of mosaic tiles with grout in between them.

- **Patchwork** reduces your image to squares filled with the predominant colors.

- **Stained Glass** is supposed to make your photo look like it's made of stained glass. The effect is usually more like a mosaic.

- **Texturizer** can be used to make your photo look like it's on canvas or brick. You can select a file to use as a texture.

Video

These filters are for use with video images.

- **De-Interlace** smoothes images captured from video by removing the odd or even interlaced lines.

- **NTSC Colors** restricts you colors to those suitable for television reproduction.

Other

This is a group of fairly technical filters.

- **Custom** lets you create your own filter.

- **High Pass** is discussed on page 185.

- **Maximum** replaces pixel brightness values with the highest and lowest values of surrounding pixels. Maximum spreads out white areas and shrinks dark areas.

- **Minimum** is the opposite of the Maximum filter. It spreads out black areas and shrinks white ones.

- **Offset** moves your selection by the number of pixels you specify.

Digimarc

Use "Read Watermark" to check for Digimarc watermarks in photos. Digimarc is a commercial system that lets subscribers enter their information in a database so that anyone who gets one of their photos can find out who the copyright holder is by searching.

View

This menu contains ways to adjust how you see your image on your screen. Adjusting the view is described on page 60.

New Window for...

This lets you create a duplicate window for your image so that you can see it at two different magnification levels at once. The new window goes away when you close your image—it doesn't create a copy of your photo.

Zoom In

To increase the view size you can choose this menu item or press Ctrl+= (⌘-=). You can also use the Zoom tool. (See page 61.)

Zoom Out

To reduce the view size, choose this menu item or press Ctrl+– (⌘--). You can also use the Zoom tool. (See page 61.)

Fit on Screen

This makes your photo as large as it can be without your having to scroll to see part of it. You can also press Ctrl+0 (⌘-0).

Actual Pixels

This view displays your image the exact size it would appear on the Web or in other programs that can't adjust view size (as Elements can). You can also press Alt+Ctrl+0 (Option-⌘-0).

Print Size

Elements makes its best guess as to how large your image would print at its current resolution. See page 64.

Selection

When this is turned on, the outlines of your selections are visible. You can toggle this setting off and on here, or by pressing Ctrl+H (⌘-H).

Rulers

If you want to see rulers around the edges of your image window, toggle them on and off here. You can adjust the unit of measurement in Edit → Preferences → Units & Rulers (Photoshop Elements → Preferences → Units & Rulers).

Grid

If you want to see a measurement and alignment grid on your photos, use this setting to toggle it on and off. You can adjust the grid size in Edit → Preferences → Grid (Photoshop Elements → Preferences → Grid).

Annotations

This is available only for files that contain voice annotations. Toggle the annotation on and off here.

Snap to Grid

When this setting is turned on, Elements automatically jumps to the nearest gridline. If the way your tools and selections keep jumping away from you bothers you, you can turn it off here. Then everything stays exactly where you place it.

Window

This menu controls which palettes and bins you see, as well as letting you adjust how your image windows display.

Images

This menu item lets you control how your images display. The choices are explained on page 60.

- **Maximize Mode.** Each image takes up the entire available space.
- **Cascade.** Image windows tile in overlapping stacks. (This is the usual view in older versions of Elements.)
- **Tile.** Your images appear edge to edge so that all windows are equally visible.
- **Match Zoom.** Choose this to make all open windows zoom to the same extent as the active window.
- **Match Location.** When you have only part of a photo visible in a window, choose this to make all open windows display the same part of their images, too, like the upper-left corner, for example.

Tools

This setting hides and shows the Toolbox. (If you've got the Windows version of Elements, you must drag the Toolbox loose from the Options bar before you can hide the Toolbox.)

Tool Options (Mac Only)

This setting hides and reveals the Options bar.

Color Swatches

Use this to show and hide the Color Swatches palette (page 180).

Histogram

Use this to show or hide the Histogram in its own palette (page 165).

How To

This setting shows or hides the How To palette, which contains step-by-step directions for popular Elements tasks and projects (page 17).

Info

Use this setting to bring up a palette with information about your photos, like the file size and dimensions, as well as color value numbers.

Layers

This is where you make the Layers palette visible or hide it. See Chapter 6.

Navigator

Turn the Navigator off and on here. The Navigator lets you adjust which portion of a large image is visible on your screen and also adjust the zoom. See page 65.

Styles and Effects

This shows and hides the Styles and Effects palette, from which you apply filters, effects, and Layer styles. See Chapter 12.

Undo History

This setting makes the Undo History palette visible or hides it. The Undo History palette shows a record of all the changes to your image up to the number of states you set in Edit → Preferences → General → History States (Photoshop Elements → Preferences → General → History States).

Palette Bin

This setting minimizes and maximizes the Palette bin (see page 13). You can also just click the edge of the bin.

Reset Palette Locations

This command returns all palettes to their original locations.

File Browser

You can show and hide the File Browser here or press Ctrl+Shift+O (⌘-Shift-O). See page 39.

Welcome

Choose this menu item to see the Welcome window that appears when Elements starts up. In Windows, you can then use the menu setting to change the component of Elements that launches when the program starts up.

Photo Bin

This setting minimizes the Photo bin for Windows and hides it for Macs. Select it again to maximize the bin (show the bin).

Image Windows

At the bottom of the View menu you see a list of all the files you have open in Elements. Choose one to bring it to the front as the active window.

Help

This menu is where you find the Elements Help files and tutorials. If you have Windows, you'll also find information about the program itself.

Help

You can call up the Elements Help application here, or press F1. Or you can click the Help button in the menu bar.

About Photoshop Elements (Windows Only)

Choose this for a window showing the version of Elements. Alt+click the menu for lots of scrolling information about the people who created Elements and the many, many patents involved in creating this program. Keep holding Alt while the window scrolls, and you'll find out what Adobe thinks of you. Click the window again to close it.

About Plug-In (Windows Only)

This contains a pop-out list of all the plug-ins in your copy of Elements. The program comes with a huge number of plug-ins—you don't have to do anything to make them work—they're all preinstalled. Choose a particular plug-in from the list to see information about it.

Glossary of Terms

The Elements Help files include a glossary of terms relating to digital imaging. If you're wondering what a term means, this menu item takes you to the glossary index so you can look it up.

Tutorials

The Elements Help files include some excellent tutorials. Choose this item to see a list of them.

System Info

Choose this for a window showing information about Elements itself and also about your operating system.

Online Support

Choose this option, and Elements launches your Web browser and attempts to go to Adobe's support Web site.

Registration

If you didn't register Elements with Adobe the first time you used the program, you can choose this to bring up the registration window again.

Photoshop Elements Online

This takes you to the main product page for Photoshop Elements on Adobe's site. Like the online support link, Elements launches your browser and offers to connect to the Internet if you're not already online when you chose this menu item.

Installation and Troubleshooting

Elements is quite easy to install and it's pretty trouble free once you're up and running. This appendix explains a couple of things you can do to ensure that your installation goes smoothly, and also provides cures for most of the little glitches that can crop up once you're using the program.

Installing Elements

There are a couple of things you should do before you install Elements, regardless of whether you're installing the program in Windows or Mac OS X.

First of all, if your computer is on a network, take it off the network temporarily. (You can go back on the network as soon as you've installed Elements.) Also, it's important to disable any antivirus software as well as any products from Norton (which tend to quarrel with Adobe software during installation). You can turn these programs back on as soon as you've finished the installation.

For both Mac and Windows, you need to install Elements from an administrative account on your computer. (If you've never done anything to change your account and you only have one account on your machine, it's almost certainly an administrative account.)

> **NOTE** If you already have a previous version of Elements, there's no need to remove it before installing Elements 3. All versions of Elements run as separate programs, and you can keep the older version, too, if you want.
>
> In Windows, however, if you decide to uninstall Elements 1 or 2 *after* installing Elements 3, you may find that you lose the Adobe Gamma utility in the process. If that happens, just reinstall Elements 3.

Also, make sure you have your Elements serial number handy. You won't be able to install the program without it. If you have a retail version of Elements, the serial number is on the label on the install disc's case. If you got it bundled (when you bought a scanner, for example), the serial number is usually on the paper sleeve the disc is in. (It's not a bad idea to write your serial number right on the disc so that you'll always have it around if you need to reinstall.)

Installing on Windows XP

Installing Elements is quite easy to do, and it's usually trouble free.

1. **Put the install disc in your computer's drive.**

   The disc window should open automatically. If for some reason it doesn't, double-click the disc's icon or right-click it and choose Open.

2. **Choose a language and accept the software agreement.**

3. **Click "Install Adobe Photoshop Elements."**

   The installation wizard launches.

4. **Enter your serial number when the installer requests it, and choose where you want Elements to install.**

5. **Select which file formats you want Elements to automatically open.**

   If you know which file formats (See Chapter 3, page xx) you want Elements to automatically open, you get a chance to tell the installer your preferences. You can also change your file associations later, as explained in Chapter 3.

6. **Click Install to begin the installation.**

   Elements installs. You may also see Windows Media Format 9 Series Runtime Setup. That's for the multimedia capabilities of the Organizer.

7. **When the Install wizard is complete, click "Finish" and restart your computer.**

The installer creates a desktop shortcut to Elements. To launch Elements, double-click the shortcut or right-click it and choose Open.

Installing on Mac OS X

To install Elements on Mac OS X, do the following:

1. **Put the install disc in your computer's drive.**

2. **Double-click the disc's icon to see the contents.**

3. **Double-click "Install Adobe Photoshop Elements."**

4. **Follow the instructions in the Installer.**

   You get asked which language you want. Then you're asked to accept the soft-ware agreement, choose your installation destination, and enter your OS X password. Finally, the installer asks for your Elements serial number before the actual installation begins.

5. **When the installer is finished, click Close.**

To launch Elements, go to Applications → Adobe Photoshop Elements 3 and double-click the Adobe Photoshop Elements 3 program icon. The first time you launch Elements, it automatically creates an icon for the program in your dock. If you don't want it there, just drag the icon out of the dock and watch it vanish in a puff of smoke.

Registration

When you first launch Elements, it asks you to register the program. You can run Elements without registering it, but there are a couple of advantages to registering. For one thing, there's a record of your serial number in your Adobe information, so if you ever misplace the number, you can get it from Adobe. Also, when Adobe releases new versions of Elements, there's usually a rebate for registered owners of previous versions.

If you don't register the program, the registration wizard keeps nagging you every time you start Elements. You can make this go away for good by letting Elements launch your Web browser and then canceling the registration process. The wizard won't try again. (You can still register Elements later on by going to Adobe's Web site and entering your information.)

Scratch Disks

Elements uses a *scratch disk* when it's busy making your photos gorgeous. The cal-culations Elements makes behind the scenes are very complex and Elements needs someplace to write stuff down while it's figuring out how to make changes to your image. It does so by using a scratch disk.

You probably have just one hard drive in your computer, and Elements automati-cally uses that drive as the scratch disk. That's fine, and Elements can run very hap-pily without a dedicated scratch disk.

> **TIP** You can make Elements *really* happy by keeping your hard drive defragmented (if you're using Windows) and making sure there's plenty of free space available for Elements to use.

If you're fortunate enough to have a computer with more than one internal drive, you can designate a separate disk as your scratch disk to improve Elements perfor-mance. Your scratch disk needs to be as fast as the drive Elements is installed on or there's no point in setting up a special scratch disk. (If you have a USB external drive, for instance, forget it and just leave your main drive as your scratch disk.)

To assign a scratch disk, go to Edit → Preferences → Plug-Ins & Scratch Disks (Photoshop Elements → Preferences → Plug-Ins &Scratch Disks) and choose your preferred disk. You can choose up to four disks to use as scratch disks.

Troubleshooting

If Elements behaves badly from the moment you install it, something probably went funky during your installation. That's easy to fix. Uninstall Elements and reinstall it.

To remove Elements in Windows, go to Control Panel → Add or Remove Programs and remove Elements. Then reinstall the program. (You can't perform a Repair Install for Elements—you just get an error message that keeps asking for the disc.)

On a Mac, go to your Applications folder and drag the Elements folder to the trash. Then go to your Home Folder → Library → Preferences and delete com. adobe.Photoshop.Elements.plist and the Photoshop Elements Preferences and Paths folders.

Fortunately, Adobe makes very good software that looks after itself very well. There is however one simple procedure you can perform if things start acting funny in Elements: delete your Elements *preferences file*. The preferences file is where Elements keeps track of your preferred settings for the program. Deleting it fixes the overwhelming majority of problems you might develop. Here's what you need to do:

1. **Quit Elements if it's currently running and relaunch the Editor (relaunch Elements).**

   As soon as you start the program, immediately press Ctrl+Alt+Shift (Shift-Option-⌘).

2. **Delete your preferences.**

   A window appears asking if you want to delete the Elements settings. Click Okay. You have to be fairly quick to press the keys in time. If you don't see the window, you were too slow. Quit Elements and try again.

This procedure resets Elements to the way it was when you launched the program for the very first time. So you will have to reenter any changes you made to your color space and your preferences. Your palettes also go back to their original locations; you'll need to rearrange them if you pulled any of them out of the bin. (Deleting the preferences doesn't affect your image files at all.)

The RAW Converter and Elements Help also have their own preference files. You can follow the same procedure to delete these preferences. For example, when launching the RAW Converter (double-click a RAW image), press Ctrl+Alt+ Shift (Shift-Option-⌘) as the converter opens.

NOTE   There's a bug in the Mac version of Elements that makes Help inaccessible from a non-administrative account. You can give administrative privileges to the other user by going to System Preferences → Accounts → Security and turning on "Allow user to administer this computer."

If you don't want to do that, there's another way, but it involves using the Terminal application, which many people find intimidating. If you want to try this method, the easiest way is to go to the forums at Mac OS X Hints (*www.macosxhints.com*) or Mac News Network (*www.macnn.com*). If you search for "Photoshop Elements 3," you'll find several threads containing scripts you can copy and paste into the Terminal window. Read the threads to see which script appeals to you.

The shareware program Panther Cache Cleaner (*www.northernsoftworks.com*) also claims to be able to fix the Help problem without the use of Terminal. There's a free trial, so you might want to give it a try.

Index

Colophon

Philip Dangler was the production editor and the proofreader for *Photoshop Elements 3: The Missing Manual*. Linley Dolby was the copyeditor. Marlowe Shaeffer and Claire Cloutier provided quality control. Julie Hawks wrote the index.

Ellie Volckhausen designed the cover of this book, based on a series design by David Freedman. Rose Cassano created the cover illustration with Adobe Illustrator CS. Ellie Volckhausen produced the cover layout with Adobe InDesign CS using Adobe's Minion and Gill Sans fonts.

Melanie Wang designed the interior layout, based on a series design by Phil Simpson. This book was converted by Andrew Savikas to FrameMaker 5.5.6 with a format conversion tool created by Erik Ray, Jason McIntosh, Neil Walls, and Mike Sierra that uses Perl and XML technologies. The text font is Adobe Minion; the heading font is Adobe Formata Condensed; and the code font is LucasFont's TheSans Mono Condensed. The illustrations that appear in the book were produced by Robert Romano, Jessamyn Read, and Lesley Borash, using Macromedia FreeHand MX and Adobe Photoshop CS.

Better than e-books

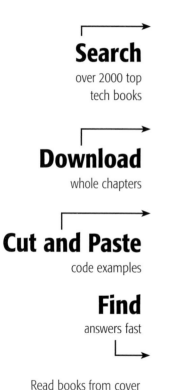

Search
over 2000 top
tech books

Download
whole chapters

Cut and Paste
code examples

Find
answers fast

Read books from cover
to cover. Or, simply click
to the page you need.

**Search Safari! The premier electronic reference
library for programmers and IT professionals**

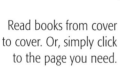

 Addison Wesley
 Sun microsystems
 ALPHA
 Java
 Microsoft Press
 Peachpit Press
 O'REILLY
 que
 macromedia PRESS
 PRENTICE HALL PTR
Adobe Press
SAMS
New Riders
Cisco Press

Part# 40421

Keep in touch with O'Reilly

1. Download examples from our books

To find example files for a book, go to:

www.oreilly.com/catalog

select the book, and follow the "Examples" link.

2. Register your O'Reilly books

Register your book at *register.oreilly.com*

Why register your books?
Once you've registered your O'Reilly books you can:

- Win O'Reilly books, T-shirts or discount coupons in our monthly drawing.
- Get special offers available only to registered O'Reilly customers.
- Get catalogs announcing new books (US and UK only).
- Get email notification of new editions of the O'Reilly books you own.

3. Join our email lists

Sign up to get topic-specific email announcements of new books and conferences, special offers, and O'Reilly Network technology newsletters at:

elists.oreilly.com

It's easy to customize your free elists subscription so you'll get exactly the O'Reilly news you want.

4. Get the latest news, tips, and tools

www.oreilly.com

- "Top 100 Sites on the Web"—PC Magazine
- CIO Magazine's Web Business 50 Awards

Our web site contains a library of comprehensive product information (including book excerpts and tables of contents), downloadable software, background articles, interviews with technology leaders, links to relevant sites, book cover art, and more.

5. Work for O'Reilly

Check out our web site for current employment opportunities:

jobs.oreilly.com

6. Contact us

O'Reilly & Associates, Inc.
1005 Gravenstein Hwy North
Sebastopol, CA 95472 USA

TEL: 707-827-7000 or 800-998-9938
(6am to 5pm PST)

FAX: 707-829-0104

order@oreilly.com
For answers to problems regarding your order or our products. To place a book order online, visit:

www.oreilly.com/order_new

catalog@oreilly.com
To request a copy of our latest catalog.

booktech@oreilly.com
For book content technical questions or corrections.

corporate@oreilly.com
For educational, library, government, and corporate sales.

proposals@oreilly.com
To submit new book proposals to our editors and product managers.

international@oreilly.com
For information about our international distributors or translation queries. For a list of our distributors outside of North America check out:

international.oreilly.com/distributors.html

adoption@oreilly.com
For information about academic use of O'Reilly books, visit:

academic.oreilly.com

Related Titles Available from O'Reilly

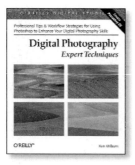

Digital Media

Adobe InDesign CS One-on-One

Adobe Encore DVD: In the Studio

Adobe Photoshop CS One-on-One

Creating Photomontages with Photoshop: A Designer's Notebook

Digital Photography: Expert Techniques

Digital Photography Hacks

Digital Photography Pocket Guide, *2nd Edition*

Digital Video Pocket Guide

DVD Studio Pro 3: In the Studio

Illustrations with Photoshop: A Designers Notebook

In the Loop with Soundtrack

iPod & iTunes: The Missing Manual, *2nd Edition*

Photo Retouching with Photoshop: A Designer's Notebook

Windows Media Hacks